Radio Program Openings
and Closings, 1931–1972

Radio Program Openings and Closings, 1931–1972

VINCENT TERRACE

McFarland & Company, Inc., Publishers

Jefferson, North Carolina, and London

LIBRARY OF CONGRESS ONLINE CATALOG

Terrace, Vincent, 1948–
    Radio program openings and closings, 1931–1972 / Vincent Terrace.
        p.   cm.
    Includes index.

    ISBN 0-7864-1485-5 (illustrated case binding : 50# alkaline paper) ∞

    1. Radio programs—United States—Dictionaries.   2. Prologues and
epilogues.   3. Credit titles (Motion pictures, television, etc.)   I. Title.
PN1991.3.U6 T44   2003
791.44'75'03 22
                                                                    2003017207

British Library cataloguing data are available

Cover photograph ©2003 Photodisc

Manufactured in the United States of America

McFarland & Company, Inc., Publishers
  Box 611, Jefferson, North Carolina 28640
    www.mcfarlandpub.com

Contents

Preface

Do you remember the immortal words of *The Shadow* ("Who knows what evil lurks in the hearts of men") or those spoken by the title character in *The Whistler* ("I am the Whistler and I know many things for I walk by night")? Do you recall the closing words of *Blackstone, the Magician* ("Good magic and goodbye") or of Orson Welles ("As always, I remain obediently yours")? Do you remember the great radio commercial jingles like "Pepsi-Cola hits the spot. Twelve full ounces, that's a lot" or "Smoke dreams from smoke rings while a Chesterfield burns?" Do you remember drinking your Ovaltine with *Little Orphan Annie* or wishing you had sent for that radio premium (like the Good Luck Swastika from *The Majestic Master of Mystery*)?

This is the kind of information you will find in this one of a kind book, the first ever attempt to document the opening and closing signatures of the programs from the golden age of radio. All types of programs have been included—from the most popular to the most obscure, and everything in between; from comedy and drama to western and sci-fi. All the memorable (and not so memorable) opening and closing themes have been reproduced here, for you to enjoy in printed form.

Each alphabetically listed entry contains a brief introductory paragraph that lists the program type, story line, sponsors, networks, years of broadcast and principal cast. There are a total of 516 opening and closing themes represented by 444 numbered entries (many shows contain multiple openings and closings to represent the changes that occurred in a series during its run).

Each theme is reproduced with music, announcer and sound effect indications just as they would occur if you were listening to the actual program. Songs and jingles have also been reproduced in this manner. Commercials have been included with sponsored programs where possible. When a commercial announcement was heard during an opening theme or right after, or before a closing theme (or during and after it), the commercial has been included. Commercials broadcast during the middle of a program have been excluded. Several problems exist regarding sponsored programs.

Not all circulating shows (programs available to the public) are complete. Some are missing openings (and/or closings) and some are missing commercials. (For example, when AFRS—The Armed Forces Radio Service—rebroadcast programs to servicemen overseas, it cut all commercials as well as the closing theme. Many shows in circulation are AFRS programs and, in many cases, are the only known existing copies of some programs.) Like people with

VCR's today, who cut out commercials from the shows they are recording, people with disk, wire and open-reel audio recorders back then cut out commercials from the radio programs they were recording. These programs eventually became circulating shows and the only indication of sponsorship may be what the announcer says in the opening theme.

Syndicated series are also a problem in more ways than one. Based on my experiences with the syndicated series used in this book, most appear to be copies of the actual disks or tapes sent to stations. While meant to be sponsored, they have no commercial messages; instead a musical selection is played for a minute or so for local stations to insert a commercial or do a voice-over announcement. The opening and closings are also brief (as they were meant to be supplemented by the local station announcer) and some syndicated series have only a musical opening and closing (providing for voice-overs by local station announcers).

In addition to an index of names and pro-grams that appears in this book, three appendices have been included. Appendix A lists all the products mentioned with the programs they sponsored. Appendix B is a brief history of radio jingles and slogans. Appendix C is a listing of World War II announcements and where to find them.

Radio, as it was so many yesterdays ago, is gone. You can relive that past through tapes of the actual programs or by reading the various reference books on radio. This is a different type of old-time radio reference book. It covers the programs of our past in a different way and explores, for the first time, advertising during that era. It took many hours to transcribe this information and, if you were to purchase the shows that appear in this book, the price would be close to $1,600. If you are a new fan of old-time radio I hope this book whets your appetite to explore it further; if you are already a fan of old-time radio, I hope some pleasant memories will be rekindled for you. You can't go back, but with old-time radio, you can relive it.

Author's Notes

ABC: The American Broadcasting Company.

AFRS: Armed Forces Radio Service.

Blue: One of two NBC networks; it eventually became ABC.

CBS: The Columbia Broadcasting System.

Mutual: The Mutual Broadcasting System. Also known as MBS, the Mutual-Don Lee Network and WOR/Mutual.

NBC: The National Broadcasting Company. Formed in 1926 and the owner of two networks: Blue and Red. NBC Red became known simply as NBC when NBC Blue became ABC in late 1944.

Sustaining: This term is listed on shows that were not meant to be sponsored.

Syndicated: Listed as Syn., it indicates programs that were sold to individual radio stations and broadcast according to the station's needs.

Various Sponsors: This term indicates programs that had numerous sponsors (much like how TV programs are broadcast today). In most cases, sponsors varied from week to week.

Recommended Book: *The Ultimate History of Network Radio Programming and Guide to All Circulating Shows* by Jay Hickerson (Box 4321, Hamden, Ct., 06514; telephone: 203-248-2887). Valuable reference book for anyone interested in old-time radio. The book lists over 6,000 radio programs with information regarding networks, dates, programs and number of episodes that are in circulation (shows available to the public). The book also lists program lengths, days and times broadcast and whether a series was network or local. There is also a section on radio societies and sources for acquiring programs.

All the openings and closings used in this book are based on circulating shows. Two sources of such shows are: *Radio Spirits* (1-800-723-4648) for well-known programs. *Vintage Broadcasts* (1-866-783-1923) for both well known as well as obscure programs.

The dates listed for the title of this book, 1931–1972, indicate the date of the earliest theme that could be found (*The Vaughn DeLeath Show*) and the date of the last broadcast of *The Devil and Mr. O.* Information prior to 1931 appears in the book, but no signatures could be found.

The 444 Radio Programs

1. The Abbott and Costello Kids' Show

Comedians Bud Abbott and Lou Costello as hosts of a program of music, songs and comedy geared to children. Sustaining. ABC, 1947–1949.

ANNOUNCER (Johnny McGovern): The American Broadcasting Company presents *The Abbott and Costello Kids' Show*, transcribed in Hollywood with our guest star, Norma Jean Nilsson, Cookie on the *Blondie* show, and featuring the Lou Costello Junior Youth Foundation Award. Every Saturday morning on this program, some lucky boy or girl will receive hundreds of dollars in valuable gifts and the Lou Costello Junior Youth Foundation gold trophy for good citizenship. Every boy and girl in the country is eligible for this award. We'll tell you how to win later in the program, but first let's have some laughs with our stars, Bud Abbott and Lou Costello.

LOU: Heeeey Abbott!

SOUND: Applause (Bud and Lou would then begin the show with a skit).

CLOSE

ANNOUNCER: The Lou Costello Junior Youth Foundation Award is given each week to a boy or girl for a civic good deed. You listeners will nominate the boy or girl each week. Anyone can write a letter nominating a boy or girl; just write to Abbott and Costello, Hollywood, California. Simply tell a story of an outstanding good deed or act of heroism by a boy or girl sixteen years of age or younger. All letters become the property of the Lou Costello Junior Youth Foundation. It will be judged by its board of directors and the judges decisions will be final. The award will be made each Saturday morning on *The Abbott and Costello Kids' Show*. Be sure to listen. The winner may be your kid or the kid next door.

BUD: Well, boys and girls, that's all for today.

LOU: Hey kids, be sure to listen next Saturday when we have two guests, really two guest stars, that great cowboy star Tim Holt and his dad, Jack Holt. Well, so long kids, till next Saturday.

THEME MUSIC: Up full then under…

ANNOUNCER: Listen to next week's award winner and remember you can nominate a winner by writing a letter to Abbott and Costello, Hollywood, California. And don't miss the regular *Abbott and Costello Show* on Wednesday nights. Johnny McGovern speaking. *The Abbott and Costello Kids' Show* is transcribed in Hollywood and is written and produced by Eddie Foreman.

MUSIC: Up full then fade out.

2. The Abbott and Costello Show

Music, songs and comedy with hosts Bud Abbott and Lou Costello. Various sponsors (Camel, Ipana and Sal Hepatica were frequent sponsors). NBC (1940; 1943–1947), ABC (1947–1949).

OPEN (NBC)

THEME MUSIC: Up full then under…

ANNOUNCER (Ken Niles): It's *The Abbott and Costello Program* with the music of Freddie Rich and his orchestra and the songs of Connie Haines. And here they are, America's favorite comedy duo, Bud Abbott and Lou Costello.

SOUND: Applause (followed by Bud and Lou introducing themselves and beginning the show).

CLOSE (NBC)

BUD: Good night folks, good night neighbors.

LOU: Good night to everybody in Paterson, New Jersey.

ANNOUNCER: Tune in again next week for another great *Abbott and Costello Show*. This is Ken Niles wishing you a very pleasant good night from Hollywood. This is NBC, the National Broadcasting Company.

OPEN (ABC)

LOU: Heeeey Abbott! What time is it?

BUD: Why, it's time for *The Abbott and Costello Show*. We're on the air for ABC here in Hollywood.

LOU: Well, what are we waiting for? Let's go with *The Abbott and Costello Show*.

THEME MUSIC: Up full then under…

ANNOUNCER (Michael Roy): Yes, it's *The Abbott and Costello Show*, produced and transcribed in Hollywood for your listening pleasure. Chuckles by the carload and music by Matty Matlock. So hold onto your chairs, folks, they're here, Bud Abbott and Lou Costello.

CLOSE (ABC)

BUD: Well, that's it for tonight. Good night folks.

LOU: Good night to everybody and good night Paterson, New Jersey. Good night.

ANNOUNCER: Listen each Wednesday night at this same time for another *Abbott and Costello Show*, produced and transcribed in Hollywood by Charles Vanda. Featured in tonight's show were Marilyn Williams and the music of Matty Matlock. Be sure to stay tuned for the outstanding enjoyment that follows throughout the evening on these ABC stations.

Note: Lou's mention of Paterson, New Jersey, in skits and in the program's closing themes referred to his home town.

3. Abie's Irish Rose

Comedy-drama about an Irish Catholic girl (Rosemary Murphy) who marries a Jewish boy (Abie Levy). Sponsored by Procter and Gamble. NBC, 1942–1944. Betty Winkler, Mercedes McCambridge, Julie Stevens and Marion Shockley played Rosemary; Richard Bond, Sydney Smith, Richard Coogan and Clayton "Bud" Collyer were Abie. The song "My Wild Irish Rose" was used as the theme.

OPEN

THEME MUSIC: Up full then under…

ANNOUNCER (Howard Petrie): Yes folks, Drene, America's largest selling shampoo, once again brings you that lovable, laughable show, Anne Nichols' *Abie's Irish Rose*. And now for tonight's visit with the Murphys and the Levys.

MUSIC: Up full then fade out.

CLOSE

ANNOUNCER: Tonight, when you go to brush your hair before you go to bed, take a good hard look in your mirror. See whether your hair is really the crowning glory it should be or just hair. Then, unless you're perfectly satisfied, make up your mind that tomorrow you'll get a bottle of our new improved special Drene. Special Drene does something no soap or shampoo can do. It reveals every bit of the natural color and luster brilliance. Special Drene never leaves any dulling film on hair; it reveals up to thirty-three percent more luster. If you haven't tried Drene lately, you'll be amazed. We know of no other shampoo that leaves hair so lusterious [*sic*] and yet so easy to manage. Ask your beauty shop to use it and be sure to specify Special Drene with hair conditioner.

THEME MUSIC: Up full then under...

ANNOUNCER: Now be sure to listen again next Saturday night at this same time for another episode of the Murphys, the Levys and their friends. *Abie's Irish Rose* is dedicated to the spirit of freedom and equality which gives to this nation the greatness that is America. *Abie's Irish Rose* is written by Anne Nichols and brought to you by Procter and Gamble, the makers of Drene, America's largest-selling shampoo. This is Howard Petrie. Good Night.

THEME MUSIC: Up full then out.

SOUND: NBC chimes. N-B-C.

4. The Adventures of Charlie Chan

Crime drama that revolves around Charlie Chan, a master Oriental detective. Various sponsors. Blue (1932–1933), Mutual (1936–1938; 1947–1948), ABC (1944–1945). Walter Connolly, Ed Begley, Santos Ortega and William Rees played Charlie Chan.

OPEN

SOUND: Chinese gong.
ANNOUNCER: *The Adventures of Charlie Chan.*
SOUND: Chinese gong.
THEME MUSIC: Up full then under...
ANNOUNCER: Right now, sit back, relax and listen to the greatest Oriental detective of them all, the incomparable Charlie Chan. Join this

famous detective of fiction, films and radio as he combines the wisdom of the East with the science of the West in a dramatic chapter in *The Adventures of Charlie Chan.*

SOUND: Chinese gong.

CLOSE

SOUND: Chinese gong.
ANNOUNCER: *The Adventures of Charlie Chan* is based on characters created by Earl Derr Biggers.
THEME MUSIC: Up full then under...
ANNOUNCER: Be sure to listen to the next exciting adventure of Charlie Chan.
SOUND: Chinese gong.

5. The Adventures of Father Brown

Crime drama about a Catholic parish priest with a penchant for solving crimes. Sustaining. NBC, 1945. Karl Swenson played Father Brown.

OPEN

ANNOUNCER (John Stanley): The National-Broadcasting Company presents *The Adventures of Father Brown.*
THEME MUSIC: Up full then under...
ANNOUNCER: From the exciting pages of G.K. Chesterton comes the best-loved detective of them all, Father Brown, played by Karl Swenson.

CLOSE

THEME MUSIC: Up full then under...
ANNOUNCER: *The Adventures of Father Brown*, based on the stories by G.K. Chesterton, is produced by Francis Shirling Oliver and directed by William M. Sweets. Karl Swenson was Father Brown. Music by Bill Wrogen. John Stanley speaking.
THEME MUSIC: Up full then under...
ANNOUNCER: Americans everywhere, please listen and seafaring men especially. Experienced seamen are now needed to man cargo and troop ships in the Pacific waters. Every available man of the sea is needed to keep every fighting man at the front well supplied. Join

the Merchant Marine as soon as possible. Wire your name, address and classification today, collect to Merchant Marine, Washington, D.C. Standby pay begins immediately upon acceptance. This announcement from the Warshipping Administration is brought to you as a public service. This is the National Broadcasting Company.

THEME MUSIC: Up full then out.
SOUND: NBC chimes. N-B-C.

6. The Adventures of Frank Merriwell

Turn-of-the-century adventure about Frank Merriwell, a student at Yale University who battles evil. Sustaining. NBC, 1946–1949. Lawson Zerbe played Frank Merriwell with Jean Gillespie as his girlfriend, Inza Burrage; Harold Studer as his friend, Bart Hodge; and Patricia Hosley as Elsie Bellwood, Bart's girlfriend. The Yale song, "Boola, Boola," was used as the theme.

OPEN

THEME MUSIC: Up full then under...
SOUND (over music): Horse trotting.
ANNOUNCER (Harlow Wilcox): There it is, an echo of the past; an exciting past, a romantic past. The era of the horse and carriage, gas-lit streets and free-for-all football games. The era of one of the most beloved heroes in American fiction, Frank Merriwell, the famous character created by Burt L. Standish. Frank Merriwell is loved as much today as he ever was. And so, the National Broadcasting Company brings him to radio in a brand-new series of stories.
THEME MUSIC: Up full then fade out.

CLOSE

THEME MUSIC: Up full then under...
ANNOUNCER: Be with us again next Saturday morning when *The Adventures of Frank Merriwell* returns to the air. Lawson Zerbe is heard in the title role with Jean Gillespie, Harold Studer and Patricia Hosley. *The Adventures of Frank Merriwell* is based on char-

acters created by Burt L. Standish; music is under the direction of Paul Taubman. Harlow Wilcox speaking for NBC, the National Broadcasting Company.

THEME MUSIC: Up full then fade out.
SOUND: NBC chimes. N-B-C.

7. The Adventures of Frank Race

The exploits of a former attorney turned undercover agent for the U.S. government. Various sponsors. Syn., 1949–1950. Tom Collins and Paul Dubov played Frank Race with Tony Barrett as his assistant, Mark Donovan.

OPEN

ANNOUNCER (Art Gilmore): *The Adventures of Frank Race* starring Tom Collins.
THEME MUSIC: Up full then under...
ANNOUNCER: Many things changed during the war. The face of the Earth was altered and the people of the Earth changed. Before the war, Frank Race was an attorney, but he traded his law books for the cloak and dagger of the O.S.S. And when it was over, his former life was over too. Adventure had become his business.
VOICE (echo effect): *The Adventures of Frank Race.*
THEME MUSIC: Up full then fade out.

CLOSE

THEME MUSIC: Up full then under...
ANNOUNCER: You have been listening to *The Adventures of Frank Race* starring Tom Collins. Tony Barrett is Mark Donovan. Music arranged and conducted by Ivan Ditmars. Art Gilmore speaking.
THEME MUSIC: Up full then fade out.

8. The Adventures of Leonidas Witherall

Crime drama about a British criminology professor (at the Meredith School for Boys) who looks like Shakespeare and solves crimes. Various sponsors. Mutual, 1944–1945. Walter Hampden played Leonidas Witherall with Agnes Moorehead and Ethel Remey as his housekeeper, Mrs. Mollet.

OPEN

THEME MUSIC: Up full then under...
ANNOUNCER (Carl Caruso): The Mutual Broadcasting System presents the distinguished American actor Walter Hampden in *The Adventures of Leonidas Witherall*. Leonidas Witherall is the New England school master who looks like shakespeare and is always getting mixed up in murders.
THEME MUSIC: Up full then fade out.

CLOSE

THEME MUSIC: Up full then under...
ANNOUNCER: Mutual has presented the distinguished American actor Walter Hampden in *The Adventures of Leonidas Witherall* with Agnes Moorehead as his housekeeper, Mrs. Mollet. The character of Leonidas Witherall is from the mystery novel by Alice Tilden. Listen against next Sunday evening at seven P.M. Eastern War Time for *The Adventures of Leonidas Witherall*. This program came to you from the studios of WOR in New York. This is the Mutual Broadcasting System.
THEME MUSIC: Up full then fade out.

9. The Adventures of Maisie

Comedy about Maisie Revere, a glamorous blonde looking for her big break in show business. Various sponsors. CBS (1945–1947), Syn. (1949–1952). Ann Sothern played Maisie Revere. Harry Zimmerman composed the theme, "Maisie."

OPEN

SOUND: Girl walking, followed by a man whistling (the wolf call).
MAN: Hi ya, babe, say how about a—
SOUND: Man's face getting slapped.
MAN: Ouch.
MAISIE: Does that answer your question, buddy?
THEME MUSIC: Up full then under...

ANNOUNCER (John Easton): *The Adventures of Maisie* starring Ann Sothern. You all remember Metro-Goldwyn-Mayer's famous *Maisie* pictures. In just a moment you'll hear Maisie on radio starring the glamorous star you all went to see and loved on the screen, Ann Sothern. And now, here's Ann Sothern as Maisie.
MAISIE: Yup, I'm Maisie like the man said, Maisie Revere of Brooklyn. They say all roads lead to Brooklyn and I believe it because I personally walked all over them. I'm in show business; it seems I'm either walking to a job that is ready to fold or walking back from one that has... [Maisie's speech would vary after the first line but all would revolve around her experiences in show business.]

CLOSE

ANNOUNCER: You have just heard *The Adventures of Maisie* starring Ann Sothern. And now again, here is Maisie.
MAISIE: Well feet, you got a new job dancing in a night club, so let's get there and get goin'.
MUSIC THEME: Up full then under...
ANNOUNCER: Maisie was written by John L. Greene. Original music was composed and conducted by Harry Zimmerman. John Easton speaking.
THEME MUSIC: Up full then fade out.

The Adventures of Michael Shayne *see* Michael Shayne

The Adventures of Nero Wolfe *see* Nero Wolfe

10. The Adventures of Ozzie and Harriet

Comical incidents in the lives of real-life marrieds Ozzie Nelson and Harriet Hilliard and their children, David and Ricky. Sponsored by General Electric, Heinz, International Silver and Lambert. CBS (1944–1948; 1949), NBC (1948–1949), ABC (1949–1954). Ozzie and Harriet Nelson played themselves; Tommy Bernard, Joel

Davis and David Nelson played David; Henry Blair and Ricky Nelson play Ricky. Basis for the television series.

OPEN

THEME MUSIC: Up full then under...

ANNOUNCER (Verne Smith): The solid silver with beauty that lives forever is International Sterling. From Hollywood, International Silver Company, creators of International Sterling, presents *The Adventures of Ozzie and Harriet* starring America's favorite young couple, Ozzie Nelson and Harriet Hilliard.

THEME MUSIC: Up full then out.

ANNOUNCER: International Silver now takes you to 1847 Rodgers Road and to the home of America's favorite young couple, Ozzie and Harriet, for a peek into their not so private lives...

CLOSE

THEME MUSIC: Up full then under...

ANNOUNCER: You have been listening to *The Adventures of Ozzie and Harriet*, presented by International Silver Company, creators of International Silver, the solid silver that lasts forever. Also heard in tonight's cast were David and Ricky Nelson, Janet Waldo, Bea Benaderet and John Brown as Thorny. *The Adventures of Ozzie and Harriet* is produced by Dave Elton and Ozzie Nelson with music by the Billy May orchestra.

THEME MUSIC: Up full then under...

ANNOUNCER: This is Verne Smith reminding you that even though the war is over, our government still needs tin to send food and medical supplies to our troops overseas. The need is great and the supply is limited. For the time being, our most valuable tin mine is the American kitchen. Please save all tin cans and prepare them in accordance with local salvage requirements. We thank you.

THEME MUSIC: Up full then out.

ANNOUNCER: This is CBS, the Columbia Broadcasting System.

11. The Adventures of Philip Marlowe

Crime drama about a hard-hitting, two-fisted Los Angeles-based private detective. Various sponsors (Ford and Lever Brothers were frequent sponsors). NBC (1947), CBS (1948–1951). Van Heflin and Gerald Mohr played Philip Marlowe.

OPEN (Van Heflin)

THEME MUSIC: Up full then under...

ANNOUNCER (Wendell Niles): Lever Brothers Company presents the Pepsodent program *The Adventures of Philip Marlowe* starring Van Heflin. Philip Marlowe, the screen's most famous private detective created by Raymond Chandler, brought to you on the air by Pepsodent and starring M-G-M's brilliant and dynamic young actor Van Heflin.

THEME MUSIC: Up full then out.

CLOSE

THEME MUSIC: Up full then under...

ANNOUNCER: You have been listening to the Pepsodent program *The Adventures of Philip Marlowe* with Van Heflin in the title role. Philip Marlowe is based on the character created by Raymond Chandler. All names used in tonight's story are fictional; any similarity to real persons, living or dead, is purely coincidental. This is Wendell Niles speaking for Lever Brothers, makers of Pepsodent Tooth Paste, reminding you to be with us again next week when Lever Brothers will present another adventure of Philip Marlowe. This is NBC, the National Broadcasting Company.

THEME MUSIC: Up full then out.

SOUND: NBC chimes. N-B-C.

OPEN (Gerald Mohr)

MARLOWE: Get this and get it straight. Crime is a sucker's road and those who travel it wind up in the gutter, the prison or the grave.

THEME MUSIC: Up full then under...

ANNOUNCER (Roy Rowan): From the pen of Raymond Chandler, outstanding author of crime fiction, comes his most famous character and crime's most deadly enemy as CBS presents *The Adventures of Philip Marlowe*. Now, with Gerald Mohr starring as Philip Marlowe, we bring you another case from the files of Philip Marlowe, Private Detective.

THEME MUSIC: Up full then out.

CLOSE

THEME MUSIC: Up full then under...

ANNOUNCER: You have been listening to Gerald Mohr starring in *The Adventures of Philip Marlowe*. Philip Marlowe is based on the character created by Raymond Chandler and is produced by Norman MacDonnell with original music composed and conducted by Richard Aurandt. All names and places in tonight's story are fictitious; any similarity to [real] persons or places is purely coincidental. Be with us again next Friday when Gerald Mohr will return in *The Adventures of Philip Marlowe*. This is Roy Rowan speaking for CBS, the Columbia Broadcasting System.

THEME MUSIC: Up full then fade out.

12. The Adventures of Rin Tin Tin

Adventure about a boy (Rusty) and his dog (Rin Tin Tin) and their experiences with the men of the Fighting Blue Devils of the 101st Cavalry. Sponsored by Nabisco Shredded Wheat and Milkbone dog biscuits. Mutual, 1955. Based on the television series of the same title.

OPEN

SOUND: Bugle call.

ANNOUNCER (Don Morrow): The National Biscuit Company presents *The Adventures of Rin Tin Tin*.

RUSTY: Yo, Rinty!

SOUND: Dog barking.

CHORUS:

Rin Tin Tin, Rin Tin Tin,
Rinty, Rinty, Rin Tin Tin.
Rin Tin Tin is brought to you by
Shredded Wheat and Milkbone too.
Rusty and Rinty, side by side,
Loyal heroics, the regiment's pride.
Action, drama, you'll find them in

The Adventures of Rin Tin Tin.

THEME MUSIC: Up full then under...

ANNOUNCER: The National Biscuit Company presents this week's *Adventures of Rin Tin Tin*.

SOUND: Dog barking.

ANNOUNCER: You know keeping up with Rin Tin Tin is a real man-sized job. Now tell me Rusty, just how do you do it?

RUSTY: Well sir, I have a man-sized breakfast, Nabisco Shredded Wheat. And boy, is Nabisco Shredded Wheat ever fun to eat. It looks just like a raft in your milk.

ANNOUNCER: Ah, you're so right, and believe me, those rafts of Nabisco Shredded Wheat are just loaded with energy, the energy you need to keep you on the go all day long. In fact, everybody needs the raft of energy in Nabisco Shredded Wheat.

RUSTY: So be like me. Every morning sail a raft of Nabisco Shredded Wheat into your breakfast bowl.

ANNOUNCER: Kids, just ask Mom to get you the package with Niagara Falls on the end and you'll be sure you're eating the kind Rusty eats, Nabisco, the original shredded wheat. Now back to *The Adventures of Rin Tin Tin*.

CLOSE

SOUND: Dog barking.

ANNOUNCER: Milkbone dog biscuits do more for your dog. Milkbone is packed with proteins, minerals and vitamins and has more energy per pound than beef steak. You can feed your dog nothing else and he'll thrive. Feed your dog Milkbone dog biscuits in the yellow and red box. It comes in three bone sizes— small, medium and large. Your dog will love Milkbone.

THEME MUSIC: Up full then under...

ANNOUNCER: Don't forget next Sunday at this same time over this same station for another exciting chapter in *The Adventures of Rin Tin Tin*, presented by the National Biscuit Company, makers of Milkbone dog biscuits, and Nabisco, the original shredded wheat. For *The Adventures of Rin Tin Tin* on television, consult your local paper for time and station. This is Don Morrow speaking and this program came to you transcribed from New York.

THEME MUSIC: Up full then fade out.

13. The Adventures of Sam Spade

Crime drama about a tough private detective who will take any case for money. Sponsored most often by Wild Root Creme Oil. ABC (1946), CBS (1946–1950), NBC (1950–1951). Howard Duff and Steve Dunne played Sam Spade with Lurene Tuttle as his secretary, Effie Perrine.

OPEN (CBS)

THEME MUSIC: Up full then under…

ANNOUNCER (Dick Joy): Dashiell Hammett, America's leading detective fiction writer, and William Spier, radio's outstanding producer-director of mystery and crime drama, join their talents to make your hair stand on end with *The Adventures of Sam Spade*, presented by the makers of Wild Root Creme Oil for the hair. And now, with Howard Duff starring as Sam Spade, Wild Root brings to the air the greatest private detective of them all in *The Adventures of Sam Spade*.

SOUND: Telephone rings.

EFFIE (picking up receiver): Sam Spade Detective Agency.

SAM: Hello, sweetheart, it's only me.

EFFIE: Oh, Sam, why so modest?

SAM: If you will only contain your feminine curiosity for a few minutes, I'll be right over to dictate my report.

THEME MUSIC: Up full then out.

CLOSE (CBS)

THEME MUSIC: Up full then under…

ANNOUNCER: *The Adventures of Sam Spade*, Dashiell Hammett's famous private detective, are produced and directed by William Spier. Sam Spade is played by Howard Duff; Laurene Tuttle is Effie. Join us next Sunday when author Dashiell Hammett and producer William Spier join forces for another adventure with Sam Spade, brought to you by Wild Root Creme Oil. Again and again, the choice for men who put good grooming first. Dick Joy speaking.

THEME MUSIC: Up full then fade out.

ANNOUNCER: This is CBS, the Columbia Broadcasting System.

OPEN (NBC)

THEME MUSIC: Up full then under…

ANNOUNCER: In response to requests representing millions of listening friends, the National Broadcasting Company is pleased to bring you again, *The Adventures of Sam Spade*. William Spier, radio's outstanding producer-director of mystery and crime drama, brings you the greatest detective of them all in *The Adventures of Sam Spade*.

THEME MUSIC: Up full then out.

CLOSE (NBC)

THEME MUSIC: Up full then under…

ANNOUNCER: The National Broadcasting Company has presented *The Adventures of Sam Spade* with Steve Dunne starring as Sam Spade. Sam Spade is based on the character created by Dashiell Hammett and produced and directed for radio by William Spier. All names and places used in tonight's story are fictional; any resemblance to actual people, living or dead, is unintentional. Be with us again next Friday when William Spier, radio's outstanding producer-director of mystery crime drama will present Mr. Stephen Dunne in another Sam Spade adventure.

THEME MUSIC: Up full then out.

ANNOUNCER: This is NBC, the National Broadcasting Company.

SOUND: NBC chimes. N–B–C.

14. The Adventures of Superman

Adaptation of the comic book story about Clark Kent, a reporter for the Metropolis *Daily Planet*, who is actually Superman, an alien (from the planet Krypton) who battles evil on Earth. Various sponsors (Kellogg's Pep cereal was a frequent sponsor). Syn. (1938–1939), Mutual (1940–1949), ABC (1949–1951). Clayton "Bud" Collyer and Michael Fitzmaurice played Clark Kent with Joan Alexander as Lois Lane, Jackie Kelk as Jimmy Olsen and Julian Noa as Perry White.

OPEN (ORIGINAL)

ANNOUNCER: Boys and girls, your attention

please. Presenting a new, exciting radio program featuring the thrilling adventures of that amazing and indestructible personality. Faster than a speeding bullet. More powerful than a locomotive. Impervious to bullets.

VOICES: Up in the sky, look! It's a giant bird! It's a plane! It's Superman!

ANNOUNCER: And now, *Superman*, a being no larger than an ordinary man but possessed of powers and abilities never before realized on Earth. Able to leap into the air an eighth of a mile at a single bound; hurtle a twenty story building with ease; race a high-powered bullet to its target; lift tremendous weights; and bend steel in his bare hands as though it were paper. Superman, the strange visitor from a distant planet, champion of the oppressed, physical marvel extraordinary who has sworn to devote his existence on Earth to helping those in need.

CLOSE

ANNOUNCER: Fellows and girls, follow *The Adventures of Superman* everyday Monday through Friday, same time, same station. *Superman* is a copyright feature appearing in *Superman-D.C. Publications*. This is Mutual.

OPEN (Revised)

ANNOUNCER: Kellogg's Pep, the super delicious cereal, presents—

NARRATOR: *The Adventures of Superman.*

ANNOUNCER: Faster than a speeding bullet.

SOUND: Bullet ricochet.

ANNOUNCER: More powerful than a locomotive.

SOUND: Train effect.

ANNOUNCER: Able to leap tall buildings in a single bound.

SOUND: Burst of wind.

VOICES: Look up in the sky! It's a bird! It's a plane! It's Superman!

ANNOUNCER: Yes it's *Superman*. Before we begin today's story here's a suggestion for you. Say gang, have you ever noticed that when fellows get together these days they often talk about aviation. That's why I want to tell you about the wonderful prizes that are in the Kellogg's Pep packages these days because it's a swell way to build up your aviation knowledge. Now this prize is a model plane made of col-

ored cardboard and it's just as easy as pie to put together. And furthermore, on the back of the plane there are lots of pointers about that particular model. Now there are 14 different models you can get altogether. Exciting planes like the British Lanchester Bomber and the Douglas Dauntless Dive Bomber and the Russian Single Sea Fighter, the 118. And best of all, you don't have to send in a single penny to get them. Not even a box top. There's a model plane right inside every single Pep package. So gang, be sure Mother gets you a package of those delicious whole wheat flakes tomorrow. See which model plane you find inside. And remember the name Pep, P-E-P. Pep, the famous cereal is made by Kellogg's of Battle Creek.

NARRATOR: And now to *The Adventures of Superman.*

CLOSE

NARRATOR: Tomorrow's episode is tense and exciting so don't miss it. Tune in and follow *The Adventures of Superman* brought to you everyday Monday through Friday, same time, same station, by the makers of that super delicious cereal, Kellogg's Pep. *Superman* is a copyrighted feature appearing in *Superman* and *D.C. Publications*. This is Mutual.

15. The Adventures of the Abbotts

Light-hearted crime drama about Jean and Pat Abbott, newlyweds fascinated by murder and mayhem. Sustaining. NBC, 1955. Claudia Morgan and Les Damon played Jean and Pat Abbott.

OPEN

THEME MUSIC: Up full then under…

ANNOUNCER (Cy Harrice): The National Broadcasting Company presents *The Adventures of the Abbotts* starring Claudia Morgan and Les Damon as Jean and Pat Abbott, those popular characters of detective fiction created by Frances Crane. NBC invites you to join Pat and Jean each week at this time for another exciting, recorded adventure in romance and crime. Here is Claudia Morgan as Jean Abbott to set the stage for tonight's puzzle in murder.

JEAN: Good evening... [She would then set up the story.]

CLOSE

THEME MUSIC: Up full then under...

ANNOUNCER: Jean and Pat Abbott will return next week at this same time with another murder mystery based on the characters created by Frances Crane. Claudia Morgan is heard as Jean with Les Damon as Pat. All names used in tonight's story were fictitious; any similarity to persons living or dead is purely coincidental. Cy Harrice speaking. This is NBC, the National Broadcasting Company,

THEME MUSIC: Up full then out.

SOUND: NBC chimes. N-B-C.

Adventures of the Thin Man *see* The Thin Man

16. The Adventures of Topper

Comical incidents in the life of Cosmo Topper (Roland Young), a droll businessman who is haunted by the ghosts of George and Marian Kerby (Paul Mann and Frances Chaney). Sponsored by Maxwell House Coffee and Post Cereals.

OPEN

GEORGE: Hey, Topper.

MARIAN: Oh Topper, darling, we're back.

TOPPER: Here we go again.

ANNOUNCER (Richard Kollmar): *The Adventures of Topper* starring Roland Young. *The Adventures of Topper*, a new comedy series based on Thorne Smith's hilarious best-seller, is brought to you by the makers of those bubbly light, crisper corn flakes, Post Toasties.

SONG (CHORUS):

> We toast 'em crisp,
> We toast 'em light,

> You can tell by the taste
> We toast 'em.
> They're a tasty treat,
> So good to eat,
> Delicious and light,
> Post Toasties, Pooost Toast-ies.

VOICE: And you know what, we like 'em!

THEME MUSIC: Up full then under...

ANNOUNCER: And now let's meet Topper.

TOPPER: Hello, my name is Cosmo Topper. I suppose some of you have a couple of friends who are considered nobody. Well, I have a couple of friends who actually have no bodies; a pair of ghosts named George and Marian Kerby. The trouble they've cause me! If things continue as they are, they'll be the death of me yet... [He would then begin the story.]

CLOSE

ANNOUNCER: I think you would like golden brown Post Toasties with fresh fruit and swimming in milk. Sounds good, doesn't it? Well it truly is. You see with Post Toasties you enjoy delicious toasted flakes that are packed with grand sunny flavor and you're gonna find that each delicious spoonful is toastfully bubbly light and crunchy down to the last tempting bite. So, for real refreshment, neighbors, buy golden brown Post Toasties. Serve them often. You'll like 'em.

THEME MUSIC: Up full then under...

ANNOUNCER: Be sure to listen to *Topper* starring Roland Young next Thursday, same time, same station. This is Richard Kollmar saying good night for the makers of those bubbly light, crisper corn flakes, Post Toasties. This program has come to you from our Radio City studios in New York. This is the National Broadcasting Company.

THEME MUSIC: Up full then fade out.

SOUND: NBC chimes. N-B-C.

17. Afloat with Henry Morgan

Serialized adventures of Henry Morgan, the notorious 17th century pirate. Sustaining. Syn., 1934. George Edwards played Henry Morgan.

OPEN

THEME MUSIC: Up full then under…

ANNOUNCER: *Afloat with Henry Morgan*, an original story written for radio by Warren Barry and a George Edwards production. History contains stories of colorful people, rogues, heroes, kings and commoners. But there were few who had such a picturesque, bloodstained career culminating in honored glory as a man named Morgan in the seventeenth century. Henry Morgan, pirate, whose foul deeds earned him the name of Colossus of the Caribbean, who eventually became Sir Henry Morgan, king's representative, governor of Jamaica.

THEME MUSIC: Up full then fade out.

CLOSE

THEME MUSIC: Up full then under…

ANNOUNCER: Don't miss the next exciting episode of *Afloat with Henry Morgan*.

THEME MUSIC: Up full then out.

18. The Aldrich Family

The misadventures of Henry Aldrich, a teenager in the town of Centerville. Various sponsors (Grape Nuts Flakes and Jell-O were frequent sponsors). NBC (1939–1944; 1946–1953), CBS (1944–1946). Ezra Stone, Norman Tokar, Raymond Ives, Dick Jones and Bobby Ellis played Henry. Sam, his father, was played by Clyde Fillmore, House Jameson and Tom Shirley. Henry's mother, Alice, was played by Lea Penman, Katherine Raht and Regina Wallace. Homer Brown, Henry's friend, was played by Jackie Kelk and Jack Grimes. Basis for the television series.

OPEN

SPONSOR'S THEME ("J-E-L-L-O"): Up full then under…

ANNOUNCER (Harry Von Zell): And now the Jell-O family presents—

ALICE (in shrill voice): Henry! Henry Aldrich!

HENRY (voice cracking): Coming Mother.

ANNOUNCER: Yes, it's *The Aldrich Family*, based on characters created by Clifford Goldsmith and starring Ezra Stone as Henry and Jackie Kelk as Homer. And yes, it's the Jell-O family—

HENRY AND HOMER SINGING:
Oh, the big red letters
Stand for the Jell-O family.
That's Jell-O, yum, yum, yum.
Jell-O puddings, yum, yum, yum.
Jell-O tap-i-oca puddings,
Yes sir-reeeee.

ANNOUNCER: and now to *The Aldrich Family* with Ezra Stone as Henry.

CLOSE

THEME MUSIC: Up full then under…

ANNOUNCER: The new Jell-O puddings are here. They're far easier and quicker to make. They have that real old-fashioned goodness, creamy, smooth, full-flavored and tempting. There are three delicious Jell-O puddings to choose from. Rich chocolate, mellow butterscotch and creamy, delicate vanilla. Yes, you'll like these new Jell-O puddings, real old-fashioned puddings made a new-fashioned way. So try them tomorrow.

THEME MUSIC: Up full then under…

ANNOUNCER: Be with us again next week for further adventures of Henry Aldrich. *The Aldrich Family* starring Ezra Stone is written by Clifford Goldsmith. Original music is composed and conducted by Jack Miller. Harry Von Zell speaking and wishing you a good night for those delicious new desserts all America is talking about—Jell-O puddings. This is the National Broadcasting Company.

THEME MUSIC: Up full then out.

SOUND: NBC chimes. N-B-C.

19. Amanda of Honeymoon Hill

Daily serial drama about a woman of a lower class status (Amanda Dyke) who marries the wealthy son of an aristocratic family (Edward Leighton). Sponsored by Phillips Milk of Magnesia. NBC Blue (1940–1942), CBS (1942–1946). Joy Hathaway played Amanda; Boyd Crawford, George Lambert and Staats Cotsworth played Edward.

THEME MUSIC: Up full then under...

ANNOUNCER (Frank Gallop): The makers of Phillips Milk of Magnesia Tablets presents *Amanda of Honeymoon Hill*, radio's drama of love and life in wartime in the romantic South. The story of a beautiful valley girl, Amanda Dyke, who married the son of an aristocratic family up on the hill, Edward Leighton.

THEME MUSIC: Up full then out.

ANNOUNCER: Today, at the end of our show, a special appeal will be made to every woman in America who is eligible to join the WAVES. Hundreds of thousands of WAVES are needed urgently—at once! Full details will be given at the end of the broadcast.

THEME MUSIC: Up full then under...

ANNOUNCER: And now for our drama, *Amanda of Honeymoon Hill*.

CLOSE

ANNOUNCER: Today we make an urgent appeal to the women of America to join the WAVES. As you know, our American Navy has now become the biggest in the world. This rapid growth of the Navy has made it necessary now, today, for the Navy to call upon the women of America for one of the most important jobs women have been asked to do in this war—to enlist by the thousands as WAVES. You're needed to put on the glorious blue uniform of the Navy, to step in and free a sailor from a shore job so he can take his place on one of the hundreds of new Navy ships and planes which now go forward to fight in one of the fiercest battles of the war. As a WAVE you may help direct the take off and landing of planes as a control tower operator; send and receive important code messages; help locate men and ships at sea; make up weather charts and so forth. The only qualifications to become a WAVE are you must be an American citizen, 20 to 35 years old with at least two years of high school or business school training and have no children under 18. For further details, go to your nearest Navy recruiting station today. Do this at once, today. Our American Navy needs you

as a WAVE in order to use its mighty strength most effectively in the days just ahead.

THEME MUSIC: Up full then under...

ANNOUNCER: *Amanda of Honeymoon Hill* is presented each day at this time by the makers of Phillips Milk of Magnesia Tablets. Don't miss our broadcast tomorrow. And please stay tuned for *Second Husband*, which follows immediately. This is CBS, the Columbia Broadcasting System.

THEME MUSIC: Up full then out.

Note: The opening and closings were taken from the episode of June 6, 1944, the day of D-Day invasion. It is one of only a few episodes that are in circulation.

Amazing Adventures of Flash Gordon *see* Flash Gordon

20. The Amazing Mr. Malone

Crime drama centering on Chicago criminal attorney John J. Malone. Sustaining. ABC (1949–1950), NBC (1950–1951). Gene Raymond and George Petrie played John J. Malone. See also *Murder and Mr. Malone*.

OPEN

ANNOUNCER (Arthur Gary): The National Broadcasting Company presents *The Amazing Mr. Malone*, an exciting half-hour of mystery starring George Petrie as the lawyer whose practice before every type of bar has become a legend. Our locale is the city of Chicago; the time, the present; and the hero of these weekly adventures, the amazing Mr. Malone.

THEME MUSIC: Up full then under...

MALONE: Malone's the name, John J. Malone, attorney and counselor-at-law. You know it's often said that no visit to Chicago is complete without taking in the field museum, the stockyards and yours truly. And as you probably guessed, I'm the one who often says it... [Malone would then begin the story].

CLOSE

THEME MUSIC: Up full then under...

MALONE: Ever hear the story of "The Incurable Gambler?" I'll tell you all about it next week, so why not pick me up at my office at this same time. I'll be waiting for you. Good night.

ANNOUNCER: George Petrie was starred as John J. Malone with Larry Haines as Lieutenant Brooks. Our program is written by Gene Wang and directed by Richard Lewis. *The Amazing Mr. Malone* is based on a character created by Craig Rice and produced by Bernard L. Schubert. The events and characters in this story were entirely fictional and any resemblance to persons living or dead is entirely coincidental. Arthur Gary speaking.

THEME MUSIC: Up full then under...

ANNOUNCER: *The Amazing Mr. Malone* has come to you from New York. Three chimes mean good times on NBC. This Sunday you're invited to meet one of your favorite families here on NBC, the Blandings. Cary Grant and Betsy Drake star every Sunday in another delightful adventure of the proud but confused owners of the famous dream house. And don't forget for mystery this Sunday, you'll hear a new private eye, *Mr. Moto*, who arrives with a swash of the buckle, an eye for a pretty girl, and a handy talent for solving murders. This is NBC, the National Broadcasting Company.

SOUND: NBC chimes. N-B-C.

21. The Amazing Mr. Smith

Comical events in the life of Geoffrey Smith, an independently wealthy, amateur sleuth. Various sponsors. CBS, 1946–1947. Alan Johnston played Geoffrey Smith with Ed Brophy as his friend Herbie.

OPEN

THEME MUSIC: Up full then under...

ANNOUNCER (Ken Niles): *The Amazing Mr. Smith* starring Alan Johnston as Geoffrey Smith and Ed Brophy as Herbie. Geoffrey Smith, so you all will know, is a young man about Hollywood who has the amazing faculty for attracting trouble in various and unexpected forms. From his family, Geoffrey

Smith has inherited a comfortable income; while from his Army career, he has inherited his ex-sergeant, Herbie, who has since become a devoted valet, chauffeur and bodyguard.

THEME MUSIC: Up full then under as a story begins.

CLOSE

ANNOUNCER: This is Ken Niles inviting you to tune in next week for another adventure with *The Amazing Mr. Smith* starring Alan Johnston and Ed Brophy. Original music is composed and conducted by Lud Gluskin. These programs are written and produced by Martin Gosch and Howard Harris and come to you from Hollywood. This is CBS, the Columbia Broadcasting System.

22. The Amos 'n' Andy Show

Comedy that centers on three best friends who live on Lexington Avenue in New York City: Amos Jones, Andrew Halt Brown and George "Kingfish" Stevens. Sponsored by Campbell's Soup, Pepsodent, Rexall and Rinso. NBC (1929–1939; 1943–1948), CBS (1939–1943; 1948–1954). Freeman Gosden played Amos and George; Charles Correll was Andy. "The Perfect Song" and "The Angels Serenade" were used as the theme.

OPEN (for Rinso)

AMOS: Andy, listen, the man is just about to say it.

ANDY: Yeah. Let's everybody listen.

ANNOUNCER (Ken Niles): Rinso, the new Rinso with Solieum, brings you *The Amos 'n' Andy Show*.

THEME MUSIC: Up full then under...

ANNOUNCER: Yes sir, Rinso, the soap that contains Solieum, the sun light ingredient, brings you a full half-hour of entertainment with the Jubalaires, Jeff Alexander's orchestra and chorus, and radio's all-time favorites, Amos and Andy.

THEME MUSIC: Up full then under...

ANNOUNCER: And now Lever Brothers Company, the makers of Rinso, invite you to sit back, relax and enjoy Amos 'n' Andy.

THEME MUSIC: Up full then out.

CLOSE (for Rinso)

THEME MUSIC: Up full then under…
ANNOUNCER: Rinso, the soap that contains Solieum, has presented *The Amos 'n' Andy Show*. Join us again next Sunday when Lever Brothers Company, makers of Rinso, will again present *The Amos 'n' Andy Show*. Ken Niles speaking. This is CBS, the Columbia Broadcasting System.
THEME MUSIC: Up full then out.

OPEN (for Rexall)

ANNOUNCER (Ken Niles): Good health to all from Rexall.
THEME MUSIC: Up full then under…
ANNOUNCER: Rexall and its participating dealers again bring you *The Amos 'n' Andy Show*. And now here they are with Jeff Alexander's orchestra and chorus, radio's all-time favorites, Amos and Andy.
THEME MUSIC: Up full then out.

CLOSE (for Rexall)

ANNOUNCER: Today, millions of men, women and children in Europe and Asia are still undernourished. In spite of all the aid given by our government, the continued help of individuals is needed to combat malnutrition and disease. You can help these people by sending a food or clothing package through CARE. Why not send your contribution to the CARE office in your community. And be sure to join us again next Sunday evening at this same time when your friendly neighborhood Rexall drug store presents *The Amos 'n' Andy Show*. This is Ken Niles speaking. This is CBS, the Columbia Broadcasting System.

Note: The series began in 1926 (and ran to 1928) as *Sam and Henry* over station WGN. It became *The Amos 'n' Andy Show* in 1928 over station WMAQ before switching to NBC. From 1954 to 1960 Freeman Gosden and Charles Correll (Amos and Andy) hosted *The Amos 'n' Andy Music Hall*. The public service announcement depicted in the close of the Rexall version is typical of what the show did each week.

23. Archie Andrews

Comical events in the life of Archie Andrews and his friends: Veronica Lodge, Jughead Jones and Betty Cooper. Various sponsors (Kraft Foods and Swift and Company were frequent sponsors). Blue (1943–1944), Mutual (1944), NBC (1945–1953). Jack Grimes, Charles Mullen, Burt Boyer and Bob Hastings played Archie; Harlan Stone and Cameron Andrews were Jughead; Rosemary Rice and Vivian Smolen were Veronica; and Doris Grundy, Joy Geffen and Yvonne Mann were Betty.

OPEN

THEME MUSIC: Up full then under…
ANNOUNCER (Bob Sherry): Yes, here he is again, the youngster millions of readers of *Archie* comics and magazines know and love so well, brought to you by Swift and Company premium franks and Swift good for you sausage, Archie and all his gang. And now for our weekly visit to Riverdale.
THEME MUSIC: Up full and out.

CLOSE

ANNOUNCER: You have been listening to another chapter in the adventures of *Archie Andrews*, based on the copyright feature in *Archie* comics magazine, and brought to you by Swift and Company. In tonight's cast were Bob Hastings as Archie, Harlan Stone as Jughead, Rosemary Rice as Veronica and Yvonne Mann as Betty. Tune in again next Saturday for more merry adventures with *Archie Andrews*. This is Bob Sherry wishing you a great weekend. So long. This is NBC, the National Broadcasting Company.
SOUND: NBC chimes. N-B-C.

24. Armstrong of the S.B.I.

Spinoff from *Jack Armstrong, the All-American Boy* that focused on Jack's exploits as the chief investigator of the S.B.I. (Scientific Bureau of Investigation). Sponsored by Wheaties. ABC, 1950–1951. Charles Flynn played Jack Armstrong with Patricia Dunlap and Dick York as his assistants, Betty and Billy Fairchild. Vic Hardy, head of the S.B.I., was played by Ken Griffin and Carlton KaDell.

OPEN

ANNOUNCER (Ed Prentiss): *Armstrong of the S.B.I.*, America's foremost scientific detective, brought to by Wheaties, breakfast of champions.

SOUND: Whistle toots.

ANNOUNCER: What sparks a champion sparks you. And champions choose Wheaties.

THEME MUSIC: Up full then under…

ANNOUNCER: Tonight we shall hear an exciting mystery of violence and murder as Armstrong, chief investigator for the famous S.B.I., brings us "The Deadliest of the Species."

SOUND: Whistle toots.

ANNOUNCER: What sparks a champion sparks you. And champions choose Wheaties. You need drive, you could use that vital spark, so remember this one outstanding fact. There's a whole kernel of wheat in every Wheaties flake; every Wheaties flake you eat builds up your power, helps spark you at whatever you do. Wheaties gives you all the grains, not only part. Not just half, but the whole rich kernel. Remember, there's a whole kernel of wheat in every Wheaties flake. What sparks a champion, sparks you. And champions choose Wheaties, breakfast of champions.

SOUND: Whistle toots.

ANNOUNCER: And now to our mystery adventure as we follow Armstrong of the S.B.I. and his never-ending fight against the enemies of justice. Names of all persons and events in tonight's story must be labeled fictitious for obvious reasons. Listen now to "The Deadliest of the Species." [Story about Jack's attempts to find the killer of an S.B.I. agent before his vengeful wife does.]

CLOSE

THEME MUSIC: Up full then under…

ANNOUNCER: Listen, America, listen next Thursday for *Silver Eagle*, radio's most powerful adventure story. Meet Jim West of the Mounties in General Mills' sensational new action-packed drama of the northland, *Silver Eagle*, riding the danger trails of Canada to adventure. *Silver Eagle*, same time, same station next Thursday.

THEME MUSIC: Up full then under…

ANNOUNCER: Listen again at this same time next Tuesday when Wheaties brings you the sensational new circus adventure series *Mr. Mercury*. And remember, what sparks a champion, sparks you. And champions choose Wheaties.

THEME MUSIC: Up full then under…

ANNOUNCER: Remember, next Tuesday, the amazing *Mr. Mercury* is coming your way and next Thursday, the first thrill-packed drama of radio's most powerful action adventure, *Silver Eagle*.

SOUND: Musical sting.

ANNOUNCER: This is Ed Prentiss. The part of Jack Armstrong is played by Charles Flynn. *Armstrong of the S.B.I.* came to you from Chicago and is written and directed by Jewel Radio and Television Productions for General Mills, makers of Wheaties, breakfast of champions.

THEME MUSIC: Up full then fade out.

25. Arthur Godfrey's Talent Scouts

Variety program that spotlighted undiscovered talent. Sponsored by Lipton Tea. CBS, 1946–1956. Hosted by Arthur Godfrey.

OPEN

ANNOUNCER (George Bryan): Lipton Tea presents *Arthur Godfrey's Talent Scouts*.

SONG (by Peggy Marshall and the Holidays):

Here comes Arthur Godfrey
Your talent scout M.C.
Brought to you by Lipton's
Brisk Lipton Tea.
You know it's Lipton Tea
If it's B-R-I-S-K.
Now here comes Arthur Godfrey,
The talent's on its way.

ANNOUNCER: *Arthur Godfrey's Talent Scouts* with the music of Archie Bleyer and his orchestra, songs by Peggy Marshall and the Holidays, and starring your master of ceremonies, Arthur Godfrey.

SOUND: Applause.

ARTHUR: Thank you George Bryan and welcome ladies and gentlemen... [At which time Arthur would begin the show.]

CLOSE

THEME MUSIC: Up full then under...

ANNOUNCER: *Arthur Godfrey's Talent Scouts* has been presented by brisk Lipton Tea and featured the music of Archie Bleyer and his orchestra and songs by Peggy Marshall and the Holidays. Be sure to see *Arthur Godfrey's Talent Scouts* on CBS television; check time and channel in your area. *Arthur Godfrey's Talent Scouts* is produced by Irving Mansfield. This is George Bryan reminding you to be with us again next Monday evening when Arthur Godfrey returns for Lipton Tea with another talent session.

THEME MUSIC: Up full then out.

ANNOUNCER: This is CBS, the Columbia Broadcasting System.

26. Aunt Jenny's Thrilling Real Life Stories

Daily series featuring serialized stories related by a kindly woman named Aunt Jenny. Sponsored by Spry (a shortening). CBS, 1937–1956. Edith Spencer and Agnes Young played Aunt Jenny. The following episode from 1946 reflects the flour and sugar shortage problems that existed at the time. The song "Believe Me, If All Those Endearing Young Charms" was used as the theme.

OPEN

ANNOUNCER (Dan Seymour): Time now for Spry's double feature treat of the day.

THEME MUSIC: Opening bars.

ANNOUNCER: *Aunt Jenny's Thrilling Real Life Stories* and—

AUNT JENNY: A luscious strawberry cream pie that needn't take a bit of sugar.

THEME MUSIC: Up full then under...

ANNOUNCER: Welcome folks, it's Spry time here at Aunt Jenny's cheery kitchen. And it's Maytime all over America. That means strawber-

ries now and loads of luscious fruits to come. Aunt Jenny, I would say there is no better time than now to tell the folks more about Spry Perfect Pastry Magic.

AUNT JENNY: You're right, Danny. Fresh, ripe fruit in a tender, mouth-watering pie crust is a treat no one can resist.

ANNOUNCER: All you need is sensational new Spry and the Spry Perfect Pastry method. That combination turns amateurs into experts.

AUNT JENNY: Yes indeed, even if you've never made a pie in your life, just try this easy method and see if you ever tasted such tender, flaky, nut-sweet pastries.

ANNOUNCER: Now folks, you'll find this wonderful Spry Perfect Pastry method on some of the Spry labels. Look for it and get to be the champion pastry maker of your neighborhood.

AUNT JENNY: And ladies, be listening for a tip on making a luscious strawberry cream pie that doesn't take a grain of your precious sugar. [The daily story would then start.]

CLOSE

ANNOUNCER (to Aunt Jenny): It's time for you to give the ladies that recipe you promised them.

THEME MUSIC: Up full then under...

AUNT JENNY: And now ladies, about that delicious sugar-saving strawberry cream pie. Make up and cool your favorite packaged vanilla pudding. Then fill a tender, flaky golden Spry shell with the pudding. Top with strawberries and sweeten with honey or corn syrup and serve.

ANNOUNCER: And hear the folks sing praises as they get to work on that swell dessert.

AUNT JENNY: You know, ladies, we're asked to save wheat flour by making only one-crust pies and this is a dandy. And by the way, the marvelous Spry Perfect Pastry method works nicely with the new emergency flour, just as well with the standard all-purpose flour.

ANNOUNCER: Say, that's more swell news. Now folks, just as soon as you can, try the surefire Spry Perfect Pastry method and see if you ever tasted pie crust so moistingly [sic] tender, flaky and nut-sweet. Yes, and Spry's extra purity and blandness assure you wonderfully delicate pastry so you get all the luscious flavor of the filling.

AUNT JENNY: Remember ladies, you can't get these superb results with just any type of shortening. A Spry Perfect method was developed especially to go with the pure creamy extra blendable Spry.

ANNOUNCER: Folks, new Spry is the biggest development in years and years of home baking. No other type of shortening has Spry's cake improver secret, and sensational new Spry improves all your baking and all your frying. So, as soon as you can find it at your grocer's, try Spry. We know it's not always easy, but keep on asking for the miracle shortening of 1946. Rely on Spry.

THEME MUSIC: First two bars.

ANNOUNCER: And now here's Aunt Jenny with a golden thought for today.

AUNT JENNY: Ladies, the secret of happiness and success in whatever we do is to keep on keeping on. Quitters never win and winners never quit.

ANNOUNCER: Well, that's a thought we need every day, Aunt Jenny. Now, folks, be sure to be on hand Monday for Spry's double feature treat of the day: the continuation of *Aunt Jenny's Thrilling Real Life Story*—

AUNT JENNY: And tender Spry oatmeal muffins.

THEME MUSIC: Up full then under...

ANNOUNCER: This is Dan Seymour again inviting you to join us Monday for *Aunt Jenny's Thrilling Real Life Stories*, brought to you by Spry, sensational new Spry with cake improver. Rely on Spry. This is CBS, the Columbia Broadcasting System.

THEME MUSIC: Up full then fade out.

27. The Avenger

Crime drama about Jim Brandon, a biochemist who battles evil as the mysterious Avenger. Various sponsors. Syn., 1945–1946. James Monks played Jim Brandon with Helen Adamson as his assistant, Fern Collier.

OPEN

ANNOUNCER: *The Avenger!*

THEME MUSIC: Up full then under...

ANNOUNCER: The road to crime ends in a trap that justice sets. Crime does not pay! The Avenger, sworn enemy of evil, is actually Jim Brandon, a famous biochemist. Through his numerous scientific experiments, Brandon has perfected two inventions to aid him in his crusade against crime as the Avenger: the telepathic indicator, by which he is able to pick up thought flashes, and the secret diffusion capsules, which cloak him in the black light of invisibility. Brandon's assistant, the beautiful Fern Collier, is the only one who shares his secrets and knows that he is the man the underworld fears as the Avenger.

THEME MUSIC: Up full then out.

CLOSE

THEME MUSIC: Up full then under...

ANNOUNCER: *The Avenger* stars James Monks as Jim Brandon with Helen Adamson as Fern Collier. *The Avenger*, written by Walter Gibson, is a Charles Michaelson production.

THEME MUSIC: Up full then fade out.

28. The Baby Snooks Show

Comedy that centers around a mischievous young girl named Baby Snooks. Sponsored by General Foods and Post Cereals. CBS (1944–1949), NBC (1949–1951). Fanny Brice played Baby Snooks with Hanley Stafford as her father, Lancelot "Daddy" Higgins.

OPEN

SONG (Chorus): J-E-L-L-Oooooooo.

ANNOUNCER (Harlow Wilcox): Jell-O in those six delicious favors, and Jell-O puddings for old-fashioned, homemade goodness, bring you Baby Snooks.

THEME MUSIC ("Rock-a-Bye Baby"): Up full then under...

ANNOUNCER: Yes, it's *The Baby Snooks Show* starring Fanny Brice as Baby Snooks with Hanley Stafford as Daddy, Carmen Dragon and his orchestra and yours truly, Harlow Wilcox, and brought to you each week by Jell-O and Jell-O puddings.

CLOSE

ANNOUNCER: We hope you'll be with us again next week when Snooks gets going in another of her amazing adventures. Remember Jell-O and Jell-O puddings. Snooks, what do you have to say about Jell-O?

SNOOKS (singing): Just a taste of Jell-O puddings or of Jell-O and you'll know, it's the one and only J-E-L-L-O. I like it.

MUSIC: Up full then under...

SOUND: Dog barking.

ANNOUNCER: Happy, healthy dogs speak for Gaines. Gaines complete meal contains everything dogs are known to need, many things meat alone cannot provide. Make Gaines the main part of every feeding to be sure you nourish every inch of your dog. And it's more economical than any other dog food. Let your dog speak for Gaines, America's largest-selling dog food.

MUSIC: Up full then under...

ANNOUNCER: Be sure to listen to *The Thin Man* which follows in just one minute. This is Harlow Wilcox speaking. This is CBS, the Columbia Broadcasting System.

MUSIC: Up full then fade out.

29. Bachelor's Children

Daily serial drama about a World War I veteran (Dr. Robert Graham) who becomes the legal guardian of two young women (Janet and Ruth Ann) after the death of their father. Sponsored by Colgate, Hostess Snack Cakes, Old Dutch Cleanser, Wonder Bread. CBS, 1936–1946. Hugh Studebaker played Robert; Patricia Dunlap was Janet; and Marjorie Hannan and Laurette Fillbrandt were Ruth Ann. The song "Ah, Sweet Mystery of Life" was used as the theme.

OPEN

THEME MUSIC: Up full then under...

ANNOUNCER (Don Gordon): Wonder Bread, the bread that's doubly fresh, fresh when you buy it and fresh when you eat it, presents *Bachelor's Children*.

THEME MUSIC: Up full then under...

ANNOUNCER: *Bachelor's Children*, radio's most beloved serial, is brought to you by the bakers of Wonder Bread and Hostess Cakes and is dedicated to the grocers of America.

THEME MUSIC: Up full then out.

ANNOUNCER: Some children don't seem to get ahead very fast. Sometimes they're tired for no other reason than they don't get enough energy food. After all, a child burns up a lot of energy in school and out. If they could only get it like a car by stepping on the gas, there would be no problem; but even at that, your child's body is like a motor; the energy comes from food instead of gasoline. And instead of a sparkplug, the body uses vitamin B-1 to help transform food into energy. So if your child needs more energy maybe all he needs to do is eat extra food with extra vitamin B-1—and that's where energy-charged Wonder Bread comes in to give that extra energy. Because not only is Wonder Bread charged with energy, but it contains extra vitamin B-1. On top of that, Wonder Bread is doubly fresh. Fresh when you buy it, fresh when you eat it. That's because it's slow baked; baked 13 percent longer than many ordinary kinds for lasting freshness. It tastes swell. Get energy-charged Wonder Bread today and serve extra slices for extra energy. Your family will love it.

THEME MUSIC: Up full then under...

ANNOUNCER: And now *Bachelor's Children*.

CLOSE

ANNOUNCER: If you don't care how long bread stays fresh you have no problem. But if you do, the bread you want is one that's fresh and stays fresh. That's energy-charged Wonder Bread, fresh when you buy it, fresh when you eat it. Remember, energy-charged Wonder Bread can help you charge up your energy. So eat extra Wonder Bread every day for extra energy. Get doubly charged Wonder Bread from your grocer today, you'll be glad you did.

THEME MUSIC: Up full then under...

ANNOUNCER: In the interest of your family's health get new Wonder Bread, made with vitamin B-1, the bread that's double fresh—fresh when you buy it, fresh when you eat it.

THEME MUSIC: Up full then under...

ANNOUNCER: If you take one quart out of a gallon, you have three quarts left. That's the story about black market gasoline. With only so much gasoline, ration coupons are issued to divide it fair and square. Stolen and counterfeit coupons for the black market trade take gasoline out of circulation. In fact, if there were no black market, A Coupons would be good for 25 percent more gasoline. Thus, you can see the wisdom of playing square with gasoline rationing. So make sure you turn coupons in for the gas you get and be sure to write your license number and state on the face of all your coupons.

THEME MUSIC: Up full then under…

ANNOUNCER: *Bachelor's Children* will return to the air tomorrow at this same time. Don Gordon speaking. This program has come to you from our Chicago studios in the Wrigley Building. This is CBS, the Columbia Broadcasting System.

THEME MUSIC: Up full then fade out.

30. Backstage Wife

Daily serial about an Iowa stenographer (Mary) who marries a Broadway star (Larry Noble) and her struggles to adjust to a new life style. Various sponsors. Mutual (1935–1936), Blue (1936), NBC (1936–1955), CBS (1955–1959). Vivian Fridell and Claire Niesen played Mary Noble with Ken Griffin, James Meighan and Guy Sorel as Larry Noble. The song "Stay As Sweet As You Are" was used as the theme.

Open

THEME MUSIC: Up full then under…

ANNOUNCER (Ford Bond): Sweetheart Soap, the soap for a brighter, lovelier complexion, presents *Backstage Wife*.

THEME MUSIC: Up full then under…

ANNOUNCER: *Backstage Wife*, the story of Mary Noble and what it means to be the wife of a famous star.

THEME MUSIC: Up full then out.

ANNOUNCER: Women who long for a brighter, smoother, more attractive complexion, listen to Sweetheart Soap's sensational guarantee. To those of you who change from careless care with wrong soap to extra care with Sweetheart Soap, Sweetheart guarantees to help you have a cleaner, fresher, smoother, brighter skin. You know how famous beauties rely on soft water for lovelier complexions, well soft water helps soap lather better and Sweetheart gives you this lather-effective soft water in ordinary water right in your own home. Either you look lovelier or mail us the wrapper and your reasons and get your money back plus postage. Get the soap that guarantees you greater loveliness, Sweetheart Soap.

THEME MUSIC: Up full then under…

ANNOUNCER: And now to today's story of *Backstage Wife*…

Close

THEME MUSIC: Up full then under…

ANNOUNCER: Sweetheart Soap for a lovelier complexion, has presented *Backstage Wife*. Be sure to be listening tomorrow for the continuing story of Mary Noble and her husband Larry. Chet Kingsbury is heard at the organ. *Backstage Wife* is produced by Frank and Anne Hummert. Ford Bond speaking. This is NBC, the National Broadcasting Company.

THEME MUSIC: Up full then out.

SOUND: NBC chimes. N-B-C.

Note: The above signatures were taken from an episode late in the series. An earlier version opened as follows:

ANNOUNCER: We present again today *Backstage Wife*, the story of Mary Noble, an Iowa girl who marries Larry Noble, handsome matinee idol, dream sweetheart of a million other women, and her struggles to keep his love in the complicated atmosphere of backstage life.

31. The Big Guy

Crime drama about private detective Joshua Sharp (Henry Calvin), a widower and the father of two children, Debbie and Joshua, Jr. (Denise Alexander, David Anderson). Various sponsors. NBC, 1950.

Open

SOUND: Joshua laughing.

DEBBIE: How tall are you, Papa? Tell me how tall.

JOSHUA: I'm twenty-foot-five in my stocking feet.

JOSHUA, JR.: How big are your shoes?

DEBBIE: What size do you wear?

JOSHUA: Size 902 in Triple Z.

DEBBIE: That's our papa, the big guy.

THEME MUSIC: Up full then under...

ANNOUNCER (Fred Collins): NBC presents *The Big Guy*, the adventures of a very unusual detective, Joshua Sharp. Joshua Sharp works for clients on a strictly cash basis to provide for the needs of his nearest and dearest; his nearest and dearest are two in number—Josh, Jr., and his daughter Debbie. To these two, Sharp is both father and mother; to his clients he is a good detective; to Josh and Debbie, he is the friendly magician, the fabulous hero, the giant among giants—the big guy.

THEME MUSIC: Up full then out.

CLOSE

THEME MUSIC: Up full then under...

ANNOUNCER: The National Broadcasting Company has presented the adventures of *The Big Guy*, played by Henry Calvin. Joshua Sharp, detective, works for his clients on a strictly cash basis to provide for the needs of his nearest and dearest, Josh, Jr. and Debbie. To them he is the friendly magician, the fabulous hero, the giant among giants—the big guy.

THEME MUSIC: Up full then under...

ANNOUNCER: *The Big Guy* features David Anderson as Josh, Jr. and Denise Alexander as Debbie. Music is by George Wright. Your announcer, Fred Collins.

THEME MUSIC: Up full then out.

SOUND: NBC chimes. N-B-C.

32. The Big Show

Performances by top-name personalities from around the world. Sponsored by Anacin, Chesterfield Cigarettes, the Ford Motor Company and RCA. NBC, 1950–1952. Tallulah Bankhead served as the host. Ted Shapiro composed the opening theme, "A Handful of Stars"; "May the Good Lord Bless and Keep You," the closing theme, was composed by Meredith Willson.

OPEN

HOST: You are about to be entertained by some of the biggest names in show business. For the next hour and thirty minutes, this program will present in person such bright stars as—

STARS (in their own voices): Fred Allen, Phil Baker, Eddie Cantor, Eddie Fisher, Ella Fitzgerald, Portland Hoffa, Ethel Waters, Meredith Willson.

HOST: And my name, dahlings, is Tallulah Bankhead.

OPENING THEME MUSIC: Up full then under...

ANNOUNCER (Ed Herlihy): The National Broadcasting Company presents *The Big Show*.

CHORUS:
> So listen America,
> The Curtain's up America,
> We're going to fill
> Your parlor full of stars.

ANNOUNCER: *The Big Show*, ninety minutes with the most scintillating personalities in the entertainment world, brought to you this Sunday and every Sunday at this same time as the Sunday feature of NBC's all-star festival. *The Big Show* is brought to you by Chesterfield, the cigarette that has for you what every smoker wants—mildness with no unpleasant after taste, the cigarette that brings you Bing Crosby and Bob Hope; and by the makers of Anacin, for relief from the pain of headache, neuritis and neuralgia; and by RCA Victor, world leader in radio, first in recorded music, first in television. The big stars on this program are Fred Allen, Phil Baker, Eddie Cantor, Eddie Fisher, Ella Fitzgerald, Portland Hoffa, Ethel Waters, Meredith Willson and the Big Show Orchestra and Chorus and every week your hostess, the glamorous, unpredictable Tallulah Bankhead.

THEME MUSIC: Up full then out.

BOB HOPE: Say Bing, got a minute?

BING CROSBY: Sure Bob, I've got all the time in the world.

BOB HOPE: Folks, better-tasting Chesterfield is the only cigarette that combines for you mildness with no unpleasant after taste. And you can prove that yourself. Just take our mildness test. Buy Chesterfield then open them and enjoy that milder, mellow aroma. Now light one up and you'll know Chesterfield's milder because it smokes milder. And Chesterfield leaves no unpleasant after taste. That fact has been confirmed by the country's first and only Cigarette Taste Panel.

BING CROSBY: Yes, mildness and no unpleasant after taste is what you and I and what every smoker wants.

CHESTERFIELD JINGLE MUSIC: Up full then under...

CHORUS:

> Chesterfield, Chesterfield
> Always takes first place.
> That milder, mild tobacco
> Never leaves an after taste.

BING (SINGING):

> Ho ho, open a pack
> and give 'em a smell.

CHORUS:

> Then you'll smoke 'em.

BIG SHOW THEME MUSIC: Up full then under...

ANNOUNCER: And here is your hostess, the glamorous, unpredictable Tallulah Bankhead.

SOUND: Applause (at which time Tallulah begins the show with a comical monologue).

CLOSE

ANNOUNCER: Here's a word from RCA Victor. Friends, if you study the room you're in right now you'll realize you can't buy furnishings piece by piece without the final picture in mind. It's that way when you buy a television too. Now, here's how to get the most out of your television dollar. Consider the complete home entertainment picture. The radio and records as well as TV. Instead of having many instruments scattered about, why not settle for one fine cabinet that costs less and contains your complete home entertainment needs? Such a one-cabinet combination is the RCA Victor Rutland. Open the doors of the Rutland's 18th century cabinet and you'll find a 17-inch television with its steady picture, AM and FM radio and the Victrola's 45 record changer as well as a changer for 78 and 33⅓ speeds. Yes, so many more families are becoming television owners this week. If

you're one of them, remember to see and listen to the exciting new Rutland at your RCA Victor dealers.

THEME MUSIC: Up full then under...

HOST: Well, dahlings, that's all the time we have for tonight. But if you're with us again next week, you're going to hear Don Cornell, Jimmy Durante, Rex Harrison, Judy Holliday, Carmen Miranda, Lili Palmer and others, and of course our very own Meredith Willson and the Big Show Orchestra and Chorus. And until then—

CLOSING THEME MUSIC: Up full then under...

TALLULAH (SINGING):

> May the Good Lord bless and keep you
> Whether near or far away.
> May the Good Lord bless and keep you
> Until we meet again.

CHORUS:

> May the Good Lord bless and keep you
> Till we meet,
> Till we meet again.

HOST: Good night dahlings and God speed to our armed forces all over the world who hear this broadcast each week.

OPENING THEME MUSIC: Up full then under...

ANNOUNCER: *The Big Show* the Sunday night feature of NBC's all-star festival has been brought to you by your local Ford dealer, who's proud to say the new 1951 Ford is the car that's built for the years ahead; by RCA Victor, world leader in radio, first in recorded music and first in television; by Chesterfield, the only cigarette that combines mildness with no unpleasant after taste; and by Anacin, for the fast relief of headache pain.

THEME MUSIC: Up full then out.

ANNOUNCER: This is NBC, the National Broadcasting Company.

SOUND: NBC chimes. N-B-C.

33. Big Sister

Daily serial about the lives of two sisters, Ruth and Sue Evans. Sponsored by Procter and Gamble and Rinso. CBS, 1936–1952. Ruth Chatterton, Nancy Marshall, Alice Frost, Marjorie Anderson, Mercedes McCambridge and Grace Matthews played Ruth; Helen Lewis,

Halia Stoddard, Dorothy McGuire, Peggy Conklin and Fran Carden played Sue.

OPEN

SOUND: Whistle of sponsor's product name (Rinso).

ANNOUNCER (Jim Ameche): Rinso presents *Big Sister*.

SOUND: Bells tolling.

ANNOUNCER: Yes, there's the clock in Glenn Falls Town Hall telling us it's time for Rinso's story of *Big Sister*, brought to you by the new soapy rich Rinso—R-I-N-S-O. You know ladies, I'm no weather profit but as a clothesline detective, I'm tops. And the thing I never miss is a Rinso white wash every time. Yes ma'am, there is just something about a Rinso wash that catches the eye. White things so shiny white and clean; colored washables, fresh and bright as can be. And here's the reason why. Rinso's grand soapy suds actually get out more dirt without hard rubbing or scrubbing either. Just a short soak in Rinso's peppy suds and a few quick rubs on the worst spots and they're ready to rinse and hang. Yes, you can see why Rinso suds are so popular. Your grocer may sometimes be out of it when you shop. If that happens, please be patient and keep asking for Rinso. There's always a shipment on its way to him.

THEME MUSIC: Up full then under...

ANNOUNCER: And now to our story of *Big Sister*, which was written by Julian Faunt.

CLOSE

SOUND: Glenn Falls clock tolling.

ANNOUNCER: We'll meet you again at big sister's tomorrow. This is Jim Ameche speaking for the new soapy rich Rinso—R-I-N-S-O. The town of Glenn Falls and the names of all characters used on this broadcast are fictitious. This is CBS, the Columbia Broadcasting System.

THEME MUSIC: Up full then fade out.

34. Big Town

Crime drama about Steve Wilson, editor of the *Illustrated Press*, a crusading newspaper in Big Town. Sponsored by Bayer Aspirin, Ironized Yeast Tablets, Lifebuoy Soap and Rinso Detergent. CBS (1937–1948; 1951–1952), NBC (1948–1951). Edward G. Robinson, Edward Pauley and Walter Greaza played Steve Wilson. Lorelei Kilbourne, the society reporter, was played by Claire Trevor, Ona Munson and Fran Carlon.

OPEN (1940)

NEWSPAPER BOY: Extra, extra, get your *Illustrated Press*. Read all about the new 1940 Rinso that washes clothes whiter and brighter. Read all about it!

THEME MUSIC: Up full then under...

ANNOUNCER (Dwight Weist): The new 1940 top-speed Rinso with its marvelous new suds booster that licks hard water and gives much richer suds in soft water too, Rinso brings you Edward G. Robinson in an exciting story from Big Town, a story of life and death on the highways of America.

THEME MUSIC: Up full then under...

ANNOUNCER: Ona Munson heads the supporting cast. Now let's see what's going on in Big Town. In tonight's presentation, Mr. Robinson is heard as Steve Wilson, managing editor of the *Illustrated Press*, where he is aided and abetted by Lorelei, the girl reporter played by Ona Munson.

THEME MUSIC: Up full then out.

CLOSE (1940)

THEME MUSIC: Up full then under...

ANNOUNCER: Rinso, the new 1940 top-speed Rinso, has presented *Big Town* with Edward G. Robinson and Ona Munson in starring roles. All names and places used in tonight's story are fictitious; any similarity to person's living or dead is coincidental. Be with us again next week at this same time for another headline story from Steve Wilson of the *Illustrated Press*. This is CBS, the Columbia Broadcasting System.

THEME MUSIC: Up full then out.

OPEN (1948)

NEWSPAPER BOY: Extra, extra, Big Town, read all about it. Extra, extra, extra.

THEME MUSIC: Up full then under...

ANNOUNCER (Dwight Weist): Ironized Yeast Tablets presents another action packed assignment for the fighting editor, Steve Wilson, of the *Illustrated Press*, whose newspaper creed stands for freedom and justice against the forces of violence and evil.

VOICE: The power and the freedom of the press is a flaming sword, that it may be a faithful servant of all the people; use it justly; hold it high and guard it well.

THEME MUSIC: Up full then out.

ANNOUNCER: It's a fact, a person can get so tired that he can't work well or sleep well or get any fun out of life. If you're tired and pale besides, your doctor may find you have a borderline anemia, resulting from a nutritional deficiency. If so, take Ironized Yeast Tablets to increase your strength, regain your color and build up red blood cells. Ironized Yeast Tablets will give you the energy you need to work, to play, to think. Take Ironized Yeast Tablets; available at your local druggist now.

THEME MUSIC: Up full then under...

ANNOUNCER: And now to Big Town and tonight's exciting headline exposé.

CLOSE (1948)

THEME MUSIC: Up full then under...

ANNOUNCER: Next week don't miss Steve Wilson's exciting *Big Town* story. *Big Town* features Edward Pawley as Steve Wilson and Fran Carlon as Lorelei Kilbourne. Music composed and conducted by John Gart.

THEME MUSIC: Up full then fade out.

OPEN (1951)

NEWSPAPER BOY: Extra, Big Town, extra!

THEME MUSIC: Up full then under...

NEWSPAPER BOY: Extra, read all about it! Murder in Big Town. Extra, Big Town, extra!

THEME MUSIC: Up full then under...

ANNOUNCER (Dwight Weist): Yes, listen to this one-page drama of *Big Town* brought to you by Lever Brothers Company, makers of Lifebuoy Health Soap.

THEME MUSIC: Up full then under...

ANNOUNCER: Another exciting assignment for the fighting editor Steve Wilson of the *Illustrated Press*, whose newspaper creed stands for freedom and justice against the forces of violence and evil.

VOICE: The power and the freedom of the press is a flaming sword, that it may be a faithful servant of all the people; use it justly, hold it high, guard it well.

THEME MUSIC: Up full then out.

ANNOUNCER: Are you safe from body odor on all 13 areas of the skin?

CHORUS:

> I'm happy and I'm singin'
> The Lifebuoy song.
> Be Lifebuoy clean on all 13,
> I'm happy and I'm singin'
> The Lifebuoy song.

ANNOUNCER: Remember, you can get odor on not one, but 13 skin areas. The cleaner you get these 13 areas, the safer you are. Lifebuoy Health Soap deodorizes these 13 skin areas. Doctors prove Lifebuoy with its purifying ingredient actually gets skin cleaner than any other leading soap. You'll love Lifebuoy's extra rich coconut oil lather, its fresh clean scent; wonderful for your complexion. Don't trust ordinary soaps, use Lifebuoy everyday.

CHORUS:

> Be Lifebuoy clean on all 13,
> I'm happy and I'm singin'
> The Lifebuoy song.

THEME MUSIC: Up full then under...

ANNOUNCER: Now to Big Town and Steve Wilson's headline story for tonight.

CLOSE (1951)

THEME MUSIC: Up full then under...

ANNOUNCER: Next week don't miss another Steve Wilson headlined story on *Big Town*. In tonight's dramatization, all names, times and places were fictional. *Big Town* featured Walter Greaza as Steve Wilson and Fran Carlon as Lorelei Kilbourne. Music composed and conducted by John Gart.

THEME MUSIC: Up full then under...

ANNOUNCER: Be sure to join us again next Tuesday at this same time when Lever Brothers Company, makers of Lifebuoy Health Soap, will again present *Big Town*. This is your narrator, Dwight Weist, wishing you a most cordial good night.

THEME MUSIC: Up full then out.

SOUND: NBC chimes. N-B-C.

35. The Billie Burke Show

Comedy about Billie Burke (herself), a well-meaning woman, her unemployed brother, Julius (Earle Ross), and their housekeeper, Daisy (Lillian Randolph). Sponsored by Listerine Toothpaste. CBS, 1944–1945.

OPEN

THEME MUSIC: Up full then under...

ANNOUNCER (Marvin Miller): Listerine Toothpaste, that quick-acting, grand-tasting dentifrice with the fresh minty tang presents *The Billie Burke Show*. In just a moment we'll visit the little white house on Sunnyview Drive to see what is happening this week at the Burke household.

THEME MUSIC: Up full then under...

ANNOUNCER: Ladies, I can tell you how you can improve your looks at top and toe. Here's how. Use the famous cleansing prescription for your teeth Listerine Toothpaste. It's designed to give you pinpoint cleansing and help bring out the natural flash and brilliance of your teeth. Yes, Listerine Toothpaste can help bring out your top smile. Next, to flatter your toes, and make your legs look prettier, try your luck at winning beautiful and flattering Nylons of Note by Hole-proof in the Listerine Toothpaste contest. Here are the rules. One, complete the following sentence in twenty-five words or less: "I Like Listerine Toothpaste Because..."; two, write or print your entry together with your name, address and stocking size. Be sure also to include your leg length, short, medium or long. Three, enclose the side or facsimile of the side from a Listerine Toothpaste box, but the side you enclose must be the one that carries the Good Housekeeping seal. Mail your entry to Listerine Contest, Post Office Box 491, Times Square, New York 18, New York. Remember, there is a different contest every week. Every week you'll have an opportunity to win twelve pairs of Nylons of Note by Hole-proof. Get in this grand contest today.

THEME MUSIC: Up full then under...

ANNOUNCER: And here she is, that bright, smiling morning star, our Miss Leading Lady, Billie Burke.

SOUND: Applause.

BILLIE: Good morning everybody, good morning... [The story would then begin.]

CLOSE

ANNOUNCER: Calling all women who like pretty clothes. Calling all women who yen for nylon stockings. Try your lady luck by winning Nylons of Note by Hole-proof in the Listerine Toothpaste Contest. Independent judges will award prizes for originality, interest and sincerity. Duplicate prizes in case of ties. The judges decisions will be final and no entries will be returned. All entries or ideas submitted become the property of Lambert Pharmical Company. The contest is open to all except employees of Lambert Pharmical Company and associated companies. Why not get in this contest today. Mail your entry with your name, address and stocking size and length on the side of a Listerine Toothpaste box bearing the Good Housekeeping seal to Listerine Contest, Post Office Box 491, Times Square, New York 18, New York.

THEME MUSIC: Up full then under...

BILLIE: Goodbye Mr. Miller, goodbye everybody, till next Saturday. And remember—

BILLIE (Singing):
To always look for the silver lining
And try to find the sunny side of life.

ANNOUNCER: *The Billie Burke Show* is produced by Axel Gruenberg. The part of Daisy is played by Lillian Randolph; Earle Ross is our Julius. Music is under the direction of Carl Bonowitz. Tune in against next Saturday when the makers of Listerine Toothpaste again present *The Billie Burke Show*. For the best in Saturday listening, don't miss *Let's Pretend*, *The Billie Burke Show* and *Armstrong's Theater of Today*. Your announcer is Marvin Miller. This is CBS, the Columbia Broadcasting System.

THEME MUSIC: Up full then out.

36. The Black Castle

Chilling stories of people trapped in dangerous situations. Sustaining. Mutual, 1943–1944. Don Douglas played all characters, including the host (the Wizard of the Black Castle) and the announcer.

OPEN

SOUND: Footsteps climbing stairs.
ANNOUNCER: Now up these steps to the iron-studded oaken door which yawns wide on rusted hinges, begging us enter.
THEME MUSIC: Up full then under...
ANNOUNCER: Music, do you hear it? Wait. It is well to stop, for here is the Wizard of the Black Castle.
WIZARD: There you are, back again, I see. Well, welcome, come in. You'll be overjoyed at the tale I have for you tonight... [The Wizard would then introduce the evening's story.]

CLOSE

THEME MUSIC: Up full then under...
ANNOUNCER: Be with us again next time when the Wizard will allow us entry into his Black Castle for another story of the unexpected.
THEME MUSIC: Up full then out.
ANNOUNCER: This is the Mutual Broadcasting System.

37. The Black Chapel

Mystery stories related by a man called the Hooded Figure (played by Ted Osborne). Sustaining. CBS, 1937–1939.

OPEN

THEME MUSIC: Up full then under...
ANNOUNCER: It is a quarter of an hour until midnight; time for us to go to the Black Chapel. Each Friday evening we come to this spot, a place of mystery and terror where a gaunt, hooded figure appears and sits at the keyboard of the ruined old organ, mumbling and delivering his fantastic tales. Tonight, "The Mahogony Coffin."

CLOSE

THEME MUSIC: Up full then under...
ANNOUNCER: It is almost midnight, time for the voice of *The Black Chapel* to recede into the world from which it came. Each Friday, at a quarter of an hour before midnight, we come to this remote place, The Black Chapel, and listen to the hooded figure who sits at the keyboard of the ruined old organ, delivering his fantastic tales. Listen next Friday evening for the tale of "The Strange Bequest."
THEME MUSIC: Up full then under...
ANNOUNCER: This is CBS, the Columbia Broadcasting System.
THEME MUSIC: Up full then out.

38. The Black Hood

Crime drama about Kip Burland, a police officer who uses the power of a black hood to battle evil. Sustaining. Mutual, 1943–1944. Scott Douglas played Kip Burland with Marjorie Cramer as newspaper reporter Barbara Sutton.

OPEN

THEME MUSIC: Up full then under...
ANNOUNCER: *The Black Hood.*
VOICE: Criminals beware! The Black Hood is everywhere.
BLACK HOOD: I, the Black Hood, do solemnly swear that neither threats nor bribes nor bullets nor death itself shall keep me from fulfilling my vow to erase crime from the face of the Earth!
THEME MUSIC: Up full then under...
ANNOUNCER: The Black Hood is, in reality, Kip Burland, a rookie police officer who uses the magical powers of a black hood to battle crime wherever he finds it. The beautiful newspaper reporter Barbara Sutton is the only other person who knows the secret of the Black Hood.
THEME MUSIC: Up full then out.

CLOSE

THEME MUSIC: Up full then under...
VOICE: Criminals beware, the Black Hood is everywhere!
ANNOUNCER: *The Black Hood* with Scott Douglas will return tomorrow at this same time. This is Mutual.
THEME MUSIC: Up full then out.

39. The Black Museum

Dramatizations based on items found in London's Black Museum. Sustaining. Mutual, 1951–1952. See also *Whitehall 1212*. Orson Welles served as the host.

OPEN

ORSON WELLES: This is Orson Welles speaking from London.

SOUND: Chimes of Big Ben.

ORSON: From The Black Museum, a repository of death. Yes, here in a grim stone structure on the Thames, which houses Scotland Yard, is a warehouse of homicide. Here, everyday objects, a silk scarf, a length of twine, a child's toy, all are touched by murder.

THEME MUSIC: Up then under...

ANNOUNCER: From the annals of the Criminal Investigation Department of the London police, we bring you dramatic stories of the crimes recorded by the objects in Scotland Yard's gallery of death, *The Black Museum*.

ORSON: Well, here we are in the Black Museum, Scotland Yard's museum of murder. Here lies death, unseen but ever present, uncatalogued but orderly, enveloping a shadow, papering the wall, carpeting the floor, death for display purposes only... [Orson would then pick up an object and tell a murder tale based on it.]

CLOSE

ORSON: And now until we meet next time in this same place and I tell you another story in *The Black Museum*, I remain, as always, obediently yours,

SOUND: Footsteps followed by the museum door opening then closing.

THEME MUSIC: Up full then fade out.

40. Blackstone, the Magic Detective

Adventure stories based on the life of stage magician Harry Blackstone. Various sponsors. Mutual, 1948–1949. Ed Jerome plays Blackstone.

OPEN

THEME MUSIC: Up full then under...

ANNOUNCER (Alan Kent): *The Magic Detective*, starring the world's greatest magician, Blackstone. He tells you the inside story of "The Frozen Lady." And right after the story, Blackstone will explain tricks that you yourself can perform, reveal the guarded secrets of the world's greatest living magician. And now, standby for *Blackstone, the Magic Detective*.

THEME MUSIC: Up full then out.

CLOSE

BLACKSTONE (after explaining a magic trick to listeners): I hope you liked that trick and now until next time, this is Blackstone. Good magic and goodbye.

THEME MUSIC: Up full then under...

ANNOUNCER: Be with us next time when the world's greatest living magician, Blackstone, tells us the story of "The Hooded Rider" and explains more tricks you yourself can perform. Listen in again to Blackstone, the world's greatest living magician.

Note: The series is also known as *Blackstone, the Magician* and *Magic Detective*.

41. Blondie

Comical incidents in the life of the Bumstead family: Blondie, a level-headed housewife; Dagwood, her scatterbrained husband; and their children, Alexander and Cookie. Sponsored by Camel Cigarettes, Lustre Creme Shampoo and Super Suds. CBS (1939–1948), NBC (1948–1949), ABC (1949–1950). Penny Singleton, Alice White, Patricia Van Cleve and Ann Rutherford played Blondie; Arthur Lake was Dagwood; Leone Ledoux, Larry Sims, Jeffrey Silver and Tommy Cook played Alexander; and Marlene Ames, Joan Rae and Norma Jean Nilsson played Cookie.

OPEN

ANNOUNCER (Howard Petrie): Uh-uh-uh-uh, don't touch that dial, listen to—

DAGWOOD: Blooooondieeeee!

THEME MUSIC: Up full then under...

ANNOUNCER: Yes folks, it's another half-hour of fun with Blondie and Dagwood, brought to you by the great new 1947 Super Suds and Lustre Creme Shampoo, the creme shampoo for true hair loveliness.

THEME MUSIC: Up full then out.

CLOSE

SOUND: Applause.

ANNOUNCER: Uh-uh-uh-uh, don't go away folks, the Bumsteads will be back in just a moment.

SOUND: Applause up full then out.

ANNOUNCER: For the shining hair all men adore, discover the magic of Lustre Creme Shampoo. Discover the remarkable way it makes hair glow with natural highlights and shadows; sparkle with silken softness; delight with clean fragrance. Not a soap, not a liquid, Lustre Creme Shampoo is an amazing new dainty cream that whips up luxurious lather like magic in hard or soft water and sweeps dullness away. Try that economical dollar jar of Lustre Creme Shampoo, sold at all cosmetic counters; also thirty cent and fifty-five cent sizes. Lustre Creme Shampoo, a cream shampoo for true hair loveliness.

THEME MUSIC: Up full then under...

ANNOUNCER: Remember folks, every Sunday over these same CBS stations, a half-hour of fun with the Bumsteads, brought to you by Lustre Creme Shampoo, a creme shampoo for true hair loveliness, and the great new 1947 Super Suds.

SONG (CHORUS):
Super Suds, great new 1947 Super Suds.

ANNOUNCER: Tell all your friends to tune in next Sunday at this same time for—

DAGWOOD: Blooooondieeeee!

ANNOUNCER: Remember, doctors proved the Palmolive Plan brings two out of three women lovelier complexions in fourteen days. And this plan was tested on women with all types of skin; dry skin, rough skin, oily skin, even skin that was not clear. Yes thirty-six doctors, leading skin specialists, proved the fourteen day Palmolive Plan improved all types of skin, bringing fresher, brighter, younger looking complexions. Start your fourteen-day Palmolive Plan now.

THEME MUSIC: Up full then under...

ANNOUNCER: *Blondie*, written by John L. Greene, stars Penny Singleton and Arthur Lake. This is Howard Petrie saying good night from Hollywood. This is CBS, the Columbia Broadcasting System.

THEME MUSIC: Up full then fade out.

42. The Blue Beetle

Crime drama about Dan Garrett, a rookie policeman who uses a suit of blue chain armour to infiltrate the underworld and destroy crime. Sustaining. Syn., 1940.

OPEN

SOUND: Police whistles.

VOICE: *The Blue Beetle.*

THEME MUSIC: Up full then under...

ANNOUNCER: Leaping down upon the underworld to smash gangland comes the friend of the unfortunate, enemy of criminals, a mysterious all-powerful character. A problem to the police, but a crusader for law; in reality Dan Garrett, a rookie patrolman. Loved by everyone but suspected by none of being the Blue Beetle. As the Blue Beetle, he hides behind a strange mask and suit of impenetrable blue chain armour, flexible as silk but stronger than steel. Giving the Green Hornet a run for his money, Dan Garrett's father was killed by a gangster's bullet. Dr. Franz, an apothecary on a side street, is the only person who knows the secret identity of the Blue Beetle. And now to today's episode of *The Blue Beetle*.

THEME MUSIC: Up full then out.

CLOSE

THEME MUSIC: Up full then under...

ANNOUNCER: *The Blue Beetle*, heard twice a week, will return Friday at this same time.

THEME MUSIC: Up full then fade out.

43. The Bob Hope Show

A mix of music, songs and comedy hosted by Bob Hope. Sponsored by American Dairy,

Chesterfield Cigarettes, General Foods, Pepsodent and Swan Soap. CBS (1941–1942), NBC (1943–1955). The song "Thanks for the Memory" was used as the theme.

OPEN

THEME MUSIC: Up full then under…

ANNOUNCER (Bill Goodwin): *The Bob Hope Show*, brought to you by Chesterfield. Chesterfield packs more pleasure because it's more perfectly packed. Thanks to Accuray, they satisfy the most.

THEME MUSIC: Up full then under…

ANNOUNCER: Yes, it's *The Bob Hope Show*, direct from Hollywood, with Les Brown and his Band of Renown and yours truly, Bill Goodwin. And here he is, the star of our show, Bob Hope.

SOUND: Applause under theme.

BOB: Good evening, ladies and gentlemen… [Bob would then begin the show with a monologue.]

CLOSE

SPONSOR'S MUSIC: Up full then under…

GIRL VOCALIST:
 Packs more pleasure,
 Packs more pleasure.
 Chesterfield packs more pleasure
 Because Chesterfield's more perfectly packed.

ANNOUNCER: It stands to reason that a cigarette made better and packed better, smokes better, tastes better and Chesterfield is more perfectly packed by Accuray. This electronic miracle removes human error in cigarette manufacture so Accuray Chesterfield is firm and pleasing to the lips; mild, yet deeply satisfying. Yes, Chesterfield gives you something no other cigarette can give you.

GIRL VOCALIST:
 Chesterfield packs more pleasure
 Because Chesterfield's more perfectly packed.

ANNOUNCER: To the touch, to the taste, Chesterfield packs more pleasure because it's more perfectly packed. Buy Chesterfield. Mild, yet they satisfy the most.

THEME MUSIC: Up full then under…

ANNOUNCER: Chesterfield has presented *The Bob Hope Show*. Chesterfield packs more pleasure because it's more perfectly packed. Smoke Chesterfield, better smoking, better tasting Chesterfield.

THEME MUSIC: Up full then under…

ANNOUNCER: Also heard on tonight's program were Jerry Colonna, Barbara Jo Allen, and the Six Hits and a Miss Chorus. Music was by Les Brown and his Band of Renown. This is Bill Goodwin inviting you to be with us next week when Chesterfield will again bring you *The Bob Hope Show*. This is NBC, the National Broadcasting Company.

THEME MUSIC: Up full then out.

SOUND: NBC chimes. N-B-C.

44. Bobby Benson and the B-Bar-B Riders

Western about Bobby Benson, a 12-year-old boy who, after the death of his parents, inherits the B-Bar-B Ranch. Various sponsors (Chicklets, Dentine, H-O Oats and Kraft Foods were frequent sponsors). CBS (1932–1936), Mutual (1949–1955). Richard Wanamaker, Ivan Curry and Billy Halop played Bobby Benson with Herb Rice, Neil O'Malley, Charles Irving, Al Hodge and Tex Ritter as Tex Mason, Bobby's guardian.

OPEN

SOUND: Horses galloping.

ANNOUNCER (Dan Seymour): They're riding fast and they're riding hard. It's time for excitement and adventure in the Modern West with *Bobby Benson and the B-Bar-B Riders*. And out in front, astride his golden palomino Amigo, is the cowboy kid himself, Bobby Benson.

BOBBY: B-Bar-Beeeeee.

CLOSE

ANNOUNCER: And so ends another thrilling adventure of *Bobby Benson and the B-Bar-B Riders*. Remember, you're riding the trail to adventure and excitement when you hear that familiar cry—

BOBBY: B-Bar-Beeeeee.

45. Bold Venture

Adventure series about Slate Shannon (Humphrey Bogart), owner of a boat (the *Bold Venture*) and hotel (Shannon's Place) in Havana, Cuba, and his ward, the beautiful Sailor Duval (Lauren Bacall). Sustaining. Syn., 1951–1952. David Rose composed the theme, "Bold Venture."

OPEN (original)

THEME MUSIC: Up full then under…
ANNOUNCER (Marvin Miller): *Bold Venture!* Adventure, intrigue, mystery, romance. Starring Humphrey Bogart and Lauren Bacall, together in the sultry setting of tropical Havana and the mysterious islands of the Caribbean. *Bold Venture!*
THEME MUSIC: Up full then out.

OPEN (revised)

THEME MUSIC: Up full then under…
ANNOUNCER (Marvin Miller): Once again the magic names of Humphrey Bogart and Lauren Bacall bring you *Bold Venture* and a tale of mystery and intrigue.
THEME MUSIC: Up full then out.

CLOSE (same for both)

THEME MUSIC: Up full then under…
ANNOUNCER: And so our two stars, Humphrey Bogart and Lauren Bacall, have brought to a close our latest *Bold Venture*. Special music was composed and conducted by David Rose. May we invite you to listen again next week at this same time for another exciting adventure starring Humphrey Bogart and Lauren Bacall, together in *Bold Venture*.
THEME MUSIC: Up full then fade out.

46. Boston Blackie

Crime drama about a master thief turned private detective. Various sponsors. NBC (1944), Mutual (1945; 1947–1950), Blue/ABC (1945–1947). Chester Morris and Richard Kollmar played Boston Blackie with Jan Miner as his girlfriend, Mary Wesley.

OPEN

THEME MUSIC: Up full then under…
ANNOUNCER (Larry Elliott): And now meet Richard Kollmar as Boston Blackie, enemy to those who make him an enemy, friend to those who have no friends.
THEME MUSIC: Up full then out.

CLOSE

THEME MUSIC: Up full then under…
ANNOUNCER: Boston Blackie! Enemy to those who make him an enemy; friend to those who have no friends. *Boston Blackie* stars Richard Kollmar with Jan Miner as Mary and Maurice Tarplan as Inspector Farraday. Be with us again next time for another exciting adventure with Boston Blackie. Larry Elliott speaking.
THEME MUSIC: Up full then fade out.

47. Box 13

Crime drama about Dan Holiday, a columnist with the *Star Times*, who quits his paper to become a mystery novelist. Various sponsors. Syn., 1948–1949. Alan Ladd starred as Dan Holiday with Sylvia Picker as Suzy, his secretary.

OPEN

ANNOUNCER: *Box 13* with the star of Paramount Pictures, Alan Ladd, as Dan Holiday.
GIRL: Box 13, Box 13, Box 13, Box 13.
ANNOUNCER: *Box 13* with Alan Ladd as Dan Holiday, the mystery writer who advertises in the *Star News* for material—
DAN: Adventure wanted. Will go anywhere, do anything. Box 13.
THEME MUSIC: Up full then under… [At this point, Dan would make various comments as he walked to pick up his mail at Box 13. The story would then begin.]

CLOSE

THEME MUSIC: Up full then under…
ANNOUNCER: *Box 13* with Alan Ladd, star of Paramount Pictures, is a Mayfair Production. Sylvia Picker is heard as Suzy.
THEME MUSIC: Up full then out.

48. Bright Star

Romantic comedy about Susan Armstrong (Irene Dunne), editor of the *Morning Star*, and her top reporter, George Harvey (Fred MacMurray). Various sponsors. Syn., 1952–1953.

OPEN

THEME MUSIC: Up full then under...

ANNOUNCER (Harry Von Zell): The Irene Dunne-Fred MacMurray Show. Starring Irene Dunne as Susan and Fred MacMurray as George, together in the gay, exciting new comedy adventure *Bright Star*.

THEME MUSIC: Up full then out.

GIRL: Have you heard what happened on the *Star*?

MAN: Did you hear what he said to her?

GIRL: Do you know what she told him?

ANNOUNCER: Yes, the whole town's talking. The "Star" they're talking about is the *Morning Star*, a newspaper. The "she" they're talking about is Susan, lovely, attractive, headstrong Susan, editor of the *Star*. And the "him," he's George, Susan's star reporter.

THEME MUSIC: Up full then out.

CLOSE

THEME MUSIC: Up full then under...

ANNOUNCER: Irene Dunne and Fred MacMurray will be back next week in another exciting comedy adventure in the gay new series *Bright Star*. This is Harry Von Zell inviting you to join us then.

THEME MUSIC: Up full then fade out.

49. The Brighter Day

Daily serial about Richard Dennis (Bill Smith), a widowed reverend in the town of Three Rivers, and his efforts to raise his four children: Liz (Margaret Draper, Grace Matthews), Barbara (Lorna Lynn), Althea (Jay Meredith) and Grayling (Billy Redfield). Sponsored by Dreft (1948–1955) then various sponsors (1955–1956). NBC (1948–1949), CBS (1949–1956).

OPEN

THEME MUSIC: Up full then under...

ANNOUNCER: Procter and Gamble, the makers of Dreft for brighter, safer cleaning of silks, nylons, woolens and dishes, presents *The Brighter Day*.

THEME MUSIC: Up full then under...

ANNOUNCER: *The Brighter Day*. Our years are as the falling leaves. We live, we love, we dream and then we go. But somehow we keep hoping that our dreams will come true on that brighter day.

THEME MUSIC: Up full then out.

ANNOUNCER: Ladies, Dreft is Procter and Gamble's amazing suds discovery for washing silks, nylons, woolens and dishes.

WOMAN: I can tell you that's true. Why Dreft's wonderful suds keep my colored things so bright and gay looking I can hardly believe my eyes. My stockings, rayons, woolens all stay as beautiful as a dream. And dishes? Dreft makes dishes shine without wiping; even glasses sparkle without touching a towel to them.

ANNOUNCER: Yes, Dreft's amazing suds rinse clean and clear. Leaves no dulling film the way all soaps do. There's no soap fading ever. No wonder colors sparkle, no wonder dishes shine without wiping. Ladies, look for Dreft in the bright green package. Dreft, the amazing suds discovery brings you faster, brighter, safer cleaning than any suds before in history. That's D-R-E-F-T, Dreft.

THEME MUSIC: Up full then under...

ANNOUNCER: And now to our story of *The Brighter Day*.

CLOSE

THEME MUSIC: Up full then under...

ANNOUNCER: Procter and Gamble, the makers of Dreft for faster, brighter, safer cleaning than any suds before in history, has presented *The Brighter Day*. Be with us again tomorrow when Procter and Gamble will present *The Brighter Day*. This is NBC, the National Broadcasting Company.

SOUND: NBC chimes. N-B-C.

50. Bringing Up Father

Comedy about Jiggs (Mark Smith, Neil O'Malley), a henpecked husband, his domineering wife Maggie (Agnes Moorehead), and their daughter Nora (Helen Shields). Sustaining. NBC, 1941.

OPEN

THEME MUSIC ("Bringing Up Father"): Up full then under...
CHORUS:
> Jiggs, stand up and be a man,
> Don't let Maggie get under
> Your collar.
> Jiggs, be a man for once
> And stand up and holler.
> Jiggs, it's time
> You make your stand,
> But it's sure not to make
> Us quit this singing of
> Bringing Up Father.

THEME MUSIC: Up full then under...
ANNOUNCER: We now have the pleasure of bringing before our microphones some old friends of yours. You've met them hundreds of times before in the pages of your newspaper, the popular brain children of George McManus in that most famous of all comic strips called "Bringing Up Father." The trials and tribulations of the lovable Jiggs, the iron rule of Maggie, his wife, and the love affairs of the beautiful Nora, their daughter. All these old acquaintances are coming into your home for the first time in real life.
THEME MUSIC: Up full then out.

CLOSE

THEME MUSIC: Up full then under...
ANNOUNCER: We'll all be wiser after the next episode of *Bringing Up Father*, which we'll be pleased to broadcast over this station next week. Till then, Jiggs and Maggie and *Bringing Up Father* bid the top of the day to you. This King Features Syndicate program, supervised by William Morris, was produced at Cameo Broadcasting and Recording Studios in New York.
THEME MUSIC: Up full then fade out.

51. Broadway Is My Beat

Crime drama about Danny Clover, a detective with the N.Y.P.D. Various sponsors (Lux and Wrigley were frequent sponsors). CBS, 1949–1954. Larry Thor played Danny Clover. The theme, "Broadway Is My Beat," was composed by Alexander Courage.

OPEN

THEME MUSIC: Up full then under...
SOUND: Traffic noises.
DANNY: Broadway is my beat. From Times Square to Columbus Circle, the gaudiest, the most violent, the lonesomest mile in the world.
THEME MUSIC: Up full then under...
ANNOUNCER (Joe Walters): *Broadway Is My Beat* with Larry Thor as Detective Danny Clover.
THEME MUSIC: Up full then under...
DANNY (speech varies by episode): Broadway, where the measured screaming of the spectacular echoes into the wilderness of the night and the cadence is the beat of a metallic and mechanical heart. This is the rhythm of the life you're assigned to on Broadway. There's nothing you can do about it. You challenge it with a whisper or a cry and there's no one to hear it because Broadway's ears are tuned to the throb of the mechanical heart. It's Broadway, my beat.
THEME MUSIC: Up full then under... (as the story would then start).

CLOSE

DANNY: It stretches out in front of you, this mere ash called Broadway. This street that offers you dreams and laughs in your face. It's crowds and cruelty, it's sound and sorrow, it's fury and a teardrop, it's Broadway, the gaudiest, the most violent, the lonesomest mile in the world. Broadway, my beat.
THEME MUSIC: Up full then out.
ANNOUNCER: *Broadway Is My Beat* stars Larry Thor as Detective Danny Clover. The program was produced and directed by Elliott Lewis with musical score composed and conducted by Alexander Courage.
THEME MUSIC: Up full then under...

ANNOUNCER: This is CBS, where you'll find *Broadway Is My Beat* every Friday night. And remember, *My Friend Irma* livens Sunday nights on the CBS Radio Network. Joe Walters speaking.

THEME MUSIC: Up full then out.

52. Buck Rogers in the 25th Century

Science fiction adventure about Buck Rogers, a 20th Century man held in suspended animation (by leaking gas in a mine) who awakens 500 years later to assist Wilma Deering and Dr. Huer in their battle against evil. Sponsored by Coco-Malt, Cream of Wheat, General Foods, Kellogg's and Posts Cereals and Popsicle. CBS (1932–1936), Mutual (1939–1947). Curtis Arnall, Carl Frank, Matt Crowley and John Larkin played Buck Rogers; Adele Ronson and Virginia Vass were Wilma Deering; and Edgar Stehli was Dr. Huer.

OPEN (1934)

SOUND: Roll of thunder on a drum.

ANNOUNCER (ECHO EFFECT): *Buck Rogers in the 25th Century!*

SOUND: Roll of thunder on a drum (followed by the announcer recapping or beginning a story).

CLOSE (1934)

SOUND: Thunder roll on a drum.

ANNOUNCER: *Buck Rogers in the 25th Century!*

SOUND: Thunder roll on a drum.

OPEN (first episode, 1939)

VOICE: *Buck Rogers in the 25th Century!*

SOUND: Thunder roll on a drum.

ANNOUNCER: Buck Rogers is back on the air— Buck and Wilma and all their fascinating friends and mysterious enemies in the super scientific twenty-fifth century. This program is brought to you by the makers of Popsicle, Fudgicle and Creamsicle, those delicious, frozen confections on a stick. Now I have a swell surprise for you. The famous winner of the typical American boy contest has become Popsicle Pete and here's a message from him.

PETE: Hello everybody, I'm sure glad to meet ya, and boy am I glad I was picked to be the typical American boy because now I'm Popsicle Pete. I always wanted to be on the radio and now I have a chance to tell you about some wonderful prizes you can get free. You get them just for saving bags from nifty Popsicle, Fudgicle and Creamsicle. You can get a wrist watch, a movie camera, table tennis, a wallet, a doll, lots of gifts. Just save the bags from Popsicle, Creamsicle and Fudgicle on a handy stick. Boy, do they taste good.

ANNOUNCER: Wholesome too, and nourishing, made fresh everyday from the finest ingredients, the biggest five cents' worth anywhere.

PETE: And say kids, get the free illustrated Popsicle gift list at your ice cream store. A free coupon comes with it, worth ten bags.

ANNOUNCER: And now for Buck Rogers and his thrilling adventures 500 years in the future. By turning a little dial to project us ahead in time, we are able to be with Buck and his friends in the wonderful world of the future— a world that sees a lot of our scientific and mechanical dreams come true. You know, there is nothing supernatural or mystical about Buck; he's just an ordinary human being who keeps his wits about him. Shall we join him there? Okay then, here we go, 500 years into the future.

CLOSE (first episode, 1939)

ANNOUNCER (following a cliff-hanging scene): Say, Buck's wish for excitement certainly came true in a hurry. I certainly hope that he, Wilma and Dr. Huer are all right. What'ya say, Pete?

PETE: I know what would make me feel all right, a great frozen Fudgicle. Jiminy, can you imagine anything better than that fresh, creamy chocolate frozen cold on a stick?

ANNOUNCER: Fellows and girls, what is the best, purest nickel's worth you can get? Right, a Fudgicle—delicious and full of healthful energy, made only from pure milk products— swell to eat and easy to digest. And don't forget to save the bags for those wonderful prizes.

SOUND: Thunder roll on a drum.

ANNOUNCER: Be with us again tomorrow, same time, same station, for more futuristic adven-

tures with (in echo effect) *Buck Rogers in the 25th Century.*
SOUND: Thunder roll on a drum.

OPEN (last episode, 1947)

ANNOUNCER: *Buck Rogers in the 25th Century.*
SOUND: Clap of thunder.
ANNOUNCER: Rocket Rangers, man your posts while Post Corn Toasties, the tender, crisper corn flakes takes you beyond rocket power—
SOUND: Rocket ship blasting off.
ANNOUNCER: Beyond the atomic bomb—
SOUND: Bomb exploding.
ANNOUNCER: Beyond the future—
SOUND: Musical Sting.
ANNOUNCER: To *Buck Rogers in the 25th Century!*

CLOSE (last episode, 1947)

ANNOUNCER: You know, boys and girls, a really good breakfast starts with a heaping bowl of the freshest, crispest corn flakes possible, Post Corn Toasties. The Post people hope you've all enjoyed the excitement and wonder of the 25th century. We hope you'll keep right on enjoying the crisper, fresher corn flakes every morning. We hope you'll start each day bright with Post Corn Toasties.
SOUND: Clap of thunder.
ANNOUNCER: Rocket Rangers, man your posts as we ride into the future.
SOUND: Announcer wrapping up the episode.
ANNOUNCER: *Buck Rogers* with John Larkin, Virginia Vass and Edgar Stehli, has been coming to you by Post Corn Toasties. Beginning next week, *Buck Rogers* will no longer be heard at this time. Instead, Mutual will present its dramatic program of best-loved children's stories, *Adventure Parade.* Be sure to tune in at this time for *Adventure Parade.* This is the Mutual Broadcasting System.

53. The Buster Brown Show

Children's program of music, songs, comedy and stories hosted by Smilin' Ed McConnell. Sponsored by Buster Brown Shoes. NBC, 1952–1953. See also *Smilin' Ed and His Buster Brown Gang.* Basis for the television series.

OPEN

BUSTER BROWN (Walter Tetley): Hey kids, it's *The Buster Brown Show.*
SOUND: A scene from the show's serial, "Gunga," is presented.
BUSTER BROWN: Kids, don't miss this exciting adventure with little Gunga and his graceful elephant, Tila. And to tell it, here is Smilin' Ed McConnell.
ED: Yes kids, you better come running as old Smilin' Ed and his Buster Brown gang are on the air.
ED (SINGING): Everybody's gotta have shoes but there's only one kind of shoe for me, good old Buster Brown.
ED (TALKING): Oh yes kids, Buster Brown is on the air out here in Hollywood with Smilin' Ed, Squeaky the Mouse, Midnight the Cat and Froggy the Gremlin. And we're going to start our program right off with a story. Once again, kids, we journey thousands of miles to India for a story about our little friend Gunga, the jungle boy, and his great charge, Tila the bull elephant ... (a dramatization follows. Following the drama, Smilin' Ed returns).
ED: Yes sir, kids, I know you're gonna like this story just as I know you're gonna like Buster Brown shoes. Yes sir, we're buddies and we stick together. You just take it from me, second-best shoes just don't pay off and that's another big reason why I want all my buddies to have Buster Brown shoes; 'cause Buster Brown shoes have what it takes for plenty of wear; good material, you bet, and they're made by men who know what my buddies like. You just can't beat that smart, grown-up looking Buster Brown style. So, anyway you look at it, Buster Brown shoes are tops. They feel swell, they look swell and they wear and wear and wear. Buster Brown shoes is the shoe all my Buster Brown gang wears. So, if you want to be a real member of my Buster Brown gang, then you do like the rest of my gang: always look for that picture of the boy and his dog inside the shoe.
SOUND: Dog barking.
BUSTER BROWN: That's my dog Tige, he lives in a shoe. I'm Buster Brown, look for me in there too.
ED: That's right, look for the picture of the boy

and his dog inside the shoe. Then you'll know they're genuine Buster Brown shoes.

CLOSE

ED: I want to tell all you kids how you can be a member of Smilin' Ed's Buster Brown gang. Yes sir-ree, I want everybody to be a member of my gang. And everybody can who wears Buster Brown shoes. You know, kids, those Buster Brown shoes are what shows we're buddies. Yes sir, we all stick together and we wear 'em because we know they're the best shoes anywhere. Now kids, I'm countin' on ya to get a pair of these swell Buster Browns the very next time mother takes you shopping for shoes. Oh, you can see some of them on our television show, but always remember, look inside the shoe for that picture of the boy and his dog, then you'll know they're genuine Buster Brown shoes.

ED (addressing the studio audience kids): Has everybody had fun today, huh?

SOUND: Audience cheers.

ED: Well that's wonderful buddies. Now don't forget church or Sunday School and be listenin' next Saturday when you'll hear "Hey kids, come a runnin."

ED (singing): The happy gang of Buster Brown now leaves the air...

ANNOUNCER (Arch Presby): *Smilin' Ed's Gang* starring Smilin' Ed McConnell is brought to you every Saturday morning by Buster Brown dealers everywhere. *Smilin' Ed's Gang* is produced in Hollywood by Frank Ferrin.

ED (singing): The happy gang of Buster Brown now leaves the air. Watch for us again when Buster Brown is on the air.

ANNOUNCER: This is NBC, the National Broadcasting Company.

SOUND: NBC chimes. N-B-C.

54. The Busy Mr. Bingle

Comical incidents in the frantic life of J.B. Bingle, owner of the Bingle Pin Company. Sustaining. Mutual, 1943. John Brown played J.B. Bingle with Ethel Owen as his secretary, Miss Pepper.

OPEN

VOICE: Mr. Bingle, what are you doing?

BINGLE: Well, I'm not sure Miss Pepper, but I'm so busy.

THEME MUSIC: Up full then under...

ANNOUNCER: WOR/Mutual presents *The Busy Mr. Bingle*, a new kind of radio pleasure for the whole family. Mr. Bingle is really J.B. Bingle, head of the Bingle Pin Company, and he keeps busy by getting the firm into and out of trouble. Now you're about to meet the happy Bingle office family: Miss Pepper, the secretary; Wizer, the master salesman; Clarence, the inventor; Tommy, the office boy; and J.B. Bingle himself, who's just entering the office... [The episode would then begin.]

CLOSE

ANNOUNCER: You have been listening to WOR/Mutual's presentation of *The Busy Mr. Bingle*. *The Busy Mr. Bingle* is heard each Thursday evening at 8:30 P.M. Eastern War Time over most of these stations. This program was an international exchange feature heard over the coast-to-coast network of the Canadian Broadcasting Corporation. If you're in or around New York and would like to see a broadcast of *The Busy Mr. Bingle*, you may secure tickets by writing "Mr. Bingle" in care of WOR, New York City. We hope you'll join us next Thursday when the busy Mr. Bingle will be busier than ever.

THEME MUSIC: Up full then under...

ANNOUNCER: The busy Mr. Bingle is played by John Brown. This is Mutual.

THEME MUSIC: Up full then fade out.

55. Call the Police

The work of law enforcement officers as seen through the investigations of Police Commissioner Bill Grant (Joseph Julian, George Petrie). Sponsored by Johnson Wax, Lifebuoy Soap and Rinso Detergent. NBC (1947–1948), CBS (1949).

OPEN

THEME MUSIC: Up full then under...

ANNOUNCER (Hugh James): New Rain Soft Rinso presents *Call the Police*.

SOUND: Police radio signals.

VOICE: Attention homicide section, crime squad detail. Murder suspect in your zone.

VOICE: Between you and the evil outside the law stands the policeman of your community. He gives up his safety that you may be safe and sometimes he gives up his life to protect yours.

THEME MUSIC: Up full then under...

ANNOUNCER: Rain Soft Rinso brings you *Call the Police*, a new series of realistic radio dramas inspired by the courageous work of police departments all over America.

THEME MUSIC: Up full then out.

GIRL VOCALIST:
> Rinso white
> Rinso bright
> Happy Washday song.

ANNOUNCER: New Rain Soft Rinso is specially made for the type of water you have in your area. Rinso's rain soft suds get out more dirt than any other type of washday product. New Rinso, the only soap that contains Solieum, now makes your water softer than rainwater. Try it. Get new Rain Soft Rinso.

GIRL VOCALIST:
> Rinso white, Rinso bright.

CHORUS:
> Rain Soft Rinso
> Rain soft suds
> Renew themselves
> As they wash your duds.

THEME MUSIC: Up full then under...

ANNOUNCER: And now to today's story of *Call the Police*.

CLOSE

THEME MUSIC: Up full then under...

ANNOUNCER: *Call the Police* starred George Petrie in the role of Police Commissioner Bill Grant. Music was composed and conducted by Ben Ludlow. This is Hugh James reminding you to be with us again next week when the Lever Brothers Company, the makers of new Rain Soft Rinso, brings you another exciting police case. All names and places used in this dramatization are fictitious. Any similarity to persons living or dead is coincidental. Be sure to listen next week for *Call the Po-*

lice. This is NBC, the National Broadcasting Company.

THEME MUSIC: Up full then out.

SOUND: NBC chimes. N-B-C.

56. Calling All Cars

Dramatizations based on the files of the Los Angeles Police Department. Sponsored by Rio Grande Oil. CBS, 1933–1939.

OPEN

ANNOUNCER (Frederick Lindsley): *Calling All Cars*, a presentation of the Rio Grande Oil Company.

VOICE: Los Angeles police calling all cars, attention all cars. Broadcast 69, a holdup. Suspect is described as five feet, eleven inches; weight about 190 pounds. Escaped in a maroon-colored coupe; license unknown. This suspect held up and robbed Mae West, motion picture actress of more than $15,000 in jewelry and cash. Go get him boys. That's all. Rosenquist.

SOUND: Sirens, then music up and under...

ANNOUNCER: Many listeners tonight have already read the story of "The Mae West Diamond Robbery" in the March issue of "Calling All Cars News." Over 300,000 motorists have already driven into the Rio Grande service stations and asked for their free copy of this unique publication. But this isn't the only free gift you get from Rio Grande. If you fill up with Rio Grande cracked gasoline you get extra speed, extra power, extra energy for emergencies, extra fast starting and all these extras are free because you pay no more for Rio Grande cracked gasoline with tetro-eythl than for uncracked gasolines which lack these extra features. Because of these extra features at no extra cost, the police department which solved the Mae West robbery has specified Rio Grande cracked gasoline for all police cars for three consecutive years. You get another free gift if you ask your Rio Grande service station for Sinclair Otholene Motor Oil. It comes in oversize cans; a quart for a quarter with two extra ounces free. You save when you buy Sinclair Otholene, yet you get complete motor protection. Sinclair Otholene Motor Oil enjoys a worldwide sale and is world famous for quality. The price is lower because the sales are larger. The independent service stations selling Rio Grande cracked gasoline and Sinclair Otholene Motor Oil are actually giving you better values for your money.

MUSIC: Up full then out.

ANNOUNCER: During 1935, it will be the policy of *Calling All Cars* to bring you from time to time rebroadcasts of outstanding cases we have dramatized in the past. Thousands of you have written to us and expressed your desire to hear the Mae West jewel robbery dramatized again. So it is with pleasure that *Calling All Cars* tonight brings you "The Mae West Robbery" with Miss Martha Wentworth playing her now famous impersonation of Miss West. What other past cases of *Calling All Cars* would you like to hear again? Write to *Calling All Cars*, care of the station to which you are now listening and tell us what preceding case you would like to hear. And now we turn the microphone over to Chief James E. Davis of the Los Angeles Police Department... [He would then begin the story.]

CLOSE

ANNOUNCER: Ladies and gentlemen, if you want further information on the Mae West diamond robbery, you can get the story illustrated in the March issue of "Calling All Cars News." Just drive into any Rio Grande service station and ask for your free copy. You are under no obligation to buy anything.

MUSIC: Up full then under...

VOICE: Los Angeles calling all cars. Attention all cars. Cancellation of Broadcast 69 regarding a holdup. Suspect described in this broadcast is now in custody. That's all. Rosenquist.

SOUND: Police sirens followed by the theme music.

NARRATOR: This is your narrator, Frederick Lindsley, bidding you good night for the Rio Grande Oil Company.

MUSIC: Up full and fade out.

57. The Campbell Playhouse

Quality dramas based on books, plays and movies. Sponsored by the Campbell Soup Company. CBS, 1939–1941. Orson Welles served as the host.

OPEN (from March 24, 1940)

THEME MUSIC: Up full then under...

ANNOUNCER (Ernest Chappell): The makers of Campbell's soups present *The Campbell Playhouse*, Orson Welles producer.

ORSON: Good evening, this is Orson Welles. It has been my custom on opening these Sunday Campbell Playhouse shows of ours to talk about, in order named, A, our offering for the evening, and B, our guest star. My task tonight is relatively easy. Our offering is our guest star, Mr. Jack Benny. Mr. Benny, not exactly unknown to the air waves as a comedian and violin virtuoso, has consented to make his radio debut as an actor, pure and simple in "June Moon." Now, for a moment or so, as Mr. Benny gets in the mood, Ernest Chappell, who is in the mood, has something to tell us about a discovery he's made. Mr. Chappell.

ERNEST: Thank you, Orson Welles. Perhaps it is hardly to be called a discovery. The taste for chicken was as keen in the year 1665 as it is with us in 1940. Now, I'm sure it must be our continued liking for chicken that has made this country take so wholeheartedly to Campbell's Chicken Soup. One after another, families have tried this chicken soup and found it rich in chicken flavor clear through. Have you tried this deep-flavored, home-like chicken soup of Campbell's? I promise you as sure as you like chicken, you'll like Campbell's Chicken Soup. And now to Orson Welles and our *Campbell Playhouse* presentation of "June Moon" starring Jack Benny. [The story of songwriter Fred Stevens, played by Jack Benny.]

CLOSE (from March 24, 1940)

ANNOUNCER: *The Campbell Playhouse* has presented "June Moon," produced by Orson Welles and starring Jack Benny. And now our producer and star of *The Campbell Playhouse*, Mr. Orson Welles.

ORSON: Ladies and gentlemen, the character of Frederick Stevens was sustained tonight by

Jack Benny. "Jane Eyre" is next week's story. It's one of the really fine, really moving romances in all literature. We are genuinely thrilled at the prospect of doing "Jane Eyre" for you and very proud indeed to announce for the name part, an old friend and very gifted actress, Madeleine Carroll. Till next Sunday night and "Jane Eyre" with Madeleine Carroll, my sponsor, the makers of Campbell soups, and all of us in *The Campbell Playhouse*, I remain as always, obediently yours.

ANNOUNCER: The makers of Campbell soups join Orson Welles in inviting you to be with us in *The Campbell Playhouse* next Sunday night when we will present "Jane Eyre" with Madeleine Carroll as our guest. In the meantime, if you enjoyed tonight's presentation, won't you tell your grocer tomorrow when you order Campbell Chicken Soup. This is Ernest Chappell saying thank you and good night. This is CBS, the Columbia Broadcasting System.

58. Can You Top This?

Game show in which a panel attempts to provide a funnier punchline to a joke sent in by a home listener. Both sustaining and sponsored (by Colgate, Kirkman's Soap Flakes and Mars Candies). Mutual (1940–1945; 1948–1950), NBC (1942–1948; 1953–1954), ABC (1951). Ward Wilson hosted; Peter Donald (then Charles Stark) read the listener's jokes; Senator Edward Ford, Harry Hershfield and Joe Laurie, Jr. comprised the panel.

OPEN

HOST: Why did the chicken cross the road?
PETER DONALD: That was no chicken, that was my wife.
HOST: Can you top that, Harry Hershfield?
HARRY: Sure.
HOST: Can you, Senator Ford?
FORD: I might.
HOST: And you, Joe Laurie, Jr.?
JOE: Maybe.
THEME MUSIC: Up full then under…
ANNOUNCER: Those expedient exclamations introduce the pint-sized author-comedian Joe

Laurie, Jr., the popular after-dinner speaker and current topic humorist Senator Ford, and well-known cartoonist and after-dinner speaker Harry Hershfield. These effervescent entertainers bring you another session of *Can You Top This?* And now, here's your master of ceremonies, Ward Wilson.
SOUND: Applause.
WARD: Good evening and welcome to *Can You Top This?*…

CLOSE

THEME MUSIC: Up full then under…
ANNOUNCER: And thus ends another laugh session of *Can You Top This?*, originated by Senator Ford. Join us again next week, same time, same station, same gang, other jokes, some new, some old. Until then, we remain yours for bigger and better laughs. This is Mutual.
THEME MUSIC: Up full then fade out.

59. The Canada Dry Ginger Ale Program

A program of music and songs hosted by comedian Jack Benny (his first radio series). Sponsored by Canada Dry. Blue (1932), CBS (1932–1933).

OPEN

SOUND: Train pulling into a station.
CONDUCTOR'S VOICE: All out, all out.
ANNOUNCER: Tonight, Canada Dry, the champagne of ginger ale, presents a series of programs to advertise the new made-to-order Canada Dry, which you can now buy by the glass at drug stores and soda fountains. This series will feature George Olsen and his music, Miss Ethel Shutta, the star of many Broadway successes, and that suave comedian, dry humorist and famous master of ceremonies Jack Benny.
JACK: Ladies and gentlemen, this is Jack Benny talking and this is my first appearance on the air professionally. By that I mean I'm finally getting paid, which of course will be a great relief for my creditors. I really don't know why I'm here. I'm supposed to be sort of a

master of ceremonies and tell you the things that will happen, which would happen anyway, and introduce the different artists who could easily introduce themselves, and also talk about Canada Dry made to order by the glass which is a waste of time because you know all about it. You drink it and like it and don't want to hear about it. So, ladies and gentlemen, a master of ceremonies is really a fellow who is unemployed and gets paid for it. I think you'll like the entertainment arranged for tonight. The first number will be a selection by George Olsen and his orchestra...

CLOSE

JACK: That, ladies and gentlemen, was the last number on our first show on the second of May. I hope you will be with us again next Wednesday. Well, good night then.

SOUND: Train bell.

CONDUCTOR'S VOICE: All aboard, away we go, all aboard, all aboard.

ANNOUNCER: Ladies and gentlemen, we are concluding the first program in a new series sponsored by Canada Dry, the ginger ale now available made to order in drug stores and soda fountains as well as in bottles. Canada Dry has presented Jack Benny, Ethel Shutta and George Olsen and his music. The same group of artists will be with you at this same time Wednesday evening. This is the National Broadcasting Company.

60. Candid Microphone

Comedy relating the reactions of people caught in prearranged situations by hidden microphones. Various sponsors. ABC (1947–1948), CBS (1950). Basis for the television series "Candid Camera." Narrated by Allen Funt

OPEN

THEME MUSIC: Up full then under...

ANNOUNCER (Ken Roberts): The *Candid Microphone*. The American Broadcasting Company presents the *Candid Microphone*, the program that brings you the secretly recorded conversations of all kinds of people as they

react in real life to all kinds of situations. No one ever knows when he's talking into the candid microphone. The candid microphone might catch you off guard; a hidden microphone might be eavesdropping on you right now. No one ever knows when he's talking into the candid microphone.

THEME MUSIC: Up full then out.

CLOSE

THEME MUSIC: Up full then under...

ANNOUNCER: So until next week, *Candid Microphone* goes back into hiding, the better to catch you in our act. Nothing is off the record when the man with the hidden mike crosses your path with the mike that hears without being seen, the candid microphone. The *Candid Microphone* is tailored for your enjoyment, so we're always glad to hear your candid comments about it. If there is someone you'd like to hear us catch off guard, tell it to candid mike. Write to *Candid Microphone* in care of the American Broadcasting Company, New York 20, New York. But whether or not you write, we invite you to please drop in again next Thursday when we'll be heard over most of these ABC stations. *Candid Microphone* is a copyrighted Allen A. Funt Production. *Candid Microphone* was transcribed. This is ABC, the American Broadcasting Company.

THEME MUSIC: Up full then fade out.

61. Candy Matson, YUkon 2-8209

Crime drama about San Francisco private detective Candy Matson (Natalie Masters). Various sponsors. NBC, 1949–1951.

OPEN

SOUND: Phone rings.

CANDY: Hello. YUkon 2-8209. Yes, this is Candy Matson.

ANNOUNCER (Dudley Manlove): From San Francisco, the National Broadcasting Company presents another yarn in the adventures of that attractive private eye, Candy Matson, YUkon 2-8209.

THEME MUSIC: Up full then out.

CLOSE

ANNOUNCER: Listen again next week at this same time. For excitement and adventure just dial—

CANDY: Candy Matson, YUkon 2-8209.

ANNOUNCER: The program stars Natalie Masters as Candy and is written and produced by Monte Masters. Eloise Rowan is heard at the organ. The characters in tonight's story are entirely fictitious; any resemblance to actual people is coincidental. The program came to you from San Francisco. Dudley Manlove speaking. You are tuned for the stars on NBC.

SOUND: NBC chimes. N-B-C.

62. Captain Midnight

Adventure series about a mysterious man who battles evil as Captain Midnight. Sponsored by Ovaltine. Mutual, 1940–1949. Ed Prentiss, Bill Bouchey and Paul Barnes played Captain Midnight. Basis for the television series.

OPEN (early)

SOUND: Gong tolling midnight followed by an airplane swooping down.

ANNOUNCER (Pierre Andre): The makers of Ovaltine present *Captain Midnight!*

SOUND: Plane flying.

ANNOUNCER: *Captain Midnight*, brought to you everyday, Monday through Friday at this same time by the makers of Ovaltine. *Captain Midnight* is a new program to many of our listeners. It is written for red-blooded young Americans, for boys and girls, and yes, mother and dad too; for everyone who's young in spirit. *Captain Midnight* will bring you plenty of excitement, mystery and suspense. Thrills galore that let you live a story of real adventure. In the air and on the ground, you'll never want to miss a single broadcast of *Captain Midnight* and you'll want to tell your friends to enjoy it too. So be sure to tell them to listen in everyday. This program is brought to you by the makers of Ovaltine, the famous food drink that is a favorite with millions of Americans young and old. Ovaltine is a fa-

vorite food drink for two reasons. First, because it is so downright good; you'll love its rich, satisfying flavor, so different from any other drink you ever tasted. And you'll never grow tired of it. Second, because Ovaltine is so good for you. It brings you loads and loads of valuable vitamins, minerals and other food elements that help build strong, healthy bodies. It gives you the pep and energy you need to be wide awake and husky. So tell mother you'd like to start drinking Ovaltine every single day and to start listening to this swell new program. And now to *Captain Midnight*.

CLOSE (early)

ANNOUNCER (after cliff-hanging scene): Don't miss the exciting adventure tomorrow. Tune in same time, same station to *Captain Midnight*. Now just a word about you. You have just heard the opening episode in a new series of exciting adventures with Captain Midnight. If you like the way the program begins keep on spreading the news to all the fellows and girls you know, will ya? And don't forget to try Ovaltine this very night. It's not only a good-tasting drink, but it's good for you too. You see, Ovaltine brings you loads of wonderful vitamins, minerals and other food elements our bodies need to fill out and grow up strong and healthy. Nobody wants to be skinny looking and tired and worn out all the time. We all want to be popular fellows and girls, full of get up and go, always ready for adventure and that's why thousands and thousands of smart fellows and girls are drinking Ovaltine every single day. Why don't you try some tonight and be sure to tune in tomorrow, same time, same station for another stirring adventure with *Captain Midnight*, brought to you everyday, Monday through Friday, by the makers of Ovaltine. See you tomorrow. And until then, this is Pierre Andre, your Ovaltine announcer, saying goodbye and happy landing.

SOUND: Plane flying.

VOICE: This is the Mutual Broadcasting System.

OPEN (later)

SOUND: Gong tolling midnight followed by an airplane swooping down.

ANNOUNCER (Pierre Andre): Cap...tain...Mid ...night! Brought to you every day, Monday through Friday, by the makers of Ovaltine. Be sure to have your pencil and paper ready at the end of today's adventure for a special Secret Squadron signal session. And now "Fighting with the Commandos" with Captain Midnight and the Secret Squadron.

CLOSE (later)

ANNOUNCER: Don't miss the thrill-packed action in the next episode of "Fighting with the Commandos."

SOUND: Telegraph signals.

VOICE: And now clear the airwaves. Stand by, the Secret Squadron signal session is on the air.

ANNOUNCER: We have a thrilling secret code message from Captain Midnight. It's an exciting clue about tomorrow night's adventure in master code number four. So write that down, code number 4, and here's the message. All right, first word is 23...13...20...4... 13. Get that? All right, here's the second word...5...26...16. One more word now. The third and last. Now here it is...15...9...3 ...7. That's all. Now remember, set your Code-O-Graph to master code four and figure out the code, a message about tomorrow's adventure and listen regularly for more of these Secret Squadron sessions and tune in tomorrow, same time, same station for *Captain Midnight*. Goodbye and Happy Landiii-iiings.

63. The Case Book of Gregory Hood

Crime drama about an importer who becomes involved with murder and mayhem. Sponsored by Petri Wines. Mutual (1946–1949), ABC (1950–1951). Gale Gordon, Elliott Lewis, Jackson Beck, Paul McGrath, Martin Gabel and George Petrie played Gregory Hood with Carl Harper and Bill Johnstone as his assistant, Sandor Taylor.

OPEN

ANNOUNCER (Harry Bartell): Petri Wine brings you *The Case Book of Gregory Hood*.

THEME MUSIC: Up full then under...

ANNOUNCER: Tonight, the Petri family, the family that took time to bring you good wine, invites you to listen to another exciting adventure from *The Case Book of Gregory Hood*. And I would like to ask you if you know one sure way to turn a simple meal into a regular feast? Just serve that meal with a good Petri dinner wine. Remember those five letters P-E-T-R-I. They spell the proudest name in the long line of fine wines.

THEME MUSIC: Up full then under...

ANNOUNCER: Well, it's Monday night in San Francisco and we have a date with Gregory Hood and his friend Sandor Taylor... [The story would then begin.]

CLOSE

THEME MUSIC: Up full then under...

ANNOUNCER: You can't go wrong with a Petri wine. Look at the long years of skill and experience that go into its making. The Petri family has been making wine for generations. Wine making is their heritage. So you can take it for granted that the Petri family really knows how to turn luscious sun-ripened grapes into clear, fragrant, delicious wine. You take it for granted too, that the name Petri on a bottle of wine is more than a trademark, it's the assurance from the Petri family that every drop of wine in that bottle is good wine. You can't go wrong with Petri wine because Petri took time to bring you good wine.

THEME MUSIC: Up full then under...

ANNOUNCER: The original music is composed and conducted by Dean Fossler. Gale Gordon played the part of Gregory Hood and Sandor Taylor is played by Carl Harper. The Petri Wine Company of San Francisco, California, invites you to tune in again next week, same time, same station. *The Case Book of Gregory Hood* comes to you from our Hollywood Studios. This is Harry Bartell saying good night for the Petri family. For a solid hour of exciting mystery drama, listen every Monday on most of these same stations at eight for *Michael Shayne*, followed immediately by *The Case Book of Gregory Hood*. This is the Mutual Broadcasting System.

THEME MUSIC: Up full then out.

Casey, Crime Photographer
see Flashgun Casey

64. Cathy and Elliott Lewis on Stage

Anthology series hosted by Cathy and Elliott Lewis. Various sponsors. CBS, 1953–1954. Ray Noble composed the theme, "Cathy and Elliott Lewis on Stage."

OPEN

THEME MUSIC: Up full then under…

ANNOUNCER (George Walsh): *Cathy and Elliott Lewis on Stage.* Cathy Lewis, Elliott Lewis, two of the most distinguished names in radio, appearing each week in their own theater, starring in a repertory of transcribed stories of their own and your choosing, radio's foremost players in radio's foremost plays. Dramas, comedy, adventure, mystery and melodrama. Ladies and gentlemen, Mr. Elliott Lewis.

ELLIOTT: Good evening, may I present my wife, Cathy.

CATHY: Good evening… [Elliott would appear next to talk about the evening's story; here is an example from January 1, 1953.]

ELLIOTT: Tonight is our opening night and tonight is the first of the new year. So we're going to do a comedy for you to start our new series.

CATHY: A story about a young man and his wife in 1953. Nice people, not rich, not poor. Happy with each other. You know, nice.

ELLIOTT: So tonight we present "String Bowtie" by Morton Fine and David Friedkin. My name in the play is Gershine Hapsmith.

CATHY: And I'm Laurie Hapsmith.

ELLIOTT: And we're married and we live in New York…

CLOSE

ANNOUNCER: "String Bowtie" starring Cathy and Elliott Lewis. Now, once again, Mr. and Mrs. Lewis.

CATHY: We'd like to thank our friends Sheldon Leonard and Mary Jane Croft who came down tonight to help us start a new year and our new series by playing Mr. and Mrs. Bill Bailey.

ELLIOTT: Now next week, Cathy.

CATHY: Just before we went into rehearsal today, we got a copy of next week's play, "The Drunken Sailor." It was written for us by a fine radio writer, Richard Chandley. It's a spy story, exciting. Thank you all for listening. Good night.

ELLIOTT: Good night.

ANNOUNCER: "The String Bowtie" was written by Morton Fine and David Friedkin. The theme for *Cathy and Elliott Lewis on Stage* was written by Ray Noble. Music for the program is composed by Fred Steiner and conducted by Lud Gluskin. *Cathy and Elliott Lewis on Stage* is transcribed and directed by Mr. Lewis. George Walsh speaking. And remember, John Lund as *Yours Truly, Johnny Dollar* will bring you colorful mystery on Friday nights on the CBS Radio Network.

65. Cavalcade of America

Dramatizations based on the lives of people who helped in the shaping of America. Sponsored by DuPont. CBS (1935–1939); NBC (1940–1953).

OPEN (1942)

THEME MUSIC: Up full then under…

ANNOUNCER (Clayton Collyer): Starring Madeleine Carroll as Amelia Earhart on the *Cavalcade of America*, sponsored by DuPont, makers of better living through chemistry.

THEME MUSIC: Up full then under…

ANNOUNCER: As these words are spoken, 22,000 woman are now piloting civil air patrol planes; others are ferrying bombers to distant places. Thousands of American women are pouring through the gates of factories, shipyards and airplane plants after a hard day's work. Today we know that there is hardly a job a woman cannot do; and if there is one woman who proved that fact once and forever, it is America's greatest woman flyer, whose thrilling story we tell this evening. For her courage, skill and persistent efforts to prove a woman's place in aviation, *Cavalcade* salutes Amelia Earhart.

THEME MUSIC: Up full then out.

CLOSE (1942)

ANNOUNCER: Thank you Madeleine Carroll. Ladies and gentlemen, next week *Cavalcade* will be proud to honor the men of our Merchant Marine in a new radio play called "Torpedo Run," a story based on the actual experiences of the heroic men who carry the goods over the seven seas fighting submarines beneath and bombers overhead. Our star will be the popular stage and screen star Dean Jagger. This is Clayton Collyer sending best wishes from DuPont.

THEME MUSIC: Up full then under...

ANNOUNCER: This is NBC, the National Broadcasting Company.

THEME MUSIC: Up full then out.

SOUND: NBC chimes. N-B-C.

OPEN (1950)

THEME MUSIC: Up full then under...

ANNOUNCER (Ted Pearson): *Cavalcade of America*, sponsored by the DuPont Company, makers of better things for better living through chemistry, and starring Elizabeth Taylor. Tonight's DuPont play, "I, Mary Peabody," is adapted from the best seller *The Peabody Sisters of Salem*, and here is our star, Elizabeth Taylor... [Elizabeth would then begin the story; here about a girl's attempts to overcome her shyness in 1833 Boston.]

CLOSE (1950)

THEME MUSIC: Up full then under...

ANNOUNCER: The DuPont *Cavalcade of America* comes to you from the stage of the Velasio Theater in New York and is sponsored by the DuPont Company of Wilmington, Delaware, makers of better things for better living through chemistry.

THEME MUSIC: Up full then out.

ANNOUNCER: This is NBC, the National Broadcasting Company.

SOUND: NBC chimes. N-B-C.

66. The CBS Radio Workshop

Anthology series that presented both fictional and real-life stories. Sustaining. CBS, 1956–1957.

OPEN

ANNOUNCER (Warren Sweeney): CBS Radio, a division of the Columbia Broadcasting System and its 217 affiliated stations, presents *CBS Radio Workshop*, dedicated to man's imagination, the theater of the mind. Tonight, a documentary in sound as recorded by Tony Swartz, a young man who walks the streets of the city as familiarly as a farmer walks his fields. He is a man who listens and what he listens to he records. Tony Swartz and his portable tape recorder have recorded "The Voice of New York."

CLOSE

ANNOUNCER: You have been listening to "The Voice of New York" as recorded by Tony Swartz and narrated by Clifton Fadiman. This is Warren Sweeney inviting you to listen to *The CBS Radio Workshop* next Friday when we will present "Report on the Unknown," a study of clairvoyancy, extra sensory perception and telepathy. *The CBS Radio Workshop* was produced and directed by Paul Roberts. This is CBS, the Columbia Broadcasting System.

67. Challenge of the Yukon

Adventure about William Preston, a Canadian Northwest Mounted Policeman, and his dog, Yukon King, as they battle evil in the Yukon of the 1890s. Sustaining. Local Detroit (1939–1947), ABC (1947–1951). Paul Sutton played Sergeant William Preston. See also *Sergeant Preston of the Yukon*. The "Donna Diana Overture" by von Reznicek was used as the theme.

OPEN

SOUND: Dog barking.

ANNOUNCER (Bill Morgan): King, the swiftest and strongest of Eskimo lead dogs, blazes the trail through storm and snow for Sergeant Preston and meets the *Challenge of the Yukon*.

THEME MUSIC: Up full then under…

ANNOUNCER: Sergeant Preston was typical of the small band of Northwest Mounted Police who preserved law and order in the Yukon during the gold rush of '98. That was the year that brought over 50,000 men swarming into the Klondike region, and the greed for gold led to frequent violence and bloodshed. But in spite of the odds against them, the force preserved a splendid record in maintaining the right. The challenge of the Northwest was answered and justice ruled triumphant.

THEME MUSIC: Up full then out.

CLOSE

THEME MUSIC: Up full then under…

ANNOUNCER: *Challenge of the Yukon*, a copyrighted feature of the Challenge of the Yukon, Inc., is brought to you every Saturday at this time and originated in the transcription studios of WXYZ, Detroit. The characters and events in tonight's drama were fictitious. Bill Morgan speaking. This is the Michigan Radio Network.

68. Chandu, the Magician

Adventure serial about Frank Chandler, an American secret agent who battles evil as Chandu, the Magician. Sponsored by Beech Nut (East Coast) and White King Soap (West Coast). Mutual, 1932–1936. Gayne Whitman played Frank Chandler, with Margaret MacDonald as his widowed sister, Dorothy Regent; Betty Webb as Dorothy's daughter, Betty; and Bob Bixby as Bob, Dorothy's son. See the following title also.

OPEN

SOUND: A gong.

THEME MUSIC: Up full then under…

ANNOUNCER: *Chandu, the Magician*. Good evening, ladies and gentlemen. The makers of the White King Granulated Soap present for your enjoyment tonight and every weekday evening at this time *Chandu, the Magician*. Listen and you will travel to strange lands, you will thrill to high adventure, romance and mystery.

THEME MUSIC: Up full then under…

ANNOUNCER: *Chandu, the Magician* is presented by the makers of White King Granulated Soap. There are many tales told on radio, but only one Chandu. There are many soaps on your grocer's counter, but none like White King. When you shop, look for White King. Now let the play begin.

THEME MUSIC: Up full then out.

CLOSE

THEME MUSIC: Up full then under…

ANNOUNCER: We pause before we say good evening to suggest that you and your family listen to *Chandu* every weekday evening at this time. Travel with us to strange places and faraway lands, into the mystery and intrigue of Egypt and the Near East. And of course we would like to have you use the soap we make, White King Granulated Soap. So on your radio, remember *Chandu, the Magician*; and at your grocer's remember White King Granulated Soap. Good night.

THEME MUSIC: Up full then out.

ANNOUNCER: This is Mutual.

69. Chandu, the Magician

Frank Chandler, the American secret agent who battles evil as Chandu, the Magician, in a revised version of the prior title that redramatized the original scripts. Various sponsors. ABC, 1948–1950. Tom Collins starred as Frank Chandler, with Irene Tedrow as his widowed sister, Dorothy Regent; Joy Terry as Betty, Dorothy's daughter; and Lee Miller as Bob, Dorothy's son.

OPEN

SOUND: A gong.

VOICE: *Chandu, the Magician*.

THEME MUSIC: Up full then under…

CHANDU: Since time began, men and women have had strange experiences for which there is no explanation, except the secrets the ancient magicians knew. But for centuries their secrets have been guarded in the hidden places of the Far East. Today, perhaps, Frank

Chandler has discovered them as people say. He is called Chandu, the Magician. Can you be sure it isn't true?

THEME MUSIC: Up full then under…

ANNOUNCER: Good evening, ladies and gentlemen, the American Broadcasting Company presents *Chandu, the Magician.*

SOUND: A gong.

ANNOUNCER: Remember that sound, that music. Remember the name Chandu, the Magician, which swept the country not so many years ago. The name that means intrigue, romance, the mystic East, the spell of Egypt. Chandu is back again on ABC's nationwide network to thrill you, to take you to faraway places, to Istanbul, to Algiers, to Cairo with lingering echoes of ancient empires—Roman, Greek and Venetian, where the Sphinx looks down upon the march of centuries over the drifting sands. Now listen to our story of mystery and magic.

SOUND: A gong.

THEME MUSIC: Up full then out.

CLOSE

SOUND: A gong.

ANNOUNCER: In a moment we'll bring you a glimpse of next week's story. Did you enjoy tonight's adventure with Chandu? Some of you businessmen will be interested to know that *Chandu, the Magician* is available to promote goodwill and sales for your business or product. In other words, you'll be glad to learn how easily you can afford to sponsor *Chandu, the Magician* in your own locality. For further details, get in touch with the manager of your local ABC station. In presenting *Chandu, the Magician*, ABC furthers its policy of bringing listeners the best in mystery dramas. For instance, in just a few moments, you'll hear the first in a new series of *The Case Book of Gregory Hood*. Heard on most of these ABC stations tonight, it's a thrill-a-minute entertainment guaranteed to keep you on the edge of your chair from start to finish. And now a word about next Saturday's story.

THEME MUSIC: Up full then under…

ANNOUNCER: Next week the desolate Sahara, a forbidding desert strongbed, a hooded desert chief who lives like a king, and a legend of ancient Egypt, become a terrifying reality.

THEME MUSIC: Up full then under…

ANNOUNCER: *Chandu, the Magician* is based on the original radio dramas created by Harry A. Earnshaw and is written by Vera Olden. Frank Chandler is played by Tom Collins. The program is a Cyril Armbruster production. We invite you to listen next week at this same time for adventure, magic, mystery— *Chandu, the Magician.*

SOUND: A gong.

THEME MUSIC: Up full then fade out.

The Charlie McCarthy Show *see* The Chase and Sanborn Hour

70. The Charlotte Greenwood Show

Comedy with singer-comedienne Charlotte Greenwood as a reporter for the small town *Post-Dispatch* who yearns to become an actress. Sponsored by Hallmark Greeting Cards. Blue, 1944. See the following title also.

OPEN

ANNOUNCER (Wendell Niles): A Hallmark card will best express your perfect tastes, your thoughtfulness.

CHORUS:
>   Welcome to our show,
>   Here's a friend you all know,
>   Charlotte Greenwood,
>   She's with us again.

ANNOUNCER: *The Hallmark Charlotte Greenwood Show*, brought to you every Sunday at this time by the makers of Hallmark greeting cards. And here is our star, that lovable lady of stage and screen, Charlotte Greenwood.

SOUND: Applause.

ANNOUNCER: Well, last week Charlotte almost got a train for Hollywood—almost, but not quite. But now we find her back in the offices of the Lake View *Post-Dispatch*. The time is one o'clock Saturday afternoon…

CLOSE

ANNOUNCER: Charlotte Greenwood will be back

in a moment. Meanwhile, I want to say just this. When you buy a card for any occasion, look for the Hallmark imprint on the back. Like Sterling Silver, that imprint, a Hallmark card, is your assurance of the finest quality. It tells your friends you cared enough to send the very best. Yes, a Hallmark card will best express your perfect taste, your thoughtfulness. And now Charlotte Greenwood.

CHARLOTTE: Friends, it's been fun visiting with you again. It's always a pleasure for all of us to visit with our friends, dropping in at their homes to chat for a moment, to laugh together and to bring back memories of good times. Today, with so many families so many miles apart, let's try to make a personal call more often in a different way, particularly to those in uniform. A card, a note to say hello will mean so much. And, if you want to get a little warmer, say darling I love you. Send this card today, will you? And now, until Sunday at this very same time, this is Charlotte Greenwood saying—

CHARLOTTE (Singing):

So long, friends, until we meet again,
So long, neighbors, until next Sunday,
Time to say so long. So long.

ANNOUNCER: *The Charlotte Greenwood Show* has been brought to you by Hallmark cards. Wendell Niles speaking. This is the Blue Network.

71. The Charlotte Greenwood Show

Revised version of the prior title about Charlotte Greenwood (herself), now the guardian of the three Barton children—Barbara, Jack and Robert (Janet Waldo, Cliff Carpenter, Dix Davis). Sponsored by Hallmark Greeting Cards. ABC, 1944–1946.

OPEN

ANNOUNCER (Wendell Niles): Whenever you have occasion to send a card, remember a Hallmark card will best express your perfect taste, your thoughtfulness.

THEME MUSIC: Up full then under…

ANNOUNCER: *The Hallmark Charlotte Green-*

wood Show. And here she is, that lovable lady of stage, screen and radio, Charlotte Greenwood. Friends, Charlotte Greenwood has as her guest today, the distinguished actor, one of the stars of Metro-Goldwyn-Mayer's *Weekend at the Waldorf,* Mr. Edward Arnold. Yes, ladies and gentlemen, Miss Charlotte Greenwood is brought to you this Sunday and every Sunday at this time by the makers of Hallmark greeting cards to remind you that whenever you want to remember someone, you'll find a Hallmark card that says what you want to say the way you want to say it. So when you choose a card, look on the back for the three identifying words "A Hallmark Card." Yes, a Hallmark card will best express your perfect taste, your thoughtfulness.

THEME MUSIC: Up full then under…

ANNOUNCER: And now to the little town of Lake View where Aunt Charlotte is bringing up the three Barton youngsters, little Robert and teenaged Jack and Barbara…

CLOSE

ANNOUNCER: Charlotte Greenwood will be back in a moment. Meanwhile I want to remind you again, the next time you buy a card for any occasion, look on the back for the identifying words "A Hallmark Card." Like Sterling on silver, those three words are your assurance of finest quality. They tell your friends that you cared enough to send the very best. Yes, a Hallmark card will best express your perfect taste, your thoughtfulness. And now Charlotte Greenwood.

CHARLOTTE: And now until next Sunday at this very same time, this is Charlotte Greenwood saying—

CHARLOTTE (SINGING):

So long until we meet again,
So long, neighbors, till next Sunday,
So until then, so long. So long.

ANNOUNCER: *The Hallmark Charlotte Greenwood Show* came to you from Hollywood. This is Wendell Niles speaking. The American Red Cross is urgently in need of young men and women to join its junior membership. When you go to school Tuesday, ask your teacher for complete information about the Junior Red Cross and join, they need you. This is the American Broadcasting Company.

72. The Chase and Sanborn Hour

Long-running variety series sponsored by Chase and Sanborn Coffee. (NBC, 1937–1948). Originally hosted by Dave Rubinoff and his orchestra (1931) then by Eddie Cantor (1931–1934). Programs from these eras are not in circulation. The series resumed production in 1937 with Don Ameche and concluded with Edgar Bergen and Charlie McCarthy as hosts. After Chase and Sanborn dropped sponsorship (1948), Edgar Bergen and Charlie McCarthy continued their own show (*The Charlie McCarthy Show*) on CBS (1948–1955) under various sponsors (most frequently Coca-Cola and Kraft Foods).

OPEN (for Don Ameche)

THEME MUSIC: Up full then under...
ANNOUNCER (Ken Carpenter): The makers of the coffee you know is fresh, Chase and Sanborn, present *The Chase and Sanborn Hour* with your host, Don Ameche.
DON: This is *The Chase and Sanborn Hour* and this is Don Ameche welcoming you from all of us. We hope you will enjoy your visit with us and we hope throughout this week you'll enjoy Chase and Sanborn coffee... [Don would then begin the show.]

CLOSE (for Don Ameche)

THEME MUSIC: Up full then under...
ANNOUNCER: You have been listening to *The Chase and Sanborn Hour* with your host, Don Ameche and presented by the makers of Chase and Sanborn, the coffee you know is fresh. This is Ken Carpenter inviting you to join us again next week when Don Ameche returns with another *Chase and Sanborn Hour*. This is NBC, the National Broadcasting Company.
THEME MUSIC: Up full then out.
SOUND: NBC chimes. N-B-C.

OPEN (for Edgar Bergen)

THEME MUSIC: Up full then under...
ANNOUNCER (Don Ameche): The makers of Chase and Sanborn coffee, the superb blend of the world's choice coffees which is so reasonably priced, present Dorothy Lamour,

W.C. Fields, Edgar Bergen and Charlie McCarthy, Robert Armbruster and his orchestra, and yours truly, Don Ameche. This is *The Chase and Sanborn Hour*.
THEME MUSIC: Up full then out.

CLOSE (for Edgar Bergen)

THEME MUSIC: Up full then under...
ANNOUNCER: The makers of Chase and Sanborn coffee have presented *The Chase and Sanborn Hour* with your hosts Edgar Bergen and his little wooden friend, Charlie McCarthy. This is Don Ameche speaking. This is NBC, the National Broadcasting Company.
THEME MUSIC: Up full then out.
SOUND: NBC chimes. N-B-C.

OPEN (for Charlie McCarthy)

THEME MUSIC: Up full then under...
ANNOUNCER (Ken Carpenter): The makers of Chase and Sanborn coffee present *The Charlie McCarthy Show*. This is Ken Carpenter, ladies and gentlemen, greeting you from Hollywood, California, on behalf of Edgar Bergen, Charlie McCarthy, Mortimer Snerd, Don Ameche and Marsha Hunt of "The Bickersons" by Bill Rapp, Ray Noble and his orchestra and Pat Patrick as Ersel Twing. Here they are, ladies and gentlemen, Edgar Bergen and his little wooden pal, Charlie McCarthy.
SOUND: Applause... (after which Edgar and Charlie would begin the show).

CLOSE (for Charlie McCarthy)

THEME MUSIC: Up full then under...
ANNOUNCER: Chase and Sanborn, that superb coffee at a reasonable price, has presented *The Charlie McCarthy Show* with Edgar Bergen, Charlie McCarthy, Mortimer Snerd, "The Bickersons" with Don Ameche and Marsha Hunt and the music of Ray Noble and his orchestra. Be with us again next week when the makers of that superb coffee, Chase and Sanborn, will present *The Charlie McCarthy Show*. Ken Carpenter speaking. This is NBC, the National Broadcasting Company.
THEME MUSIC: Up full then out.
SOUND: NBC chimes. N-B-C.

73. Chick Carter, Boy Detective

Spinoff from *Nick Carter, Master Detective* about the crime-fighting adventures of Nick's adopted son, Chick. Sustaining. Mutual, 1943–1945. Bill Lipton and Leon Janney played Chick Carter, with Jean McCoy and Joanne McCoy as Sue, his assistant.

OPEN

SOUND: Telegraph transmission.
ANNOUNCER (Ken Powell): Mutual to Y-O-U. Sending. Are you ready?
VOICE: Y-O-U to Mutual, go ahead.
ANNOUNCER: Then listen to the adventures of *Chick Carter, Boy Detective.*
THEME MUSIC: Up full then under…
ANNOUNCER: Yes, time for another case from the files of Chick Carter, the adopted son of that most famous master detective, Nick Carter. And now, *Chick Carter, Boy Detective.*
THEME MUSIC: Up full then out.

CLOSE

THEME MUSIC: Up full then under…
ANNOUNCER: Join us again tomorrow and every weekday at this time for the adventures of *Chick Carter, Boy Detective.* Leon Janney is heard as Chick Carter with Jean McCoy as Sue; Ken Powell speaking. This is the Mutual Broadcasting System.
THEME MUSIC: Up full then fade out.

74. Chip Davis, Commando

The adventures of an American member of Britain's World War II fighting squadron the Commandos. Sustaining. CBS, 1942–1943. Charles Paul composed the theme, "Commando."

OPEN

THEME MUSIC: Up full then under…
ANNOUNCER: Out of the night, grim shadows rise; the steel of vengeance finds its mark. The Commandos have struck again! Columbia presents *Chip Davis, Commando*, the story of an American and his exciting adventures in Britain's famous fighting unit.

CLOSE

ANNOUNCER: You have been listening to *Chip Davis, Commando*, Columbia's weekly series about an American in Britain's famous fighting unit. *Chip Davis, Commando* is directed by John Deats with music by Charles Paul and is produced by Robert Lewis Shallot. Join us again next Sunday at seven P.M. Eastern War Time for another story with Chip Davis and the men of the United Nations who share his adventures in the Commandos.
THEME MUSIC: Up full then under…
ANNOUNCER: This is the Columbia Broadcasting System.
THEME MUSIC: Up full then fade out.

75. Christopher London

Crime drama about a troubleshooter for hire. Various sponsors. NBC, 1950. Glenn Ford played Christopher London. Lyn Murray composed "The Christopher London Theme."

OPEN

THEME MUSIC: Up full then under…
ANNOUNCER: The National Broadcasting Company presents *Christopher London*, created especially for radio by the world's foremost mystery writer, Erle Stanley Gardner. Produced and directed by William N. Robson and starring Mr. Glenn Ford as Christopher London, the loner who will go anywhere and take any case to solve the problems of others. *Christopher London.*
THEME MUSIC: Up full then out.

CLOSE

THEME MUSIC: Up full then under…
ANNOUNCER: That was *Christopher London* starring Glenn Ford and created especially for radio by the world's most widely read mystery writer, Erle Stanley Gardner. Music was composed and conducted by Lyn Murray. Mystery fans, you'll find two other great pulse-

packed adventure programs on most of these NBC stations every Monday night. Listen tomorrow night for *Night Beat* and *Dangerous Assignment* in one hour of intrigue and adventure on NBC. And be with us again next week at this same time when *Christopher London* returns with another exciting excursion against crime. Stay tuned for the Phil Harrises, then *Sam Spade* on NBC.

THEME MUSIC: Up full then out.

SOUND: NBC chimes. N-B-C.

76. City Hospital

Drama that centers on the work of Barton Crane (Melville Ruick), a doctor at City Hospital. Various sponsors. CBS, 1951–1958.

OPEN

THEME MUSIC: Up full then under…

ANNOUNCER (John Cannon): *City Hospital*. City Hospital, where life begins and ends, where around the clock, twenty-four hours a day, men and women are dedicated to the war against suffering and pain.

THEME MUSIC: Up full then under…

ANNOUNCER: *City Hospital* is presented by Carter's Little Liver Pills.

THEME MUSIC: Up full then out.

ANNOUNCER: A doctor's advice. If you're in excellent health there is no need for you to take laxatives regularly. Five New York doctors now have proved you can break the laxative habit. Eighty-three percent of his cases tested did it. So can you. Stop taking whatever you now take. Instead do this. Every night for one week take two Carter's Little Liver Pills. Second week, one each night. Third week, one every other night. Then nothing. Every day drink plenty of liquid. Put yourself on schedule. When overwork, overeating or worry get you off stride temporarily, take Carter's temporarily and don't get the laxative habit. Get Carter's Little Liver Pills; only 43 cents and break the laxative habit.

THEME MUSIC: Up full then under…

ANNOUNCER: And now to Melville Ruick as Dr. Barton Crane and *City Hospital*.

CLOSE

THEME MUSIC: Up full then under…

ANNOUNCER: Carter's Little Liver Pills has presented *City Hospital*. Be with us again next week at this same time for another presentation of *City Hospital*. City Hospital, where life begins and ends, where around the clock, twenty-four hours a day, men and women are dedicated to the war against suffering and pain. This series of programs is produced and directed by Ira Ashley and features Melville Ruick as Dr. Crane.

THEME MUSIC: Up full then fade out.

77. Cloak and Dagger

Dramatizations based on the files of the O.S.S. (Office of Strategic Services). Various sponsors. NBC, 1950. Colonel Corey Ford, co-author of the book *Cloak and Dagger*, served as the host.

OPEN

THEME MUSIC: Up full then under…

HOST: Are you willing to undertake a dangerous mission for the United States knowing in advance you may never return alive?

THEME MUSIC: Up full then under…

ANNOUNCER: What you have just heard is the question asked during the war of agents to the O.S.S., ordinary citizens who to this question answered yes. We have the honor at this time to present a former O.S.S. officer, co-author of the book *Cloak and Dagger*, upon which this series is based, Colonel Corey Ford.

FORD: Thank you. The O.S.S., the Office of Strategic Services, was America's top secret intelligence agency during the war. It was this country's first all-out effort in black warfare; dropping undercover operatives behind enemy lines, organizing local partisans to blow bridges and dynamite tunnels, outwitting the best spy business systems of Europe and Asia. The success of the O.S.S. is known, but the story behind that success, the story of the everyday, average Americans of every race, creed and color, who risked their lives knowing all too well that if they were caught they would face torture and probably death, is what Alistair McBain and I have tried to tell in *Cloak and Dagger*. We feel it is a story in which every American can take deep pride.

ANNOUNCER: The National Broadcasting Company takes you behind the scenes of a war that nobody knew. This is—

VOICE: *Cloak and Dagger.*

THEME MUSIC: Up full then out.

CLOSE

THEME MUSIC: Up full then under...

ANNOUNCER: *Cloak and Dagger* with your host Colonel Corey Ford is based on the book *Cloak and Dagger* by Colonel Ford and Alistair McBain. Actual names and places have been changed to protect the innocent. Be with us again next Sunday for another behind-the-scenes story of *Cloak and Dagger*. This is NBC, the National Broadcasting Company.

THEME MUSIC: Up full then out.

SOUND: NBC chimes. N-B-C.

78. The Clyde Beatty Show

Adventure series based on the experiences of wild animal trainer Clyde Beatty. Various sponsors. Mutual, 1950–1952.

OPEN

ANNOUNCER (Jackson Beck): *The Clyde Beatty Show.*

THEME MUSIC: Up full then under...

ANNOUNCER: The world's greatest wild animal trainer, Clyde Beatty, with an exciting adventure from his brilliant career. The circus means thrills, excitement, snarling jungle beasts. The circus means fun for young folks and old. But under the big top you see only part of the story; the real drama comes from behind the scenes, where 500 people live as one family, where Clyde Beatty constantly risks death in the world's most dangerous acts on earth. This master of the big top has journeyed to Africa and India, hunting down his beasts in their native jungle. All this is part of the Clyde Beatty story.

CLOSE

THEME MUSIC: Up full then under...

ANNOUNCER: All stories are based upon incidents in the career of the world-famous Clyde Beatty and the Clyde Beatty Circus. *The Clyde Beatty Show* is produced by Shirley Thomas. All names used were fictional and any resemblance to persons living or dead is purely coincidental. This is a Commodore Production.

THEME MUSIC: Up full then fade out.

79. Coast-to-Coast on a Bus

Children's program wherein passengers rode the imaginary White Rabbit Bus to a different locale each week (where they sang, danced and acted in skits). Sustaining. Blue (1927–1944), ABC (1945–1948). Originally aired locally in New York (as "The Children's Hour") 1924–1927. Milton Cross played the conductor of the White Rabbit Bus (the slogan of which is "Jumps anywhere, anytime").

OPEN

SOUND: Bus horn.

VOICE: *Coast-to-Coast on a Bus.* The White Rabbit Line jumps anywhere, anytime.

SONG (children singing):
> Oh, we just roll along,
> takin' her up, takin' her down,
> Takin' her up and down,
> All day long.
> And we don't care a lot,
> Maybe it's hot,
> Maybe it's cold.
> Maybe it's cold or hot,
> Let us ride.
> When our big bus jumps around,
> That don't worry us,
> 'Cause we just roll along,
> Takin' her up, takin' her down,
> Takin' her up and down
> All day long.

CONDUCTOR: Good morning little and big folks, children and grownups, passengers on the White Rabbit Bus... [He would then begin the show by mentioning the bus's destination.]

CLOSE

THEME MUSIC: Up full then under...

ANNOUNCER: *Coast-to-Coast on a Bus* features Milton Cross as our conductor with Madge Tucker as the Lady Next Door. Music is by Walter Fleischer, and the entire production is under the supervision of Miss Tucker. *Coast-to-Coast on a Bus*, created and written by Madge Tucker, will return next Sunday morning. Be with us for another ride on the famous White Rabbit Bus, the bus that jumps anywhere, anytime. This is the Blue Network.
THEME MUSIC: Up full then out.
SOUND: NBC chimes. N-B-C.

80. The Coke Club

Variety series sponsored by Coca-Cola beverages. Mutual, 1943–1951.

OPEN

MORTON DOWNEY SINGING:
> La-la- dee ya dum
> La-dee ya-dee dum dee.

ANNOUNCER: Yes friends, it's time for another transcribed session of *The Coke Club* which brings you the romantic voice of Morton Downey with Leah Ray as your hostess, Jimmy Lytell and his orchestra, the Coke Club Quartet and yours truly, David Ross.

CLOSE

ANNOUNCER: You have been listening to *The Coke Club*, transcribed, with the romantic voice of Morton Downey. This is David Ross inviting you to be with us again when the makers of Coca-Cola bring you another session of *The Coke Club*. Good night. This is Mutual.

81. The Colgate Sports Newsreel

Sports program with a different touch— dramatizations of events in the lives of people in the field of athletics or of those related to athletes. Sponsored by Colgate Shave Creme. NBC, 1939–1951. Hosted by sportscaster Bill Stern. The program is also known as *Bill Stern's Col-*

gate Sports Newsreel, The Colgate Shaving Creme Sports Newsreel and *The Bill Stern Review.* When Colgate dropped sponsorship in 1951, the show continued as *Bill Stern Sports* as a sustaining program on NBC (1953–1954) and as a sponsored series on ABC (Budweiser Beer, 1953–1954; various sponsors, 1954–1956).

OPEN

CHORUS:
> C-O-L-G-A-T-E,
> Colgate presents Bill Stern.

ANNOUNCER (Arthur Gary): With The Colgate Shave Creme Sports Newsreel.
CHORUS:
> Bill Stern the Colgate shave creme
>   man is on the air
> Bill Stern the Colgate shave creme
>   man with stories rare
> Take his advice and you'll look keen
> You'll get a shave that's smooth and clean
> You'll be a Colgate brushless fan.

BILL: Good evening, ladies and gentlemen, this is Bill Stern bringing you the 354th edition of *The Colgate Shave Creme Sports Newsreel* featuring strange and fantastic stories, some legends, some mere heresay, but all so interesting we'd like to pass them onto you.

CLOSE

BILL: And that's the "Three-O-Mark" for tonight. Next Friday we'll be back, same time, same station, with another edition of *The Colgate Shave Creme Sports Newsreel.* This is Bill Stern for Colgate Shave Creme wishing you all a good, good night.
CHORUS:
> Bill Stern the Colgate shave creme
>   man is on his way
> Bill Stern the Colgate shave creme
>   man has lots to say
> He told you tales of sports heroes
> The inside dope he really knows.
> So listen in next Friday night as
> Colgate presents Bill Stern.

ANNOUNCER: *The Bill Stern Show* tonight came from New York City. This is Arthur Gary wishing you a pleasant good night.
THEME MUSIC: Up full then out.

ANNOUNCER: This is NBC, the National Broadcasting Company.
SOUND: NBC chimes. N-B-C.

82. The Columbia Workshop

A showcase for aspiring actors, writers, producers and directors. Sustaining. CBS, 1936–1947.

OPEN

THEME MUSIC: Up full then under...
ANNOUNCER (Sandy Becker): Presenting radio's foremost laboratory of new writing and production techniques, *The Columbia Workshop. The Columbia Workshop* presents Irwin Shaw's story "Act of Faith," as adapted by Charles S. Monroe and directed by John Deats. [Story about American soldiers in France following World War II.]

CLOSE

THEME MUSIC: Up full then under...
ANNOUNCER: You have just heard "Act of Faith." This was written by Irwin Shaw and appeared originally in the *New Yorker* magazine. It was adapted for *The Columbia Workshop* by Charles S. Monroe of the CBS program writing division. The original musical score was composed and conducted by Alexander Semelar. Today's cast included Richard Nelson, Martin Wilson, Robert Dryden and Frank Butler. "Act of Faith" was produced and directed by John Deats. Next week *The Columbia Workshop* will present an adaptation of Damon Runyon's story "A Very Honorable Guy." It will be directed by Jack Mosman. Your announcer is Sandy Becker for CBS, the Columbia Broadcasting System.
THEME MUSIC: Up full then fade out.

83. Command Performance

Variety series tailored for the military. AFRS, 1942–1950.

OPEN

ANNOUNCER (Harry Van Zell): *Command Per-*

formance, USA, the greatest entertainers in America as requested by you, the men and women of the United States Armed Forces throughout the world. *Command Performance*, presented this week and every week till its over over there. Okay there gang, this is Harry Von Zell reminding you that it's time to join us once again for another session dedicated to answering your requests to *Command Performance*, Armed Forces Radio, Los Angeles, U.S.A.

CLOSE

THEME MUSIC ("Over There"): Up full then under...
ANNOUNCER: Harry Von Zell speaking for *Command Performance*.
VOICE: This is the Armed Forces Radio Service.
THEME MUSIC: Up full then fade out.

84. The Continental Celebrity Club

Variety series sponsored by the Continental Can Company. CBS, 1945–1946.

OPEN

ANNOUNCER (Bud Collyer): The Continental Can Company presents *The Continental Celebrity Club* with our own young comedy star, Jackie Kelk, the songs of Margaret Whiting, the music of Ray Bloch's orchestra, yours truly, Bud Collyer, and our special guest this evening, the glamorous radio and supper club star Hildegarde. [Margaret Whiting would be introduced and the show would begin with a song. This program aired May 26, 1946.]

CLOSE

ANNOUNCER: *The Continental Celebrity Club* is produced and directed by Mark Slobb and written by Will Glickman. Hildegarde appeared through a courtesy of Kool cigarettes. Next week, in addition to Jackie Kelk, Margaret Whiting and Ray Bloch's orchestra, we will have as our special guest, the brilliant young Hollywood comedian Eddie Bracken. This is Bud Collyer inviting you to join us then. *The Continental Celebrity Club* is brought to you by the 25,000 men and women of the Continental Can family, producing for the health, happiness and welfare of the nation. This is CBS, the Columbia Broadcasting System.

85. The Count of Monte Cristo

Adventure series about Edmond Dantes (Carleton Young), a mysterious figure who fights for justice in 18th century France as the Count of Monte Cristo. Various sponsors. Mutual, 1946–1947. "The Sylvia Ballet" by Dilibes was used as the theme.

OPEN

ANNOUNCER (Dick Wynn): *The Count of Monte Cristo.*

THEME MUSIC: Up full then under…

ANNOUNCER: From Hollywood, the Don Lee Network presents Carleton Young in another exciting adventure of *The Count of Monte Cristo.*

THEME MUSIC: Up full then under…

ANNOUNCER: More than a century ago, King Louis Philippe of France was constantly on guard against the intrigues that threatened his country. From across the borders came spies who added coal to the fire of discrimination that burned within the homeland. The King would trust few men, but he numbered among his confidantes, the daring patriot whose keen mind and flashing sword never failed the cause of justice and the common citizen. This hero of many a twice-told legend was Edmond Dantes, the fabulous Count of Monte Cristo.

THEME MUSIC: Up full then out.

CLOSE

THEME MUSIC: Up full then under…

ANNOUNCER: *The Count of Monte Cristo* stars Carleton Young in the title role with Parley Baer as René Michon. This adaptation is based on the characters created by Alexandre Dumas. Music by Dean Fossler. This is Dick

Wynn inviting you to join us next week at this same time for another adventure of *The Count of Monte Cristo.* This is the Mutual-Don Lee Broadcasting System.

THEME MUSIC: Up full then fade out.

86. Counterspy

Adventure series about David Harding, a U.S. government counterspy. Sponsored by Anahist, Gulf Oil, Mail Pouch, Pharmacraft, Pepsi Cola and Schutter Candy. Blue/ABC (1942–1950), NBC (1950–1953), Mutual (1954–1957). House Jameson and Don MacLaughlin played David Harding.

OPEN (World War II episodes)

SOUND: Morse Code Transmission.

ANNOUNCER (Roger Krupp): Washington calling Counterspy.

HARDING: Harding, Counterspy, calling Washington.

ANNOUNCER: The Blue Network presents *Counterspy.* Germany has its Gestapo, Italy its Zobra and Japan its Black Dragon. But matched against all these secret enemy agents are Uncle Sam's highly trained counterspies. Visualize ace Counterspy of them all, David Harding.

CLOSE (World War II episodes)

ANNOUNCER: The Blue Network has presented *Counterspy* with Don MacLaughlin. Tune in every week for *Counterspy.* This is the Blue Network.

OPEN (postwar)

ANNOUNCER (Bob Shepherd): Pepsi Cola. P-E-P-S-I, that's your smart cola buy. Pepsi Cola presents *Counterspy.*

VOICE: Washington calling David Harding, Counterspy; Washington calling David Harding, Counterspy.

HARDING: Harding, Counterspy, calling Washington.

ANNOUNCER: United States counterspies, especially appointed to investigate and combat the enemies of our country both here and abroad.

Tonight, "The Case of the Visiting Vultures," another *Counterspy* report to the American people brought to you each Tuesday and Thursday by Pepsi Cola.

SONG (CHORUS):

> Pepsi Cola hits the spot,
> Two full glasses that's a lot,
> Why take less when Pepsi's best.

ANNOUNCER: And now to Counterspy.

CLOSE (postwar)

ANNOUNCER: Pepsi Cola has presented Don MacLaughlin as *Counterspy*. Tune in every Tuesday and Thursday at this same time, same station, to *Counterspy*, produced by Phillips H. Lord with music by Jesse Crawford. Bob Shepherd speaking. This is ABC, the American Broadcasting Company.

87. The Couple Next Door

Comedy dialogue with an unnamed married couple (Peg Lynch, Alan Bunce) who converse about everyday life. Sustaining. CBS, 1957–1960. Madeleine Pierce played their six-and-a-half-year-old daughter, Betsy.

OPEN

THEME MUSIC: Up full then under...
ANNOUNCER (Warren Sweeney): *The Couple Next Door*, written by Peg Lynch and starring Peg Lynch and Alan Bunce. A view of everyday life as seen by the couple next door.
THEME MUSIC: Up full then out.

CLOSE

THEME MUSIC: Up full then under...
ANNOUNCER: *The Couple Next Door* is written by Peg Lynch and stars Peg Lynch and Alan Bunce with Madeleine Pierce as Betsy and is produced by Walter Hart. This is Warren Sweeney inviting you to listen tomorrow to *The Couple Next Door*.
THEME MUSIC: Up full then fade out.

88. Cousin Willie

Comedy about Willard O. Knott (Billy Idelson), a happy-go-lucky young man who moves in with his cousins, Marvin and Fran Sample (Marvin Miller, Patricia Dunlap). Sustaining. NBC, 1953.

OPEN

ANNOUNCER (Jimmy Wallington): It's now *Cousin Willie* on NBC.
THEME MUSIC: Up full then under...
ANNOUNCER: This is the one about Cousin Willie. Billy Idelson is Cousin Willie. Believe it or not, our Cousin Willie came to California from Milwaukee, Wisconsin. He is staying, temporarily, with his cousins, the Marvin Sample family, at 2164 Mariposa Avenue, Glendale. So far he has been with them, temporarily, for seven weeks. Cousin Willie sleeps, temporarily, on the davenport in Marvin's den. And he had a job, temporarily, selling reconditioned vacuum cleaners. And now, *Cousin Willie*.

CLOSE

THEME MUSIC: Up full then under...
ANNOUNCER: This has been *Cousin Willie*, an NBC Network production. *Cousin Willie* is written by Frank and Doris Hursley. Marvin Miller was heard as Marvin with Patricia Dunlap as Fran. Music is by Robert Armbruster. This is Jimmy Wallington speaking for NBC, the National Broadcasting Company.
THEME MUSIC: Up full then out.
SOUND: NBC chimes. N-B-C.

89. Crime and Peter Chambers

Crime drama about Peter Chambers (Dane Clark), a New York based private detective. Various sponsors. NBC, 1954.

OPEN

THEME MUSIC: Up full then under...
ANNOUNCER (Fred Collins): *Crime and Peter Chambers*, created by Henry Kane, transcribed and starring as Peter Chambers, Dane Clark.

THEME MUSIC: Up full then under...

PETER: You're a private eye, that's your business. Anything else, that's for laughs.

THEME MUSIC: Up full then out.

CLOSE

THEME MUSIC: Up full then under...

ANNOUNCER: And there you've had *Crime and Peter Chambers*. Dane Clark was starred as Peter Chambers. *Crime and Peter Chambers*, transcribed, was created and written by Henry Kane. This is Fred Collins inviting you to tune in next week, same time, same station for Dane Clark in *Crime and Peter Chambers*.

THEME MUSIC: Up full then out.

ANNOUNCER: This is NBC, the National Broadcasting Company.

SOUND: NBC chimes. N-B-C.

90. The Crime Cases of Warden Lawes

Anthology that dramatized cases from the files of Sing Sing Prison. Sponsored by Clipper Craft Clothes. Mutual, 1946–1947.

OPEN

SOUND: Bell ringing.

VOICE: Lock cell block, lock cell block, lock cell block.

SOUND: Prison door closing.

ANNOUNCER (Cy Harrice): *The Crime Cases of Warden Lawes*. The makers of Clipper Craft Clothes for men and 924 leading retail stores from coast to coast, tonight present from the files of Lewis E. Lawes, former warden of Sing Sing Prison, case number 45837-M—"M for Murder."

CLOSE

ANNOUNCER: Next week, *The Crime Cases of Warden Lawes* will present the dramatic story of a girl who risked her life to pay a debt she did not owe. All names of persons and places mentioned in today's case are fictitious. Now stay tuned for that famous racket busting program *Special Investigator* which follows immediately over most of these Mutual stations.

The Crime Cases of Warden Lawes is produced by Bernard Proctor. Cy Harrice speaking. This is the Mutual Broadcasting System.

91. Crime Classics

Dramatizations of crime stories from "the records of newspapers of every land from every time." Sustaining. CBS, 1953–1954. Lou Merrill played the host, Thomas Hyland. Bernard Herrmann composed the theme.

OPEN

THEME MUSIC: Up full then under...

HOST: Good evening, this is *Crime Classics*. I am Thomas Hyland with another true story of crime.

THEME MUSIC: Up full then under...

ANNOUNCER (Bob Lemond): *Crime Classics*, a series of true crime stories from the records and newspapers of every land from every time. Your host each week, Mr. Thomas Hyland, connoisseur of crime, student of violence and teller of murders.

CLOSE

THEME MUSIC: Up full then under...

ANNOUNCER: You have been listening to *Crime Classics*, true stories from the records and newspapers of every land and every time. Your host, Thomas Hyland, was played by Lou Merrill. Original music was composed and conducted by Bernard Herrmann. The entire production was under the supervision of Elliott Lewis. Bob Lemond speaking. Be with us again next Monday evening for another *Crime Classics*. This is CBS, the Columbia Broadcasting System.

THEME MUSIC: Up full then fade out.

92. Crime Club

Dramatizations based on stories that appeared in *Crime Club* books. Sustaining. Mutual, 1946–1947. Raymond Edward Johnson played the Crime Club librarian.

OPEN

SOUND: Phone ringing.

HOST (picking up receiver): Hello … I hope I haven't kept you waiting … Yes, this is the Crime Club. I'm the librarian … "Death at 7:10" … Yes, we have that Crime Club book for you. Come right over.

THEME MUSIC: Up full then under…

SOUND: Door bell rings; door opens.

HOST: Ah, you're here, good. Take the easy chair by the window. Comfortable? The book is on this shelf. Here it is, "Death at 7:10" by H.F.S. Moore. A very intriguing story of a beautiful woman who is in love—with death.

SOUND: Musical sting.

HOST: Let's look at it under the reading lamp.

SHOW MUSIC: Up full then under as the story begins (here, about the police investigation into the mysterious death of a woman who died suddenly while on a train).

CLOSE

THEME MUSIC: Up full then under…

HOST: And so closes tonight's *Crime Club* book, "Death at 7:10" based on a story by H.F.S. Moore. Steadman Coles did the radio adaptation; Roger Bower produced and directed it. Raymond Edward Johnson played the part of Mark Kent, Helen Shields was Susan Ward, Eleanor Phelps was Claire Ellis and Reese Taylor was heard as Robert Ward.

SOUND: Phone ringing.

HOST (to listeners): I beg your pardon.

SOUND: Host picking up the phone.

HOST: Hello, I hope I haven't kept you waiting? Yes, this is the Crime Club, I'm the librarian … Yes, come over a week from tonight. Good. Yes, we have the very exciting story of a night that was made for fun and remade for murder. It's called "Coney Island Nocturne." In the meantime, well in the meantime, there's a new Crime Club book available this week and every week at bookstores. Yes, it's available now. Fine. We'll look for you next week.

THEME MUSIC: Up full then under…

ANNOUNCER: This program came from New York. This is the Mutual Broadcasting System.

THEME MUSIC: Up full then fade out.

93. The Crime Files of Flamond

Crime drama about Flamond (Everett Clarke), a private detective who is also a psychologist and character analyst. He is assisted by his secretary, Sandra Lake (Muriel Bremner). Each episode is called a "Card" followed by a number. Various sponsors. Mutual, 1953–1957.

OPEN

THEME MUSIC: Up full then under…

ANNOUNCER (Bob Cunningham): Card Number 240 from *The Crime Files of Flamond*. Flamond, the most unusual detective in criminal history. Flamond, famous psychiatrist and character analyst. Flamond, who looks beyond laughter and tears, jealousy and greed in order to discover the reason why. Flamond, starring Everett Clarke as Flamond with Muriel Bremner as Miss Lake. And now to Card Number 240, "The Fiend Who Walks But Can't Be Seen." [Story about a young couple who believe their new home is haunted by a ghost. Miss Lake calls it "The Case of the Suspicious Scream."]

CLOSE

THEME MUSIC: Up full then under…

ANNOUNCER: And so closes another case in *The Crime Files of Flamond*. All names and places used in this story are fictitious. Any similarity to actual persons is purely coincidental. This is Bob Cunningham inviting you to be with us again next week for Card Number 241 on *The Crime Files of Flamond*. This is Mutual.

THEME MUSIC: Up full then fade out.

94. Crime on the Waterfront

Crime drama about Lou Kagel (Myron Wallace), an N.Y.P.D. lieutenant whose beat is the waterfront. Sustaining. NBC, 1949.

OPEN

SOUNDS: Tugboat whistles; footsteps approaching a phone booth; receiver being picked up; number dialed.

VOICE: Waterfront. Kagel calling.

THEME MUSIC: Up full then under...

ANNOUNCER (George Stone): The National Broadcasting Company presents Lou Kagel, detective, fighting ... *Crime on the Waterfront*.

THEME MUSIC: Up full then out.

CLOSE

THEME MUSIC: Up full then under...

ANNOUNCER: *Crime on the Waterfront* stars Myron Wallace as Lou Kagel with Muriel Bremner as reporter June Sherman. Listen again next week to another *Crime on the Waterfront*. This is George Stone speaking.

THEME MUSIC: Up full then fade out.

Crime Photographer *see* Flashgun Casey

95. The Cuckoo Hour

Comedy coupled with music and songs from the wacky staff of radio station KUKU. Sustaining. NBC Blue, 1930–1936. Raymond Knight played station manager Ambrose J. Weems.

OPEN

THEME MUSIC ("Crazy People"): Up full then under...

ANNOUNCER (Ward Wilson): Good evening, friends, the next fifteen minutes are to be devoted to *The Cuckoo Hour*, radio's oldest network comedy program, and if you don't think that is something—well, maybe you're right. *The Cuckoo Hour* features Raymond Knight, the radio humorist, as station KUKU's master of ceremonies and a lot of other disreputable characters. We now turn you over to station KUKU.

KNIGHT: Good evening, fellow pixies, this is Raymond Knight ... [at which point the show would begin].

CLOSE

THEME MUSIC: Up full then under...

ANNOUNCER: It's time to end the broadcast day of station KUKU until next week at this same time when your master of ceremonies, Ambrose J. Weems, returns with another cuckoo session. Raymond Knight stars as Ambrose J. Weems with Adelina Thompson as Mrs. George T. Pennyfeather. Music is by Robert Armbruster and his orchestra with songs by Mary McCoy. *The Cuckoo Hour* is written, produced and directed by Mr. Knight. Your announcer is Ward Wilson. This is the Blue Network.

THEME MUSIC: Up full then out.

96. Curtain Time

Anthology series sponsored by General Mills Cereals and Mars Candies. Mutual (1938–1939), ABC (1945–1946), NBC (1946–1950).

OPEN

ANNOUNCER (Don Gordon): Kellogg's Kix brings you *Curtain Time*.

THEME MUSIC: Up full then under...

ANNOUNCER: Once again it's *Curtain Time*. Tonight we present the powerful drama of a mother who fought against blind justice and of a man who loved an adopted boy. The story of two fiercely determined wills in a brilliant play, "Beautiful Lady."

THEME MUSIC: Up full then out.

VOICE: On stage, on stage please. Warning for first act. On stage please, on stage.

SOUND: A gong.

ANNOUNCER: Again a gay and fashionable audience crowds every seat of our playhouse. A splendid cast awaits cues and we're ready for that most thrilling moment in theater, curtain time. Remember, this play is presented for your entertainment by General Mills, makers of America's brand-new cereal sensation, Kix. K-I-X, Kix. In just a moment, the house lights will dim, but first let's look through our playbill for tonight. "Beautiful Lady" was written for *Curtain Time* by one of radio's best authors, Arch Oboler, and stars two outstanding actors, Margaret Hillias and Hugh Studebaker. The orchestra is under the baton of Henry Weber and the entire production is directed by Blair Wallacer. Now Mr. Weber steps to the stand and the show is on.

ANNOUNCER: Kellogg's Kix has presented for your entertainment *Curtain Time*. Be with us again next week for another dramatic presentation on *Curtain Time*. Until then this is Don Gordon bidding you a good night. This is Mutual.

97. The Damon Runyon Theater

Adaptations of stories written by Damon Runyon and related by Broadway (John Brown), an underworld character who hangs out at Mindy's Bar. Sustaining. Syn., 1949–1950.

OPEN

ANNOUNCER: *The Damon Runyon Theater.*
THEME MUSIC: Up full then under…
ANNOUNCER: Once again *The Damon Runyon Theater* brings you another story by the master storyteller Damon Runyon, and this one, "The Brain Goes Home." And to tell it to you, here is Broadway.
BROADWAY: Thanks. This is a story about a guy we call "The Brain" …

CLOSE

ANNOUNCER: And so ends the famous Damon Runyon story "The Brain Goes Home." Listen in again next week for *The Damon Runyon Theater*. *The Damon Runyon Theater* with John Brown as Broadway is directed by Richard Sandville and the stories are adapted for radio by Russell Hughes. This is a Mayfair Production.

98. Danger, Dr. Danfield

Crime drama about Daniel Danfield (Michael Dunne), a brilliant criminal psychologist, and his secretary, Rusty Fairfax (JoAnne Johnson). Various sponsors. ABC, 1946–1951.

OPEN

ANNOUNCER: *Danger, Dr. Danfield.*
THEME MUSIC: Up full then under…
DANFIELD: The human mind is like a cave. Beyond the light there are dark passageways and mysterious recesses. I, Dr. Daniel Danfield, have explored those unknown retreats and know their secrets.
ANNOUNCER: Dr. Daniel Danfield, authority on crime psychology, has an unhappy facility for getting himself mixed up in hazardous predicaments because of his astounding revelations regarding the workings of the criminal mind. As our story opens, we find Dr. Danfield in his office dictating to his pretty secretary, Rusty Fairfax…

CLOSE

THEME MUSIC: Up full then under…
ANNOUNCER: *Danger, Dr. Danfield* stars Michael Dunne as Dr. Daniel Danfield with JoAnne Johnson as Rusty Fairfax. Be with us again next week, same time, same station, for another crime-solving adventure on *Danger, Dr. Danfield*. This is the American Broadcasting Company.
THEME MUSIC: Up full then fade out.

99. Danger with Granger

Crime drama about Steve Granger, a private detective who doesn't mind ruffling feathers to get the job done. Various sponsors. Mutual, 1956–1957.

OPEN

THEME MUSIC: Up full then under…
ANNOUNCER: *Danger with Granger.*
STEVE: This is Steve Granger, private detective. I protect the innocent. If you tell me the whole story and it holds together, I'll take the case.
ANNOUNCER: *Danger with Granger.*
THEME MUSIC: Up full then out.

CLOSE

THEME MUSIC: Up full then under…

STEVE: Steve Granger again. You have just heard one of the most interesting cases from my files. I'll have another one for you next week at this same time, so be around next time.

THEME MUSIC: Up full then fade out.

100. Dark Venture

Dramatizations about people propelled into unexpected situations. Sponsored by Wild Root Creme Oil. ABC, 1946–1947.

OPEN

THEME MUSIC: Up full then under…

ANNOUNCER (John Laing): *Dark Venture*, presented by Wild Root Creme Oil for the hair. Over the minds of mortals come many shadows. Shadows of greed and hate, jealousy and fear, darkness, the absence of light. Throw in the sudden shadows that spark the minds of men and women; or bound them with strange impulses which urge them into the unknown. *Dark Venture*.

SPOKESMAN (Harry Walstrom): *Dark Venture* is brought to you by the Wild Root Company, makers of Wild Root Creme Oil for the hair. There are a lot of reasons why Wild Root Creme Oil is again and again the choice of men who put grooming first. And here's one that every man appreciates. It gives you the successful, well-groomed look that helps you get ahead on the job. Wild Root Creme Oil does this by keeping your hair handsomely in place, relieving dryness and removing loose ends. Wild Root Creme Oil is non-alcoholic and the only leading oil hair tonic that contains soothing lanolin. So get the big economy-sized bottle at your drug or toilet goods counter. And ask your barber for Wild Root Creme Oil again and again. The choice of men who put good grooming first.

ANNOUNCER: And now to tonight's *Dark Venture*.

CLOSE

ANNOUNCER: Next week at this same time, the Wild Root Company, makers of Wild Root Creme Oil for the hair, will bring you another original *Dark Venture* story. And now a word

to the men. If you want the girls to make you their choice, better make Wild Root Creme Oil your choice. Wild Root Creme Oil is again and again the choice of men who put good grooming first. Smart fellows know it grooms their hair the way girls like to see it and relieves dryness and removes loose dandruff too. Tonight take Wild Root's closeup test. If a closeup look in the mirror reveals unruly hair, dryness or loose dandruff, you need Wild Root Creme Oil again and again, the choice of men who put good grooming first.

THEME MUSIC: Up full then under…

ANNOUNCER: Original music for *Dark Venture* is by Dean Fossler. Your narrator has been John Laing. Until next Tuesday, remember smart girls use Wild Root Creme Oil too for great grooming and to relieve dryness between permanents. Mothers say it's great for training children's hair too. This is ABC, the American Broadcasting Company.

THEME MUSIC: Up full then fade out.

101. Darrow of the Diamond X

Western about John Darrow, owner of the Diamond X Ranch. Sustaining. NBC, 1950. Curt Martell plays John Darrow with Mary Barnett as Mary Harrison, his romantic interest. The song "On Top of Old Smokey" was used as the theme.

OPEN

THEME MUSIC: Up full then under…

ANNOUNCER (Phil Walker): *Darrow of the Diamond X*.

SOUND: Horse galloping.

ANNOUNCER: *Darrow of the Diamond X*, exciting tales of the Old West with John Darrow, the ranch owner who lends a hand to people in trouble. Join us now for *Darrow of the Diamond X* with Curt Martell as John Darrow and Mary Barnett as Mary Harrison.

THEME MUSIC: Up full then out.

CLOSE

THEME MUSIC: Up full then under…

ANNOUNCER: You have just heard *Darrow of the Diamond X*, written and directed by Samuel Dickson. Listen to the next episode Friday night at 8:30. Music was arranged and directed by Tony Freeman with guitar solo by Paul Miller. Sound effects were created by Bill Brownell. Phil Walker speaking.

THEME MUSIC: Up full then out.

ANNOUNCER: This is NBC, the National Broadcasting Company.

SOUND: NBC chimes. N-B-C.

102. A Date with Judy

Comedy that revolves around Judy Foster, a pretty high school girl. Sponsored by Ford, Pepsodent, Revere Cameras, Sal Hepatica and Tums. NBC (1941–1948), ABC (1948–1950). Dellie Ellis, Louise Erickson and Ann Gillis played Judy; Paul McGrath, Stanley Farrar and John Brown were her father, Melvyn; Margaret Brayton, Lois Corbett and Mary Marsh were her mother, Dora; and Harry Harvey and Dick Crenna were Judy's boyfriend, Oogie Pringle.

OPEN (for Sal Hepatica)

THEME MUSIC: Up full then under...

ANNOUNCER (Ken Niles): Sal Hepatica for the smile of health presents for your listening pleasure *A Date with Judy* with Louise Erickson as Judy Foster, the cutest date in town. Your date with Judy each Wednesday at this time is arranged by the makers of Sal Hepatica for the smile of health.

THEME MUSIC: Up full then out.

CLOSE (for Sal Hepatica)

ANNOUNCER: This is Ken Niles inviting you to be with us next week at this same time to keep your date with Judy. Louise Erickson is starred as Judy with John Brown as Father and Dick Crenna as Oogie. This program came to you transcribed from Hollywood. This is ABC, the American Broadcasting Company.

OPEN (for Tums)

ANNOUNCER (Ralph Langley): By Transcription.

SONG (By Dick Crenna):
> I've got a date with Judy,
> A big date with Judy,
> Oh jeepers and gee.
> I've got a date with Judy,
> And Judy's got one with me.

ANNOUNCER: The American Broadcasting Company presents *A Date with Judy* starring Louise Erickson as Judy with John Brown as Father and sponsored by Tums, for quick relief of acid indigestion. And now, let's look in on the Foster home as we prepare for our date with Judy.

CLOSE (for Tums)

ANNOUNCER: This is Ralph Langley inviting you to be with us next week at this same time to keep your date with Judy. *A Date with Judy* stars Louise Erickson as Judy with John Brown as Father and Dick Crenna as Oogie Pringle and is brought to you by Tums, famous for quick acid relief. Helen Mack is the director. This is ABC, the American Broadcasting Company.

103. David Harum

Daily serial about a philosopher and banker in the town of Homeville. Sponsored by Bab-O. NBC (1936–1942; 1943–1947; 1950–1951), CBS (1942–1943; 1947–1950). Wilmer Walter, Craig McDonnell and Cameron Prud'Homme played David Harum. The song "Sun Bonnet Sue" was used as the theme.

OPEN

THEME MUSIC: Up full then under...

ANNOUNCER (Ford Bond): Once again we present *David Harum*, one of the most beloved stories of American fiction. For David Harum is America. It is the story of every one of us, of our search for love, for happiness and the good way of life.

THEME MUSIC: Up full then out.

ANNOUNCER: Remember, ladies, do not confuse Bab-O, the modern grease dissolving formula, with outdated cleansers which leave most of the hard work for you. There is a vast difference between ordinary sluggish cleansers and fast-acting Bab-O. And here's the reason. Today, ninety percent of scouring is caused by grease. Bab-O dissolves grease and in addition, has a miraculous combination of other cleaning ingredients. So, when you wipe Bab-O on, dirt and stains wipe gently away. It's fast, tough and easy. You're through with astounding speed. Try grease dissolving Bab-O for cleaning baby bassinets, painted wood work, pots and pans, bathtubs and kitchen sinks. Try it for all your household cleaning. See what a precious saving in time and energy it means. Today, ask your grocer for gentle, grease dissolving Bab-O. You'll know it by the green can with the big white B-A-B dash O.

THEME MUSIC: Up full then under...

ANNOUNCER: And now to *David Harum*.

CLOSE

THEME MUSIC: Up full then under...

ANNOUNCER: Ladies, if you want to finish your housework quicker, have extra time for your family and friends, take this tip about cleaning from over a thousand housewives just like yourself. In actual tests, these women compared the cleaning speed of Bab-O with that of their former cleansers. And here are the amazing facts they discovered. In just cleaning a wash basin, Bab-O saves time on the average of two full minutes. What's more, they reported minute after minute saved in cleaning pots and pans, bathtubs, kitchen sinks, refrigerators—savings, which applied to your cleaning jobs, can easily mean one half-hour for extra leisure every day. So today make your own time-saving tests. Compare grease dissolving Bab-O with your former lazy cleanser, then see if you can ever go back to any less modern method. Remember, when you buy, be sure you get the genuine article. No other cleaner gives you the same miraculous combination of ingredients that Bab-O gives you; hence, no other cleaner cleans as Bab-O cleans. Insist on genuine Bab-O—spelled B-A-B dash O.

THEME MUSIC: Up full then under...

ANNOUNCER: *David Harum* will be on the air at this same time Monday, 11:45 A.M. Eastern War Time. Ford Bond speaking for B.T. Bab-bit, Incorporated, the makers of the grease dissolving cleanser, Bab-O.

THEME MUSIC: Up full then out.

ANNOUNCER: This is the National Broadcasting Company.

SOUND: NBC chimes. N-B-C.

Note: An earlier version of the theme opened as follows:

ANNOUNCER: We bring you the story that has thrilled Americans for generations, the true-to-life story of David Harum, the kindly country philosopher who makes life worth living by helping those who need help and by outwitting those who are too clever and scheming in helping themselves.

104. A Day in the Life of Dennis Day

The mishaps of Dennis Day as a soda jerk at the Willoughby Drugstore. Sponsored by the Colgate Palmolive Company. NBC, 1946–1951. The song "Yours Is My Heart Alone" was used as the theme.

OPEN

THEME MUSIC: Up full then under...

ANNOUNCER: Dennis Day is brought to you by Colgate Lustre Creme Shampoo for soft, glamorous dream-girl hair. *The Dennis Day Show* with Barbara Eiler, Bea Benaderet, Dink Trout, John Brown, Charles Dant and his orchestra and yours truly, Verne Smith, is written by Frank Galen and stars our popular young singer in *A Day in the Life of Dennis Day*.

CLOSE

DENNIS: Good night everybody.

ANNOUNCER: Dennis Day is brought to you every Wednesday by the Colgate Palmolive Company.

SONG (Male Vocalist):
> Dream girl, dream girl,
> Beautiful Lustre Creme girl,
> Hair that gleams and glistens
> From a Lustre Creme Shampoo.

ANNOUNCER: Yes, Lustre Creme Shampoo leaves hair with new three-way loveliness. One, fragrantly clean; two, glistening with sheen; three, soft, easy to manage. Lustre Creme is not a soap, not a liquid, but an utterly new rich lathering creme shampoo, a blend of secret ingredients plus lanolin. Try Lustre Creme Shampoo; four-ounce jar only one dollar, at all cosmetic counters. Also in smaller sizes. Be a dream girl, a lovely Lustre Creme girl.

SONG (Male Vocalist):
>   Dream girl, dream girl,
>   Beautiful Lustre Creme girl,
>   You owe your crowning glory to
>   A Lustre Creme Shampoo.

ANNOUNCER: This is Verne Smith reminding you to join us again next week for another Dennis Day show brought to you by Lustre Creme Shampoo for soft, glamorous dream-girl hair. Good night. This is NBC, the National Broadcasting Company.

SOUND: NBC chimes. N-B-C.

105. Deadline Mystery

Crime drama about newspaper columnist, Lucky Larson (Steven Dunne). Sponsored by the Knox Company. ABC, 1947.

OPEN

THEME MUSIC: Up full then under…

ANNOUNCER (Frank Hemingway): From Hollywood, the Knox Company, world-wide distributors of scientifically compounded pharmaceutical products, presents Steven Dunne, star of Columbia Pictures, in *Deadline Mystery*.

LUCKY: Lucky Larson's the name, columnist for over 250 newspapers syndicated all over the world… [He would then begin the story.]

CLOSE

LUCKY: That's 30.

ANNOUNCER: Listen next week at this same time when the Knox Company, world-wide distributors of Cistex, the modern kidney diuretic, and Mendaco for recurring attacks of bronchial asthma, presents another exciting adventure of Lucky Larson starring Steven Dunne through arrangement with Columbia Pictures, producers of *Down to Earth*. The events and characters depicted in this story were entirely fictional and any resemblance to actual places or people, living or dead, is entirely coincidental. Frank Hemingway speaking. This program came to you from Hollywood. This is ABC, the American Broadcasting Company.

106. The Dean Martin and Jerry Lewis Show

Music, songs and comedy with hosts Dean Martin and Jerry Lewis. Various sponsors. NBC, 1949–1951.

OPEN

THEME MUSIC: Up full then under…

ANNOUNCER (Johnny Jacobs): From Hollywood we present *The Dean Martin and Jerry Lewis Show*, brought to you by Chesterfield—sound off for Chesterfield; by Anacin for fast relief of headaches; and by Dentine, the gum with breathtaking flavor. And now, ladies and gentlemen, it gives me great pleasure to introduce our master of ceremonies, Mr. Dean Martin.

DEAN: Hi folks, this is Dean Martin… [Audience applause follows and Dean begins the show with a song.]

CLOSE

ANNOUNCER: From Hollywood you have just heard transcribed *The Dean Martin and Jerry Lewis Show* written by Ed Simmons and Norman Lear. Brought to you by Chesterfield—sound off for Chesterfield, Anacin for fast headache relief; and by Dentine, the breathtaking gum. Johnny Jacobs speaking. This is NBC, the National Broadcasting Company.

Note: Prior to being called *The Dean Martin and Jerry Lewis Show* (1951–1953), the series was titled *The Martin and Lewis Show* and opened as follows:

ANNOUNCER (Ben Alexander): It's *The Martin and Lewis Show*. The National Broadcasting Company brings you transcribed from New

York, *The Martin and Lewis Show* featuring Florence MacMichael, Dick Stabile and his orchestra and starring Dean Martin and Jerry Lewis.

107. Death Valley Days

Tales of the old West as told by the host, the Old Ranger (Tim Frawley, George Rand, Harry Humphrey, Jack MacBryde). Sponsored by the Pacific Coast Borax Company. NBC (1930–1931; 1932–1936; 1940–1941), Blue (1931–1932; 1936–1939), CBS (1944–1945). "Bugle Call" by Josef Bonine was used as the theme.

OPEN

THEME MUSIC: Up full then under...

ANNOUNCER (George Hicks): As the old morning bugle call of the covered wagon train dies away among the echoes, another true story of *Death Valley Days*. *Death Valley Days* is brought to you by the Pacific Coast Borax Company, who give you the miracle of Borax in three convenient forms. There is Twenty Mule Team Borax for household use; Twenty Mule Team Borax Soap Chips for washing clothes and dishes; and Boraxo for bathroom use. Before you become absorbed in the Old Ranger's story for tonight, we would like to take just a moment of your time to tell you something about Boraxo. Boraxo was created in response to the insistent demands from women for a product that would cleanse the skin as safely as Twenty Mule Team Borax cleanses painted woodwork or bathroom porcelain or your fine china and glassware. The letters we receive every day praising Boraxo tell us that we have succeeded in meeting this demand. For, say our new customers who have discovered Boraxo, your Boraxo does just what we wanted. It cleanses dirty hands and the children's knees and elbows like magic; it works so fast that children no longer have any excuse to be late for meals. They can, you can wash up in a jiffy with Boraxo and best of all I know they will come to the table not only really clean but with smooth, soft skin. Your Boraxo cleanses the skin as quickly as your Twenty Mule Team Borax cleans your house. And like Twenty Mule Team Borax, it cleanses without doing any damage. Thank you for your wonderful new product, Boraxo, and thank you too for *Death Valley Days*, which all of us love. And now here is the Old Ranger to begin tonight's story.

CLOSE

ANNOUNCER: The Pacific Coast Borax Company, makers of Twenty Mule Team Borax, has presented another story of the Old West on *Death Valley Days*. This is George Hicks speaking on behalf of Twenty Mule Team Borax and inviting you to be with us again next week at this same time. This is the Blue Network.

108. December Bride

Humorous incidents in the life of Lily Ruskin (Spring Byington), an elderly widow who lives with her daughter, Ruth (Doris Singleton), and son-in-law, Matt (Hal March). Various sponsors. CBS, 1952–1953. Basis for the television series.

OPEN

ANNOUNCER (Johnny Jacobs): And now *December Bride*, the story of a guy who likes his mother-in-law. Created and transcribed by Parke Levy and featuring Hal March and Doris Singleton.

THEME MUSIC: Up full then under...

ANNOUNCER: *December Bride*, starring the beloved lady of the screen Spring Byington as Lily Ruskin, the mother-in-law.

THEME MUSIC: Up full then fade out.

CLOSE

THEME MUSIC: Up full then under...

ANNOUNCER: You have just heard Spring Byington in *December Bride* with Hal March and Doris Singleton. *December Bride* is created by Parke Levy with original music composed and conducted by Wilbur Hatch. Johnny Jacobs speaking. This is CBS, the Columbia Broadcasting System.

THEME MUSIC: Up full then fade out.

109. Defense Attorney

Crime drama about Martha Ellis Bryan (Mercedes McCambridge), a female defense attorney. Sponsored by Clorets, Goodyear and Kix. ABC, 1951–1952.

OPEN

THEME MUSIC: Up full then under…

ANNOUNCER (Orville Anderson): The makers of Kix, tasty, crispy corn puffs, food for action; and the makers of Clorets, the new chlorophyll chewing gun that makes your breath kissing sweet, present *Defense Attorney*.

DEFENSE ATTORNEY: Ladies and gentlemen, to depend upon your judgment and to fulfill my known obligation, I must submit the facts, fully aware of my responsibility to my client and to you as defense attorney.

ANNOUNCER: And now we proudly present Miss Mercedes McCambridge as *Defense Attorney*. When Martha Ellis Bryan chose law as her career, she accepted the challenge of defending the defenseless.

THEME MUSIC: Up full then out.

ANNOUNCER: And now let's listen to a man who sings the blues because he doesn't take time to eat breakfast.

SAD SONG:

It's a shame to be a Nixee like me.
I suffer from a lack of en-er-gy.
Won't somebody tell me why I fail
At everything I try
It's a shame to be a Nixee like me.

ANNOUNCER: People who are always weary, always dreary are Nixees, so different from active, cheery Kixees. Kixees are men of action who eat Kix, food for action; lively boys, girls and grownups who always eat breakfast built around a bowl of Kix. How fine everyone feels because Kix is an eighty-three percent energy food. Are Kix good? You bet. Crispy Corn puffs so tender and tasty. Eat Kix, food for action.

HAPPY SONG:

Oh, it's grand to be a Kixee like me,
Full of pep and energy.

Every morning I eat Kix
So I'm never in a fix,
Oh, it's grand to be a Kixee like me.

ANNOUNCER: And now the curtain rises on act one of tonight's *Defense Attorney* story.

CLOSE

ANNOUNCER: You have just heard *Defense Attorney* starring Mercedes McCambridge. Next week another exciting adventure with Mercedes McCambridge, defense attorney—be sure to listen. *Defense Attorney* is presented by the makers of Kix, tasty, crispy corn puffs, food for action, and by Clorets, the new chlorophyll chewing gum that makes breath kissing sweet.

MERCEDES: This is Mercedes McCambridge reminding you to stay tuned to your ABC station for that entertaining program, *The Amateur Hour*, by that great showman and grand person Ted Mack.

ANNOUNCER: This program came to you from Hollywood. America is sold on the American Broadcasting Company.

110. Destination Freedom

Stories involving "the American Negro people." Sustaining. NBC, 1948–1951.

OPEN

ANNOUNCER (Harry Cook): Station WMAQ brings you *Destination Freedom*, dramatizations of the democratic heritage of the American Negro people and the part of America's own "destination freedom." Today, *Destination Freedom* tells the story of one of America's outstanding modern composers, the famous Edward Kennedy "Duke" Ellington in a chapter entitled "Echoes of Harlem."

VOICE: He had the songs in his head long before he knew how to write the notes. He was a boy on Logan Street in Washington, D.C., looking for a way to play the tune he was whistling, a tune that called his gang together on a hot summer evening…

CLOSE

ANNOUNCER: You have just heard *Destination*

Freedom's dramatization of the life of the great Negro composer and conductor Duke Ellington. *Destination Freedom* is written by Richard Durham and produced under the direction of Homer Hecht with Larry Auerback assisting. The role of Duke Ellington was played by Oscar Brown, Jr. Others in the cast were Gladys Williams, Charles Mountain, Cliff Norton, Tony Parrish, Fred Pinkard and Len Spears. Music of Duke Ellington's band heard on this program was recorded; other music was arranged by Emil Sodestrom and played by Elwin Owen and Bobby Christian. This is Henry Cook inviting you to be with us again next week when *Destination Freedom* will tell the story of the beloved Negro educator Mary McCloud Bethune. This is NBC, the National Broadcasting Company.

SOUND: NBC chimes. N-B-C.

111. The Devil and Mr. O

Updated stories originally broadcast on *Lights Out*. Sustaining. Syn., 1971–1972. Arch Oboler served as the host, Mr. O.

OPEN

THEME MUSIC: Up full then under...

ANNOUNCER: It's long ago, it's also now. Like a vintage brew that gets tastier by the years, the radio mysteries of the thirties, forties and fifties, although resting in the dusty archives, are still fresh and vibrant. Let's sit back now as the listener did so many yesterdays ago and try to figure out whodunit.

THEME MUSIC: Up full then out.

VOICE: Light's out for (in echo effect): *The Devil and Mr. O.*

SOUND: Bell tolling.

VOICE: It...Is...Later...Than...You...Think. Turn out your lights now!

MR. O: We bring you stories of the supernatural and the super-normal, dramatizing the fantasies and the mysteries of the unknown. We tell you this, frankly, so if you wish to avoid the excitement and tension of these imaginative plays, we urge you calmly but sincerely turn off your radio now. This is Mr. O, Arch Oboler. Once upon a long time ago in

New York City on top of the Empire State Building, I met a pair of very young and very much in love honeymooners. I remembered those two when I wrote the play you're about to hear. It's not a horror story and yet there is terror in it. I give you now a story about one of the strangest days since our planet began to circle the sun. (The story, "Alone in New York City," is set during World War II. A young couple, Michael and Eve are in the observation deck of the Empire State Building when a series of mysterious clouds engulfs the city. Soon they discover the city is deserted and they are the only ones left.)

CLOSE

MR. O: This is Arch Oboler. Our play has ended and may it always continue to be just that, a play.

THEME MUSIC: Up full then under...

ANNOUNCER: Every week we'll reach into the dusty files, brush it off and present a still up-to-date replica of a whodunit of yesterday.

THEME MUSIC: Up full then fade out.

112. Dial Dave Garroway

Music, light comedy, chatter and songs with humorist Dave Garroway. Sponsored by Dial Soap. NBC, 1949–1953.

OPEN

ANNOUNCER (Jack Haskell): And now Dial, the soap that stops odor before it starts, presents *Dial Dave Garroway*.

THEME MUSIC ("Sentimental Journey"): Up full then under...

DAVE: Hello friends, we've got one of the best-sounding little gangs you ever heard: Constance Russell, Jack Haskell and Art Van Damme. Dial Soap, the famous deodorant soap, brings you confidence these warm June days, any day throughout the year. Just get Dial Soap and feel fresh and clean all over.

SONG:

> Dial, that's D-I-A-L,
> Dial Soap.
> The newest, nicest

Way to stay free
And odor safe all day.
DAVE: Good morning ladies and welcome…

CLOSE

THEME MUSIC: Up full then under…
DAVE: We'll be talking to you again tomorrow. Until then, love and peace.
ANNOUNCER: Tomorrow and each weekday at this time, Arrow and Company, the makers of Dial Soap, invite you to *Dial Dave Garroway*. Jack Haskell speaking. This is NBC, the National Broadcasting Company.
THEME MUSIC: Up full then out.
SOUND: NBC chimes. N-B-C.

113. Dick Tracy

Crime drama about the investigations of master detective Dick Tracy. Various sponsors. CBS (1935), Mutual (1935–1937), NBC (1938–1939), Blue/ABC (1943–1948). Ned Wever, Matt Crowley and Barry Thompson played Dick Tracy.

OPEN (Ned Wever)

ANNOUNCER (George Gunn): Boys and girls, here's *Dick Tracy*!
SOUND: Police car departing followed by a siren's wail.
ANNOUNCER: Presenting Detective Inspector Dick Tracy, protector of law and order.

CLOSE (Ned Wever)

ANNOUNCER (following a cliff-hanging scene): What is Dick Tracy going to do? You'll know tomorrow, so tune in same time, same station for the adventures of *Dick Tracy*. This is George Gunn speaking.

OPEN (Barry Thompson)

ANNOUNCER (Dan Seymour): And now … *Dick Tracy*!
SOUND: Radio code signals.
TRACY: This is Dick Tracy. Stand by for action. Let's go men.
SOUND: Car departing followed by a siren's wail.

ANNOUNCER: Yes, it's Dick Tracy, protector of law and order. And now *Dick Tracy*!

CLOSE (Barry Thompson)

ANNOUNCER (following a cliff-hanging scene): What is Dick going to do? You'll know tomorrow, so tune in same time, same station for the adventures of *Dick Tracy*. Any tough detective lives the life of danger. He must be on the alert at all times because tough characters know that the best way of keeping out of his clutches is to get him first. Well, Tracy fans, I guess you know that goes double for Dick Tracy because he's so very tough. That's one of the reasons you can be sure that the adventures of *Dick Tracy* will keep you on the edge of your seats. *Dick Tracy* is on the air Monday through Friday over more than one hundred radio stations throughout the country. Listen to another chapter as Dick Tracy tangles with the underworld tomorrow at this same time over this same station. Dan Seymour speaking. This is ABC, the American Broadcasting Company.

114. Dimension X

Dramatizations of science-fiction stories by noted authors. Various sponsors. NBC, 1950–1951. Norman Rose is the series narrator.

OPEN

THEME MUSIC: Up full then under…
ANNOUNCER (Fred Collins): Adventures in time and space told in future tense.
VOICE: *Dimension X*.
ANNOUNCER: The National Broadcasting Company in cooperation with Street and Smith, publishers of *Astounding Science Fiction* magazine, bring you *Dimension X*… [The evening's story would then be introduced.]

CLOSE

THEME MUSIC: Up full then under…
ANNOUNCER: You have just heard another adventure into the unknown world of the future, the world of *Dimension X*. Be sure to be with us next week for another *Dimension X*.

Dimension X is produced by Van Woodward with music by Albert Buhrmann. Fred Collins speaking. This is NBC, the National Broadcasting Company.
THEME MUSIC: Up full then out.
SOUND: NBC chimes. N-B-C.

115. Dr. Christian

Drama about Paul Christian, a doctor in the small town of River Bend, Minnesota. Sponsored by Vaseline. CBS, 1937–1954. Jean Hersholt played Dr. Paul Christian with Lurene Tuttle, Dorothy Lowell, Rosemary DeCamp and Helen Claire as his nurse, Judy Price. Also known as *The Vaseline Program*. The series was unique in that it used scripts submitted by listeners (who received $500 each).

OPEN

SOUND: Telephone ringing.
NURSE (picking up receiver): Dr. Christian's office.
THEME MUSIC ("Rainbow in the River"): Up full then under…
ANNOUNCER (Art Gilmore): *The Vaseline Program*, the only show in radio where the audience writes the scripts. Jean Hersholt is starred as Dr. Christian with Rosemary DeCamp in the role of Judy Price.
THEME MUSIC: Up full then under…
ANNOUNCER: Folks, do you know somebody whose hair never seems to lie down? Then do him a good turn, tell him about Vaseline Hair Tonic. For just a few drops of Vaseline Hair Tonic every morning will keep a man's hair neat and well-groomed all day. Vaseline Hair Tonic cares for the scalp too, loosens dandruff, relieves that tight, itchy feeling. Vaseline Hair Tonic is good for the scalp because it supplements natural oil. Good to use on the hair because it contains no alcohol or other drying ingredient. Vaseline Hair Tonic gives double care to scalp and hair. It's a double-purpose hair tonic, the first choice of American men today. Get Vaseline Hair Tonic tonight and try it tomorrow.
THEME MUSIC: Up full then under…
ANNOUNCER: Now to the small town of River Bend and the story of Dr. Paul Christian.

CLOSE

THEME MUSIC: Up full then under…
ANNOUNCER: And the curtain comes down on another *Dr. Christian* with our star, Jean Hersholt, waiting to greet you. But first a message from Judy Price.
JUDY: Friends, here's an interesting letter Dr. Christian and I received from a young mother. "Recently my three-year-old fell against the hot-cold range. Her palms and fingertips on both hands were badly burned. I grabbed her up and dashed for my tube of Vaseline Petroleum Jelly. I covered both hands freely then bandaged them. Her screams subsided and she was soon ready to go to sleep. Next day I applied fresh Vaseline Petroleum Jelly and bandaged it [sic]. By evening she was playing as if nothing had happened and the burns healed perfectly thanks to Vaseline Petroleum Jelly. Signed Mrs. Edward J. Cramer, Portland, Oregon." Friends, wasn't it fortunate this young mother had Vaseline Petroleum Jelly on hand. It has so many uses in the home; there's probably nothing so important in the medicine cabinet that does so much yet costs so little. Insist on Vaseline Petroleum Jelly—only 15 cents for the popular size; 25 cents for the large economy size.
ANNOUNCER: Thank you Rosemary DeCamp. And now here is Jean Hersholt.
JEAN: Thank you very much. We invite you to join us again next Wednesday evening, same time, same station. Till then I'll say good night.
THEME MUSIC: Up full then under.
ANNOUNCER: Men, have hair that stays good-looking all day, use just a few drops of Vaseline Hair Tonic every morning. Vaseline Hair Tonic tames hard to manage hair, keeps it looking soft and well-groomed. Tomorrow morning try Vaseline Hair Tonic.
THEME MUSIC: Up full then out.
ANNOUNCER: Art Gilmore speaking. This is CBS, the Columbia Broadcasting System.

116. The Doctor Fights

Dramatizations based on the experiences of

combat doctors during World War II. Sponsored by Schenley Laboratories. CBS, 1944–1945.

Open

ANNOUNCER: Schenley Laboratories presents *The Doctor Fights* starring Lieutenant Commander Robert Montgomery, United States Naval Reserve, in a thrilling, true story of a doctor in World War II. *The Doctor Fights* starring Robert Montgomery.

VOICE: The eternal providence has appointed me to watch over the life and death of all Thy creatures. May I always see in the patient, a fellow creature in pain; grant me strength and opportunity always to extend the domain of my craft.

ANNOUNCER: This is the prayer of every doctor. It is ages old and yet today it is as new as the heroism of tomorrow's battles. This is a doctor at war.

Close

ANNOUNCER: Schenley Laboratories has presented *The Doctor Fights* starring Lieutenant Commander Robert Montgomery—true stories of doctors at war. All names used in this dramatization are fictional. Any resemblance to persons, living or dead, is coincidental. This is CBS, the Columbia Broadcasting System.

117. Dr. Six Gun

Western about Ray Mattson, a doctor of the old West who packs a six gun but puts healing before killing. Various sponsors. NBC, 1954–1955. Karl Weber played Ray Mattson with Bill Griffis as his friend Pablo.

Open

ANNOUNCER: *Dr. Six Gun.*
SOUND: Horse galloping.
ANNOUNCER: Across the rugged Indian territory rides a tall young man on a mission of mercy. His medical bag strapped on one hip; his six shooter on the other. This is Dr. Six Gun, the first episode in the exciting adventure series

Dr. Six Gun. Ray Mattson, M.D. was the gun-toting frontier doctor who roamed the length and breadth of the old Indian territory. Friend and physician to white man and Indian alike; the symbol of justice and mercy in the lawless West of the 1870s. This legendary figure was known to all as Dr. Six Gun.

THEME MUSIC: Up full then under…
VOICE: Dr. Six Gun was my friend. Me? They call me Pablo. It's as good a name as any for a Gypsy. I am a peddler and I have many things in my pack. There is not much of which I am proud; but there is one thing—I can call Doc Six Gun my friend. [At this point Pablo would begin to tell a story, and a flashback sequence would be used to relate it to the audience.]

Close

THEME MUSIC: Up then under…
ANNOUNCER: You have been listening to *Dr. Six Gun.* Dr. Six Gun is played by Karl Weber and Pablo by Bill Griffis.
THEME MUSIC: Up full then under…
ANNOUNCER: *Dr. Six Gun* starring Karl Weber as the frontier doctor with William Griffis as Pablo, the wandering Gypsy, has come to you through the world-wide facilities of the United States Armed Forces Radio and Television Service.
THEME MUSIC: Up full then fade out.

118. Dragnet

Realistic police dramas based on the files of the Los Angeles Police Department. Sponsored by Chesterfield and Fatima Cigarettes. NBC, 1949–1957. Basis for the television series. Jack Webb played Sgt. Joe Friday with Barton Yarborough as Officer Ben Romero and Ben Alexander as Officer Frank Smith. Walter Schumann composed the theme, "The Dragnet March."

Open (for Fatima)

ANNOUNCER (George Fenneman): Fatima Cigarettes, best of all king size cigarettes, brings you *Dragnet* on both radio and television.

THEME MUSIC: Up full then under...

ANNOUNCER: Ladies and gentlemen, the story you are about to hear is true; the names have been changed to protect the innocent. *Dragnet*, the documented drama of an actual crime. For the next thirty minutes, in cooperation with the Los Angeles Police Department, we will travel step by step on the side of the law through an actual case transcribed from official police files. From beginning to end, from crime to punishment, *Dragnet* is the story of your police force in action.

THEME MUSIC: Up full then under...

FRIDAY: It was Wednesday, May 9th. It was hot in Los Angeles. We were working the night watch out of homicide. My partner is Ben Romero; the boss is Captain Norman, my name is Friday...

CLOSE (for Fatima)

ANNOUNCER: The story you have just heard is true; the names were changed to protect the innocent.

THEME MUSIC: Up full then under...

ANNOUNCER: You have just heard *Dragnet*, a series of authentic cases from official files. Technical advice comes from the office of Chief of Police W.H. Parker, Los Angeles Police Department.

THEME MUSIC: Up full then under...

ANNOUNCER: *Dragnet*, sponsored by Fatima, best of the long cigarettes. Fatima has stood for the best in cigarette quality for thirty years and now Fatima is the best of long cigarettes. If you smoke a long cigarette, smoke the best of the long cigarettes, smoke Fatima.

THEME MUSIC: Up full then under...

ANNOUNCER: Jack Webb is heard as Sergeant Joe Friday with Barton Yarborough as Officer Ben Romero. Original music is composed and conducted by Walter Schumann. George Fenneman speaking. Be with us again next Thursday evening at this same time for another case from the files of the Los Angeles Police Department on *Dragnet*. This is NBC, the National Broadcasting Company.

THEME MUSIC: Up full then out.

SOUND: NBC chimes. N-B-C.

OPEN (for Chesterfield)

THEME MUSIC: Up full then under...

ANNOUNCER (Hal Gibney): Ladies and gentlemen, the story you are about to hear is true, the names have been changed to protect the innocent.

VOICE: *Dragnet* is brought to you by Chesterfield, made by Liggett and Myers, first major tobacco company to bring you a complete line of quality cigarettes.

THEME MUSIC: Up full then under...

ANNOUNCER: Meet Peter Lind Hayes and Mary Healy, America's favorite husband-and-wife comedy team. They are typical of smokers everywhere who are saying Chesterfield's for me. Mary says—

MARY: I've smoked regular size Chesterfields for about seven years. Guess that ought to prove how I feel about Chesterfield's taste and mildness.

ANNOUNCER: Peter says Chesterfield's for me too.

PETER: As far as I'm concerned, king is the only size and like Mary says, Chesterfield is the only cigarette.

MARY: Either way you like them; I'll bet you'll find Chesterfield is best for you.

ANNOUNCER: Yes, smoke America's most popular two-way cigarette, regular and king size Chesterfield, for the taste you want, the mildness you want, join the thousands now changing to Chesterfield. Always say, Chesterfield's for me.

THEME MUSIC: Up full then under...

ANNOUNCER: *Dragnet*, the documented drama of an actual crime. For the next thirty minutes in cooperation with the Los Angeles Police Department, you'll travel step by step on the side of the law through an actual case transcribed from official police files. From beginning to end, from crime to punishment, *Dragnet* is the story of your police force in action.

THEME MUSIC: Up full then under...

FRIDAY: It was Wednesday, February 10th. It was cold in Los Angeles. We were working the day watch out of juvenile. My partner is Frank Smith, the boss is Captain Powers, my name is Friday...

CLOSE (for Chesterfield)

ANNOUNCER: Tobacco has been one of man's basic pleasures for over 400 years. And the

Chesterfields you smoke today are the best cigarettes ever made. And when I say that I mean Chesterfield regular, I mean Chesterfield king size. Remember this is the cigarette that's tested and approved by 30 years of scientific tobacco research. The cigarette that gives you proof of highest quality, low nicotine. The taste you want, the mildness you want. Yes, friends, the Chesterfield that you smoke today is the best cigarette ever made. So join the thousands now changing to Chesterfield. Regular or king size, always say Chesterfield's for me.

THEME MUSIC: Up full then under...

ANNOUNCER: You have just heard *Dragnet*, a series of authentic cases from official files. Technical advice came from the office of Chief of Police W.H. Parker, Los Angeles Police Department. Music by Walter Schumann. Hal Gibney speaking.

THEME MUSIC: Up full then under...

ANNOUNCER: Watch an entirely different *Dragnet* case history on your local NBC television station. Please check your newspaper for the day and time. Chesterfield has brought you *Dragnet*, transcribed from Los Angeles.

THEME MUSIC: Up full then out.

SOUND: NBC chimes. N-B-C.

119. Duffy's Tavern

Comedy centered around a shady character named Archie who runs a shabby New York bar on Third Avenue called Duffy's Tavern. Sponsored by Blatz Beer, Bristol Myers, Ipana Toothpaste, Sanka Coffee and Schick Razor Blades. CBS (1941–1942), NBC (1943–1955). Ed Gardner played Archie with Shirley Booth, Florence Halop, Gloria Eilanger, Florence Robinson, Sandra Gould and Hazel Shermit as Miss Duffy (daughter of the never-seen tavern owner) and Charlie Cantor as Clifton Finnegan, Archie's dim-witted friend. The song "When Irish Eyes Are Smiling" was used as the theme.

OPEN

THEME MUSIC: Up full then under...

ANNOUNCER (Rod O'Connor): It's Wednesday evening so we take you now to *Duffy's Tavern* and to the man who runs the bar for Duffy, Archie himself, Ed Gardner.

THEME MUSIC: Up full then under...

ANNOUNCER: *Duffy's Tavern* is brought to you by Bristol Myers, makers of Trushay for softer, lovelier hands, and Vitalis for well-groomed hair.

SOUND: Phone rings followed by Archie picking up the receiver.

ARCHIE: Hello, Duffy's Tavern, where the elite meet to eat. Archie the manager speaking, Duffy ain't here. Oh, hello Duffy... [Archie then sets the stage for the episode by telling Duffy what has been happening.]

CLOSE

THEME MUSIC: Up full then under...

ANNOUNCER: It's time now to leave *Duffy's Tavern* for this evening. So let's meet here again at this same time next Wednesday. Until next Wednesday, then, this is Rod O'Connor reminding you that for well-groomed hair, remember Vitalis, and for softer, lovelier hands, remember Trushay. Each Wednesday Bristol Myers brings you *Duffy's Tavern* and *Mr. District Attorney* which follows immediately over most of these stations. This is NBC, the National Broadcasting Company.

THEME MUSIC: Up full then out.

SOUND: NBC chimes. N-B-C.

120. The Eddie Cantor Pabst Blue Ribbon Show

Variety series mixing music and songs with sketches and jokes. Sponsored by Pabst Blue Ribbon Beer. NBC, 1946–1949. Comedian Eddie Cantor hosted.

OPEN

ANNOUNCER (Harry Von Zell): Pabst Blue Ribbon Beer, finest beer served anywhere, proudly presents—

CHORUS: *The Eddie Cantor Pabst Blue Ribbon Show*—

ANNOUNCER: With Dinah Shore, the Sportsmen Quartet, Cookie Fairchild's Orchestra, Alan Reed, Frank Nelson, yours truly, Harry Von

Zell, and starring your man Friday, Eddie Cantor.

SOUND: Applause.

EDDIE: Thank you, ladies and gentlemen, and good evening…

CLOSE

BARTENDER: What will you have?

VOICE: Pabst Blue Ribbon.

CHORUS: Pabst Blue Ribbon Beer.

ANNOUNCER: Just before our program tonight, you heard your radio, those NBC chimes. You know, that Bing-Bong-Bell. Now, you probably heard that NBC musical signal 150 times or more. And every time you hear it, it makes exactly the same sound. Well, I can't think of a better way to illustrate the uniformity of Pabst Blue Ribbon. If you enjoy a good glass of beer, you probably ordered Pabst Blue Ribbon a 150 times or more. And I'm sure you noticed every glassful was exactly alike. Not too heavy, not too light, but fresh, clear, sparkling, with the real beer flavor coming through just the way you like it. Now, how does Pabst keep it that way year after year? Well, its thirty-three fine brews blended into one great beer. Yes, that Pabst blending process is costly and takes infinite patience, but the result—I'll leave it to your sense of taste. Why not order a few cans or bottles and learn why millions the world over have settled down to blended, splendid Pabst Blue Ribbon.

THEME MUSIC: Up full then under…

ANNOUNCER: Pabst Blue Ribbon Beer, the finest beer served anywhere, has presented *The Eddie Cantor Show* starring your man Friday, Eddie Cantor. This is Harry Von Zell reminding you to be with us again next Friday when Pabst Blue Ribbon will again present *The Eddie Cantor Show*. This is NBC, the National Broadcasting Company.

THEME MUSIC: Up full then out.

SOUND: NBC chimes. N-B-C.

121. Ellery Queen

Crime drama about a gentleman detective operating out of New York City. Various spon-

sors. CBS (1939–1940; 1945–1947), NBC (1942–1944; 1947), ABC (1947–1948). Hugh Marlowe, Carleton Young, Sydney Smith and Lawrence Dobkin played Ellery Queen.

OPEN

THEME MUSIC: Up full then under…

ANNOUNCER: *Ellery Queen.* In the interest of a safer American home, a happier American community, a more United States, the American Broadcasting Company and its affiliated stations bring you *Ellery Queen*, celebrated fighter of crime. As usual, Ellery invites you to match wits with him as he relates the mystery, and before revealing the solution, he gives you a chance to solve it. Tonight, Ellery's guest "Armchair Detective," who will represent you home armchair detectives, is the popular vocalist Miss Peggy Lee. And now here's Ellery Queen, your host for the next half-hour.

ELLERY: Thank you Paul Masterson and good evening ladies and gentlemen… [Ellery would then begin the story.]

CLOSE

ELLERY (after solving the crime): And there, ladies and gentlemen, you have the solution to our mystery. Thank you, Peggy Lee for serving as our guest "Armchair Detective" this evening. As mementoes of the occasion, I have for you a copy of my latest mystery anthology, *The Queen's Awards, 1947*, and a subscription to *Ellery Queen Mystery Magazine*. This is Ellery Queen saying good night till next week and enlisting all Americans every night and every day in the fight against bad citizenship, bigotry and discrimination, the crimes which are weakening America.

ANNOUNCER: All names used on this program are fictitious and do not refer to real people either living or dead. The entire production was under the supervision of Ellery Queen. This is ABC, the American Broadcasting Company.

122. Emotion

Stories that place subjects in emotional situations that require clear thinking to overcome. Sustaining. NBC, 1949.

OPEN

HOST: Ladies and gentlemen, good evening, this is Joseph Schildkraut speaking. For the next half hour, an unusual story will be presented to you. You may find it disturbing; yes, you may even find it shocking. However, we do promise you one thing, we promise you an *Emotion*.

THEME MUSIC: Up full then under...

ANNOUNCER: This is *Emotion* starring Joseph Schildkraut.

THEME MUSIC: Up full then out.

CLOSE

HOST: Ladies and gentlemen, this evening you have heard our first experiment in *Emotion*. In the weeks to come, we invite you to explore with us the shadows of literature. We promise you an exciting journey along strange and seldom traveled paths of Emotion. Good night.

THEME MUSIC: Up full then under...

ANNOUNCER: Original music was composed and conducted by Dr. Albert Harris. The entire production was under the direction of Andrew C. Love.

THEME MUSIC: Up full then out.

ANNOUNCER: This is NBC, the National Broadcasting Company.

SOUND: NBC chimes. N-B-C.

123. Eno Crime Clues

Crime drama about Spencer Dean, a famous detective who is known as the Manhunter. Sponsored by Eno Effervescent Salts. CBS (1931–1932), Blue (1933–1936). Edward Reece and Clyde North played Spencer Dean with Helen Choate as Jane Elliott, Dean's romantic interest, and Jack MacBryde as Dan Cassidy, Dean's assistant.

OPEN

SOUND: Gong sounding three times.

ANNOUNCER: *Eno Crime Clues*. The makers of Eno Effervescent Salts present another thrilling "Manhunter" mystery.

SOUND: Gong tolls.

ANNOUNCER: And now another thrill-a-minute "Manhunter" mystery; another action-packed radio riddle giving you a chance to play detective yourself. Match wits with the Manhunter; see how great a sleuth you really are. Listen carefully, you can solve the puzzle from the clues given in tonight's story.

CLOSE

SOUND: Gong sounds three times.

ANNOUNCER: Eno Effervescent Salts has presented another "Manhunter" mystery. Clyde North is heard as the Manhunter. Also in the cast are Helen Choate and Jack MacBryde. Be with us again next time for another chance to solve the mystery on *Eno Crime Clues*. This is the Blue Network.

SOUND: Gong tolls.

124. Escape

Suspense stories in which people are trapped in life-and-death situations. Various sponsors. CBS, 1947–1954.

OPEN (original)

NARRATOR (William Conrad): Fed up with the everyday grind? Tired of the dull routine? Want to get away from it all?

ANNOUNCER (Roy Rowan): We offer you *Escape*! *Escape*, designed to free you from the four walls of today for a half-hour of high adventure.

NARRATOR: You're speeding through the English countryside, the fast express train rocking beneath your feet. And you know somewhere in the dark ahead of you, a band of men are plotting the destruction of the train—and the moment of your death.

ANNOUNCER: Today, we escape to England at the turn of the century and the story of a complete train that vanished from the face of the earth as Sir Arthur Conan Doyle told it in his fascinating tale "The Lost Special."

CLOSE (original)

ANNOUNCER: Next week—

NARRATOR: You are aboard the Orient Express rushing through the European night, bound for Constantinople. And in your compartment with you, a gun is pointed at your head; a small, mysterious figure is about to take your life!

ANNOUNCER: Next week we escape with Graeme Greene's exciting novel of intrigue *Orient Express*. Goodbye then, until this same time next week when CBS again offers you *Escape*. This is Roy Rowan speaking for CBS, the Columbia Broadcasting System.

OPEN (revised)

THEME MUSIC ("Night on Bald Mountain" by Moussorgsky): Up full then under...

ANNOUNCER (Chip Corning): You are isolated on a remote plantation in the crawling Amazon jungle and an immense army of ravenous ants is closing in on you, swarming to eat you alive—a deadly black army from which there is no escape!

NARRATOR (Paul Frees): We offer you *Escape*, designed to free you from the four walls of today for a half-hour of high adventure. Tonight we escape to the Amazon jungle and to a creepy, crawling terror as Carl Stevenson told it in his famous story "Leinigen vs. the Ants."

CLOSE (revised)

ANNOUNCER: *Escape* this week was dramatized by Richard Sanville and tonight brought you "Leinigen vs. the Ants" by Carl Stevenson. Adapted for radio by Robert Rice with Tudor Owen as Leinigen and Gerald Mohr as the Commissioner. Music was conducted by Wilbur Hatch. Next week—

VOICE: You are standing at the doorway of a cabin on Cashier Creek. Up on the ridge, the bloodhounds have caught your scent and between you and a fortune, between you and escape, yawns the white jaws of a deadly snake—a cottonmouth moccasin. Next week we escape with Irvin S. Cobb's ironic story "Snake Doctor." Be with us next week at this same time when we once again offer you *Escape*. Ethelbert, Ann and Casey will be along

in a few moments with tonight's *Crime Photographer* drama entitled "Sellout." All year long, *Casey, Crime Photographer* has been one of radio's top-rating shows. You're sure to enjoy the proceedings, coming up over most of these CBS stations. Chip Corning speaking. This is CBS, the Columbia Broadcasting System.

125. Everyman's Theater

Dramatizations based on stories written by Arch Oboler. Sponsored by Oxydol. NBC, 1940–1941. "Death and Transfiguration" by Richard Strauss was used as the theme.

OPEN

THEME MUSIC: Up full then under...

ANNOUNCER: *Everyman's Theater*, written especially for radio by Arch Oboler. Tonight our star is the celebrated actor of stage and screen Mr. Raymond Massey in an adventure of our times, "The Precious Freedom," the second of an exciting series of plays especially written for radio and brought to you each Friday at this time and over this station by Oxydol. And now here is Mr. Oboler to tell you about tonight's program on *Everyman's Theater*.

ARCH: This is a fictional story, a play about crimes which should never happen ... (a story about preserving freedom for us and our children).

CLOSE

ANNOUNCER: You know you don't care how often your favorite cotton prints have been washed if they still look bright and colorful, which is one reason why you should wash your colored cottons with Oxydol, ladies, because Oxydol leaves them that way: bright and colorful week after week. But say, here's another reason. Clothes washed in Oxydol last two to three times longer when it comes to wash day wear and tear than clothes washed by old-fashioned scrub-boil methods. Because with Oxydol there's no scrubbing or boiling; instead, just an easy ten-minute soaking with a few gentle, quick rubs on the dirty spots and you're through, ready for a good douse in the rinse. So look, you save your clothes a lot of washday wear and tear when you use Oxydol. That's still another reason why you should ask for Oxydol today. Your dealer has it in the bright orange and blue bullseye box. Just ask for Oxydol.

THEME MUSIC: Up full then under...

ARCH: This is Arch Oboler. Tonight it has been a great privilege to bring you Mr. Raymond Massey in "This Precious Freedom." Until next week, good night.

ANNOUNCER: Be with us again next Friday evening when Oxydol will present *Everyman's Theater*. This is NBC, the National Broadcasting Company.

THEME MUSIC: Up full then out.

SOUND: NBC chimes. N-B-C.

126. Everything for the Boys

Wartime anthology series "dedicated to the men and women fighting for the cause of freedom the world over." The program combined variety with dramatizations (original stories and short adaptations of films and classic books). Sponsored by Auto Lite. NBC, 1944–1945. Hosted by Ronald Colman then Dick Haymes. The example used here, from April 25, 1944, features Ronald Colman and Ingrid Bergman in an adaptation of *Death Takes a Holiday* and a shortwave broadcast to Italy reuniting soldiers with their families.

OPEN

THEME MUSIC: Up full then under...

ANNOUNCER (Frank Martin): From Hollywood, California, and Naples, Italy, Auto Lite brings you *Everything for the Boys*, the command theater of the air, starring Mr. Ronald Colman and our guest for tonight, Miss Ingrid Bergman.

THEME MUSIC: Up full then under...

ANNOUNCER: *Everything for the Boys* is presented by the Electric Auto Lite Company and its 22 great manufacturing plants, builders of precision equipment for 35 years, world famous for Auto Lite Spark Plugs, batteries, wires, cables and electrical systems for automotive, aviation and marine use. Now, here's your host, Mr. Ronald Colman.

SOUND: Applause.

RONALD: Good evening, ladies and gentlemen... [He would then introduce the evening's program.]

CLOSE

ANNOUNCER: American flyers have nicknamed it Elmer; the British call it George. We on the homefront refer to it as an automatic pilot, and perhaps a name like Elmer or George is more fitting because it's almost human. It has a brain and muscles; its control over a plane and flight is far more precise than that of any pilot; it's nerveless and unexcitable. The brain transmits an accurate signal to the hydraulic muscle to pilot the plane on a straight and level flight. But an automatic pilot is not born, it's man-made, an ingenious example of precision manufacturing by the Auto Lite aviation plant in Toledo, Ohio. They're working long hours every day, accurately building automatic pilots everyday for Navy dive bombers. The lives of many Allied fliers, the success of operations depend in great measure on the performance of this and other precision instruments. That's why accuracy to within 25-one millionth [25 millionths] of an inch in the manufacture of certain vital parts is required. This is indeed engineering know-how—another example of the name Auto Lite meaning precision manufacturing.

THEME MUSIC: Up full then under...

RONALD: You all heard of the magnificent life saving work the Red Cross is doing attending to the sick and wounded, but there is another kind of sickness the Red Cross takes care of— homesickness. To millions of men overseas, the Red Cross clubs mean a glimpse of home. Naturally, such clubs cost to maintain. But if your contribution could ease the heart of a single homesick boy, could you find it in your heart to turn him down? I think not.

THEME MUSIC: Up full then under...

ANNOUNCER: Join us next week when the Electric Auto Lite Company again presents *Everything for the Boys*, your new global half-hour uniting the home front with the fighting front overseas. Your host, Mr. Ronald Colman, will have as his guest Miss Ruth Chatterton in Arch Oboler's radio adaptation of the comedy *Holy Matrimony*. Following the play, Mr.

Colman and Miss Chatterton will speak by shortwave with two United States Marines stationed somewhere in the Central Pacific.

RONALD: Until next week when Ruth Chatterton will be our guest, as well as two fighting Marines in the Pacific, this is Ronald Colman saying good night to you and the boys and God be with you.

THEME MUSIC: Up full then under…

ANNOUNCER: This program is shortwaved all over the world. This is Frank Martin saying good night for Auto Lite. Ingrid Bergman appears tonight through the courtesy of David O. Selznick, whose newest picture, *Since You Went Away*, will soon be released. This program came to you from Hollywood and Naples, Italy. This is NBC, the National Broadcasting Company.

THEME MUSIC: Up full then out.

SOUND: NBC chimes. N-B-C.

127. Exploring Tomorrow

Stories exploring the future of mankind. Various sponsors. Mutual, 1957–1958. Hosted by John Campbell, Jr.

OPEN

ANNOUNCER: The program you are about to hear is fiction, science fiction. We make no guarantees, however, how long it will remain fiction.

VOICE: *Exploring Tomorrow.*

THEME MUSIC: Up full then under…

ANNOUNCER: And now, here is your guide to these adventures of the mind, the editor of *Astounding Science Fiction* magazine, John Campbell, Jr.

HOST: We all believe pretty solidly that sooner or later any problem you can name is going to be solved. So, apparently, all you have to do is stand by and wait and it will soon be solved for you. I don't think that works right. There is another thing to consider—

ANNOUNCER: *Exploring Tomorrow.* Presented by the Mutual Broadcasting System in cooperation with L&M, today's most exciting cigarette. L&M smokes cleaner, tastes best. Live modern, smoke modern L&M. And the Kraft

Foods Company, makers of delicious new Kraft jellies and preserves; and Cape Coral, a beautiful waterfront wonderland on the western coast of Florida. In a moment, John Campbell returns with tonight's story.

SPOKESMAN (Bill Stern): Hello everybody, this is Bill Stern and I'd like to tell you about a tropical paradise where living is so easy that I intend to settle down and stay for the rest of my life. The name of my dream city is Cape Coral on the unspoiled western coast of Florida. Just think, two thousand acres of high dry palm and honey combed with fifty miles of navigable waterways just teaming with fish they write books about. You can buy a large 80 by 125 foot home site for only $990. Only $20 down and $20 a month and live here like a king on a retirement budget or purchase now for possible profitable resale later. The complete Cape Coral kit story has been compiled for you in easy-to-read literature; it's yours free of charge—a post card is all you need. Send it to me, Bill Stern now. I'll be seeing you at Cape Coral, Florida.

ANNOUNCER: To get your free literature, write Bill Stern, Cape Coral, Post Office Box 230, New York 18, New York.

THEME MUSIC: Up full then under…

ANNOUNCER: And now Mr. Campbell. [John Campbell would begin the evening's story.]

CLOSE

ANNOUNCER: Remember how grandma used to boil jellies and preserves on the stove in the kitchen? What a wonderful aroma. But you know that wonderful aroma was really flavor boiling away. And lots of folks still boil flavor away when they're making jellies and preserves. Not Kraft. Kraft jellies and preserves are cool cooked at temperatures below boiling to keep the flavor many others boil away. Kraft jellies and preserves have that true fresh-picked flavor, a flavor you can add to your favorite foods. There are so many ways to use these fresh, delicious flavors. It tells you how in the free recipe folder—"Flavor Magic for Your Favorite Foods with Kraft Jellies and Preserves." Just write to Kraft Jellies and Preserves, Box 5310, Chicago 77, Illinois. Do it now before you forget. And be sure to get Kraft jellies and preserves.

THEME MUSIC: Up full then under...

ANNOUNCER: *Exploring Tomorrow* was presented by the Mutual Broadcasting System in cooperation with L&M, today's most exciting cigarette, the Kraft Foods Company, makers of delicious jellies and preserves, and by Cape Coral, a beautiful waterfront wonderland on the western coast of Florida.

THEME MUSIC: Up full then under...

ANNOUNCER: Join us each Wednesday and Friday night for fascinating adventures in *Exploring Tomorrow*. Produced and directed by Sanford Marshall here in New York. This is Mutual, the world's largest network.

THEME MUSIC: Up full then fade out.

128. The Fabulous Dr. Tweedy

Comical incidents in the life of Dr. Thaddeus Q. Tweedy (Frank Morgan), dean of men at Potts College. Sustaining. NBC, 1946. Also in the cast were Gale Gordon as Alexander Potts, head of the college, and Janet Waldo as Mary Potts, Alexander's daughter.

OPEN

THEME MUSIC: Up full then under...

ANNOUNCER: *The Fabulous Dr. Tweedy*, written by Robert Riley Crutcher, and starring Frank Morgan as Dr. Thaddeus Q. Tweedy, dean of men at Potts College, who is always eager to help, but whose advice is often not helpful.

THEME MUSIC: Up full then under...

ANNOUNCER: We now take you to Potts College for our weekly visit with the befuddled but fabulous Dr. Tweedy.

CLOSE

THEME MUSIC: Up full then under...

ANNOUNCER: *The Fabulous Dr. Tweedy*, written by Robert Riley Crutcher, stars Frank Morgan with Gale Gordon and Janet Waldo. Music is by Elliot Daniel. Bud Heistand Speaking.

THEME MUSIC: Up full then out.

ANNOUNCER: This is NBC, the National Broadcasting Company.

SOUND: NBC chimes. N-B-C.

129. The Falcon

Crime drama about Michael Waring, a private detective known as the Falcon. Various sponsors (Gem Blades and Kraft Foods were frequent sponsors). Blue/ABC (1943–1945), Mutual (1945–1950; 1953–1954), NBC (1950–1952). Berry Kroger, James Meighan, Les Damon, Les Tremayne and George Petrie played Michael Waring.

OPEN (for Gem)

SOUND: Ticking clock.

ANNOUNCER (Russ Dunbar): Avoid five o'clock shadow.

VOICE: Use Gem Blades, use Gem Blades, use Gem Blades.

ANNOUNCER: Gem Razors and Gem Blades present the adventures of *The Falcon*.

SOUND: Phone rings.

FALCON (Picking up receiver): Hello. Yes, this is the Falcon.

ANNOUNCER: Once again Gem Blades, the razor blades that help you avoid five o-clock shadow, bring you the adventures of *The Falcon*. The Falcon, as you know, is Michael Waring, freelance detective, who's always ready with a hand for oppressed men and an eye for repressed women.

THEME MUSIC: Up full then out.

ANNOUNCER: I can tell you that nine out of ten men will stay face neat right around the clock by shaving the Gem way, that is with a Gem Razor and genuine Gem Blades. I know it takes a definite effort on your part to change your shaving method, but I promise you that if you shave the Gem way your effort will be repaid everyday of your life. Gem Razors are again available at your dealers; get one if you haven't one already and begin immediately to enjoy Gem's famous features: such as the clever face-fitting bevel which compels you to use the master barber's long, gliding stroke; and you'll like the way the super keen Gem blade gets the beard at skin level, so close, clean and comfortable. So try the Gem way, won't you? Avoid five o'clock shadow with Gem Razors and Gem Blades.

THEME MUSIC: Up full and under...

ANNOUNCER: Now back to the adventures of *The Falcon*.

CLOSE (for Gem)

THEME MUSIC: Up full then under...

ANNOUNCER: Be sure to listen next week at this time to another gay, exciting adventure of *The Falcon*. And, in the meantime, avoid five o'-clock shadow with Gem Razors and Gem Blades. The adventures of *The Falcon* are based on the famous character created by Drexell Drake. James Meighan was starred as the Falcon. This is the Mutual Broadcasting System.

THEME MUSIC: Up full then fade out.

OPEN (for Kraft)

THEME MUSIC: Up full then under...

ANNOUNCER: This is Ed Herlihy, friends, inviting you on behalf of the Kraft Foods Company to listen to the adventures of *The Falcon* starring Les Damon. You met the Falcon first in his best-selling novels, then you saw him in his thrilling motion picture series. Now, join him on the air.

THEME MUSIC: Up full then out.

ANNOUNCER: Friends, in just a moment or two we'll join *The Falcon*. But first, let me tell you about nine ways you can save time in the kitchen. Just discover the nine handy Kraft cheese spreads and enjoy snacks and sandwiches, salad toppings and appetizers that are really easy and quick to fix. There are sharp-tasting Kraft cheese spreads and mild-tasting ones too. You can depend on them all to be delicious and you can depend on them to be the finest quality because they are made by Kraft. Try some of these handy helpers tomorrow.

THEME MUSIC: Up full then under...

ANNOUNCER: And now *The Falcon*.

CLOSE (for Kraft)

ANNOUNCER: It's wonderful as a spread, delicious as a seasoning, superb as a flavor shortening. Parkay margarine, that all-purpose margarine made by Kraft. Yes, millions prefer Parkay to any other spread. It tastes so good and it tastes so good because it's always fresh. In states where the law permits, get yellow Parkay in its new aluminum foil flavor savor wrap; elsewhere get the regular package or color quick bag. That's P-A-R-K-A-Y,

Parkay margarine made by Kraft. It tastes so good.

THEME MUSIC: Up full then under...

ANNOUNCER: Be sure to listen at this same time next week for another adventure of *The Falcon*, brought to you by the Kraft Foods Company. The adventures of *The Falcon* are based on the famous character created by Drexell Drake and are produced by Bernard L. Schubert. Les Damon was starred as the Falcon with Ken Lynch as Sergeant Corbett. This is Ed Herlihy speaking for the Kraft Foods Company.

THEME MUSIC: Up full then out.

SOUND: NBC chimes. N-B-C.

130. The Fat Man

Crime drama about Brad Runyon, an overweight private detective known as the Fat Man. Sponsored by American Chicle, Norwich Pharmaceutical and R.J. Reynolds. ABC, 1946–1951. J. Scott Smart played Brad Runyon.

OPEN

ANNOUNCER (Charles Irving): When your stomach's upset, don't add to the upset, take soothing Pepto Bismol and feel good again.

THEME MUSIC: Up full then under...

WOMAN: There he goes into that drugstore. He's stepping on the scales.

SOUND: Coin dropping into the weighing machine.

WOMAN: Weight 237 pounds.

SOUND: Fortune card dropping into slot.

WOMAN: Fortune ... Danger! Who is it?

MAN: *The Fat Man*.

ANNOUNCER: *The Fat Man*, Dashiell Hammett's fascinating and exciting character. *The Fat Man*, a fast-moving criminologist who tips the scales at 237 pounds, brought to you by the Norwich Pharmaceutical Company, Limited, makers of Pepto Bismol, Unguentine and other fine drug products.

THEME MUSIC: Up full then out.

ANNOUNCER: When you overeat or eat too fast, you're looking for trouble with your digestion. That's no time to add to the upset, instead try a better way, a gentle way, take soothing Pepto Bismol. Yes, when you're bothered by heartburn, nervous indigestion and other common digestive disturbances, Pepto Bismol promptly helps to calm and quiet the upset. It settles and sweetens it; you feel good again. Next time you eat too much or too fast, try soothing Pepto Bismol and feel good again.

THEME MUSIC: Up full then under…

ANNOUNCER: And now from New York, *The Fat Man* starring J. Scott Smart.

CLOSE

ANNOUNCER: Before you go to bed tonight, look in your medicine cabinet. See if you have a bottle of Pepto Bismol. If you haven't make a note to stop in at your druggist tomorrow morning. With Pepto Bismol on hand you're ready to help relieve the distress of acid indigestion, heartburn or that uneasy feeling that follows overeating. Anybody can take Pepto Bismol anytime. Pepto Bismol contains no sugars. It doesn't add to the upset; take soothing Pepto Bismol and feel good again.

THEME MUSIC: Up full then under…

ANNOUNCER: Next Week, the Norwich Pharmaceutical Company presents that exciting and fascinating character *The Fat Man* in another exciting adventure. Charles Irving speaking. This is ABC, the American Broadcasting Company.

THEME MUSIC: Up full then out.

Note: In some openings, Brad is said to be 239 pounds and the parts described here as being said by a woman are spoken by a man.

131. Father Knows Best

Comedy that centered on the lives of Jim and Margaret Anderson and their children, Betty, Bud and Kathy. Sponsored by General Foods. NBC, 1949–1954. Robert Young played Jim Anderson with June Whitley and Jean VanderPyl as Margaret; Rhoda Williams as Betty; Ted Donaldson as Bud; and Norma Jean Nilsson and Helen Strong as Kathy. Basis for the television series.

OPEN

BETTY: Mother, are Post Forty Percent Brand Flakes really the best-tasting cereal of them all?

MARGARET: Well, your father says so, and Father knows best.

THEME MUSIC: Up full then under…

ANNOUNCER (Bill Forman): Yes, it's *Father Knows Best*, transcribed in Hollywood and starring Robert Young as Father. A half-hour visit with your neighbors, the Andersons, and brought to you by America's largest-selling bran flakes, Post Forty Percent Bran Flakes, and by Instant Postem, the good-tasting drink that's entirely caffeine free.

THEME MUSIC: Up full then out.

ANNOUNCER: I know something every mother takes seriously, the family breakfast, so let's talk about that for a moment. You've probably known all along that bran is good for you. Maybe you tried bran but weren't too keen about the taste. Well, things are different now. Something wonderful has happened to bran. The Post cereals people have given Post Forty Percent Bran Flakes a wonderful new flavor, a magic oven flavor and crisp texture that's really delicious. You can serve new Post Bran Flakes with its ounce of prevention, its important keep-regular benefits, and know that the family will get these vital extras in a cereal they'll really enjoy.

SONG (girl vocalist):
> For goodness sakes
> Eat Post Bran Flakes,
> So good and so good for you.

ANNOUNCER: When you do your weekend shopping, buy new Post Forty Percent Bran Flakes. They're America's largest-selling bran flakes. They're so good and so good for you.

THEME MUSIC: Up full then under as the story begins.

CLOSE

THEME MUSIC: Up full then under…

ANNOUNCER: Join us next week when we'll be back with *Father Knows Best* starring Robert Young as Jim Anderson. Until then, good night and good luck from the makers of Post Forty Percent Bran Flakes, America's largest-selling bran flakes, and Instant Postem, the drink that's entirely caffeine free. Also in the cast were Norma Jean Nilsson as Kathy, Jean VanderPyl as Margaret, Rhoda Williams as

Betty and Ted Donaldson as Bud. Ladies, for a happy family at the start of each day, start serving breakfast the Post Ten's way. It's the handy, thrifty way to let everybody choose his own favorite cereal. Post Ten's brings you ten individual packages of seven Post cereals: Raisin Bran, Forty Percent Bran Flakes, Post Toasties, Grape Nuts and Grape Nuts Flakes. And Post Ten's is the only assortment with two leading sweet-coated cereals: popular new Kringles and delicious candy-coated Sugar Crisp. Try this popular assortment of famous Post cereals. Get Post Ten's today.

THEME MUSIC: Up full then under...

ANNOUNCER: *Father Knows Best* has been transcribed in Hollywood. This is Bill Forman speaking. This is NBC, the National Broadcasting Company.

THEME MUSIC: Up full then out.

SOUND: NBC chimes. N-B-C.

132. The FBI in Peace and War

Crime drama about the FBI's relentless battle against crime. Various sponsors (Brylcream, Lava and Nescafe were frequent sponsors). CBS, 1944–1958. "March for Love for Three Oranges" by Richard Strauss was used as the theme.

OPEN (early)

THEME MUSIC: Up full then under...

ANNOUNCER (Bob Wright): *The FBI in Peace and War. The FBI in Peace and War*, brought to you by Brylcream, the original creme hair-grooming discovery that instantly improves your appearance. Brylcream, the creme that's really not greasy, not messy, and—

SONG: L-A-V-A, L-A-V-A.

ANNOUNCER: Lava, the soap that gets grimy hands cleaner faster than ordinary soaps ever can; and by Nescafe Instant Coffee, the coffee with the richer, heart-of-the-bean flavor. And now another great story based on Frederick L. Collins' copyrighted book *The FBI in Peace and War*. Drama, thrills, action. It's *The FBI in Peace and War*.

CLOSE (early)

ANNOUNCER: The radio dramatizations of *The FBI in Peace and War* are written by Louis Pelletier and Jacques Finke. These programs are produced and directed by Betty Manderville. All names and characters used on the program are fictitious. Any similarity to persons living or dead is purely coincidental. This program is based on Frederick L. Collins' copyrighted book *The FBI in Peace and War* and is not an official program of the FBI. This is the CBS radio network.

OPEN (later)

THEME MUSIC: Up full then under...

ANNOUNCER (Warren Sweeney): *The FBI in Peace and War*. Another great story from Frederick L. Collins' copyrighted book, *The FBI in Peace and War*. Drama, thrills, action. *The FBI in Peace and War*!

CLOSE (later)

ANNOUNCER: All names and characters used on this program are fictitious. Any similarity to persons living or dead is purely coincidental. This program is based upon Frederick L. Collins' copyrighted book *The FBI in Peace and War*. This broadcast does not imply endorsement or authorization or approval of the Federal Bureau of Investigation. This is Warren Sweeney inviting you to listen in again next week for *The FBI in Peace and War*, same time, same station. This is the CBS radio network.

133. Fibber McGee and Molly

Comedy about Fibber McGee (Jim Jordan), the world's greatest liar, and his patient wife, Molly (Marian Jordan), residents of the town of Wistful Vista. Sponsored by Johnson Wax and Reynolds. NBC, 1935–1956.

OPEN (early)

THEME MUSIC: Up full then under...

ANNOUNCER (Harlow Wilcox): The makers of

Johnson Auto Wax present a new show featuring Rico Martellis, Kathleen Wells, those two harmoniacs, Ronny and Van, and starring that humbug of the highways, Fibber McGee with his constant companion and severest critic, Molly.

CLOSE (early)

ANNOUNCER: don't forget next week at this same time you have a bright and shining date with Johnson's Auto Wax and Fibber McGee and Molly. This is Harlow Wilcox speaking. Good night. This is the National Broadcasting Company.

Note: At this time, Fibber McGee and Molly (Jim Jordan, Marian Jordan) were only minor characters whose comic adventures as they drove across the country were depicted. Singer Kathleen Wells and orchestra leader Rico Martellis were the stars. When Johnson wax changed from auto wax to floor polish, they gave the McGees a home at 79 Wistful Vista to enable them to advertise their new product. These shows are also known as "The Johnson Wax Program."

OPEN (later)

THEME MUSIC: Up full then under...
ANNOUNCER (Harlow Wilcox): *The Johnson Wax Program* with Fibber McGee and Molly. The makers of Johnson Wax and Johnson Self-Polishing Glo Cote present *Fibber McGee and Molly*, written by Don Quinn, music by the Kingsmen and Billy Mills Orchestra.
THEME MUSIC: Up full then out.

CLOSE (later)

ANNOUNCER: Did you ever stop to think of the health advantage of a waxed home? Besides beauty and protection for your things, your home is cleaner and more sanitary if you keep your floors regularly polished with Johnson Wax. Whether your things are old or new, it will pay you to polish them regularly with genuine Johnson Wax.
FIBBER: Ladies and gentlemen, the traditional sentiment of people from Missouri has always been "Show me."
MOLLY: So let's all show our new President, Mr. Harry Truman of Missouri, that he has our complete loyalty and support in his difficult

task of winning the war and leading our nation to peace and security.
FIBBER: Good night.
MOLLY: Good night all.
ANNOUNCER: This is Harlow Wilcox speaking for the makers of Johnson Wax for home and industry inviting you to be with us again next Tuesday night. Good night. This is the National Broadcasting Company.
SOUND: NBC chimes. N-B-C.

134. The Fire Chief

Early comedy-variety series that featured a live studio audience and host Ed Wynn in full costume and makeup (based on the sponsor's, Texaco's, Fire Chief Gasoline). NBC, 1932–1935.

OPEN

SOUND: Sirens.
ANNOUNCER (Graham McNamee): For speed, for power and action, Texaco Fire Chief, the gasoline that's bought by more tourists than any other brand. And for a sweeter running engine, Texaco, the motor oil that lasts longer and saves you money.
THEME MUSIC: Up full then under...
ANNOUNCER: Texaco service stations and dealers in all our 48 states present for your entertainment Eddie Duchin and his music, yours truly, Graham McNamee, and Ed Wynn, *The Fire Chief...* [Applause would follow and Ed would then begin the show.]

CLOSE

SOUND: Sirens.
ANNOUNCER: Texaco Fire Chief, the brand that's bought by more tourists than any other brand of gasoline, has presented Ed Wynn as *The Fire Chief*. Remember also, for a sweeter running engine, use Texaco motor oil. This is Graham McNamee speaking for Texaco service stations and dealers in all our 48 states and reminding you to be with us again next Tuesday night when Ed Wynn returns as *The Fire Chief*. This is NBC, the National Broadcasting Company.
SOUND: NBC chimes. N-B-C.

135. First Nighter

Anthology series set at the Little Theater Off Times Square where the host, Mr. First Nighter, introduces three-act plays from his seat (fourth row center). Various sponsors. Blue (1930–1933), NBC (1933–1936), CBS (1937–1942; 1945–1949), Mutual (1944). Charles P. Hughes, Bret Morrison, Marvin Miller, Don Briggs and Ed Prentiss played Mr. First Nighter. The song "Neapolitan Nights" was used as the theme.

OPEN

THEME MUSIC: Up full then under…

ANNOUNCER (Larry Keating): Campana's First Nighter program from the Little Theater Off Times Square. Starring Olan Soule and Barbara Luddy with an all-star cast sent to you by Campana, the quality name in cosmetics.

THEME MUSIC: Up full then under…

ANNOUNCER: Broadway, theater time, and this evening there is a special date on the theater calendar because a new play is scheduled for its opening night performance at the Little Theater Off Times Square. What's more, you have front-row seats with the genial First Nighter himself as your host. And here he is.

FIRST NIGHTER: Good evening, everybody. They say it's going to be a prompt curtain tonight, so let's be off shall we? Here's my cab, won't you step in.

SOUND: Mr. First Nighter entering the cab.

FIRST NIGHTER: All right driver, let's go.

SOUND: Traffic noises.

ANNOUNCER: Up Broadway, across 42nd Street and into the famous Times Square district. Theater and supper clubs cluster in this area like pins in a pin cushion.

FIRST NIGHTER: Well, here we are.

VOICE: Have your tickets ready. Have your tickets ready, please.

VOICE: Good evening, Mr. First Nighter. The usher will show you to your seat.

FIRST NIGHTER: Thank you, we'll go right in. Here we are inside the theater, ladies and gentlemen, and I wish I had the time to name all the notables in the audience tonight … but about the play. It's a farce called "There's

Something in the Air," written by Anthony Wayne. And, according to reports from those in the know, it promises a half-hour of hilarious entertainment. Olan Soule and Barbara Luddy headline the all-star cast. I see Frank Worth and his First Night Orchestra in the pit, and it's just about time for the first curtain.

VOICE: Curtain time, curtain time.

FIRST NIGHTER: There's the signal for first curtain. The house lights are out and here's the play.

CLOSE

THEME MUSIC: Up full then under…

ANNOUNCER: The curtain falls on the final act of another original play from the Little Theater Off Times Square. Next week, ladies and gentlemen, we want to issue a special invitation to you and your family to join us again when another brand-new play entitled "The Green Leprechaun" will be presented in the Little Theater Off Times Square. It's a love story, the kind that tugs at your heartstrings as it puts a smile on your lips. Your whole family will enjoy it. Be sure to join us next week, same time, same station. And ladies, you'll never know how pretty you can be until you try Magic Touch. Now we move out of the theater and into the street.

SOUND: Mr. First Nighter entering his cab.

FIRST NIGHTER: Good night.

ANNOUNCER: This is CBS, the Columbia Broadcasting System.

THEME MUSIC: Up full then out.

136. The Fitch Bandwagon

Variety series sponsored by Fitch Shampoo. NBC, 1938–1948. Programs broadcast from 1938–1944 featured the music of various orchestras. Regular hosts were Dick Powell (1944–1945), Cass Daley (1945–1946) and Phil Harris and Alice Faye (1946–1948).

OPEN (Cass Daley)

CHORUS:

Laugh a while
Let a song be your style

Use Fitch Shampoo.
Don't despair
Use your head, save your hair
Use Fitch Shampoo.

GIRL:

Fitch, it makes you feel so grand,
Fitch, you'll sing to beat the band.
We'll make the pitch,
Then it's up to you
To make the switch
To Fitch, Fitch, Fitch.

ANNOUNCER (Larry Keating): *The Fitch Band-wagon*, brought to you by the F.W. Fitch Company, makers of those fine Fitch products, with yours truly, Larry Keating, Henry Russell, Dink Trout, and our special guest for today, Glen Gray and the Casa Loma Orchestra. And starring Cass Daley... [Applause would follow with Cass then beginning the show.]

CLOSE (Cass Daley)

ANNOUNCER: You have been listening to *The Fitch Bandwagon*, brought to you by the F.W. Fitch Company, makers of those fine Fitch products. Be with us again next week, same time, same station. This is Larry Keating inviting you to join us then. This is NBC, the National Broadcasting Company.

OPEN (Phil Harris)

CHORUS:

Laugh a while
Let a song be your style,
Use Fitch Shampoo.

ANNOUNCER (Bill Forman): The F.W. Fitch Company, makers of those fine Fitch products, presents *The Fitch Bandwagon* starring Alice Faye and Phil Harris.

CLOSE (Phil Harris)

ANNOUNCER: *The Fitch Bandwagon* with Phil Harris and Alice Faye has been brought to you by the F.W. Fitch Company. Also in the cast were Myra Marsh, Jeanine Roos and Ann Whitfield with Walter Tetley as Julius. Original music was composed and conducted by Walter Sharp. Bill Forman speaking. This is NBC, the National Broadcasting Company.

137. Flash Gordon

Adventure series based on the comic strip by Alex Raymond that relates the exploits of Flash Gordon, Dale Arden and Dr. Zarkoff as they battle evil. Two series were produced. The first, *The Amazing Adventures of Flash Gordon*, starred James Meighan (Flash Gordon), Irene Watson (Dale Arden) and Owen Jordan (Dr. Zarkoff). The series was sponsored by Groves Emulsified Nose Drops and aired on Mutual (1935–1936).

The second series, *The Amazing Interplanetary Adventures of Flash Gordon*, starred Gale Gordon (Flash Gordon), Franc Hale (Dale Arden) and Maurice Franklin (Dr. Zarkoff). The program was sponsored by Hearst Newspapers and was syndicated in 1939.

OPEN (1935)

THEME MUSIC: Up full then under...

ANNOUNCER: *The Amazing Adventures of Flash Gordon*. Groves Emulsified Nose Drops bring to your radio the further interplanetary adventures of Flash Gordon. It is the same daring and resourceful Flash Gordon whose exploits have held you spellbound in the newspapers. Now through your loudspeakers, every Monday, Tuesday, Wednesday and Thursday at this same time, travel with Flash Gordon, Dale Arden and Dr. Zarkoff to the lost continent of Atlantis on the ocean floor.

THEME MUSIC: Up full then out.

ANNOUNCER: For any head cold or nose cold you want to get mother to let you try Groves Emulsified Nose Drops. Then you'll get the relief you want and you won't have to go through any suffering to get it. Groves Emulsified Nose Drops do not bite or sting; neither do they run down your face and throat. These drops stay put so that you get a much more prolonged effect than ordinary oil drops. It's wise to use Groves Emulsified Nose Drops. They are on sale at all drugstores. And now back to *Flash Gordon*.

CLOSE (1935)

ANNOUNCER: Mother knows what a battle it is to get you to take nose drops. When she sees how willingly you stand for Groves Emulsified

Nose Drops, she feels a service has been done to her. Mothers write and tell us every day how grateful they are for Groves Emulsified Nose Drops. They find them not only more acceptable but more effective. Groves Nose Drops are something new, a decided improvement on the old nose drops. They are made by the makers of Groves Bromo Quinine. Mother knows that guarantees their quality. Maybe if you suggest it after this program, Mother will get a bottle in the house tonight to have them ready the next time a head cold shows.

THEME MUSIC: Up full then under...

ANNOUNCER: Come with us every Monday, Tuesday, Wednesday and Thursday at this same time for further interplanetary adventures with Flash Gordon.

THEME MUSIC: Up full then fade out.

OPEN (1939)

THEME MUSIC: Up full then under...

ANNOUNCER: Presenting *The Amazing Interplanetary Adventures of Flash Gordon.*

THEME MUSIC: Up full then under...

ANNOUNCER: These thrilling adventures come to you as they are pictured each Sunday in the big, full-page *Comic Weekly*, the world's greatest pictorial supplement of humor and adventure. The full-page *Comic Weekly*, each page printed in full color, is distributed everywhere as an integral part of your Hearst Sunday newspaper.

THEME MUSIC: Up full then out.

CLOSE (1939)

THEME MUSIC: Up full then under...

ANNOUNCER: These amazing adventures are graphically portrayed in full color action pictures in the *Comic Weekly*, the big, full-page picture supplement distributed each Sunday with your Hearst newspaper. Don't miss the *Comic Weekly* next Sunday. For, in addition to Flash Gordon you will find many other characters of fun and adventure waiting to entertain you. And don't forget our date next week for the next chapter in *The Amazing Interplanetary Adventures of Flash Gordon.*

THEME MUSIC: Up full then fade out.

138. Flashgun Casey, Press Photographer

Crime drama about Jack Casey, a crime photographer for the *Morning Express*. Sustaining (American Hocking Glass, Philip Morris and Toni were sponsors 1947–1950). CBS, 1943–1955. Matt Crowley and Staats Cotsworth played Jack Casey with June Allison, Alice Reinheart, Betty Furness, Lesley Woods and Jan Miner as reporter Anne Williams. The series was also called *Press Photographer*, *Crime Photographer* and *Casey, Crime Photographer*.

OPEN (original)

ANNOUNCER (Bob Hite): *Flashgun Casey, Press Photographer.*

THEME MUSIC: Up full then under...

ANNOUNCER: Out of a big city's roaring life; out of a newspaper's pounding heart come the exciting adventures of a man with a camera— *Flashgun Casey, Press Photographer.*

THEME MUSIC: Up full then under...

ANNOUNCER: Columbia presents the new adventure character Flashgun Casey, press photographer; tough, daring, typical of the men who often risk their lives so you may see the news as well as read it. Their salaries are not large and they seldom get much credit, but their lives are packed with danger and thrills. Tonight and every Wednesday night at this time, Columbia invites you to follow the story of Flashgun Casey and the people who pass in swift parade before the shutters of his camera.

THEME MUSIC: Up full then out.

CLOSE (original)

THEME MUSIC: Up full then under...

ANNOUNCER: You have been listening to *Flashgun Casey, Press Photographer*, based on the fiction character created by George Harmon Cox. The program was produced for Columbia by Chester Renair. Join us next Wednesday night at this same time for another swift-moving story of a press photographer, Flashgun Casey.

THEME MUSIC: Up full then under...

ANNOUNCER: This is CBS, the Columbia Broadcasting System.

THEME MUSIC: Up full then fade out.

OPEN (revised)

THEME MUSIC: Up full then under...
ANNOUNCER (Tony Marvin): Columbia presents *Casey, Crime Photographer*. Good evening, ladies and gentlemen, this is Tony Marvin inviting you to listen to *Casey, Crime Photographer*, ace cameraman who covers the crime news of a great city.
THEME MUSIC: Up full then out.

CLOSE (revised)

THEME MUSIC: Up full then under...
ANNOUNCER: You have been listening to *Casey, Crime Photographer*, ace cameraman of the *Morning Express*. Staats Cotsworth is heard as Casey with Jan Miner as Anne Williams and John Gibson as Ethelbert, the bartender. This is Tony Marvin inviting you to be with us again next week for another exciting adventure on the Columbia series, *Casey, Crime Photographer*.
THEME MUSIC: Up full then fade out.

139. Flywheel, Shyster and Flywheel, Attorneys-at-Law

Comedy with Groucho Marx as less than honorable lawyer Waldorf T. Flywheel and his associate Emmanuel Ravelli (Chico Marx). Sponsored by the Standard Oil Company. NBC, 1932–1933.

OPEN

ANNOUNCER (George Hicks): *The Five Star Theater* presents Groucho and Chico Marx. *The Five Star Theater*, sponsored by the Standard Oil Company of New Jersey, Pennsylvania and Louisiana, and the Colonial Beacon Oil Company through 30,000 Esso—spelled E-S-S-O—stations, which form a network of convenient service to the motorist all the way from Maine to Louisiana. Monday night is comedy night on *The Five Star Theater*. We are about to hear those mad Marxmen in another of their three act comedies concerning the adventures of Flywheel, Shyster and Fly-

wheel, attorneys-at-law. Both are coming onto the platform now, dressed just as you remember them on stage and screen. Groucho, in his little black moustache, red tie and top coat; and Chico and his bushy hair, little green hat and corduroy coat. Our orchestra conductor, Leonard Joy, is lifting his stick and the show is about to begin.

CLOSE

ANNOUNCER: You have been entertained tonight on *The Five Star Theater* by Groucho and Chico Marx in their three-act comedy, *Flywheel, Shyster and Flywheel, Attorneys-at-Law*. *The Five Star Theater* is sponsored by the Standard Oil Company of New Jersey, Pennsylvania and Louisiana and the Colonial Beacon Oil Company. George Hicks announcing. This is the National Broadcasting Company.

140. Forever Ernest

Comical incidents in the life of Ernest Fudge, a clerk at Spencer's Pharmacy. Sustaining. CBS, 1946. Jackie Coogan played Ernest Fudge with Lurene Tuttle as his girlfriend, Candy Lane, and Arthur Q. Bryan as his friend, Duke.

OPEN

ANNOUNCER (Dick Joy): Here is *Forever Ernest*, a new radio series starring Jackie Coogan, Lurene Tuttle and Arthur Q. Bryan.
THEME MUSIC: Up full then under...
ANNOUNCER: The place? Oh, that's as familiar as Niagara Falls, as American as apple pie a la mode. Sure, you know Spencer's Drugstore all right, but it's possible you don't know Ernest Fudge. Ernest, played by Jackie Coogan, is assistant clerk, pharmacist and soda jerk; in fact, assistant everything in the place. And, as usual, he is the one who needs assistance. Let's join Ernest, his girlfriend, Candy Lane, and our friend Duke at Spencer's Drug Store.
THEME MUSIC: Up full then out.

CLOSE

THEME MUSIC: Up full then under...

ANNOUNCER: You have been listening to *Forever Ernest* with Jackie Coogan as Ernest, Lurene Tuttle as Candy Lane and Arthur Q. Bryan as Duke. Original music composed and conducted by Billy May. Be with us again next week when we pay another visit to Spencer's Drugstore on *Forever Ernest*. Dick Joy speaking. This is CBS, the Columbia Broadcasting System.

THEME MUSIC: Up full then fade out.

141. Fort Laramie

Western about Lee Quince (Raymond Burr), captain of a cavalry unit stationed at Fort Laramie during the 1880s. Various sponsors. CBS, 1956. Amerigo Moreno composed the theme, "Fort Laramie."

OPEN

THEME MUSIC: Up full then under…

ANNOUNCER (Dan Cubberly): L&M, the modern cigarette that lets you get full exciting flavor through the modern miracle of the pure white miracle tip, presents *Fort Laramie*.

THEME MUSIC: Up full then under…

ANNOUNCER: *Fort Laramie* starring Raymond Burr as Captain Lee Quince. Specially transcribed tales of the dark and tragic ground of the wild frontier. The saga of fighting men who rode the rim of empire and the dramatic story of Lee Quince, captain of cavalry.

THEME MUSIC: Up full then out.

CHORUS:
Why don't you live modern,
Live modern, live, live modern
Change to L&M.

ANNOUNCER: Only with L&M can you enjoy the full exciting flavor of today's finest tobaccos through the modern miracle of the L&M miracle tip. Through the pure white miracle tip, L&M tastes richer, smokes cleaner, draws easier. No other cigarette, plain or filter, gives you all the flavor you want, the rich and exciting flavor you get only from L&M. So light up, free up, let your taste come alive, live modern, smoke L&M.

CHORUS:
Make today your day,

Your big red letter day
And start to live the modern way.
Live, live, live modern
Get L&M to-daaaay.

THEME MUSIC: Up full then under…

ANNOUNCER: And now to Lee Quince, captain of cavalry at Fort Laramie…

CLOSE

LEE: Company, attention! Dismissed!

THEME MUSIC: Up full then under…

ANNOUNCER: Next week L&M, the modern cigarette that lets you get full, exciting flavor through the modern miracle of the pure white miracle tip, will present another transcribed story of the Northwest frontier and the troopers who fought under Lee Quince, captain of cavalry. Original music for *Fort Laramie* composed and conducted by Amerigo Moreno. Norman MacDonnell is the producer. Dan Cubberly speaking for CBS, the Columbia Broadcasting System.

THEME MUSIC: Up full then fade out.

142. Four Star Playhouse

Dramatizations based on stories appearing in *Cosmopolitan* magazine. Sustaining. NBC, 1949. Robert Cummings, Rosalind Russell, Fred MacMurray and Loretta Young comprised the four stars of the "Playhouse" (performing on a rotating basis).

OPEN

THEME MUSIC: Up full then under…

ANNOUNCER: Here's another in NBC's outstanding parade of new shows, dramatically transcribed. *Four Star Playhouse*, a repertory company of four great Hollywood stars:

ROBERT CUMMINGS: This is Robert Cummings.

ROSALIND RUSSELL: This is Rosalind Russell.

FRED MACMURRAY: This is Fred MacMurray.

LORETTA YOUNG: This is Loretta Young.

ANNOUNCER: Yes, these are the stars heard weekly on *Four Star Playhouse*. Ladies and gentlemen, one of our stars, and the star of tonight's play, Robert Cummings.

ROBERT: On behalf of Rosalind Russell, Fred MacMurray and Loretta Young, let me welcome you back to our *Four Star Playhouse*. As you know, every Sunday night at this time, Roz, Fred, Loretta and I appear in a dramatization selected from *Cosmopolitan* magazine, stories by the world's leading writers of popular fiction. (Robert would then introduce the audience to the evening's story.)

CLOSE

ANNOUNCER: And so ends another of our *Four Star Playhouse* presentations adapted from the pages of *Cosmopolitan* magazine. Our star for tonight was Robert Cummings. Next week our star will be Loretta Young. *Four Star Playhouse* is produced and directed by Warren Lewis with music by Albert Harris. Be with us again next Sunday evening for *Four Star Playhouse*. This is NBC, the National Broadcasting Company.

SOUND: NBC chimes. N-B-C.

143. The Fred Allen Show

Jokes, music, skits and songs hosted by comedian Fred Allen. Sponsored by Blue Bonnett Margarine, the Ford Motor Company, Ipana Toothpaste, Sal Hepatica Mouthwash and Tender Leaf Tea. NBC, 1939–1940; 1945–1949. See also *Texaco Star Theater* and *Town Hall Tonight*.

OPEN

CHORUS: Mister Allen, Mister Allen.

ANNOUNCER (Kenny Delmar): The makers of Blue Bonnett Margarine and Tender Leaf Tea present *The Fred Allen Show* with Portland Hoffa, Minerva Pious as Mrs. Nussbaum, Alan Reed as Falstaff Openshaw, Parker Fennelly as Titus Moody with the DeMarco Sisters and Al Goodman and his orchestra. And, until I show up as Senator Claghorn, my name is Kenny Delmar. And here he is, Fred Allen.

SOUND: Applause.

FRED: Good evening, ladies and gentlemen and welcome to our show…

CLOSE

ANNOUNCER: At this season of the year as the

sun settles down to rather serious business, we all have the same problem—how to cool off. Millions do it the gracious way with iced Tender Leaf Tea in a tall, tall frosty glass. Frosty outside, delicious within. It's cooling delight, refreshing, relaxing, satisfying, but take the precaution to get Tender Leaf brand tea because in ice tea season flavor is what counts. It's more important than ever. The finer and richer your tea is to start off with, the better your ice tea will be. So it stands to reason that a flavor favorite that makes superb hot tea will give you just what it takes to offset the melting ice, yet with a big margin of goodness to spare. Get a supply of Tender Leaf Tea so there's no chance of running out. Have plenty of tea and plenty of flavor. Enjoy it often with meals and between. Ask your grocer for delicious Tender Leaf Tea.

THEME MUSIC: Up full then under…

FRED: We hope, ladies and gentlemen, that you enjoyed tonight's presentation and you'll remember to be with us again next Sunday night. This is Fred Allen saying good night.

ANNOUNCER: *The Fred Allen Show* has been presented tonight by the makers of Blue Bonnett Margarine and Tender Leaf Tea. This is NBC, the National Broadcasting Company.

SOUND: NBC chimes. N-B-C.

144. The Fresh Up Show

Comedy with Bert Wheeler as a clerk at Doc Fickett's Drugstore. Sponsored by 7-Up. Mutual, 1945–1946.

OPEN

ANNOUNCER (Jerry Lawrence): Fresh up with 7-Up, you like it, it likes you. The makers and distributors of 7-Up, America's fresh up drink, bring you *The Fresh Up Show* starring Bert Wheeler. Doc Fickett's Drugstore in Sunnydale is just like thousands of other drugstores throughout the United States. And the only reason you can't get service is because of the clerk who works there, Bert Wheeler. Now let's join Bert as he begins work at Doc Fickett's Drugstore.

CLOSE

ANNOUNCER: *The Fresh Up Show* starring Bert Wheeler features Walter Kinsella as Doc Fickett, Annette Warren as Viola Fickett, and Lee Brady as Melville Fickett. Artie Elmer is heard as Mr. Fuddle. The Fresh Up Orchestra and Chorus is under the direction of Dave Terry. Ruth Davey is our vocalist. This is Jerry Lawrence wishing you the best of the evening from 7-Up, America's fresh up drink, and saying good night. This is the Mutual Broadcasting System.

145. Front Page Farrell

Serial about David Farrell, a reporter for the *Daily Eagle* whose impressive record has earned him the nickname "Front Page," and his wife (and assistant) Sally. Various sponsors. Mutual (1941–1942), NBC (1942–1954). Richard Widmark, Staats Cotsworth and Carleton Young played David Farrell with Florence Williams, Virginia Dwyer and Betty Garde as Sally. The song "You and I Know" was used as the theme.

OPEN

THEME MUSIC: Up full then under...

ANNOUNCER (James Fleming): The Whitehall Pharmaceutical Company, makers of Anacin for fast headache relief, presents the unforgettable radio drama *Front Page Farrell*.

THEME MUSIC: Up full then under...

ANNOUNCER: *Front Page Farrell*, the story of a crack newspaper reporter and his wife. The story of David and Sally Farrell.

THEME MUSIC: Up full then out.

ANNOUNCER: Every day you hear more and more about a remarkable way to reduce the pain of headaches, neuritis and neuralgia. The name is Anacin, spelled A-N-A-C-I-N. Thousands of men and women discovered this way when their own physicians or dentists handed them an envelope containing Anacin tablets. Now, the reason Anacin acts so incredibly fast is that it is like a doctor's prescription. That is, it is not composed of just one, but a combination of medically proven active ingredients in convenient tablet form. Next time you have

pain from headache, neuritis and neuralgia, try Anacin instead of the way you are now using. You'll be delighted with its incredibly fast, effective action. Try it with this money back guarantee. If the first few tablets don't give complete satisfaction, you may return the unused portion and your money will be refunded. Ask for Anacin today. It's sold in all drugstores in the United States and Canada. Use only as directed. If pain persists or is unusually severe, see your doctor. Easy-to-take Anacin tablets come in handy boxes of 12 and 30 and economical family size bottles of 50 and 100.

THEME MUSIC: Up full then under...

ANNOUNCER: And now to our story of *Front Page Farrell*.

CLOSE

THEME MUSIC: Up full then under...

ANNOUNCER: *Front Page Farrell* has been brought to you by the Whitehall Pharmaceutical Company, makers of Anacin and many other dependable high quality drug products. *Front Page Farrell* is produced by Frank and Anne Hummert with original organ music by Ann Leax. James Fleming speaking. Be sure to be with us again tomorrow for another exciting adventure in the unforgettable radio drama *Front Page Farrell*. This is NBC, the National Broadcasting Company.

THEME MUSIC: Up full then out.

SOUND: NBC chimes. N-B-C.

146. Frontier Gentleman

Western about J.B. (Jeremy Bryan) Kendall, a British reporter for the *London Times* who covers the American West of the 1880s. Various sponsors. CBS, 1958. John Dehner starred as J.B. Kendall. Jerry Goldsmith composed the theme, "Frontier Gentleman."

OPEN

ANNOUNCER (Johnny Jacobs): L&M, the cigarette with the patented miracle tip, presents *Frontier Gentleman*.

THEME MUSIC: Up full then under...

ANNOUNCER: *Frontier Gentleman.* Here with an Englishman's account of life and death in the West. As a reporter for the *London Times,* he writes his colorful and unusual stories; but as a man with a gun, he lives and becomes part of the violent years in the new territories. Now, starring John Dehner, this is the story of Jeremy B. Kendall, frontier gentleman.

THEME MUSIC: Up full then out.

CHORUS:

> L&M has found the secret
> That unlocks the flavor,
> Unlocks the flavor,
> Unlocks the flavor,
> L&M has found the secret
> That unlocks the flavor
> In a filter cigarette.

ANNOUNCER: Now is the time to reach for flavor, reach for L&M because L&M has found the secret that unlocks the flavor in a filter cigarette in today's L&M with the patented miracle tip. Fine tobaccos can be blended, not just filtered to suit your taste. So you get taste, more taste, more taste by far. So reach for flavor, reach for L&M.

CHORUS:

> L&M has found the secret
> That unlocks the flavor
> In a filter cigarette.

THEME MUSIC: Up full then under…

ANNOUNCER: And now to J.B. Kendall and today's story of *Frontier Gentleman.*

CLOSE

THEME MUSIC: Up full then under…

ANNOUNCER: You have been listening to *Frontier Gentleman* with John Dehner as Jeremy B. Kendall. *Frontier Gentleman* has been brought to you by L&M, the cigarette with the patented miracle tip to unlock the flavor. So reach for flavor, reach for L&M. Music for *Frontier Gentleman* is composed by Jerry Goldsmith and conducted by Wilbur Hatch. Tony Ellis is the producer. This is Johnny Jacobs inviting you to join us next week for another report from the *Frontier Gentleman.* This is the Columbia Broadcasting System.

THEME MUSIC: Up full then fade out.

147. Gangbusters

Crime drama about police law enforcement efforts to defeat crime. Sponsored by Chevrolet, Cue Magazine, Palmolive, Post Grape Nuts, Sloan's Liniment, Tide, Wrigley's Chewing Gum. Blue (1935), CBS (1936–1940; 1949–1954), Blue/ABC (1942–1948), Mutual (1955–1957).

OPEN (early)

SOUND: Marching feet, machine-gun fire, wailing sirens.

VOICE: Calling the police! Calling the G-Men! Calling all Americans to war on the underworld!

ANNOUNCER (Charles Stark): *Gangbusters!* With the cooperation of leading law enforcement officials of the United States, *Gangbusters* presents facts in the relentless war of the police on the underworld. Authentic case histories that show the never-ending activity of the police in their work of protecting our citizens.

OPEN (mid years)

ANNOUNCER (Don Gardner): Now, *Gangbusters,* presented in cooperation with police and federal law enforcement departments throughout the United States. The only national program that brings you authentic police case histories.

SOUND: Marching feet, machine-gun fire, police whistles.

ANNOUNCER: Sloan's Liniment presents *Gangbusters.* At war, marching against the underworld, from coast to coast, Gangbusters. Police, the G-Men, our government agents marching toward the underworld.

OPEN (late)

ANNOUNCER (Jay Jackson): And now Grape Nuts, the heart of your B-E-B, present *Gangbusters. Gangbusters,* presented in cooperation with police and federal law enforcement departments throughout the United States, the only national program that brings you authentic police case histories.

SPOKESMAN: Hey mister, and you madame, sitting in front of your radio, do you feel droopy in the morning? Wouldn't you rather feel on your toes? Full of zip and ready to go?

FEMALE: Who wouldn't.

SPOKESMAN: Then what you need is B-E-B.

FEMALE: B-E-B, B-E-B, B-E-B, wow!

SPOKESMAN: One bowl of Grape Nuts gives you more nourishment than an egg and a slice of bacon. That's why Grape Nuts is the best cereal for your B-E-B, your basic energy breakfast, the kind of breakfast that gives you more energy to beat that droopy morning let you down. And you'll like the taste of Grape Nuts immediately. So, if you're droopy before noon, if you don't feel lively in the morning, make sure you get your B-E-B and make sure you make Grape Nuts the heart of your basic energy breakfast. Ask your grocer for Grape Nuts tomorrow.

FEMALE: Tomorrow is Sunday.

SPOKESMAN: Oh, so it is. Go to church tomorrow and buy Grape Nuts on Monday. And now Grape Nuts takes you back to *Gangbusters*.

SOUND: Police sirens, machine-gun fire.

VOICE (echo effect): Tonight *Gangbusters* presents "The Case of the Surprised Safecrackers." [Story about how surveillance enables the police to capture criminals.]

Note: Closings for all eras are basically the same: a case summary by the announcer, a mention of the cast, the episode's writers and the producer. This would be followed by the announcer identifying himself and the network. This closing from the opening directly above is typical.

CLOSE (late)

VOICE (echo effect): Next week, "The Case of the Masquerading Gunmen," who staged the biggest bank robbery in Oregon history but found that when the masks were down, the prize for the best performance went to the men in police uniforms.

ANNOUNCER: Listen next week, same time, same CBS station to the amazing facts in "The Case of the Masquerading Gunmen" on *Gangbusters*. Tonight's case was dramatized by Stanley Niss and directed by William Sweets with Frank Reddick and Larry Haines in leading roles. Jay Jackson speaking. *Gangbusters* is a Phillips H. Lord production and has been presented by Grape Nuts, the delicious multigrain cereal that gives you nourishment plus. So make Grape Nuts the heart of your B-E-B, the heart of your basic energy breakfast. This is CBS, the Columbia Broadcasting System.

148. Gentleman Adventurer

The story of Alan Drake (James Meighan), owner of a marine and ocean insurance company. Sustaining. Mutual, 1946. Morris Mamorsky composed the theme, "Gentleman Adventurer." John Larkin plays Alan's assistant, Steve Lawlor.

OPEN

THEME MUSIC: Up full then under...

ANNOUNCER (Don Fredericks): Mutual presents *Gentleman Adventurer* starring James Meighan as Alan Drake. The man called Alan Drake is the last of his name. He earns his living in a remarkable way. He's a troubleshooter, an investigator for the ancient company, Drake and Company, insurers of shipping who protect all comers against piracy on the high seas or robbery on the open road anywhere in the world.

THEME MUSIC: Up full then out.

CLOSE

THEME MUSIC: Up full then under...

ANNOUNCER: You have heard a complete episode of *Gentleman Adventurer*, the life of Alan Drake, starring James Meighan in the title role. Featured was John Larkin as Steve Lawlor. The entire program is under the direction of Herbert Rice. Don Fredericks speaking.

THEME MUSIC: Up full then under...

ANNOUNCER: This is the Mutual Broadcasting System.

149. The G.I. Journal

Variety series geared to the armed services. Sustaining. AFRS, 1943–1946.

OPEN

ANNOUNCER (Harry Mitchell): *The G.I. Journal* goes to press.

CHORUS: *G.I. Journal*, it's *The G.I. Journal.*

ANNOUNCER: Yes sir, it's *The G.I. Journal*, your radio newspaper of the air, the paper that prints the jokes and poems sent in by you men overseas. Here is tonight's editor in chief, our guest star, Bob Hope… [Bob would then begin the show with a monologue before introducing skits based on letters and poems.]

CLOSE

ANNOUNCER: *The G.I. Journal* with our guest Bob Hope also featured Mel Blanc and Arthur Q. Bryan. Harry Mitchell speaking. This is the Armed Forces Radio Service.

150. The Goldbergs

Serialized stories about the Goldbergs, a Jewish family living at 1038 Tremont Avenue in the Bronx. Sponsored by Colgate, General Foods, Oxydol and Pepsodent. Blue (1929–1931), NBC (1931–1934), Mutual (1936), CBS (1938–1950). Gertrude Berg played the mother, Molly Goldberg, with James R. Waters as her husband, Jake; Roslyn Siber, as their daughter, Rosalie; and Alfred Ryder and Everett Sloane as their son, Sammy. Basis for the television series. "Serenade" by Toselli was used as the theme.

OPEN

MOLLY: Yoo hoo, is anybody?

ANNOUNCER (Don Hancock): There's Molly folks, that means your friends the Goldbergs are here.

THEME MUSIC: Up full then under…

ANNOUNCER: Procter and Gamble, the makers of the new high-test Oxydol, bring you *The Goldbergs.*

THEME MUSIC: Up full then out.

ANNOUNCER: You know, I heard a woman say she had the best luck imaginable with her wash. Everything turned out just right. I mean all her linens and towels and things as white as snow. And best of all the children's cotton prints and plaids were bright and gay, fresh as a daisy. You don't need luck nowadays to turn out wash like that. You need only Oxydol because Oxydol will give you washes like that every single wash day. You see Oxydol is a new high-test laundry soap, the result of an amazing formula that it whiter washing and yet keeps it safe. And Oxydol is just as safe for your hands too; it doesn't make them all rough and red. But remember, safe as the new high-test Oxydol is, it's whiter washing now than ever before. So ladies, don't count on lady luck for success on wash day, get Oxydol and make sure you'll have dazzling whiter washes that are really safe.

THEME MUSIC: Up full then under…

ANNOUNCER: And now *The Goldbergs.*

CLOSE

THEME MUSIC: Up full then under…

ANNOUNCER: Be sure to listen to the next episode, won't you? And now this is Don Hancock saying goodbye for the makers of high-test Oxydol. Have you heard *The O'Neills* recently? They come to you immediately over this station and we invite you all to listen for this entertaining and exciting story of family life. This is the Columbia Broadcasting System.

THEME MUSIC: Up full then fade out.

151. Granby's Green Acres

Comedy about John Granby, a city dweller who moves to the country to operate a farm. Various sponsors. CBS, 1950. Gale Gordon played John Granby with Bea Benaderet as his wife, Martha; Louise Erickson as their daughter, Janice; and Parley Baer as their handyman, Eb. The song "Old MacDonald Had a Farm" is used as the theme. Served as the basis for the "Green Acres" television series.

OPEN

THEME MUSIC: Up full then under…

ANNOUNCER (Bob Lemond): *Granby's Green Acres* starring Gale Gordon as John Granby.

JOHN (singing): Old John Granby had a farm.

ANNOUNCER: With Bea Benaderet as Martha Granby.

MARTHA (singing): And on that farm he had a wife.

ANNOUNCER: Louise Erickson as Janice.

JANICE (singing): With a daughter here.

ANNOUNCER: Parley Baer as Eb.

EB (singing): And a hired hand there.

JOHN (singing): Old John Granby had a farm.

ANNOUNCER: And now to *Granby's Green Acres.* Today, Mr. Granby plants a crop [this line would vary by episode].

CLOSE

ANNOUNCER: You have just heard *Granby's Green Acres* starring Gale Gordon with Bea Benaderet, Louise Erickson and Parley Baer. Tune in next week when Mr. Granby discovers electricity. *Granby's Green Acres* was written by Jay Sommers and Jack Harvey and was directed by Jay Sommers. Music was composed and conducted by Opie Cates. This is Bob Lemond speaking. Now stay tuned for *Leave It to Joan* which follows immediately on most of these CBS stations. This is CBS, the Columbia Broadcasting System.

152. Grand Central Station

Stories set against the background of New York City. Sponsored by the Campbell Soup Company, Cream of Wheat, Listerine, Rinso, Pillsbury and Toni Home Permanents. Blue (1937–1938; 1940–1941), CBS (1938–1940; 1944–1952), NBC (1941–1942), ABC (1954).

OPEN

ANNOUNCER (Tom Shirley): The Campbell Soup Company, makers of delicious Campbell's Tomato Soup, presents *Grand Central Station.*

SOUND: Train effect (chugging steam locomotive).

ANNOUNCER: As a bullet seeks its target, shining rails in every part of our great country are aimed at Grand Central Station, heart of the nation's greatest city. Drawn by the magnetic force of the fantastic metropolis, day and night great trains rush toward the Hudson River, sweep down its eastern bank for 140 miles, flash briefly by the long row of tenement houses south of 125th Street, dive with a roar into the 2½-mile tunnel which burrows beneath the glitter and swank of Park Avenue and then...

SOUND: Steam escaping from locomotive drivers.

ANNOUNCER: Grand Central Station, crossroads of a million private lives, a gigantic stage on which are played a thousand dramas daily. Grand Central Station. *Grand Central Station* is presented by the Campbell Soup Company.

THEME MUSIC: Up full then out.

ANNOUNCER: If I were to ask each one of you to name aloud right now your favorite soup and if I could hear you reply, I'm almost certain the soup that would top them all would be Campbell's Tomato Soup. The reason of course is the magic matchless flavor of tomato soup as Campbell makes it. A flavor that speaks to every appetite. Watch a hungry man enjoy to the last drop the rich flavor of this smooth blend of luscious tomatoes, delicate seasonings and fine table butter. It's always the happy choice for the main dish at lunch or supper; a welcome beginning for the day's main meal. That's why Campbell's Tomato Soup is the steady favorite of most families; the soup served often and enjoyed always. Have it again soon, won't you. Perhaps tomorrow. And now to *Grand Central Station.*

CLOSE

THEME MUSIC: Up full then under...

ANNOUNCER: The Campbell Soup Company, makers of delicious Campbell's Tomato Soup, has presented this week's episode of *Grand Central Station.* Be with us again next week when Campbell's Tomato Soup will present *Grand Central Station* and another story set against the backdrop of a great metropolis. Tom Shirley speaking. This is CBS, the Columbia Broadcasting System.

THEME MUSIC: Up full then fade out.

153. Grand Marquee

Various stories featuring rotating male leads (Jim Ameche, Olan Soule). Various sponsors. NBC, 1946–1947.

OPEN

THEME MUSIC: Up full then under...

ANNOUNCER (George Stone): The National

Broadcasting Company's *Grand Marquee*. *Grand Marquee*, lighted by stars, twinkling, glowing, blazing with various lights and colors against the sky. The National Broadcasting Company's mammoth billboard announces another exciting evening in the world of make-believe. To greet you and to set the scene for tonight's merriment, here is your *Grand Marquee* star, Jim Ameche.

SOUND: Applause.

JIM: Thank you, thank you, George Stone, and good evening ladies and gentlemen... [Jim would then introduce the audience to the evening's drama.]

CLOSE

THEME MUSIC: Up full then under...

ANNOUNCER: *Grand Marquee* with Jim Ameche as its star is a presentation of the National Broadcasting Company. Music was composed and conducted by Joseph Gallichio. George Stone speaking. Be with us again next week when Olan Soule will be our *Grand Marquee* star.

THEME MUSIC: Up full then out.

ANNOUNCER: This is NBC, the National Broadcasting Company.

SOUND: NBC chimes. N-B-C.

154. The Great Gildersleeve

Comical incidents in the life of Throckmorton P. Gildersleeve, water commissioner of Summerfield, and the bachelor uncle of his niece and nephew, Marjorie and Leroy Forrester. Sponsored by Kraft Foods. NBC, 1941–1957. Harold Peary and Willard Waterman played Gildersleeve with Louise Erickson and Marylee Robb as Marjorie and Walter Tetley as Leroy.

OPEN (original)

ANNOUNCER (Ken Carpenter): The Kraft Foods Company presents Harold Peary as the Great Gildersleeve.

THEME MUSIC: Up full then under...

ANNOUNCER: *The Great Gildersleeve* is brought to you by the Kraft Foods Company, makers of Parkay Margarine.

THEME MUSIC: Up full then out.

ANNOUNCER: Millions of women all over America serve Parkay because it tastes so good and now in many states you can buy this delicious Parkay Margarine in yellow quarter pound sticks. Yes, this same spread that tastes so good now comes in handy quarter pound sticks already colored a rich golden yellow and ready to serve. That's Parkay—P-A-R-K-A-Y—Parkay Margarine, made by Kraft.

THEME MUSIC: Up full then under...

ANNOUNCER: Well, let's see what's going on at the Great Gildersleeve's house on this fine spring morning...

CLOSE (original)

ANNOUNCER: The Kraft Foods Company has presented *The Great Gildersleeve* starring Hal Peary.

THEME MUSIC: Up full then under...

ANNOUNCER: Women all over America are using Parkay Margarine for cooking and as a spread too. Parkay is nutritious and economical too; costs only about half as much as the most expensive spread. Parkay tastes so good. Parkay is the delicious margarine made by Kraft. And remember, in many states you can now buy Parkay Margarine in yellow quarter pound sticks.

THEME MUSIC: Up full then under...

ANNOUNCER: Also in tonight's cast were Louise Erickson as Marjorie and Walter Tetley as Leroy with Lillian Randolph as Birdie. Music is under the direction of Billy Mills. Ken Carpenter speaking. Be with us again next Wednesday evening when the Kraft Foods Company, makers of Parkay Margarine and other fine food products, brings you *The Great Gildersleeve* starring Harold Peary. This is the National Broadcasting Company.

THEME MUSIC: Up full then out.

SOUND: NBC chimes. N-B-C.

OPEN (revised)

ANNOUNCER (Ken Roberts): The Kraft Foods Company presents *The Great Gildersleeve*.

THEME MUSIC: Up full then under...

ANNOUNCER: Yes, it's *The Great Gildersleeve* starring Willard Waterman and brought to you by the Kraft Foods Company, makers of Parkay Margarine and a complete line of quality food products.

THEME MUSIC: Up full then out.

ANNOUNCER: Here's news. You can now get yellow Parkay Margarine in all states where laws permit. Yes Parkay, the same delicious spread with the wonderful flavor, now comes in handy quarter pound sticks, already colored a rich golden yellow. You'll find yellow Parkay costs a little more, largely because of the Federal Coloring Tax, but it's a real saving for you in time and trouble. Try the new yellow Parkay in quarter pound sticks. Remember, where state laws permit, you can get this delicious spread, golden yellow and ready to spread. Of course, you can still buy white Parkay at the low economy price. That's P-A-R-K-A-Y, Parkay Margarine made by Kraft.

THEME MUSIC: Up full then under...

ANNOUNCER: Now let's peep into the world of Summerfield and see what goes on there...

CLOSE (revised)

ANNOUNCER: You'll like the pleasant quick way of making leftovers more delicious. Just add a little Kraft Prepared Mustard and you'll add a lot of tang. Hidden flavors in broiled ham, sausage, most any meat, pop right out, every bite tastes better. Now you can get two kinds of Kraft Mustard: Salad Mustard, delicately spiced for those who prefer a milder flavor, and Kraft Mustard with snappy horseradish added. Have both kinds in your pantry. Then with every meat dish, hot or cold, just add a little mustard and you'll add a lot of tang. Kraft Prepared Mustard.

THEME MUSIC: Up full then under...

ANNOUNCER: You have been listening to Willard Waterman as the Great Gildersleeve. Also in the cast were Marylee Robb as Marjorie and Walter Tetley as Leroy. This is Ken Roberts inviting you to join us next week when the Kraft Foods Company will again present *The Great Gildersleeve*. This is NBC, the National Broadcasting Company.

THEME MUSIC: Up full then out.

SOUND: NBC chimes. N-B-C.

155. The Green Hornet

Crime drama about Britt Reid, owner-pub-

lisher of the *Daily Sentinel*, who avenges crimes as the mysterious Green Hornet. Various sponsors. Local Detroit (1936–1938), Mutual (1938–1939; 1940–1941), Blue (1939–1940; 1942–1944), ABC (1945–1952). Al Hodge, A. Donovan Faust, Robert Hall and Jack McCarthy played Britt Reid. Raymond Hayashi, Rollon Parker and Michael Tolan played his aide, Kato. "Flight of the Bumblebee" by Rimsky-Korsakov was used as the theme.

OPEN

THEME MUSIC: Up full then under...

ANNOUNCER (Bob Hite): *The Green Hornet*.

SOUND: Hornet buzz.

ANNOUNCER: He hunts the biggest of all game, public enemies that even the G-Men cannot reach.

THEME MUSIC: Up full then under...

ANNOUNCER: *The Green Hornet*. With his faithful aide, Kato, Britt Reid, daring young publisher, matches wits with the underworld, risking his life that criminals and racketeers, within the law, may feel its weight by the sting of the Green Hornet.

SOUND: The Hornet's car, the *Black Beauty*, pulling out.

ANNOUNCER: Ride with Britt Reid as he races toward another thrilling adventure as the Green Hornet rides again.

THEME MUSIC: Up full then out.

CLOSE

THEME MUSIC: Up full then under...

ANNOUNCER: The story you have just heard is a copyright feature of the Green Hornet, Incorporated. The events depicted in the drama are fictitious. Any similarity to persons living or dead is purely coincidental. Jack McCarthy is heard as the Green Hornet. This is ABC, the American Broadcasting Company.

THEME MUSIC: Up full then fade out.

156. The Green Lama

Crime drama about Jethro DuMont, a wealthy young American who fights for justice as the mysterious Green Lama. Sustaining. CBS, 1949. Paul Frees plays Jethro DuMont with Ben

Wright as his aide, Toku. Richard Aurandt composed the "Green Lama" theme.

OPEN

THEME MUSIC: Up full then under...

ANNOUNCER: Time now for another exciting adventure from the files of Jethro DuMont. Jethro DuMont, a wealthy young American who, after ten years in Tibet, returned as the Green Lama to amaze the world with his amazing powers in his single-handed fight against injustice and crime. *The Green Lama.*

THEME MUSIC: Up full then out.

CLOSE

THEME MUSIC: Up full then under...

ANNOUNCER: *The Green Lama* stars Paul Frees with Ben Wright as Toku. Music for *The Green Lama* is composed and conducted by Richard Aurandt. Larry Thor speaking. Be with us again next time for another exciting adventure taken from the files of Jethro Du-Mont—*The Green Lama.* This is CBS, the Columbia Broadcasting System.

THEME MUSIC: Up full then fade out.

157. Guest Star

Public service anthology series sponsored by the Treasury Department to promote the sale of U.S. savings bonds. Programs featured guests performing in short dramatic or musical sketches. Syn., 1947–1962.

OPEN

THEME MUSIC: Up full then under...

ANNOUNCER (Jeff Barker): The United States Savings Bond Division presents *Guest Star.* How do you do, ladies and gentlemen? This is Jeff Barker greeting you on behalf of *Guest Star,* the transcribed feature program brought to you by this station and the United States savings bond as a public service. With it we bring you this message—a secure future for yourself and your family is yours if you save for it through the regular purchase of United States savings bonds. [The guest would then be introduced.]

CLOSE

THEME MUSIC: Up full then under...

ANNOUNCER: You have been listening to *Guest Star,* a transcribed feature program brought to you by this station each week at this time as a public service. For yourself, for your family's future, buy United States savings bonds. The Savings Bond Orchestra was under the direction of David Rose. Jeff Barker speaking. Join us again next week when we'll have another fine star on our program.

THEME MUSIC: Up full then fade out.

158. Gunsmoke

Western about Matt Dillon, marshal of Dodge City, Kansas. Various sponsors (Chesterfield and L&M Cigarettes and Post Cereals were frequent sponsors). CBS, 1952–1961. William Conrad played Matt Dillon with Parley Baer as Deputy Chester Proudfoot, Georgia Ellis as Long Branch Saloon owner Kitty Russell and Howard McNear as Doc Adams. Rex Koury composed the theme, "The Old Trail." Basis for the television series.

OPEN

SOUND: Horse galloping followed by a gunshot.

ANNOUNCER (George Walsh): *Gunsmoke,* brought to you by L&M Filters. This is it, L&M is best, stands out from all the rest.

THEME MUSIC: Up full then under...

ANNOUNCER: Around Dodge City and the territory out west, there is just one way to handle the killers and the spoilers and that is with the U.S. marshal and the smell of gunsmoke.

THEME MUSIC: Up full then under...

ANNOUNCER: *Gunsmoke,* starring William Conrad, the transcribed story of the violence that moved west with young America, and the story of a man who moved with it.

MATT: I'm that man, Matt Dillon, United States marshal, the first man they look for and the last they want to meet. It's a chancy job and it makes a man watchful and a little lonely.

THEME MUSIC: Up full then out.

L&M JINGLE MUSIC: Up full then under...

GIRL VOCALIST: This is it, L&M Filters.

MALE VOCALIST: It stands out from all the rest.

TOGETHER: Miracle tip, much more flavor.

GIRL (speaking): L&M's got everything.

TOGETHER (singing): It's the best.

ANNOUNCER: Yes, L&M is best, stands out from all the rest.

GIRL: The miracle tip draws easy. You'll enjoy all the taste.

ANNOUNCER: Light and mild, America's best filter-tip cigarette.

THEME MUSIC: Up full then under…

ANNOUNCER: And now *Gunsmoke* with William Conrad as Matt Dillon.

CLOSE

ANNOUNCER: And now our star, William Conrad.

CONRAD: Thank you, George. You filter tip smokers. When you change to L&M filters, the first thing you'll notice is how mild they are, how easy they draw. Yes, L&M's pure white miracle tip lets you enjoy all the taste; no filter compares with it for quality or effectiveness. Try L&Ms right now. They're great.

ANNOUNCER: *Gunsmoke*, produced and directed by Norman MacDonnell, stars William Conrad as Matt Dillon, U.S. marshal. Parley Baer is Chester, Howard McNear is Doc and Georgia Ellis is Kitty.

SONG: Chesterfield Jingle.

CHORUS:

> Stop, start smoking with a smile
> With Chesterfield.
> Smiling all the while
> With Chesterfield.
> For the smile in your smoking,
> Just give 'em a try,
> Light up a Chesterfield, they satisfy.

ANNOUNCER: Put a smile in your smoking, buy Chesterfield. So smooth, so satisfying. Chesterfield. You'll also enjoy Chesterfield's great radio shows—Perry Como sings all the top tunes on CBS radio every Monday, Wednesday and Friday; Jack Webb stars in *Dragnet* on Tuesday nights—check your local listings. Remember, listen again next week for another transcribed story of the Western frontier when Matt Dillon, Chester Proudfoot, Doc and Kitty, together with all the other hard-living citizens of Dodge, will be with you once more; it's America growing West in the 1870s. It's drama, it's *Gunsmoke*, brought to you by L&M Filters. This is CBS, the Columbia Broadcasting System.

159. The Hall of Fantasy

Stories of the supernatural hosted by Richard Thorne. Sustaining. Mutual, 1952–1953.

OPEN

ANNOUNCER: *The Hall of Fantasy.*

THEME MUSIC: Up full then under…

HOST: Welcome to *The Hall of Fantasy.* Welcome to this series of radio dramas dedicated to the supernatural, the unusual and the unknown. Come with me, my friends, we shall descend to the world of the unknown and forbidden, down to the depths where the veil of time is lifted and the supernatural reigns as king. Come with me and listen to the tale of "The Shadow People."

THEME MUSIC: Up full then out.

CLOSE

THEME MUSIC: Up full then under…

ANNOUNCER: Tonight's story, "The Shadow People," was written and directed by Richard Thorne. Be with us next week same time, same station, when we descend to the world of the unknown and forbidden in *The Hall of Fantasy*. This is the Mutual Broadcasting System.

THEME MUSIC: Up full then fade out.

160. The Halls of Ivy

Comedy about the faculty and students of mythical Ivy College in Ivy, U.S.A. Various sponsors. NBC, 1950–1952. Ronald Colman played college president Dr. William Todhunter Hall with Benita Hume as his wife, Victoria. The song "The Halls of Ivy" was used as the theme.

OPEN

THEME MUSIC: Up full then under…

ANNOUNCER (Ken Niles): Ladies and gentlemen, the Joseph Schlitz Brewing Company of Milwaukee, Wisconsin, presents *The Halls of Ivy* starring Mr. and Mrs. Ronald Colman.

RONALD: Good evening, this is Ronald Colman inviting you to join Mrs. Colman and me for the next half-hour.

VOICE: I was curious. I tasted it. Now I know why Schlitz is the beer that made Milwaukee famous.

ANNOUNCER: If you like good beer, you'll find it pays to be curious and learn about Schlitz for yourself. Schlitz, the beer that made Milwaukee famous.

THEME MUSIC: Up full then under…

CHORUS:
> Oh, we love the Halls of Ivy
> That surround us here today.
> And we will not forget
> Though we be far, far away.

ANNOUNCER: Welcome again to Ivy, Ivy College that is, in the town of Ivy, U.S.A. Ivy College is co-educational and nonsectarian and its age is indicated by the fact that until recently, the curriculum required two years of Greek. Ivy is all-American; its student body is a pretty fair cross section of the country's youthful seekers of knowledge. Dr. William Todhunter Hall, Ph.D., LL.D. and M.A. is president of Ivy. He lives on campus at number one Faculty Row with his wife, Victoria, a former showgirl of the British stage. And now, *The Halls of Ivy*.

CLOSE

VOICE: I was curious. I tasted it. Now I know why Schlitz is the beer that made Milwaukee famous.

ANNOUNCER: If you like good beer, you'll find it pays to be curious and learn about Schlitz for yourself. Schlitz, the beer that made Milwaukee famous.

THEME MUSIC: Up full then under…

ANNOUNCER: We'll be seeing you next week at this same time at *The Halls of Ivy* starring Mr. and Mrs. Ronald Colman. *The Halls of Ivy* was created by Don Quinn with music composed and conducted by Henry Russell and was presented by the Joseph Schlitz Brewing Company of Milwaukee, Wisconsin.

CHORUS:
> Oh, we love the Halls of Ivy
> That surround us here today.
> And we will not forget
> Though we be far, far away.

ANNOUNCER: This is NBC, the National Broadcasting Company.

SOUND: NBC chimes. N-B-C.

161. Hannibal Cobb

Daily crime drama about a private detective who takes a personal interest in his clients. Sustaining. ABC, 1950–1951. Santos Ortega plays Hannibal Cobb.

OPEN

THEME MUSIC: Up full then under…

ANNOUNCER (Les Griffith): *Hannibal Cobb* starring Santos Ortega. Each weekday at this time, the American Broadcasting Company brings you *Hannibal Cobb* as you'll find him in the "Photocrime" pages of *Look* magazine. And now, a dramatic story of human conflict told from the point of view of the client, rather than the detective.

THEME MUSIC: Up full then out.

CLOSE

THEME MUSIC: Up full then under…

ANNOUNCER: Be sure to be with us each weekday at this same time when *Hannibal Cobb* will bring you another exciting story of human conflict. Santos Ortega starred as Hannibal Cobb; Rosa Rio is heard at the organ. Les Griffith speaking. This is ABC, the American Broadcasting Company.

THEME MUSIC: Up full then fade out.

162. Happy Island

Variety series with Ed Wynn as King Bubbles, ruler of an island filled with music, songs and comedy. Sponsored by Borden Milk. ABC, 1944–1945.

OPEN

THEME MUSIC: Up full then under…

ANNOUNCER (Paul Masterson): Borden Milk welcomes everybody to *Happy Island* with Ed Wynn as King Bubbles, the song stylings of Evelyn Knight and Jerry Wayne, the music of Mark Warnow and his orchestra, and yours truly, Paul Masterson. And here he is for Borden Milk, the hilarious majesty of Happy Island, Ed Wynn as King Bubbles.

SOUND: Applause... [Ed would begin the show with an exchange of jokes with the announcer.]

CLOSE

ANNOUNCER: Borden Milk has presented *Happy Island* with Ed Wynn as King Bubbles, the song stylings of Jerry Wayne and Evelyn Knight, the music of Mark Warnow and his orchestra and featuring Lorna Lynn as Beulah, the King's niece. Paul Masterson speaking. This is the American Broadcasting Company.

163. The Hardy Family

Adaptation of the motion picture series about Andy Hardy, the mischievous son of Judge James Hardy. Sustaining. Mutual, 1952–1953. Mickey Rooney played Andy Hardy with Lewis Stone as Judge Hardy and Fay Holden as Andy's mother, Emily.

OPEN

THEME MUSIC: Up full then under...

ANNOUNCER (Jack McCoy): From Hollywood, here's Mickey Rooney, Lewis Stone and Fay Holden, *The Hardy Family*. We're proud to present *The Hardy Family* based on the famous Metro-Goldwyn-Mayer motion picture series, which brought to life to millions and reflected the common joys and tribulations of the average American family. And now, here they are, the same great stars in the parts they created on the screen, Lewis Stone, Mickey Rooney and Fay Holden, *The Hardy Family*.

THEME MUSIC: Up full then out.

CLOSE

THEME MUSIC: Up full then under...

ANNOUNCER: *The Hardy Family* starring Lewis Stone, Mickey Rooney and Fay Holden is presented by arrangement with Metro-Goldwyn-Mayer, producers of *Malaya* starring Spencer Tracy, James Stewart, Valentina Cortesa, Sydney Greenstreet and John Hodiak. This program was written by Jameson Brewer, direction is by Joel Bigelow. Original music was composed and conducted by Jerry Fielding. Jack McCoy speaking.

THEME MUSIC: Up full then fade out.

164. The Harold Peary Show—Honest Harold

Comical incidents in the life of Harold Hemp, host of a radio program called "The Homemaker." Sustaining. CBS, 1950–1951. Harold Peary played Harold Hemp with Jane Morgan and Kathryn Card as his mother, Emily; Sammy Ogg as his nephew, Marvin; Gloria Holiday as Gloria, the station switchboard operator; and Joseph Kearns as Hal's friend, Dr. Yak Yak.

OPEN

THEME MUSIC: Up full then under...

ANNOUNCER (Bob Lemond): *The Harold Peary Show*. And now Harold Peary as Honest Harold, the homemaker. Harold Hemp, known as Honest Harold, hosts "The Homemaker" radio program in Melrose Springs. He sings, tells jokes and offers advice. Let's join Harold as his honesty sometimes does more harm than good.

THEME MUSIC: Up full then out.

CLOSE

THEME MUSIC: Up full then under...

ANNOUNCER: You have just heard *The Harold Peary Show—Honest Harold* with Harold Peary as Honest Harold Hemp. Also in the cast were Jane Morgan as Mrs. Hemp, Sammy Ogg as Melvin, Gloria Holliday as Gloria and Joseph Kearns as Dr. Yak Yak. Original music is composed and conducted by Jack Meakin. Bob Lemond speaking. This is CBS, the Columbia Broadcasting System.

THEME MUSIC: Up full then fade out.

165. Hashknife Hartley and Sleepy Stevens

Western adventures with roaming cowboys Hashknife Hartley (Frank Martin) and Sleepy Stevens (Barton Yarborough). Sustaining. Mutual, 1950–1951.

OPEN

THEME MUSIC: Up full then under...

ANNOUNCER (Don McCall): This is W.C. Tuttle's famous adventure story of *Hashknife Hartley and Sleepy Stevens* starring Frank Martin as Hashknife Hartley and Barton Yarborough as Sleepy Stevens. Here now is the creator of these rough and tumble cowboys, W.C. Tuttle himself, ready to begin today's story called "Range War."

TUTTLE: Howdy, folks. Hashknife Hartley and Sleepy Stevens are riding through the fertile delta basin on their way to Clarkdale. At the south end of the basin they come across a half-completed cabin on the bank of the river... [The story follows their efforts to prevent a range war between ranchers and cattlemen.]

CLOSE

ANNOUNCER: W.C. Tuttle's famous adventures of *Hashknife Hartley and Sleepy Stevens* will be on the air again next week at this same time. Be sure to be with us. This is Mutual.

166. The Harry Richman Show

Variety series sponsored by Florida Treat. Syndicated, 1937.

OPEN

ANNOUNCER: It's Florida Treat. The state of Florida invites you to join the transatlantic troubadour Harry Richman, Freddie Rich and his orchestra, and those foolish fun makers the Sisters of the Skillet in fifteen minutes of entertainment.

CLOSE

ANNOUNCER: Florida Treat has presented Harry Richman, that transatlantic troubadour in fifteen minutes of music and laughter. The state of Florida invites you to be with us again next week at this same time, same station.

167. Have Gun—Will Travel

Western about a debonair, professional gunman for hire who goes by the name of Paladin. Various sponsors. CBS, 1958–1960. Based on the television series. John Dehner plays Paladin with Ben Wright as Hey Boy, his servant at the Hotel Carlton.

OPEN

CHORUS:
Why don't you live modern,
Live modern, live, live modern,
Change to L&M.

ANNOUNCER: L&M, the modern cigarette with the pure white miracle tip filter, presents *Have Gun—Will Travel.*

THEME MUSIC: Up full then under...

ANNOUNCER: *Have Gun—Will Travel* starring Mr. John Dehner as Paladin.

THEME MUSIC: Up full then under...

ANNOUNCER: San Francisco, 1875, the Hotel Carlton, headquarters of the man called Paladin.

THEME MUSIC: Up full then under... (as the episode begins.)

CLOSE

CHORUS:
Why don't you live modern,
Live modern, live, live modern,
Change to L&M.

ANNOUNCER: Yes, have an L&M and enjoy a really modern cigarette, a cigarette that gives you the full, exciting flavor of today's finest tobaccos. No other cigarette, plain or filter, gives you the flavor you get through the modern miracle of the L&M miracle tip. Through the pure white tip L&M tastes richer, smokes cleaner, draws easier. So light up, free up, let your taste come alive. Live modern, smoke L&M today.

CHORUS:

> Make today your day
> Your big red letter day
> And start to live the modern way.
> Live, live, live modern,
> Get L&M today.

THEME MUSIC: Up full then under...

ANNOUNCER: *Have Gun—Will Travel*, created by Herb Meadow and Sam Rolfe, is produced by Norman MacDonnell and stars John Dehner as Paladin. Ben Wright is heard as Hey Boy with Virginia Gregg as Miss Wong. This is Hugh Douglas inviting you to join us again next week when L&M will present more *Have Gun—Will Travel*.

THEME MUSIC: Up full then out.

ANNOUNCER: This is CBS, the Columbia Broadcasting System.

168. Hawk Larabee

Western about Texas cattleman then wanderer Hawk Larabee. Sustaining. CBS. 1946–1948. The original concept found Hawk Larabee (Elliott Lewis) as the owner of the thousand acre Flying H Ranch in Black Mesa. Brazos John (Barton Yarborough) assisted him and he rode a horse named Flame. In the revised version, Hawk Larabee (Barton Yarborough) left his old stomping grounds in Sunset Wells to travel west (and help people in trouble). Hawk called himself a "Fiddlefoot" ("A guy who can't stay put and is always bumping into trouble") and was accompanied by Sombre Jones (Barney Phillips), a former marshal (of Mulberry Creek) who was mournful about everything. The series was originally called *Hawk Durango*.

OPEN (Elliott Lewis)

SOUND: A whistle.

ANNOUNCER: The hawk is on the wing.

SOUND: Horse galloping followed by a whistle.

CHORUS:

> Come along folks and listen for a spell
> Here's Hawk Larabee with a tale to tell.

ANNOUNCER: The hawk's whistle signals another exciting episode in the story of *Hawk Larabee*. Starring Elliott Lewis with Barton Yarborough and the Plainsmen and produced and

directed by William N. Robson. Yes, the hawk is on the wing and Hawk Larabee's riding high in the saddle.

CHORUS:

> We're in for excitement
> So why don't you stay,
> This Larabee fellow has plenty to say.

ANNOUNCER: And now another exciting story of *Hawk Larabee*.

CLOSE

ANNOUNCER: Each week at this time we invite you to ride into the West with *Hawk Larabee* starring Elliott Lewis with Barton Yarborough. Produced and directed by William N. Robson with vocal interludes by Andy Parker and the Plainsmen. Next week at this same time *Hawk Larabee* rides your way with another exciting adventure. So be with us next week when—

SOUND: A whistle.

ANNOUNCER: The hawk is on the wing.

CHORUS:

> The hawk is on the wing
> And headin' your way
> With another great story
> Just a week from today.

ANNOUNCER: This is CBS, the Columbia Broadcasting System.

OPEN (Barton Yarborough)

CHORUS:

> Come along folks and listen to the tale
> Of Hawk Larabee on the western trail.

HAWK: Larabee's the name, Hawk Larabee.

CHORUS:

> He rode every trail
> Across the lone prairie
> As sure as his name's Hawk Larabee.

ANNOUNCER (Jack McCoy): Yes, it's *Hawk Larabee* starring Barton Yarborough with his exciting stories of the timeless West. Stories of men and women, famous and infamous, who loved and hated, lived and died in the colorful drama of the American West. Stories chronicled for you by *Hawk Larabee*.

CLOSE

CHORUS:

> Hawk Larabee gained more renown

As he rode the trail
From town to town.
Until next week,
That's the end of the tale of
Hawk Larabee on the western trail.
ANNOUNCER: This is Jack McCoy saying tune in again next week at this very same time for *Hawk Larabee*. This is CBS, the Columbia Broadcasting System.

169. Hearthstone of the Death Squad

Crime drama about a brilliant inspector with the Death Squad Division of Scotland Yard. Sustaining. CBS, 1951–1952. Alfred Shirley played Inspector Hearthstone.

OPEN

ANNOUNCER (Harry Cramer): And now, *Hearthstone of the Death Squad* with Alfred Shirley as the brilliant Inspector Hearthstone.
THEME MUSIC: Up full then under...
ANNOUNCER: Tonight we again present the famous Hearthstone of the Death Squad, implacable manhunter of the Metropolitan Police Department in London.
THEME MUSIC: Up full then out.

CLOSE

ANNOUNCER: And thus, Hearthstone of the Death Squad writes "solved" in the files of his latest case. The part of Inspector Hearthstone was played by Alfred Shirley. *Hearthstone of the Death Squad* is written by Frank Hummert, directed by Henry Howard and is a presentation of CBS Radio.
THEME MUSIC: Up full then under...
ANNOUNCER: Your announcer is Harry Cramer. Remember *Hollywood Sound Stage* brings you top film stars and top drama Thursday on the CBS Radio Network.
THEME MUSIC: Up full then fade out.

170. A Helping Hand

Dramatizations of real life problems cou-

pled with advice on how to solve the problem presented in a vignette. Sponsored by Ironized Yeast Tablets. CBS, 1941–1942. John J. Anthony served as the host.

OPEN

ANNOUNCER (Don Hancock): The makers of Ironized Yeast presents *A Helping Hand*.
THEME MUSIC: Up full then under...
ANNOUNCER: *A Helping Hand* is a new program dedicated to public service and conducted by John J. Anthony, nationally famous counselor on human problems, author of the well-known book *Marriage and Family Problems and How to Solve Them*, and founder of the Marital Relations Institute. And now, here is Mr. Anthony... [He would then begin the program with a dramatized problem.]

CLOSE

ANNOUNCER: It's strange but it's true. A person can get so tired he can't work well, he can't even get any fun out of life. Now, if you're that tired and pale, your doctor may find you have a borderline anemia resulting from a nutritional blood deficiency. If so, take Ironized Yeast Tablets. Ironized Yeast Tablets help increase your strength, regain your color by building up red blood cells. So take Ironized Yeast Tablets to get the energy you need to work, to play, to think. Ironized Yeast Tablets.
THEME MUSIC: Up full then under...
ANNOUNCER: The makers of Ironized Yeast Tablets have presented *A Helping Hand* with John J. Anthony, nationally known counselor on human problems. Be with us again tomorrow for another *Helping Hand*. Elsie Thompson is heard at the organ; Don Hancock speaking. This is the Columbia Broadcasting System.
THEME MUSIC: Up full then fade out.

171. The Henry Morgan Show

Variety series coupling music and songs with skits and jokes. Sponsored by Adler Elevator Shoes, Bristol Meyers, Camel Cigarettes, Eversharp Razor Blades, Ironized Yeast, Lifebuoy Soap, Pall Mall Cigarettes, Shell Gasoline. Local N.Y./Mutual (1940–1945), ABC (1945– 1948), NBC (1949–1950). Also titled *Here's Morgan*.

OPEN (*Here's Morgan*)

THEME MUSIC ("For He's a Jolly Good Fellow"): Up full then under...
HENRY: Good evening, anybody.
ANNOUNCER: *Here's Morgan*.

CLOSE (*Here's Morgan*)

HENRY: Morgan'll be on this same corner in front of the cigar store next week at this same time. Good night everybody.

OPEN (*The Henry Morgan Show*)

THEME MUSIC ("For He's a Jolly Good Fellow"): Up full then under...
ANNOUNCER (Ed Herlihy): *The Henry Morgan Show*. Yes, *The Henry Morgan Show* with Arnold Stang, Pert Kelton, Art Carney, Milton Katims and the orchestra, the Billy Williams Quartet and Ed Herlihy. And here's the star of *The Henry Morgan Show*, standing on his favorite corner in front of the cigar store.
HENRY: Good evening, anybody. Here's Morgan.

CLOSE (*The Henry Morgan Show*)

ANNOUNCER: Morgan himself will be back on this corner in front of the cigar store next week at this same time. This is Ed Herlihy. Good night everybody.

172. Here Comes McBride

Crime drama about Rex McBride (Frank Lovejoy), a Los Angeles-based private insurance investigator. Sustaining. NBC, 1949.

OPEN

THEME MUSIC ("Here Comes the Bride"): Up full then under...
SOUND: Gunshots.

ANNOUNCER (Art Ballinger): *Here Comes McBride*! Out of the pages of Cleave F. Adams' popular novels, NBC presents an exciting new detective series, *Here Comes McBride* starring Frank Lovejoy as Rex McBride, free-lance private investigator.
THEME MUSIC: Up full then out.

CLOSE

THEME MUSIC: Up full then under...
ANNOUNCER: You have been listening to *Here Comes McBride* starring Frank Lovejoy and based on the popular fiction character created by Cleave F. Adams. This is NBC, the National Broadcasting Company.
SOUND: NBC chimes. N-B-C.

173. The Hermit's Cave

Tales of horror and suspense as told by the Hermit, a character who lives in a cave and warns people with weak hearts not to listen. Sustaining. Syn., 1940–1943. Mel Johnson played the Hermit.

OPEN

THEME MUSIC: Up full then under...
ANNOUNCER: And now the Hermit.
SOUND: Howling dogs, crackling wind.
HERMIT: Hee, hee, hee, hee, hee, hee. Ghost stories, weird stories, murder too. Hee, hee, hee, hee. The Hermit knows of them all. Turn out your lights, turn them out. Ahhhhh, have you heard the story "The Blackness of Terror?" Hmmmmmmmmm? Then listen while the Hermit tells you the story. Hee, hee, hee, hee.

CLOSE

HERMIT: Turn on your lights, turn them on. Hee, hee, hee, hee. I'll be back next week, until then, pleasant dreams. Hee, hee, hee, hee.
ANNOUNCER: All characters, places and occurrences mentioned in *The Hermit's Cave* are fictitious and similarities to persons, places or occurrences are purely coincidental.
THEME MUSIC: Up full then fade out.

174. The Hinds Honey and Almond Creme Program

Variety (music, songs, jokes) with hosts George Burns and Gracie Allen. Sponsored by Hinds Honey and Almond Hand Creme. CBS, 1939–1940. In 1940, comedienne Gracie Allen ran for the presidency of the United States. She campaigned on this series as well as on other comedy and variety programs. Circulating programs in this series reflect that campaign. The following information comes from the episode of March 13, 1940.

OPEN

ANNOUNCER (Truman Bradley): Hello-lotion my friends, *The Hinds Honey and Almond Creme Program.*

CHORUS:
> Vote for Gracie, vote for Gracie,
> Vote for Gracie, vote for Gra-ceee.

ANNOUNCER: Starring George Burns and Gracie Allen with Frank Parker, Ray Noble and his orchestra and Truman Bradley speaking.

CHORUS:
> A hundred million strong
> That's why you can't go wrong,
> Vote for Gracie
> Keep voting all day long.

ANNOUNCER: Presenting our presidential candidate who just flew back from Washington where she was the honored guest at the Women's National Press Club's annual dinner, Hinds Honey, Gracie Allen.

SOUND: Applause.

GRACIE: Thank you very much.

ANNOUNCER: And now her partner, who just got back from the opening of a meat market, George Burns... [Applause would follow with George and Gracie exchanging dialogue.]

CLOSE

ANNOUNCER: Wash day is certainly hard on your hands. Harsh cleansers and hard water and raw wind when you're hanging clothes on the line certainly make your skin look red and chapped. So for real comfort, keep a bottle of Hinds Honey and Almond Creme near your washtub. Smooth Hinds all over your hands, arms and wrists before you start and the minute you finish washing. Right away, good creamy Hinds smoothes your tender skin. Remember Hinds, H-I-N-D-S, and use it faithfully for softer, prettier hands.

GRACIE: George wants me to do my campaign song again on account he sings the chorus in it.

CAMPAIGN MUSIC: Up full then under...

GRACIE (singing):
> Vote for Gracie,
> Vote for Gracie,
> She's the best little
> Skipper in the land.
> Vote for Gracie,
> Vote for Gracie,
> Won't you please
> Give this little girl a hand.
> Even big politicians
> Don't know what to do,
> Gracie doesn't know what to do
> But neither do you.
> So vote for Gracie
> To win the presidential race.
> A hundred million strong,
> That's why you can't go wrong.
> Vote for Gracie,
> Keep voting all day long.

CAMPAIGN MUSIC: Under...

ANNOUNCER: Would you like a copy of Gracie's campaign song, "Vote for Gracie?" Yes, I mean the actual sheet music complete with lyrics and verses? Well, here's how you can get a copy of this song. Just write your name and address on the back of a Hinds Honey and Almond Creme carton, the twenty-five, fifty cent or dollar size carton, or two ten cent sized cartons and mail it to Gracie Allen, Hollywood, California. That's all. And in a few days you'll receive your copy of Gracie's campaign song, "Vote for Gracie." Oh, I almost forgot. This sheet music has a swell picture of Gracie on the cover too, which shows how sweet and lovable Gracie really is in person. Get a bottle of Hinds tonight and use it for softer, smoother hands.

GEORGE: Well Gracie, say good night.

GRACIE: Good night. And when I'm in the White House you're all invited to come and have tea with me. But don't forget to bring your own lemons as I'm cutting down on the budget you know.

GEORGE: Good night.

ANNOUNCER: Have you tried the new hand cream in jars made by the makers of the famous Hinds Honey and Almond Creme? Just like the creamy Hinds that you know so well. The new Hinds hand cream is a quick softener for rough hands. It's fragrant too and not a bit sticky; it makes hands lovely.

CAMPAIGN MUSIC: Up full then under...

ANNOUNCER: Next Wednesday at this same time over these same stations, George and Gracie and all of the rest of us will be back again and don't forget for honeymoon hands, it's Hinds Honey and Almond Creme. This is the Columbia Broadcasting System.

CAMPAIGN MUSIC: Up full then fade out.

175. His Honor, the Barber

Comical incidents in the life of Bernard Fitz (Barry Fitzgerald) barber and judge in the small town of Vincent County, Colorado. Sponsored by Ballantine Ale. NBC, 1945–1946.

OPEN

THEME MUSIC: Up full then under...

VOICE: District Court Number One in the court house of Vincent County on the twenty-seventh day of November 1945 is convened. Judge Bernard Fitz presiding.

ANNOUNCER (Frank Martin): Ballantine, America's largest-selling ale, presents Barry Fitzgerald starring in *His Honor, the Barber*, written and produced by Carlton E. Morse.

THEME MUSIC: Up full then out.

ANNOUNCER: On the street, a striped pole means a barbershop as Judge Fitz would be the first to tell you. Further, a marquee over the sidewalk is a symbol for the theater, the movies. And another symbol that means pleasure ahead is famous for wherever folks get thirsty—it's the Three Ring symbols for Ballantine Ale, largest-selling ale in America. One ring means purity; one ring means body; one ring means Ballantine flavor. Put together the three rings and it means complete ale satisfaction. Millions will tell you it's the best ale man can make or money can buy. Always ask for Ballantine, America's largest-selling ale.

THEME MUSIC: Up full then under...

ANNOUNCER: And now to our story.

CLOSE

ANNOUNCER: Ballantine Ale, America's favorite, is a grand tradition to any good meal, the table-mate to any sandwich and a beautiful death to the worst of thirsts. That's three times to enjoy the three ring beverage, America's largest-selling ale. Ask for it. Ballantine.

THEME MUSIC: Up full then under...

ANNOUNCER: *His Honor, the Barber*, written and directed by Carlton E. Morse, stars Barry Fitzgerald. *His Honor, the Barber* is presented by Ballantine Ale. Orchestra and music under the direction of Opie Cates. This is Frank Martin speaking. This is the National Broadcasting Company.

SOUND: NBC chimes. N-B-C.

176. Hobby Lobby

Human interest series that spotlighted people who came to lobby their hobbies. Various sponsors. CBS (1937–1938; 1939–1946), NBC (1938–1939), Mutual (1949). Dave Elman served as the host.

OPEN

SOUND: Phone ringing.

VOICE (after picking up receiver): Who? *Hobby Lobby*? It's for you, ladies and gentlemen, it's for you.

ANNOUNCER: *Hobby Lobby*, conducted by the dean of hobbyists, the originator of *Hobby Lobby*, Dave Elman.

DAVE: Thank you Ted Brown and greetings friends, welcome to *Hobby Lobby*.

CLOSE

ANNOUNCER: *Hobby Lobby* with the dean of hobbyists, Dave Elman, can be heard again next week at this same time. This is Ted Brown bidding you a good evening. This is CBS, the Columbia Broadcasting System.

177. Hogan's Daughter

Comedy about Phyllis Hogan (Shirley

Booth), a young woman trying to find her place in life. Sponsored by Philip Morris cigarettes and Revelation Pipe Tobacco. NBC, 1949. Philip Morris was represented by Johnny the Bellboy.

OPEN

SPONSOR'S THEME ("On the Trail"): Up full then under...

ANNOUNCER (Ken Roberts): Philip Morris presents *Hogan's Daughter* starring Shirley Booth.

SPOKESMAN (Johnny Roventini): Call for Philip Mor-rees, call for Philip Mor-rees.

ANNOUNCER: It's a wonderful, wonderful feeling to wake up fresh with no cigarette hangover. Yes, you'll be glad tomorrow when you smoke Philip Morris today.

JOHNNY: Call for Philip Mor-rees.

HOGAN'S DAUGHTER THEME: Up full then under...

ANNOUNCER: And now for our weekly visit with *Hogan's Daughter* starring Shirley Booth as Phyllis, with Howard Smith and Betty Garde as her parents, Tom and Kate.

THEME MUSIC: Up full then out.

CLOSE

ANNOUNCER: Listen again next week for *Hogan's Daughter*. Until then—

JOHNNY: Call for Philip Mor-rees.

ANNOUNCER: Friends, remember this. If you're tired of cigarette hangover, call for the one cigarette that gives you a milder, fresher, cleaner smoke. Yes, from now on—

JOHNNY: Call for Philip Mor-rees.

SPONSOR'S THEME: Up full then under...

ANNOUNCER: Good night, Johnny, see you next Tuesday, same time, same station when Philip Morris will again present Shirley Booth as *Hogan's Daughter*. Until then—

JOHNNY: Call for Philip Mor-rees.

ANNOUNCER: Smoke a pipe? You get real solace, comfort and pleasure from Revelation Pipe Tobacco, plus smooth burning, plus what a swell aroma. This Revelation Pipe Tobacco is a revelation in pleasure. Only 15 cents. Try Revelation.

SPONSOR'S THEME: Up full then under...

ANNOUNCER: All names used in this program are fictitious. Any similarity to persons living or dead is purely coincidental. This is Ken Roberts saying good night for Philip Morris. This is NBC, the National Broadcasting Company.

SPONSOR'S THEME: Up full then out.

SOUND: NBC chimes. N-B-C.

178. Honeymoon in New York

Daily variety series that saluted honeymooners. Various sponsors. NBC, 1945–1947. Hosted by Durward Kirby and Ed Herlihy.

OPEN

THEME MUSIC: Up full then under...

ANNOUNCER (Wayne Howell): Hold hands and hearts for a happy *Honeymoon in New York*. Here it is Wednesday again and time for your midweek mixture of mirth and matrimony as Ed Herlihy leads honeymooners around the nation on a thrill-filled NBC *Honeymoon in New York*. We're all here and waiting for you and to find us, all you have to do is follow the Lover's Lane that leads to your honeymoon host; here he is, you found him, big Ed Herlihy.

ED: Thank you Wayne, and a happy Wednesday morning everybody, everywhere...

CLOSE

THEME MUSIC: Up full then under...

ED: We'll be back bright and early tomorrow morning, neighbors, when another *Honeymoon in New York* will be at your doorstep; so come around will ya? This is Ed Herlihy wishing you the top of the morning from the bottom of my heart. Goodbye.

ANNOUNCER: this is NBC, the National Broadcasting Company.

SOUND: NBC chimes. N-B-C.

Note: Ed Herlihy became the host in 1947 with Eve Young as the vocalist. Durward Kirby was the original host and Joy Hodges was the vocalist. Programs with these performers are not in circulation.

179. Hop Harrigan

Aviation adventure about Hop Harrigan, a daring air ace. Various sponsors. Blue/ABC

(1942–1945), Mutual (1946–1948). Chester Stratton, Albert Aley and Matt Crowley played Hop Harrigan.

OPEN

ANNOUNCER (Glenn Riggs): Presenting *Hop Harrigan*, America's ace of the airwaves.

SOUND: Airplane in flight.

HOP: CX-4 calling control tower. CX-4 calling control tower. Standing by. Okay, this is Hop Harrigan coming in.

ANNOUNCER: Yes, it's America's ace of the airwaves coming in for another transcribed episode in the adventures of *Hop Harrigan*.

CLOSE

ANNOUNCER: You have been listening to another transcribed episode in the adventures of *Hop Harrigan*, America's ace of the airwaves. Chester Stratton is heard in the title role. Be sure to be with us again tomorrow, same time, same station when *Hop Harrigan* returns to the airwaves. This is the Blue Network.

180. Hopalong Cassidy

Western about Hopalong Cassidy (William Boyd), foreman of the Bar 20 Ranch in Arizona. Various sponsors. Mutual (1950), CBS (1950–1952).

OPEN (original)

ANNOUNCER (Bob Moon): From Hollywood, California, the Columbia Broadcasting System presents *Hopalong Cassidy*, the great western character created by Clarence E. Mulford and brought to the screen for Paramount Pictures by Harry Sherman.

SOUND: Horse trotting.

CHORUS:
> Hear that rovin' cowboy
> Ridin' down
> That lonesome trail.

ANNOUNCER: A rovin' cowboy like a knight riding out of the West. A lone figure gallops through the prairies and mountains of the land he loves, lending a hand to those who need him, solving problems in his own way.

The greatest cowboy in fact or fancy, the foreman of the Bar 20 Ranch.

SOUND: Horse galloping.

ANNOUNCER: Here he comes, Hopalong Cassidy. Hopalong Cassidy, everywhere in the West that name is feared by law breakers; wherever there is trouble, Hopalong Cassidy is the man to fix it.

CHORUS:
> We'll roam, roam, roam
> Onto an unseen goal,
> Swinging along
> To the song of the pio-o-neers.

ANNOUNCER: The whole West is Hopalong Cassidy's reign. But Hoppy and his pals are happiest when they're at home on the Bar 20, the famous Buck Peters ranch in Arizona where Hoppy is foreman... [The story would then begin.]

CLOSE (original)

SOUND: Hoppy and his sidekick riding back to the Bar 20 after solving a crime.

CHORUS:
> See those rovin' cowboys
> Ridin' down that lonesome trail.
> Well, they're ridin' home.

ANNOUNCER: You have been listening to *Hopalong Cassidy*. Tonight's production was written and directed by Paul Pierce with music by Wilbur Hatch.

THEME MUSIC: Up full then under...

ANNOUNCER: William Boyd stars as Hopalong Cassidy with Andy Clyde as California. Bob Moon speaking. This is the Columbia Broadcasting System.

OPEN (revised)

THEME MUSIC: Up full then under...

ANNOUNCER: With action and suspense out of the old West comes the most famous hero of them all, *Hopalong Cassidy*, starring William Boyd.

SOUND: Cowboy walking.

ANNOUNCER: The ring of the silver spurs heralds the most amazing man ever to ride the prairies of the early West, Hopalong Cassidy. The same Hoppy you cheer in motion pictures and the same California you've laughed at a million times. Raw courage and quick shooting have built a legend around this famous hero.

Hopalong Cassidy is a name to be feared, respected and admired, for this great cowboy rides the trails of adventure and excitement. William Boyd as Hopalong Cassidy and Andy Clyde as California.

THEME MUSIC: Up full then out.

CLOSE (revised)

ANNOUNCER: And so an exciting adventure ends for Hoppy and California. They'll get back to the Bar 20 just around round-up time and settle down to a peaceful ranch life. But we've a hankering [sic] it won't last for very long. Somewhere there'll be trouble and that's when Hoppy will ride out into another dangerous escapade. *Hopalong Cassidy* starring William Boyd is transcribed and produced in the West by Walter White, Jr. All stories are based upon the characters created by Clarence E. Mulford. This is a Commodore Production.

181. I Deal in Crime

Crime drama about Ross Dolan (William Gargan), a Los Angeles-based private detective. Various sponsors. ABC, 1945–1947. Skitch Henderson composed the theme, "I Deal in Crime."

OPEN

VOICE: *I Deal in Crime.*

THEME MUSIC: Up full then under…

ANNOUNCER (Dresser Dahlstead): The American Broadcasting Company presents *I Deal in Crime* starring William Gargan as Ross Dolan.

ROSS: My name is Ross Dolan, I'm a private investigator. I have offices in the Melrose Building and I charge twenty-five dollars a day plus expenses. [After this opening speech, which would change with each episode, Ross would begin the story.]

CLOSE

ANNOUNCER: Don't forget to listen again next week, same time, same station, when you'll hear William Gargan say—

ROSS: *I Deal in Crime.*

THEME MUSIC: Up full then under…

ANNOUNCER: *I Deal in Crime* starring William Gargan as Ross Dolan is a presentation of the American Broadcasting Company. Dresser Dahlstead speaking. *I Deal in Crime* came to you from Hollywood. This is ABC.

THEME MUSIC: Up full then fade out.

182. I Fly Anything

Adventures of Dockery Crane, pilot of a DC-4 who will fly any cargo anywhere as long as it is legal. Various sponsors. ABC, 1950–1951. Dick Haymes played Dockery Crane with Georgia Ellis as his secretary, June.

OPEN

THEME MUSIC: Up full then under…

SOUND: Airplane in flight.

ANNOUNCER (Lou Cook): *I Fly Anything* starring Dick Haymes as air cargo pilot Captain Dockery Crane.

CRANE: Cargo 91743 to LaGuardia tower, requesting landing instructions, please. Over.

VOICE: LaGuardia to 91743. You're number two to land. Visibility seven miles. Wind northwest 290 degrees, 20 miles. Altimeter setting of 025. You will be clear to land on runway two-one. Is that you Crane?

CRANE: That's me, Dockery Crane.

VOICE: What are you bringing to our fair city this time, Crane? Cabbages, kings or crumbuns?

CRANE: No, you're wrong all the way, Buster. I'm bringing in a dent in my rudder, a gram of drugs and a date with death. You know me, I fly anything.

ANNOUNCER: Transcribed, the American Broadcasting Company presents Dick Haymes as fast-moving, hard-hitting, romantic air cargo pilot Captain Dockery Crane in *I Fly Anything*.

CRANE: My name is Dockery Crane and my business is the Wild Blue Yonder Business— the pickup and delivery business by air. You get yourself a crew, a hangar, a secretary, a teletype machine and a certificate from the C.A.B. and a great big pile of hope and your motto is "Anything, anywhere, any time. I fly anything."

THEME MUSIC: Up full then out.

CLOSE

ANNOUNCER: You have been listening to the fifth in a series starring Dick Haymes as air cargo pilot Dockery Crane in *I Fly Anything*.

SOUND: Teletype machine.

ANNOUNCER: And there goes the teletype with next week's cargo load—

JUNE: Doc, an urgent on the teletype. A man by the name of Brad Barton wants to know if you will fly up to the timber country of northern Minnesota to pick up a passenger.

CRANE: Tell him sure. Anything, any time, anywhere, I fly anything.

ANNOUNCER: *I Fly Anything* starring Dick Haymes was produced by Frank Cooper and Sy Fisher in cooperation with the American Broadcasting Company. The part of June is played by Georgia Ellis. Music was composed and conducted by Basil Adlam. This transcribed program was directed by Dwight Hauser. This is Lou Cook speaking. This program has come to you from Hollywood and was transcribed from ABC, the American Broadcasting Company.

THEME MUSIC: Up full then fade out.

183. I Love Lucy

Humorous incidents in the lives of nightclub entertainer Ricky Ricardo (Desi Arnaz), his wife, Lucy (Lucille Ball) and their friends, Fred and Ethel Mertz (William Frawley, Vivian Vance). Sponsored by Philip Morris Cigarettes. CBS, 1952. Based on the television series. Philip Morris is represented by its trademark, Johnny the Bellboy (Johnny Roventini).

OPEN

SPONSOR'S THEME ("On the Trail"): Up full then under...

ANNOUNCER (John Stevenson): Philip Morris, America's most enjoyable cigarette, presents Lucille Ball and Desi Arnaz in *I Love Lucy*.

JOHNNY: Call for Philip Mor-rees, call for Philip Mor-rees.

ANNOUNCER: Ladies and gentlemen, you can stop worrying about cigarette irritation and start smoking for pleasure. Remember this important fact, Philip Morris and only Philip

Morris is entirely free of a source of irritation used in the manufacture of all other leading cigarettes. You'll be glad tomorrow that you smoked Philip Morris today.

JOHNNY: Call for Philip Mor-rees, call for Philip Mor-rees.

***I LOVE LUCY* THEME:** Up full then under...

ANNOUNCER: And now by transcription, let's join Lucille Ball and Desi Arnaz as Lucy and Ricky Ricardo in *I Love Lucy*.

RICKY: Hello, I'm Ricky Ricardo and I'm the guy who loves Lucy. The whole thing started ten years ago. I had just come to this country from Cuba and I didn't know much about your customs. The first girl I had a date with was Lucy. It was a romantic night and after all, I had a reputation to live up to as a Latin lover. I kissed her good night. It was right then that she told me that under the Constitution of the United States, if a man kisses a girl he had to marry her. Then I found out that she tricked me; but I didn't care because after all, if I didn't marry her I would have married someone else. And Lucy, just like any other American girl, was pretty, charming, witty and partly insane. She's always doing these crazy things... [at which point the episode would begin.]

CLOSE

SPONSOR'S THEME: Up full then under...

JOHNNY: Call for Philip Mor-rees, call for Philip Mor-rees.

ANNOUNCER: Stop worrying about cigarette irritation and start smoking for pleasure, pure pleasure and nothing but pleasure. Philip Morris is entirely free of the source of irritation used in the manufacture of all other leading cigarettes. For your own protection, for your own greater smoking pleasure, enjoy Philip Morris. You'll be glad tomorrow you smoked Philip Morris today.

***I LOVE LUCY* THEME:** Up full then under...

ANNOUNCER: *I Love Lucy* starring Lucille Ball and Desi Arnaz features Vivian Vance and William Frawley as Ethel and Fred Mertz. Tonight's program was written by Jess Oppenheimer, Madelyn Paugh and Bob Carroll, Jr. John Stevenson speaking. This is the CBS Radio Network.

THEME MUSIC: Up full then fade out.

184. I Want a Divorce

Drama with Joan Blondell as the leading lady in stories about the incidents that lead a couple to seek a divorce. Various sponsors. Mutual, 1940–1941.

OPEN

ANNOUNCER (Herb Allen): Starring Joan Blondell in *I Want a Divorce*.

VOICE: Judge, I want a divorce.

JUDGE: Divorce granted.

VOICES: I want a divorce, I want a divorce, I want a divorce.

ANNOUNCER: Faster, faster, ever faster does the divorce mill grind away yesteryear's happiness. Why? Why? Why?, ask millions. Listen to *I Want a Divorce*, the copyrighted program approved by many leaders of church and state, the program that dramatizes the real-life happenings in other people's marriages. Broadcast coast to coast from Hollywood each week at this hour.

THEME MUSIC ("Wedding March"): Up full then under…

ANNOUNCER: And now here is Cal York, Hollywood correspondent of *Photoplay Movie Mirror* magazine, to tell you about tonight's *I Want a Divorce* play. [Cal would appear next and tell the audience about the play and Joan's role.]

CLOSE

ANNOUNCER: And so ends another *I Want a Divorce* play. All names mentioned in tonight's play are fictitious. Any similarity to actual persons is purely coincidental. Music was scored and conducted by David Rose. Joan Blondell is soon to appear with Dick Powell in the Universal picture *Model Wife*. Herb Allen speaking. This is the Mutual Broadcasting System.

THEME MUSIC: Up full then fade out.

185. I Was a Communist for the FBI

Drama about Matt Cvetic, an FBI under-cover agent who infiltrated the Communist Party in the U.S. Various sponsors. Syn., 1952–1954. Dana Andrews played Matt Cvetic.

OPEN

VOICE: *I Was a Communist for the FBI.*

THEME MUSIC: Up full then under…

ANNOUNCER: Starring Dana Andrews in an exciting tale of danger and espionage, *I Was a Communist for the FBI.*

THEME MUSIC: Up full then under…

ANNOUNCER: You are about to hear a strange story; names, dates and places are, for obvious reasons, fictional, but many of these incidents are based on the actual experiences of Matt Cvetic who, for nine fantastic years, lived as a Communist for the FBI. Here is our star, Dana Andrews as Matt Cvetic.

MATT: I was a part of the whole dirty mess. For nine years I lied. For nine years I cheated and betrayed my country in word and deed. For nine years I was everything decent people hate. For nine years I was a Communist working as an undercover man for the FBI. This story may help you understand why I felt my job was important to everyone in America.

THEME MUSIC: Up full then under…

ANNOUNCER: And now here is Dana Andrews as Matt Cvetic, undercover man, in this story from the confidential file marked "Draw the Red Curtain."

CLOSE

MATT: So there it was, another Red plan gone wrong. But there were more plans and behind them all, the deadly threat of their master plan, their historic mission. Until this threat was gone, I knew my work had to go on—and I would continue to be a man who walks alone.

SOUND: Footsteps in echo effect.

THEME MUSIC: Up full then under…

DANA: This is Dana Andrews. The names, places and organizations mentioned in this story are fictional, but the danger is a very real one. So be on your guard; don't let your organization fall into Red hands—it can happen and it has happened. But you can keep it from happening again. Next week we'll bring you another story based on the true life adventures of Matt Cvetic. Join us for it, won't you.

THEME MUSIC: Up full then fade out.

186. Information Please

Game show in which a panel attempts to answer questions submitted by listeners. Various sponsors (Canada Dry, Heinz and Lucky Strike were frequent sponsors). Blue (1938–1940), NBC (1940–1946), CBS (1946–1947), Mutual (1947–1951). Clifton Fadiman served as the host.

OPEN

SOUND: Rooster crowing.

ANNOUNCER (Ben Grauer): It's half-past eight, New York time, time to wake up, America and stump the experts. Each week at this time, Lucky Strike sets up a board of four know-it-alls to answer the questions you have submitted. For every question we use, Lucky Strike pays out $10 plus a copy of the new *Information Please Quiz Book*. If your question stumps us, you get $25 more plus a 24-volume set of the current *Encyclopedia Britannica*. And now light up a Lucky Strike as I present our master of ceremonies, the literary critic of the *New Yorker* magazine, Clifton Fadiman.

CLIFTON: Good evening, ladies and gentlemen. Let me remind you again, *Information Please* is completely unrehearsed and ad-libbed from beginning to end... [Clifton would then begin the show by asking the panel a question.]

CLOSE

THEME MUSIC: Up full then under...

ANNOUNCER: And that brings to a close this session of *Information Please*. *Information Please* has been presented by Lucky Strike. Lucky Strike means fine tobacco, so round, so firm, so fully packed, so fine and easy on the draw. For a taste you'll like, light up a Lucky.

THEME MUSIC: Up full then under...

ANNOUNCER: This is Ben Grauer reminding you again that if you would like to submit a question to us, please write to Information Please, 480 Lexington Avenue, New York City. If our editorial staff edits your question a bit, don't fret over it. In case of duplications, *Information Please* uses the question that was received first. This is Ben Grauer reminding you to be with us again next Friday evening at 8:30 for another *Information Please*. This is NBC, the National Broadcasting Company.

THEME MUSIC: Up full then out.

SOUND: NBC chimes. N–B–C.

187. Inner Sanctum Mysteries

Grisly, sometimes unsettling stories of mystery and suspense. Sponsored by Bromo Seltzer, Carter's Liver Pills, Colgate-Palmolive Company, Lipton Tea and Lipton Soup, Mars Candies, Pearson Pharmaceutical Company. Blue (1941–1943), CBS (1943–1950; 1952), ABC (1950–1951). Raymond Edward Johnson, Paul McGrath and House Jameson played the Host; Mary Bennett was the commercial spokeswoman.

OPEN

ANNOUNCER (Ed Herlihy): Lipton Tea and Lipton Soups present *Inner Sanctum Mysteries*.

SOUND: squeaking door opening.

HOST: Good evening friends of the *Inner Sanctum*, this is your Host to welcome you through the squeaking door to another half-hour of horror. Come in, won't you, you'll be delighted at the story I have for you tonight. Oh, by the way, if you feel a cold, thin sliver of steel across your neck in the next half-hour, sit perfectly still, someone's got an edge on you.

MARY: Gracious, Mr. Host, I'm afraid I'd have to move—fast.

HOST: Oh Mary, you must sit still, you wouldn't want to lose your head.

MARY: I'll remember your advice, Mr. Host, but right now I have some advice for our Lipton listeners. You know a teapot can't talk, but if it could I think it would tell you the same thing I do about Lipton Tea. I think it would probably say the most delicious tea is the tea with the most flavor. And I bet it would cast its vote to Lipton Tea because Lipton has that grand, brisk flavor, the flavor that's so different from other teas, the flavor that fills your cup with pleasure. So make that next pot of tea you brew at your house Lipton Tea.

HOST: And now here's a little tale of horror that speaks for itself, "The Edge of Death" [about a man who uses an ancient rapier to commit murder].

CLOSE

THEME MUSIC: Up full then under.

HOST: This month's *Inner Sanctum* mystery novel is *The Pavilion* by Hilda Lawrence. And next week, the makers of Lipton Tea and Lipton Soups bring you another grisly tale entitled "The Confession." Until next Tuesday then, good night, pleasant dreams?

SOUND: squeaking door closing.

MARY: Got tomorrow's meal on your mind? Well how about letting me make a suggestion? And now here's a real menu masterpiece that the whole family will love. It's Lipton's Noodle Soup, a grand soup chock-full of fresh noodles cooked in chicken goodness. Lipton's Noodle Soup is prepared with ease and ready to please in just a few quick minutes. It's economical too; costs less than canned soups. So ask your grocer for Lipton's Noodle Soup mix.

SOUND: Musical sting.

MARY: And don't forget to tune in next Tuesday night for another *Inner Sanctum Mystery*.

THEME MUSIC: Up full then out.

ANNOUNCER: This is CBS, the Columbia Broadcasting System.

188. Inspector Thorne

Crime drama with Karl Weber as a homicide bureau inspector. Sustaining. NBC, 1951.

OPEN

ANNOUNCER: The National Broadcasting Company presents *Inspector Thorne*.

THEME MUSIC: Up full then under...

ANNOUNCER: Tonight, the National Broadcasting Company presents the exploits of the spectacular young Inspector Thorne of the Homicide Bureau. Inspector Thorne's investigations rank with many of the most celebrated ones in the annals of crime fiction. Inspector Thorne, an investigator smart enough to claim he is dumb and modest enough to believe it.

THEME MUSIC: Up full then out.

CLOSE

THEME MUSIC: Up full then under...

ANNOUNCER: The National Broadcasting Company has presented *Inspector Thorne*. Karl Weber is starred in the title role with Danny Ocko as Sergeant Muggin. Be with us again next week for another adventure with *Inspector Thorne*. This is NBC, the National Broadcasting Company.

SOUND: NBC chimes. N-B-C.

189. It Pays to Be Ignorant

Game in which three "ignorant" panelists attempt to answer simple questions (for example, "What color is the White House?"). Various sponsors (Chrysler and DeSoto cars and Philip Morris cigarettes were frequent sponsors). Mutual (1942–1944), CBS (1944–1950), NBC (1950–1952). Tom Howard served as the host with Lulu McConnell, Harry McNaughton and George Shelton as the panelists. Philip Morris was represented by its trademark, Bellboy Johnny Roventini.

OPEN

SPONSOR'S THEME ("On the Trail"): Up full then under...

JOHNNY: Call for Philip Mor-rees, call for Philip Mor-rees.

ANNOUNCER (Ken Roberts): It's a wonderful feeling to wake up fresh without cigarette hangover. Yes, you'll be glad tomorrow if you smoke Philip Morris today.

JOHNNY: Call for Philip Mor-rees, call for Philip Mor-rees.

ANNOUNCER: Johnny presents—

THEME MUSIC: Up full then under...

ANNOUNCER: *It Pays to Be Ignorant*, a zany half-hour with those masters of insanity, Harry McNaughton, Gene Shelton and Lulu McConnell, with the Townsmen Quartet, Doc Novak's Orchestra and the man who proves *It Pays to Be Ignorant*, Tom Howard.

TOM: Thank you Ken Roberts and good evening ladies and gentlemen, welcome to another edition of *It Pays to Be Ignorant*...

CLOSE

THEME MUSIC ("It Pays to Be Ignorant"): Up full then under...

SONG:

It pays to be ignorant,
To be dense, to be dumb,
To be ignorant just like me...

ANNOUNCER: You have been listening to *It Pays to Be Ignorant*, presented by Philip Morris. It's a wonderful, wonderful feeling to wake up fresh with no cigarette hangover. You'll be glad tomorrow if you smoke Philip Morris today.

SPONSOR'S THEME: Up full then under...

JOHNNY: Call for Philip Mor-rees, call for Philip Mor-rees.

THEME MUSIC: Up full then under...

ANNOUNCER: This is Ken Roberts reminding you to be with us again next week, same time, same station for more zany fun on *It Pays to Be Ignorant*.

SONG:

It pays to be ignorant,
Have no brain, be insane,
Just ignorant.
It pays to be ignorant,
Just like me.

THEME MUSIC: Up full then out.

ANNOUNCER: This is CBS, the Columbia Broadcasting System.

190. It Pays to Be Married

Game show in which married couples reveal facts about their lives for prizes. Various sponsors. NBC, 1953–1955.

OPEN

THEME MUSIC: Up full then under...

HOST (Jay Stewart): Hi everybody, this is Jay Stewart inviting you to *It Pays to Be Married*, the show that honors the American home. Each weekday we hear the stories of interesting couples from all walks of life who have met the problem of their marriages and solved them. Hear their true stories revealed from their married lives. They have an opportunity to win our family fortune jackpot. Now meet our first couple for today. From Los Angeles, Mr. and Mrs. Erwin Porter...

CLOSE

THEME MUSIC: Up full then under...

HOST: *It Pays to Be Married*, created and produced by Steve Hatis and Henry Hoople, is an NBC Radio production and transcribed in Hollywood. Be sure to be with us again tomorrow for more interesting couples and their true stories of their married lives. Until then, this is Jay Stewart reminding you that it pays to be married.

THEME MUSIC: Up full then out.

SOUND: NBC chimes. N-B-C.

191. It's a Crime, Mr. Collins

Crime drama about husband-and-wife private detectives Greg and Gail Collins. Various sponsors. Mutual, 1956–1957. Tom Collins and Mandell Kramer played Greg Collins, with Gail Collins as Gail.

OPEN

THEME MUSIC: Up full then under...

VOICE: *It's a Crime, Mr. Collins.*

ANNOUNCER: *It's a Crime, Mr. Collins* with Tom and Gail Collins, as the husband-and-wife team of detectives who solve the most puzzling crimes.

VOICE: *It's a Crime, Mr. Collins.*

GAIL: It surely is. Yes, Gail Collins here to set the stage for tonight's puzzling crime... [Gail then sets up the story.]

CLOSE

THEME MUSIC: Up full then under...

GREG: Well folks, Gail and I hope you enjoyed our adventure. Be sure to visit us next week for another puzzling murder. Where there's crime and romance, there you will find Mr.—

GAIL: and Mrs. Collins.

THEME MUSIC: Up full then fade out.

192. It's Higgins, Sir

Comedy about an American family (the Roberts) who inherit a prim and proper British butler (Higgins). Sustaining. NBC, 1951. Harry McNaughton plays Higgins with Vinton Hayworth and Arthur Cole as Philip Roberts; Peggy

Allenby and Vera Allen as his wife, Elizabeth; and Denise Alexander, Charles Nevil and Pat Hosley as their children, Debbie, Tommy and Nancy. Basis for the "Our Man Higgins" television series.

OPEN

THEME MUSIC ("Higgins Theme"): Up full then under…

HIGGINS: There's no Mister. It's just Higgins, sir.

ANNOUNCER: The National Broadcasting Company presents a new comedy series, *It's Higgins, Sir*, created and transcribed by Paul Harrison and starring Harry McNaughton as Higgins, butler to the Roberts, an average American family. The Roberts, you see, not only inherited a valuable Queen Ann silver service, but a butler as well, a prim and proper butler named:

HIGGINS: Higgins, just Higgins, sir.

THEME MUSIC: Up full then out.

CLOSE

THEME MUSIC: Up full then under…

ANNOUNCER: This has been *It's Higgins, Sir*, a new comedy series starring Harry McNaughton and tonight Arthur Cole and Vera Allen as Mr. and Mrs. Roberts. *It's Higgins, Sir* was directed and transcribed by Paul Harrison.

THEME MUSIC: Up full then out.

SOUND: NBC chimes. N-B-C.

193. Jack Armstrong, the All-American Boy

Adventure series that originally dealt with the exploits of Jack Armstrong, a super athlete and honor student at Hudson High School. He was later joined by his cousins, Billy and Betty Fairfield, and their uncle, Jim Fairfield, a pilot of a plane called the Silver Albatross. In 1946, Jim was dropped and replaced by Vic Hardy, chief investigator for the S.B.I. (Scientific Bureau of Investigation). Jack, Billy and Betty now worked with Vic; in 1950, these characters were spunoff into a series called *Armstrong of the S.B.I.*

(*see* entry). Sponsored by Wheaties. CBS (1930–1936), NBC (1936–1941), Mutual (1941–1942), Blue/ABC (1942–1950). St. John Terrell, Jim Ameche, Don Ameche, Stanley Harris, Michael Rye and Charles Flynn played Jack Armstrong; Billy Fairfield was played by Murray McLean, John Gannon, Roland Butterfield, Milton Guion and Dick York. Scheindel Kalish, Sarajane Wells, Loretta Poynton and Patricia Dunlap played Betty Fairfield. James Gross was Jim Fairfield and Ken Griffin was Vic Hardy.

OPEN (1935)

SOUND: Cheers and "Rah, rah, rah."

CROWD VOICES: Jack Armstrong, Jack Armstrong, hooray!

ANNOUNCER (David Owen): *Jack Armstrong, the All-American Boy* is on the air in person to get you to eat Wheaties. Fellows, girls, hang in for thrills, excitement, adventure. Today, Wheaties brings you a story of champions in action. And now, *Jack Armstrong, the All-American Boy*.

CLOSE (1935)

ANNOUNCER: Be sure to listen in at this same time tomorrow evening to find out what happens next. Fellows, girls, ask your mother for Wheaties right now. Fix that famous breakfast of champions with plenty of milk, cream and sugar and some bananas. You'll say, just like Jack Armstrong says, Wheaties and bananas are a great combination. And just one more thing. When your mother gets Wheaties call her attention to the famous seal of acceptance of the Committee on Foods of the American Medical Association. That seal is mighty important to your mother for it tells her Wheaties are pure and truthfully advertised. By the way, many grocers are featuring specials on Wheaties and bananas this month. Ask your mother to buy you some bananas when she buys Wheaties for you. Eat Wheaties and sliced bananas for breakfast some morning soon. You'll say it's a marvelous combination. This is David Owen saying goodbye for *Jack Armstrong, the All-American Boy*.

OPEN (1940)

VOICES (ECHOING): Jack Armstrong, Jack Armstrong, Jack Armstrong, the all-American boy.

CHORUS:

> Wave the flag for Hudson High boys,
> Show them how we stand!
> Ever shall our team be champion,
> Known throughout the land.

ANNOUNCER (Franklyn McCormick): Wheaties, breakfast of champions, brings you this thrilling adventure of *Jack Armstrong, the All-American Boy*. Listen fellows and girls, today is a really good news day. Today Jack Armstrong starts on a brand new radio adventure, one of the most exciting and dangerous he's ever had. I know you won't want to miss a single episode of this thrilling Jack Armstrong adventure. Right now, at the very beginning of a new school year and the start of a new Jack Armstrong series, is a mighty fine time to start making Wheaties your regular year-round breakfast dish. So, would you do this for me? Would you eat Wheaties, breakfast of champions, the next four mornings in a row. Then ask yourself if you've ever found any other breakfast dish that gives you as much pleasure and satisfaction as this combination of Wheaties, milk and fruit. It's my bet you'll say Wheaties have a flavor that's absolutely different and better than any other breakfast dish you've ever tasted. And now, *Jack Armstrong, the All-American Boy*.

CLOSE (1940)

ANNOUNCER (after cliff-hanging scene): Say, looks like Jack, Billy and Betty have really stumbled into some excitement, doesn't it? Listen in all of you at this same time tomorrow and see what happens next with *Jack Armstrong, the All-American Boy*. The thrilling adventures of *Jack Armstrong, the All-American Boy* has [sic] been presented by Wheaties, the breakfast cereal for champions.

CHORUS:

> Have you tried Wheaties?
> They're whole wheat
> With all of the bran.
> Won't you try Wheaties?
> They're crispy, they're crunchy
> The whole year through.
> Jack Armstrong never tires of them
> And neither will you.
> So just buy Wheaties,
> The best breakfast food in the land.

ANNOUNCER: This is Franklyn McCormick saying goodbye until tomorrow for General Mills, makers of Wheaties, breakfast of champions, who have just presented another episode of *Jack Armstrong, the All-American Boy*.

CHORUS:

> So just try Wheaties,
> The best breakfast food in the land.

OPEN (1948)

ANNOUNCER (Bob McKee): A famous Jack Armstrong adventure story.

THEME MUSIC: Up full then under...

VOICES: Jack Armstrong, Jack Armstrong, Jack Armstrong.

ANNOUNCER: The all-American boy. Brought to you by Wheaties, breakfast of champions. Why don't you eat Wheaties? Champions do, why don't you?

THEME MUSIC: Up full then under...

ANNOUNCER: And now Wheaties presents Jack Armstrong in another of his new, complete adventures. Today's half-hour story, "Clear the Tracks."

THEME MUSIC: Up full then out.

ANNOUNCER: If you like good things to eat, you'll like Wheaties and like 'em a lot because Wheaties are awfully good. They're flakes, crackling golden flakes with a wonderful flavor, plenty nourishing too; they're flakes of 100 percent whole wheat, filled with vitamins, minerals and energy, a kind of nourishment that'll help you perform like a champion. Pick up a couple of packages of those orange and blue boxes of Wheaties at your grocer's today.

ANNOUNCER: And now on with our Jack Armstrong adventure story... [In "Clear the Tracks," Jack tries to save passengers on a runaway train.]

CLOSE (1948)

ANNOUNCER: Listen Monday at this same time for another complete adventure with *Jack Armstrong, the All-American Boy*, brought to you by Wheaties, breakfast of champions. And tomorrow morning, start your day the way so many coaches and athletes do—eat Wheaties, breakfast of champions.

THEME MUSIC: Up full then under...

CHORUS:

> Have you tried Wheaties,
> They're whole wheat
> With all of the bran.

ANNOUNCER: Listen Monday through Friday to your ABC station from 5:30 to 6. Make this the most exciting half-hour of your day. Tomorrow, a thrilling story with *Sky King*. And Monday, another famous Jack Armstrong champion adventure story. Yes, make 5:30 to 6 on ABC, the most exciting time of the day. This is Bob McKee speaking for General Mills, makers of Wheaties, breakfast of champions.

THEME MUSIC: Up full then out.

ANNOUNCER: Can you imagine having nothing but rags to wear? Not even being able to play outside because you don't have enough clothes to keep you warm? Well, listen, millions of children in countries overseas are dressed in rags right now. And that's why the Girl Scouts of the U.S.A. are devoting this whole year to a program called Clothes for Friendship. They've promised to send 100,000 complete sets of clothing to the needy children of Europe and Asia. So won't you girls and fellows too, won't you help the Girl Scouts make good on their promise? Offer your services to your local Girl Scouts today. They'll appreciate it.

VOICE: This is ABC, the American Broadcasting Company.

194. The Jack Benny Program

Comedy-variety series that revolved around the home and working life of comedian Jack Benny. Sponsored by Canada Dry (NBC, 1932–1933; see *The Canada Dry Ginger Ale Program*), Chevrolet (as *The Chevrolet Program*, NBC, 1933–1934), General Tire (as *The General Tire Program*, NBC, 1934), Jell-O (NBC, 1934–1942; see *The Jell-O Program*), Grape Nuts (as *The Grape Nuts and Grape Nuts Flakes Program*, NBC, 1942–1944) and Lucky Strike Cigarettes (called both *The Jack Benny Program* and *The Lucky Strike Program*, NBC, 1944–1948; CBS, 1949–1955). The songs "Love in Bloom"

and "Yankee Doodle Dandy" were combined to form the theme song.

OPEN (NBC)

ANNOUNCER (Don Wilson): *The Jack Benny Program*, presented by Lucky Strike.

SPOKESMAN: Smoke a Lucky Strike to feel your level best. That's how you'll feel when you light up a Lucky because Lucky's fine tobacco picks you up when you're low, calms you down when you're tense. Puts you in the right level to feel and do your best. It's important for you to know as a smoker, that fine tobacco can do this for you and as you know—

VOICE: L.S.M.F.T., L.S.M.F.T.

SPOKESMAN: Lucky Strike Means Fine Tobacco. No wonder more independent tobacco experts smoke Lucky Strike regularly than the next two leading brands combined. So smoke a Lucky to feel your level best. Yes, the next time you buy cigarettes, remember, Lucky's fine tobacco puts you on the right level, the Lucky level, to feel your level best and do your level best. Smoke a Lucky to feel your Lucky best. Get a carton of Lucky's and get started today.

THEME MUSIC: Up full then under...

ANNOUNCER: *The Lucky Strike Program* starring Jack Benny with Mary Livingston, Phil Harris, Rochester, Dennis Day, and yours truly, Don Wilson.

THEME MUSIC: Up full then under...

ANNOUNCER: And now, ladies and gentlemen, we bring you our master of ceremonies, Jack Benny.

JACK (over applause): Good evening, ladies and gentlemen, and welcome to our show...

CLOSE (NBC)

JACK: Next week, ladies and gentlemen, we'll be with you at this same time with the same cast on another network. However, I want to take this opportunity to thank everyone connected with NBC for a very pleasant association.

SPOKESMAN: Smoke a Lucky to feel your level best. Lucky's fine tobacco picks you up when you're low, calms you down when you're tense, puts you on the right level to feel and do your best. So smoke a Lucky to feel your level best.

JACK: Good night everybody.

ANNOUNCER: Ladies and gentlemen, listen again next Sunday for *The Jack Benny Program* which will be heard on another network at this same time. This is NBC, the National Broadcasting Company.

SOUND: NBC chimes. N-B-C.

OPEN (CBS)

ANNOUNCER (Don Wilson): *The Jack Benny Program*, transcribed and presented by Lucky Strike, the cigarette that tastes better.

CHORUS: Light up a Lucky

GIRL VOCALIST: It's light-up time.

CHORUS: Be happy, go Lucky

GIRL VOCALIST:

> It's light-up time.
> For the taste that you like,
> Light up a Lucky Strike.

CHORUS: Relax, it's light-up time.

ANNOUNCER: This is Don Wilson, friends, and I certainly agree. There's no time like right now to light up a Lucky and find out firsthand what real deep down smoking enjoyment is. So right now, while the show gets under way, or whenever it's light-up time for you, be happy, go Lucky. Enjoy Lucky Strike, the best-tasting cigarette you ever smoked.

GIRL VOCALIST:

> For the taste that you like,
> Light up a Lucky Strike.

CHORUS: Right now

GIRL VOCALIST: Light up a Lucky

CHORUS: It's light-up time.

THEME MUSIC: Up full then under...

ANNOUNCER: *The Lucky Strike Program* starring Jack Benny, with Mary Livingston, Rochester, Dennis Day, Bob Crosby and yours truly, Don Wilson. And here he is ladies and gentlemen, the star of our program, Jack Benny.

JACK (over applause): Thank you, thank you, this is Jack Benny and welcome to our show...

CLOSE (CBS)

THEME MUSIC: Up full then under...

JACK: Good night folks, see you next week.

ANNOUNCER: *The Jack Benny Program* was produced and transcribed by Hilliard Marks.

SPOKESMAN: Filter smokers, here's the true tobacco taste you've been looking for. Filter tip Taryton gives you all the full rich flavor of Taryton's famous quality tobacco and real filtration too. Filter-tip Taryton incorporates actual charcoal, renowned for its power of selective filtration and used far and wide to purify the air we breathe, the water we drink. Look for the red, white and blue stripe on the package; they identify filter-tip Taryton, the best in filtered smoking.

ANNOUNCER: *The Jack Benny Program* is brought to you by the American Tobacco Company, America's leading manufacturer of cigarettes.

THEME MUSIC: Up full then fade out.

195. The Jack Webb Show

Comedy series coupling skits with music and songs. Sustaining. ABC, 1946. Only two episodes are in circulation. Based on these, the opening and closing signatures varied greatly from week to week. The episode of April 10, 1946, has a complex opening of one-line jokes. The episode of April 17, 1946, is less complex and best describes this skit show.

OPEN

THEME MUSIC: Up full then under...

ANNOUNCER (John Galbraith): This week, the major league baseball season opens. In keeping with this, the American Broadcasting Company brings you the first foul ball of the season, *The Jack Webb Show* in its fifth consecutive strikeout. Nothing new has been added. The Ragadiers will play tonight but without their director, Phil Vivaro, who only confused the men anyway. That spirited singer Clancy Hayes will conduct his usual contest with the orchestra. She's young, she's pretty, she sings. That's three runs for our side, vocalist Nora McNamara. Oh yes, a wonderful gal with a wonderful voice has made a terrible mistake tonight. Midge Williams has agreed to set her career back ten years with a guest appearance on *The Jack Webb Show*. I'm gonna find a nice quiet room until this whole thing blows over. Why don't you do the same thing. [The show would then begin.]

CLOSE

JACK: This is Jack Webb. Give us another chance

next Wednesday at nine-thirty, won't ya? Good night, gang.

ANNOUNCER: This is ABC, the American Broadcasting Company.

196. Jason and the Golden Fleece

Adventure series centered around Jason, a bar owner who also captains the *Golden Fleece*, a 60-foot boat. Various sponsors. ABC, 1952–1953. Macdonald Carey played Jason with William Conrad as Louis DuMont, his bartender and first mate.

OPEN

SONG (MALE PEDDLER):
　　A load of coal upon my back,
　　I sells my coal, two bits a sack.
SONG (FEMALE PEDDLER):
　　　　Rasp-berr-ies.
　　　　Rasp-berr-ies.
THEME MUSIC: Up full then under…
JASON: The New Orleans waterfront is old, dirty and damp, but I like it here. I like the chant of the coal peddler as he walks past my bar on Bourbon Street. I like the call of the blackberry woman who is still singing the same song she sang when pirates hid their loot in Jean Lafitte's blacksmith shop in the French Quarter. And I like the Mississippi, where a man and his boat can find a dream. Yea, I like New Orleans. They call me Jason; I call my boat the *Golden Fleece*.
THEME MUSIC: Up full then out.

CLOSE

THEME MUSIC: Up full then under…
ANNOUNCER: *Jason and the Golden Fleece*, starring Macdonald Carey with Bill Conrad as Louie DuMont, is written by Cleave Herman and Herb Ellis and directed by Arthur Jacobson. Portions transcribed. Original music is composed and conducted by Frank Worth. This is NBC, the National Broadcasting Company.
THEME MUSIC: Up full then out.
SOUND: NBC chimes. N-B-C.

197. Jeff Regan, Investigator

Crime drama about a tough private detective named Jeff Regan. Sustaining. CBS, 1948–1950. Jack Webb and Frank Graham played Jeff Regan with Wilms Herbert and Frank Nelson as his boss, Anthony J. Lyon; and Laurette Fillbrandt as Melody, Lyon's receptionist.

OPEN

JACK WEBB: I'm Jeff Regan, a private eye, his private eye. I work for Anthony J. Lyon, head of the International Detective Bureau. He doesn't care where the money comes from, so long as it comes to him. He cashes in on trouble, and for him it pays off; for me, it's work.
THEME MUSIC: Up full then under…
ANNOUNCER (Marvin Miller): Here's the kind of adventure you've been waiting to hear. Hardboiled action and mystery with radio's most exciting private detective—Jeff Regan. So stand by for trouble and suspense. And now, here's Jack Webb as Jeff Regan. [The episode would then begin.]

CLOSE

JEFF: He doesn't care whether it's arson, homicide, a lost daughter or just people getting kicked around. He makes money on it. I help him.
MELODY: Why do you do it?
JEFF: I don't know, Melody.
THEME MUSIC: Up full then under…
ANNOUNCER: Jack Webb is featured as *Jeff Regan, Investigator* with Wilms Herbert as Anthony J. Lyon and Laurette Fillbrandt as Melody. Remember it's CBS, same time next week for hard-boiled action and mystery with radio's most exciting private detective, Jeff Regan. *Jeff Regan, Investigator* is produced and directed by Gordon P. Hughes with original music by Del Castillo. This is CBS, the Columbia Broadcasting System.
THEME MUSIC: Up full then out.

198. The Jell-O Program

Comedy-variety series that looked at the

home and working life of comedian Jack Benny. Sponsored by Jell-O. NBC, 1934–1942.

OPEN

CHORUS: J-E-L-L-Oooooooooo.

ANNOUNCER (Don Wilson): *The Jell-O Program*, brought to you by Jell-O and Jell-O Puddings, starring Jack Benny with Mary Livingston, Phil Harris, Dennis Day, Rochester and yours truly, Don Wilson.

THEME MUSIC: Up full then out.

ANNOUNCER: Jell-O spells grand enjoyment friends, whether you find it on a box of Jell-O or on a package of those other wonderful dessert flavors. Jell-O Puddings, Jell-O Chocolate, Vanilla and Butterscotch puddings, you know are made by the makers of Jell-O and like Jell-O, they're easy to prepare, thrifty to serve and delightfully good. They give you all the mellow richness of homemade pudding, the tempting old-fashioned goodness of Grandma's creamy masterpiece. Yet, how much less time and trouble they take to make. You can make a variety of desserts with Jell-O Pudding—butterscotch pie, for instance. All you do is prepare a package of Jell-O Butterscotch Pudding according to directions. Then cook, cool and turn into a baked eight-inch pie shell. Serve plain or garnish with whipped cream. And you'll say you never made an easier butterscotch pie or tasted one more delicious. So get a package of Jell-O Butterscotch Pudding and make the family this rich golden butterscotch pie for tomorrow night's dinner. In a pie or pudding, you'll find Jell-O Butterscotch Pudding a swell treat. Just like grandma's only more so.

THEME MUSIC: Up full then under… [Jack is announced and begins the show.]

CLOSE

CHORUS: J-E-L-L-Ooooooooo.

ANNOUNCER: *The Jell-O Show* is written by Bill Morrow and Eddie Molloy.

THEME MUSIC: Up full then under…

ANNOUNCER: Tomorrow, when you order Jell-O, be sure to order Jell-O Puddings too. Jell-O Puddings are rich, luscious puddings that you make with milk and they come in three swell flavors—chocolate, vanilla and butter-

scotch. There's Jell-O Chocolate Pudding, delightfully smooth and mellow, a pudding that's simply tops for a grand, creamy taste with a distinctive chocolate flavor developed exclusively for Jell-O Puddings by the famous Walter Baker Chocolate people. So tomorrow, when you order Jell-O, ask for Jell-O Pudding, they're just like Grandma's only more so.

THEME MUSIC: Up full then under…

ANNOUNCER: Be sure to listen next week at this same time for *The Jell-O Program*. This program came to you from Hollywood. This is NBC, the National Broadcasting Company.

THEME MUSIC: Up full then out.

SOUND: NBC chimes. N-B-C.

199. The Jimmy Durante–Garry Moore Show

Variety series mixing music and songs with skits and jokes. Sponsored by Rexall. CBS, 1945–1947.

OPEN

ANNOUNCER (Howard Petrie): Your Rexall Drugstore presents Jimmy Durante and Garry Moore.

THEME MUSIC: Up full then under…

ANNOUNCER: *The Jimmy Durante-Garry Moore Show* with Jeri Sullivan, Roy Bargy and his orchestra and yours truly, Howard Petrie. Brought to you by your friendly Rexall Drugstore. Rexall, an old familiar name that has always stood for quality and value.

THEME MUSIC: Up full then out.

CLOSE

GARRY: Good night, Mr. Durante.

JIMMY: Good night, Mr. Moore.

GARRY: Good night, everybody.

JIMMY: Good night, folks.

ANNOUNCER: We'll be looking for you next Friday night, same time, same station when we'll be back with another *Jimmy Durante-Garry Moore Show* for Rexall Drugstores. In the meantime, visit the friendly Rexall druggist who brings you these fine programs. And remember, you can depend on any drug product that bears the Rexall name. Remember, in drugs, if it's Rexall, it's right. Tune in again next Friday night for Roy Bargy and his orchestra, Jeri Sullivan, yours truly, Howard Petrie—

JIMMY: And Jimmy Durante.

GARRY: And Garry Moore.

JIMMY: In person.

ANNOUNCER: This is CBS, the Columbia Broadcasting System.

200. The Jimmy Durante Show

Variety series of music, songs and comedy skits sponsored by Camel Cigarettes and Rexall Drugs. NBC, 1947–1950.

OPEN

CHORUS: Good health to all from Rexall.

ANNOUNCER (Howard Petrie): It's *The Jimmy Durante Show*.

JIMMY (Singing): Ink a dink, a dink, a dink a do, a dink a dee, oh what a tune for me...

ANNOUNCER: Yes, ten thousand Rexall Drugstores who carry the complete line of quality Rexall drug products brings you *The Jimmy Durante Show* with Peggy Lee, Candy Candito, Roy Bargy and his orchestra, the Crew Chiefs Quartet, yours truly Howard Petrie and our special guest again, the lovable Victor Moore. And here he is, ladies and gentlemen, the one, the only Jimmy Durante in person... [Jimmy would then begin the show with a song.]

CLOSE

ANNOUNCER: Remember, twenty-five percent of America buys its drug needs in Rexall Drugstores. Remember, Rexall is that large and respected family of more than 2,000 different drug products. Remember, you can always depend on any drug product bearing the name Rexall. Remember, Rexall drug products are available in Rexall Drugstores everywhere.

JIMMY: Touché, Professor Petrie and I'd be glad to ad—

JIMMY (singing):
I do my shopping at a Rexall store,

Buying Rexall drugs and further more,
We buy Rexall, that's all, how about you?

ANNOUNCER: Well, Rexall for the night and we'll be back next week. For Victor Moore, Peggy Lee, Candy Candito, Roy Bargy and yours truly, Howard Petrie, good night.

JIMMY: Good night Mrs. Calabash, wherever you are.

ANNOUNCER: This program was produced and directed by Phil Cohan. Good health to all from Rexall. This is NBC, the National Broadcasting Company.

SOUND: NBC chimes. N-B-C.

201. The Joan Davis Show

Comedy with Joan Davis as the owner of Joanie's Tea Room in Swanville, U.S.A. Sponsored by Swan Soap. CBS, 1945–1947.

OPEN

THEME MUSIC: Up full then under...

ANNOUNCER (Harry Von Zell): *The Joan Davis Show*.

SONG:
Poor Joan
Ain't got nobody,
She's nobody's sweetheart now.

THEME MUSIC: Up full then under...

ANNOUNCER: Featuring the romantic singing of Andy Russell.

ANDY (singing): Amore, Amore, A-moooore.

ANNOUNCER: With a great comedy cast including Verna Felton, Shirley Mitchell, the music of Paul Weston and his orchestra, and here's the star of our show, America's queen of comedy, Joan Davis.

JOAN: Thank you, thank you very much... [Joan would then begin the show in her tea room.]

CLOSE

THEME MUSIC: Up full then under...

ANNOUNCER: Tune in again next week when Lever Brothers, the makers of Swan, will present another half-hour of comedy with Joan Davis, Andy Russell, Verna Felton, Shirley Mitchell, the music of Paul Weston and his orchestra and yours truly, Harry Von Zell. This is CBS, the Columbia Broadcasting System.

THEME MUSIC: Up full then fade out.

202. Joan Davis Time

A revised version of the prior title with Joan Davis as the owner of Joanie's Tea Room in the small town of Swanville. Various sponsors. CBS, 1947–1949.

OPEN

FEMALE VOICE: It's *Joan Davis Time*.

ANNOUNCER (Ben Gage): Well there's no question about it. From coast to coast, it's *Joan Davis Time*.

CHORUS: It's *Joan Davis Time*.

THEME MUSIC: Up full then under…

ANNOUNCER: During the time you'll spend with Joan Davis tonight, you'll hear the voice of her special guest, that talented young man who's been spreading laughter from coast to coast Peter Lind Hayes, plus a supporting cast featuring Lionel Stander, Hans Conried, the music of John Rarig's orchestra, the Choraleers singing quintet and yours sincerely, Ben Gage. And now it's time to meet the star of our show, America's queen of comedy, Joan Davis.

CLOSE

CHORUS: Joan, Joan, Joan.

ANNOUNCER: Don't forget there's more good fun and music coming up next week, coast to coast, when a very special guest will drop in to see Joanie. So, remember, if anybody asks you what time it is next week at this time, tell them it's *Joan Davis Time*.

CHORUS: It's *Joan Davis Time*.

ANNOUNCER: *Joan Davis Time* is produced and directed by Dick Mack and is written by Larry Marks and Arthur Stander. This is CBS, the Columbia Broadcasting System.

203. Joe and Mabel

Comedy that centered on a manicurist (Mabel Stooler) and her boyfriend, Joe Sparton, a cab driver. Various sponsors. NBC, 1941–1942.

Ann Thomas was Mabel with Ted de Corsia as Joe; Betty Garde as Adele (Mabel's mother); Jack Grimes as Sherman (Mabel's brother); and Walter Kinsella as Mike (Joe's friend).

OPEN

THEME MUSIC: Up full then under…

ANNOUNCER (George Putnam): It's time to meet Joe and Mabel, those very human beings. Irving Gaynor Neiman brings you another story of the far-from-placid lives of Joe, loquacious cabbie, and his spirited girlfriend Mabel. And throw in for good measure another glimpse of Sherman, Mabel's kid brother, and of course, Joe's cabbie friend, Mike. *Joe and Mabel* starring Ted de Corsia as Joe with Ann Thomas as Mabel.

THEME MUSIC: Up full then under…

ANNOUNCER: And now for another look into the not-so-private lives of our two young lovers, Joe and Mabel.

THEME MUSIC: Up full then under… (as the story begins.)

CLOSE

THEME MUSIC: Up full then under…

ANNOUNCER: You have just heard another episode in the new radio series *Joe and Mabel*, written by Irving Gaynor Neiman. Also in the cast were Betty Garde, Jack Grimes and Walter Kinsella. This program has been brought to you by the National Broadcasting Company, RCA Building, Radio City, New York. George Putnam speaking.

THEME MUSIC: Up full then under…

SOUND: NBC chimes. N–B–C.

204. Johnny Desmond Follies

Variety series sponsored by Philip Morris Cigarettes and Ronson Lighters. NBC, 1949.

OPEN

FEMALE VOICE: Here's Johnny Desmond, brought to you by Ronson, world's greatest lighter specialists.

ANNOUNCER: Ronson all, Ronson all, lights any flint lighter best of all.

FEMALE VOICE: And here's another helpful hint: use a Ronson Red Skin Flint.

HOST: Hi there friends, this is Johnny Desmond coming your way with Jack Fascinato's trio.

SOUND: Applause. [Johnny would then begin the show with a song.]

CLOSE

THEME MUSIC: Up full then under...

ANNOUNCER: Ronson has presented *Johnny Desmond Follies* with Johnny Desmond and the Jack Fascinato Trio. Remember Ronson, the world's greatest lighter specialists. This is the National Broadcasting Company.

THEME MUSIC: Up full then out.

SOUND: NBC chimes. N-B-C.

205. A Johnny Fletcher Mystery

Crime drama about Johnny Fletcher and Sam Kragg, men who devise schemes to make money and always encounter beautiful women in trouble. Various sponsors. NBC (1945), ABC (1947). Albert Dekker and Bill Goodwin played Johnny Fletcher with Mike Mazurki and Sheldon Leonard as Sam Kragg.

OPEN

SAM: Johnny, I don't like this. Somethin' tells me we shudda minded our own business.

JOHNNY: Look Sam, helping a damsel in distress is your business, my business, everybody's business.

THEME MUSIC: Up full then under...

ANNOUNCER (John Storm): Yes, it's time for another *Johnny Fletcher Mystery*, brought to you by the National Broadcasting Company and starring Albert Dekker as Johnny Fletcher and Mike Mazurki as Sam Kragg.

THEME MUSIC: Up full then out.

CLOSE

THEME MUSIC: Up full then under...

ANNOUNCER: Be sure to be with us next week when we bring you *A Johnny Fletcher Mystery*

starring Albert Dekker and Mike Mazurki. Original music composed and conducted by Buzz Adlam; John Storm speaking. This program was produced in Hollywood's Radio City. This is NBC, the National Broadcasting Company.

THEME MUSIC: Up full then out.

SOUND: NBC chimes. N-B-C.

206. Johnny Madero, Pier 23

Crime drama about a private detective based on San Francisco's waterfront. Various sponsors. Mutual, 1947. Jack Webb played Johnny Madero. The song "I Cover the Waterfront" was used as the theme.

OPEN

THEME MUSIC: Up full then under...

JOHNNY: Yea, I'm Johnny Madero, Pier 23.

THEME MUSIC: Up full then under...

ANNOUNCER: *Johnny Madero, Pier 23.*

JOHNNY: Here in San Francisco, the piers stretch out like a big yawn from south of the Ferry Building clear to the docks. Here you'll find Pier 23. From there it's a short walk to Johnny Madero's Boat Shop, my place. The sign outside looks honest. I rent boats and do anything else to make a buck.

ANNOUNCER: *Johnny Madero, Pier 23.*

THEME MUSIC: Up full then out.

CLOSE

THEME MUSIC: Up full then under...

ANNOUNCER: *Johnny Madero, Pier 23* starring Jack Webb as Johnny Madero has been presented by the Mutual Network. Bill Conrad played Inspector Worcheck of Homicide. Original music was composed and conducted by Harry Zimmerman and the entire production was directed by Nat Wolfe. Tony LaFano speaking.

THEME MUSIC: Up full then out.

ANNOUNCER: This is the Mutual Broadcasting System.

207. Jonathan Brixton

Crime drama about a San Francisco lawyer

who helps people with problems far beyond the norm. Sustaining. Mutual, 1945. Michael Raffetto plays Jonathan Brixton with Barton Yarborough as James, his assistant.

OPEN

THEME MUSIC: Up full then under…

ANNOUNCER (Marvin Miller): C&F Radio Productions present Michael Raffetto as Jonathan Brixton.

THEME MUSIC: Up full then under…

ANNOUNCER: Jonathan Brixton, criminal lawyer, San Francisco, bachelor of uncertain habits, brilliant in court, yet capable of amazing indulgence. But then he has Fong to feed him and get him out of bed, and James to do all the tedious work of looking up the law. Yes, James is the studious type, but don't let his quiet way deceive you; he's a brawny fellow with a mean wallop.

THEME MUSIC: Up full then under…

ANNOUNCER: Jonathan Brixton, his business is crime, a sordid life but never dull because you never know what to expect… [The announcer would then set up the evening's story.]

CLOSE

ANNOUNCER: We have presented *Jonathan Brixton* starring Michael Raffetto with Barton Yarborough as James. We must confess that Jonathan Brixton is not a model man, he doesn't lead a pretty life and he's no knight in shining armor. If you're looking for a conventional hero, Jonathan Brixton is not your man.

THEME MUSIC: Up full then under…

ANNOUNCER: *Jonathan Brixton* is a C&F Radio Production.

THEME MUSIC: Up full then fade out.

208. Joyce Jordan, M.D.

Serial drama about a young doctor with a practice in the small town of Preston; later as a doctor in a large city hospital. Rita Johnson, Ann Shepherd, Betty Winkler, Elspeth Eric, Gertrude Warner and Fran Carlon portrayed Joyce. Sponsored by General Foods and Procter and Gamble. (CBS (1938–1944), NBC (1944–1948; 1954–1955), ABC (1951–1952).

OPEN

THEME MUSIC: Up full then under…

ANNOUNCER (Ron Rawson): Dreft, America's favorite brand for dishes, presents *Joyce Jordan, M.D..* If doing dishes gets you down, you'll love that new Dreft. It does dishes far quicker, far easier, far better than any soap in the world. This new Dreft is wonderfully mild, too. If dishwashing is a headache, you'll love that new Dreft. And now to the dramatic story of *Joyce Jordan, M.D.*

THEME MUSIC: Up full then out.

CLOSE

THEME MUSIC: Up full then under…

ANNOUNCER: Well, if you have to do dishes, try new Dreft. It does dishes easier, quicker, better than the best soap on the market. Try it and you'll see what I mean. You'll see suds like you've never seen before. And these suds are so thick, so hard-working; they wash dishes cleaner than soap—even glassware shines without wiping; pots and pans come clean without scouring. If dishwashing is a headache, you'll love that new Dreft. This is Roy Rawson inviting you to listen again to *Joyce Jordan, M.D.*, brought to you by Procter and Gamble, makers of Dreft, America's favorite brand for dishes. It's new, it's improved, it's better than ever, Dreft. Listen tomorrow at this same time for *Joyce Jordan, M.D.* and be sure to stay tuned now for *This Is Nora Drake*, which follows immediately over most of these NBC stations. This is NBC, the National Broadcasting Company.

SOUND: NBC chimes. N-B-C.

209. The Judy Canova Show [1944]

Comedy with Judy Canova as a country girl from the rural town of Cactus Junction who moves to California to improve her social status and find a husband. Sponsored by Colgate. CBS (1943–1944 as "Rancho Canova"), NBC (1944–1945).

OPEN

ANNOUNCER (Verne Smith): From Hollywood,

The Judy Canova Show, brought to you each week by the Colgate-Palmolive-Pete Company, makers of Palmolive Soap and Colgate Tooth Powder.

THEME MUSIC: Up full then under...

ANNOUNCER: Palmolive Beauty Soap, your beauty hope, and Colgate Tooth Powder for a breath that's sweet, present *The Judy Canova Show* with Mel Blanc, Ruby Dandridge, Joe Kearns, Ruth Perrot, George Dietz, the Sportsmen, Opie Cates and his orchestra, and starring Judy Canova.

THEME MUSIC: Up full then under...

ANNOUNCER: And now a message from Colgate Tooth Powder.

CHORUS:

> Use Colgate Tooth Powder
> Keep smilin' just right.
> Use it each morning
> And use it each night.
> Don't take a chance
> With your romance,
> Use Colgate Tooth Powder.

ANNOUNCER: A breath of trouble can retard the career of secretary, salesman or big financier. So ask yourself, are you the victim of a breath of trouble, I mean unpleasant breath? Do this. Brush your teeth night and morning and before every date with Colgate Tooth Powder for Colgate Tooth Powder clears your breath as it cleans your teeth. Remember to buy it first thing and remember the name, Colgate Tooth Powder with the accent on powder.

CHORUS:

> Don't take a chance
> With your romance,
> Use Colgate Tooth Powder.

THEME MUSIC: Up full then under...

ANNOUNCER: And now *The Judy Canova Show* starring Judy Canova [at which time the program begins].

CLOSE

ANNOUNCER: Remember, doctors prove Palmolive's beauty results. It's true, doctors prove Palmolive soap can bring two out of three women a more beautiful complexion in just 14 days. And this test was conducted on women with all types of skin. Thirty-six doctors, leading skin specialists, have proved the 14-day Palmolive plan improves all types of skin. Start your 14-day Palmolive plan now. It's as simple as one, two, three. Here's all you do. One—

GIRL: Wash your face with Palmolive soap.

ANNOUNCER: Two—

GIRL: Then massage your face for 60 seconds with Palmolive's soft, lovely lather.

ANNOUNCER: Three—

GIRL: Then rinse. Do this just three times a day for 14 days.

ANNOUNCER: And that's all. So get Palmolive soap. See what Palmolive can do for your complexion in only 14 days.

THEME MUSIC: Up full then under...

JUDY: Folks, I'm sure most of us wouldn't worry about things if we remember worrying is just like sittin' in a rockin' chair. All you do is agitate yourself without gettin' anywhere.

ANNOUNCER: This is Verne Smith asking you to follow the 14-day Palmolive plan for a lovelier complexion and don't take a chance with your romance, use Colgate Tooth Powder night and morning and before every date. [Pause] Keep it up ladies, keep on saving your used cooking fat. Secretary of Agriculture Clinton P. Anderson says it's just as important now as when fats and oils were rationed, to save and turn in every bit of used kitchen fat. Used fats continue to be one of our most important sources of supply for the manufacture of soap and other industrial uses. It may be many months before we can obtain an adequate surplus of imported fats and oils for these uses. Remember too, fat is needed in the manufacture of nylons, textiles, electrical appliances, baby carriages and scores of other peacetime products. Well ladies, now that you can get more meat, you'll have more surplus cooking fat. Don't waste it. Sell it to your butcher; he'll give you four cents a pound. Just remember, where there's fat, there's soap and other products you need. Now here's Judy.

THEME MUSIC: Up full then under...

JUDY: Folks, it was awfully nice bein' with you tonight. And I hope we'll all be together again next Saturday night. In the meantime, please don't forget the two products that bring us together each week, Palmolive Soap and Colgate Tooth Powder—the bestest in the world. This is Judy Canova from Hollywood singing—

Go to sleep-y, little baby,
Go to sleep-y, little baby...

ANNOUNCER: *The Judy Canova Show* is written by Fred Fox and Henry Hoople. This is NBC, the National Broadcasting Company.

SOUND: NBC chimes. N-B-C.

210. The Judy Canova Show [1945]

A revised version of the prior title with Judy Canova as a film actress with her own weekly radio series. Sponsored by the Colgate Palmolive Company. NBC, 1945–1951.

OPEN

THEME MUSIC: Up full then under...

ANNOUNCER (Howard Petrie): From Hollywood, *The Judy Canova Show*, brought to you each week by the Colgate Palmolive Company, makers of Halo Shampoo to glorify your hair, and the new 1948 Super Suds with extra suds for extra whiteness. *The Judy Canova Show* with Mel Blanc, Ruby Dandridge, Joe Kearns, Gale Gordon, George Neise, Verna Felton, the Sportsmen, Charles Dant and his orchestra and starring Judy Canova. Judy will return in a moment.

THEME MUSIC: Up full then out.

CHORUS:

Halo, everybody, Halo.
Halo is the shampoo
That glorifies your hair,
So Halo everybody, Halo.

ANNOUNCER: Use Halo Shampoo if you want naturally bright and beautiful hair. Halo reveals the true color and brilliance of your hair the very first time you use it, leaves it shimmering with glorious, natural highlights. Use Halo on your children's hair too. Say hello Halo Shampoo, goodbye to dulling soap film. Get Halo at any cosmetics counter. And remember, soaping dulls hair, Halo glorifies it.

CHORUS:

So Halo everybody, Halo,
Halo Shampoo, Halo.

ANNOUNCER: And now back to Judy Canova [at which time she would begin the show with a song.]

CLOSE

FEMALE VOICES: It's unbelievable! It's amazing! Astounding! Am I seeing things?

ANNOUNCER: Look, it can't be, but it is, a huge freight car full of suds. Yes, just one box of Super Suds filled that freight car to overflowing with suds. Proof that Super Suds gives you extra suds for extra whiteness. It's the suds that do the work. That's why no other soap in the world can wash clothes whiter or get out more dirt than Super Suds. Yes, extra suds for extra whiteness and no bleach needed. So buy a box at your grocer's and carry home a carload of suds.

CHORUS:

Super Suds now gives more suds,
Extra suds for whiter duds.
No other soap can wash clothes whiter,
Get out more dirt and wash 'em brighter.

THEME MUSIC: Up full then under...

ANNOUNCER: *The Judy Canova Show* is written by Fred Fox and Henry Hoople with John Ward and is produced and directed by Joe Rines. This is Howard Petrie asking you to use Halo Shampoo to glorify your hair, and the new 1948 Super Suds with extra suds for extra whiteness. And now, here's Judy.

JUDY: Thank you, Howard. And folks, it was awfully nice being with you tonight; and I hope we'll all be together again next Saturday night. In the meantime, please don't forget the two products that bring us together each week, Halo Shampoo and Super Suds. This is Judy Canova from Hollywood singing—

Go to sleep-y, little baby,
Go to sleep-y, little baby,
When you wake,
You'll patty-patty cake,
And ride a shiny little pony.

ANNOUNCER: Colgate Dental Cream cleans your breath while it cleans your teeth. No other toothpaste cleans teeth better. Colgate cleans teeth thoroughly, safely; reveals natural sparkle and beauty. After you eat and before every date, use Colgate Dental Cream to clean your breath while you clean your teeth. Stay tuned to Kay Kyser with his comedy of errors in his *Kollege of Musical Knowledge*. This is NBC, the National Broadcasting Company.

SOUND: NBC chimes. N-B-C.

211. The Jumbo Fire Chief

Variety series based on Billy Rose's stage play *Jumbo* (about two feuding circus owners and their children, who loved each other). Sponsored by Texaco Fire Chief Gasoline. NBC, 1935–1936.

OPEN

SOUND: A siren.

ANNOUNCER (Louis Witten): Texaco is on the air. Texaco service stations and dealers from coast to coast present the new *Jumbo Fire Chief* program. We are broadcasting from the Sawdust Ring of the New York Hippodrome, scene of the most spectacular theatrical venture of all time. An actual audience of 4,500 people is present and we have asked them not to laugh or applaud so that you may better enjoy the program. The story is written by Ben Hecht and Charles MacArthur with original songs by Richard Rodgers and Lorenz Hart. The cast stars Jimmy Durante in a new and lovable comedy role, Claudius B. Bowers—the "B" stands for Brains; Arthur Sinclair, dean of the Irish theater, as John A. Considine, owner of the Jumbo Show; Donald Novis as Matt Mulligan, son of Considine's bitterest business rival; A.P. Kaye, prominent Theater Guild actor as Jellico; Miss Gloria Grafton in the part of Considine's daughter; with Charles Henderson's Singing Razorbacks, Adolph Deutsch, musical director—all under the personal supervision of Billy Rose.

CLOSE

ANNOUNCER: Louis A. Witten speaking for the Texaco Company, inviting you to tune in again next Tuesday for the *Jumbo Fire Chief* program for the further adventures of the Considine Wonder Show. And remember, whenever you hear the siren and bells, think of Texaco.

SOUND: Siren and bells.

ANNOUNCER: This is the National Broadcasting Company.

SOUND: NBC chimes. N-B-C.

212. The Jungle Adventures of Frank Buck

Adventure series based on the RKO feature film *Bring 'Em Back Alive*, that details the exploits of wild animal trapper Frank Buck. Sustaining. NBC Blue, 1934.

OPEN

SOUND: Lion roaring.

ANNOUNCER: From the tangled wilds of Borneo—

SOUND: A gong.

ANNOUNCER: To the majestic mountains of Tibet—

SOUND: A gong.

ANNOUNCER: To the fierce jungles of Malaya—

SOUND: Lion growling.

ANNOUNCER: Bring 'Em Back Alive!

SOUND: A gong.

ANNOUNCER: RKO Radio Pictures presents *Bring 'Em Back Alive*. Filmed in the depths of the Malayan Jungle, the only wild animal picture which can never be duplicated, Frank Buck's original *Bring 'Em Back Alive* is authentic, thrilling, packed with action and suspense. The dramatic story of the jungle, the land of the short shadows where survival of the fittest is the law of life. See Frank Buck in *Bring 'Em Back Alive*. And now, for the first time on the air, RKO presents *The Jungle Adventures of Frank Buck*.

CLOSE

SOUND: A gong.

ANNOUNCER: Killers of the jungle!

SOUND: A gong.

ANNOUNCER: A fight to death with a crocodile!

SOUND: A gong.

ANNOUNCER: A mad elephant on the rampage!

SOUND: A gong.

ANNOUNCER: A battle royal between a 30 foot python and a tiger!

SOUND: Lion growling.

ANNOUNCER: *Bring 'Em Back Alive*! RKO Radio Pictures has presented a jungle adventure of Frank Buck. In this series of original radio dramas, all characters are impersonated. See and hear Frank Buck in person in his great wild animal picture, the original *Bring 'Em Back Alive*. Filmed in the depths of the Malayan jungle, the only wild animal picture which can never be duplicated. *Bring 'Em Back Alive* is authentic, thrilling, packed with action, danger, suspense. It's a picture for every member of the family; an exciting experience in motion picture entertainment. See the most ferocious jungle killers in their native haunt. See *Bring 'Em Back Alive*. It's another great RKO Radio picture.

SOUND: A gong.

Note: The series is also known as *Bring 'Em Back Alive* and *Frank Buck's Adventures*.

213. Jungle Jim

Adventure based on the comic strip by Alex Raymond about Jim Bradley, an African safari guide known as Jungle Jim, and his sidekick Kolu. Sponsored by Hearst Newspapers. Syn., 1935–1954. Matt Crowley played Jungle Jim with Juano Hernandez as Kolu.

OPEN

THEME MUSIC: Up full then under…

ANNOUNCER (Roger Krupp): Presenting the adventures of *Jungle Jim*. The thrilling adventures of *Jungle Jim* are presented each Sunday in the *Comic Weekly*, the world's greatest pictorial supplement of humor and adventure. In *Comic Weekly*, each page is printed in full color and is distributed everywhere as an integral part of your Hearst Sunday newspaper. And now to today's exciting episode in the adventures of *Jungle Jim*.

THEME MUSIC: Up full then out.

CLOSE

THEME MUSIC: Up full then under…

ANNOUNCER: These amazing adventures are graphically portrayed in full color action pictures in the *Comic Weekly*, the big, full-page picture supplement distributed each Sunday with your Hearst newspaper. Don't miss the *Comic Weekly* next Sunday. And don't forget our date next week for the next exciting adventure of *Jungle Jim*.

THEME MUSIC: Up full then out.

214. Junior Miss

Comical incidents in the life of Judy Graves, the mischievous teenage daughter of Harry and Grace Graves. Various sponsors. CBS, 1948–1954. Barbara Whiting played Judy Graves with Elliott Lewis and Gale Gordon as Harry and Margaret Lansing and Sarah Selby as Grace.

OPEN

JUDY: Philosophers have said that there's a place for everything and everyone in this world. I wish we 15 year olds could be located.

THEME MUSIC: Up full then under…

ANNOUNCER (Johnny Jacobs): It's time for *Junior Miss*, another in the transcribed series of programs based on the delightful characters created by Sally Benson with Gale Gordon as Harry Graves and starring Barbara Whiting.

THEME MUSIC: Up full then under…

ANNOUNCER: Our Junior Miss is 15-year-old Judy Graves. Judy lives with her father and mother and older sister, Lois, in an apartment house at 36 East 82nd Street in New York City. [The story would then begin.]

CLOSE

THEME MUSIC: Up full then under…

ANNOUNCER: *Junior Miss*, based on the famous stories by Sally Benson, is written for radio by Henry Garson. Mr. Garson directed. In tonight's cast were Barbara Whiting as Judy Graves, Peggy Knudsen as Lois and Gale Gordon and Sarah Selby as Harry and Grace Graves. The music was composed and conducted by Bill Saborinsky. This is Johnny Jacobs inviting you to listen to *Junior Miss* transcribed again next week at this same time. This is CBS, the Columbia Broadcasting System.

Note: An earlier CBS version was produced in 1942 with Shirley Temple as Judy Graves.

215. Just Plain Bill

Daily serial about Bill Davidson, a philosophical barber, his married daughter, Nancy Donovan, and Nancy's husband, Kerry. Various sponsors. CBS (1933–1936), NBC (1936–1955). Arthur Hughes played Bill Davidson with Ruth Russell as Nancy and James Meighan as Kerry. The song "Polly Wolly Doodle" was used as the theme.

OPEN

THEME MUSIC: Up full then under…

ANNOUNCER (Felden Ferguson): Now *Just Plain Bill.* Here is the music that brings you one of radio's best-loved stories, just plain Bill Davidson, barber of Hartville, a tender real-life story of people who might be your own next door neighbors.

THEME MUSIC: Up full then out.

ANNOUNCER: Ladies, those flies buzzing around your kitchen aren't as innocent as they look. They carry germs, spread disease. Get rid of them fast, use Black Flag Insect Spray. Black Flag contains active ingredients which spell sudden death for insects. Keeps on knocking 'em dead for weeks when used as directed. Harmless to fabrics, furniture and wall paper, designed for quick knockdown and lasting effect at amazingly low prices. Get Black Flag Insect Spray today.

THEME MUSIC: Up full then under…

ANNOUNCER: And now *Just Plain Bill.*

CLOSE

THEME MUSIC: Up full then under…

ANNOUNCER: Why suffer from the pain of headache, neuritis or neuralgia when Anacin gives such incredibly fast, effective relief. Anacin is like a doctor's prescription; that is, it contains not just one, but a combination of medically proven active ingredients in easy-to-take tablet form. Ask for Anacin, that's A-N-A-C-I-N, Anacin.

THEME MUSIC: Up full then under…

ANNOUNCER: This is Felden Ferguson saying goodbye for *Just Plain Bill* and for the White-hall Pharmaceutical Company, makers of Anacin and many other dependable high quality drug products.

THEME MUSIC: Up full then out.

216. Kay Fairchild, Stepmother

Daily serial about a stepmother's efforts to raise her husband's children from a previous marriage. Sponsored by Colgate. CBS, 1938–1942. Sunda Love, Janet Logan and Charlotte Munson played Kay Fairchild.

OPEN

THEME MUSIC ("Minute Waltz"): Up full then under…

ANNOUNCER (Roger Krupp): Can a stepmother successfully raise another woman's children? Colgate All-Purpose Tooth Powder presents the real-life story of Kay Fairchild, our stepmother who tries.

THEME MUSIC: Up full then out.

ANNOUNCER: Colgate Tooth Powder cleans your teeth and freshens your mouth. You'll find Colgate Tooth Powder safe and ever so pleasant for gum massage. Yes, it's an all-purpose tooth powder with benefits for all members of the family. And right now, Colgate Tooth Powder is smashing all time records in sales because you can buy a large can for only one penny when you buy the giant-sized Colgate Tooth Powder at the regular forty cents price. But when dealers' limited supplies are gone, this exciting one cent sale is over. Wouldn't it be too bad if you missed out? Now Colgate Tooth Powder presents *Kay Fairchild, Stepmother.*

CLOSE

ANNOUNCER: Now here are the facts, plain facts in plain language. Colgate Tooth Powder is a safe, rich-foaming, smooth dentifrice. It loosens dingy film stains on teeth with amazing speed, leaves teeth sparkling bright, radiant with natural luster. Then Colgate's flavorsome foam cleans your mouth and sweetens your breath. And for final good measure, Colgate Tooth Powder is safe for gum massage. With all these benefits you'll agree that Colgate Tooth Powder, even at its regular price, is a swell value. But listen, our big one cent sale is still on and you can actually buy a large can of Colgate Tooth Powder for one cent.

Yes, one modest penny when you buy the giant can at the regular forty cent price. That's 50 percent more tooth powder for only one penny more. Why, it's colossal!

THEME MUSIC: Up full then under...

ANNOUNCER: Tune in again tomorrow and every day, Monday through Friday, for *Kay Fairchild, Stepmother*, brought to you by Colgate All-Purpose Tooth Powder. This is Roger Krupp. This is CBS, the Columbia Broadcasting System.

THEME MUSIC: Up full then out.

ANNOUNCER: Wouldn't you call yourself lucky to get a gift from Wayne King, America's most popular orchestra leader? The gift is a free 25 cent jar of Casmere Cold Creme for cleansing when you buy one jar at the regular 25 cent price. And you also receive free a photograph of Wayne King. Discover for yourself the thrilling result of Casmere Bouquet Face Creme. See how this light, refreshing cream leaves your skin radiant clean, soft and smooth to your touch and scented with Casmere Bouquet, the fragrance men love. These Wayne King gift packages of Casmere Bouquet Face Creme are now at cosmetic counters and they're going like mad, so get yours today.

217. Land of the Lost

Children's adventure about Isabel and Billy (Betty Jane Tyler, Raymond Ives), a young sister and brother who explore an underwater kingdom called Land of the Lost. Sustaining. ABC (1944–1945; 1947–1948), Mutual (1945–1946). Bosco sponsored the program for one year (1947–1948). Isabel Manning Hewson hosted; Junius Matthews, William Keene and Art Carney played Red Lantern, the fish who guides Isabel and Billy. Listeners were called Pollywogs.

OPEN

ANNOUNCER (Michael Fitzmaurice): Lost anything lately, you listeners? Then stay tuned to this station. You may hear surprising news about it in our fantasy, *Land of the Lost*, with prizes for lucky winners at the end.

THEME MUSIC: Up full then under...

ANNOUNCER: The Mutual Broadcasting System presents the *Land of the Lost* and its discoverer, the well-known storyteller Isabel Manning Hewson.

THEME MUSIC: Up full then out.

ISABEL: Time to catch an ocean current everyone, time to travel down, down to the bottom of the sea, to that enchanted kingdom, the Land of the Lost. No wonder all lost things from up on Earth come to life there. For it is the loveliest place you ever dreamed of. With its white sand and pearly palaces, all a-shimmer with pale green light. My brother Billy and I never tired of visiting the Land of the Lost. Every week our faithful friend, the wise-talking fish Red Lantern, would take us down through the tunnel under our lake that led to the ocean. Soon we'd be speeding along on an express current and before you could say "Popping Perriwinkles," we'd reach our destination.

RED LANTERN: All off, Pollywogs, it's the Land of the Lost.

ISABEL: And there's the magic seaweed curtain waiting to open for us... [The story would then begin.]

CLOSE

ISABEL: Remember our motto, "Never Say Lost."

ANNOUNCER: Remember too, at this same time next week, you may be hearing your name as a winner on "Lucky Seven Time." Get your letters off as soon as possible telling us about anything you've lost. It makes no difference whether it's a collar button or a diamond ring. You'll receive the nearest possible duplicate if, in the opinion of our judges, you've sent in one of the most interesting letters telling us why you want a lost possession returned. You can send your letter in separately, or if you're ordering a *Land of the Lost* book, just enclose it with your order. Of course, you can buy *Land of the Lost* books at stores all over the country. It's a best-seller, but since Isabel Manning Hewson wrote it especially at the request of our radio listeners, she sends you a present with each book ordered through this program. The present is a Red Lantern badge with a picture of the one and only Red Lantern in his green coat. It's fun to wear the badge and the book makes a year-round present because when you hear the *Land of the Lost* program, you can look right at the characters while you listen to the show. To get your book and badge, send two dollars in check or money order to the Land of the Lost, care of the Mutual Broadcasting System, Box 222, Times Square Station, New York. Print your name and address plainly. Do this too when you write about those treasures you lost and want returned.

THEME MUSIC: Up full then under...

ANNOUNCER: Be with us again next week, same time, same station, when Isabel Manning Hewson takes you again to the Land of the Lost. The *Land of the Lost* is an original story by Isabel Manning Hewson. The director is Cyril Armbruster. Vocal arrangements by Peggy Marshall; lyrics by Barbara Miller; musical background, Gene Porozzo. Michael Fitzmaurice speaking.

THEME MUSIC: Up full then out.

ANNOUNCER: This is the Mutual Broadcasting System.

218. The LaRosa Hollywood Theater of Stars

Anthology series that featured top Hollywood stars in stories ranging from comedies to tense dramas. Sponsored by LaRosa Macaroni. Mutual, 1948–1951.

OPEN

THEME MUSIC: Up full then under...

ANNOUNCER (Wendell Niles): The *LaRosa Hollywood Theater of Stars* with your host, Mr. C.P. MacGregor.

SOUND: Applause.

C.P.: Thank you, thank you and greetings from Hollywood, ladies and gentlemen. This is C.P. MacGregor speaking. Welcome to *The LaRosa Hollywood Theater of Stars*, radio's greatest daytime radio program. Every day, a complete thirty-minute drama from Hollywood; every day, a famous Hollywood star. Today our star is Vincent Price in a tense drama, "Endless Journey." Act one in just a moment, but first a word from our announcer, Wendell Niles for LaRosa.

NILES: There's never been anything like it. This year's wheat crop is the finest ever produced and that means LaRosa brings you the most delicious spaghetti and egg noodles you ever tasted. Tonight take the LaRosa three-way quality test: see, taste, compare. See LaRosa's natural golden color; taste LaRosa's luscious flavor—richer, smoother and more delicate, with that just right, firmer texture. Once you try LaRosa, you'll never serve anything but LaRosa. And now once again our producer.

C.P.: Now act one of "Endless Journey" starring Vincent Price.

CLOSE

THEME MUSIC: Up full then under...

C.P.: Tomorrow in our *LaRosa Hollywood Theater*, Elliott Lewis and Elaine Barrymore co-star in a bright, romantic fantasy called "Devil Taketh." Be sure to join us, won't you. Till tomorrow then, thanks for listening and cheerio from Hollywood.

THEME MUSIC: Up full then out.

219. Lassie

Adventure about a wandering collie who helps people and animals she finds in trouble. Sponsored by Red Heart Dog Food. ABC (1947–1948), NBC (1948–1950).

OPEN

SOUND: Lassie barking.

ANNOUNCER (Charles Lyon): From Hollywood, John Morrill and Company, makers of Three Flavor Red Heart, America's favorite dog food, presents Metro-Goldwyn-Mayer's lovable motion picture star *Lassie*. And here to tell you today's story is your storyteller, Lassie's trainer, Rudd Weatherwax. [Rudd would then begin the story.]

CLOSE

THEME MUSIC: Up full then under...

ANNOUNCER: Lassie is presented each week at this time by John Morrill and Company, makers of Three Flavor Red Heart, the taste-tested food that your dog will enjoy; the

health-tested food that will keep him in good shape. Lassie appeared by arrangement with Metro-Goldwyn-Mayer, who invite you to see their Technicolor musical *Annie Get Your Gun* starring Betty Hutton and Howard Keel. The *Lassie* show is produced and transcribed in Hollywood by Frank Perrin and directed by Harry Stewart. This is Charles Lyon for NBC, the National Broadcasting Company.
SOUND: NBC chimes. N-B-C.

220. Last Man Out

Anthology series based on the files of various U.S. government agencies. Sustaining. NBC, 1953–1954.

OPEN

ANNOUNCER: The National Broadcasting Company presents *Last Man Out*, a series of true stories, transcribed and documented from the official files of United States government agencies. Ladies and gentlemen, here is your narrator for *Last Man Out*, the well-known writer Mr. Richard English.
ENGLISH: Thank you. Tonight, ladies and gentlemen, you are going to hear one of the most important programs in the entire *Last Man Out* series. There has been a lot of criticism lately directed at government committees, which have attempted to expose the Communist infiltration of our American schools. Tonight, we're going to prove that the Communist infiltration did happen here. Our subject tonight is Dorothy K. Fund, a New York City school teacher. Miss Fund joined the Communist Party in 1939, left in 1946. Dorothy Fund actually saw the poison that was being injected into our school system— the attempt to mold the minds of our children into the Communist pattern. Now, the subject report of a former Communist Party member, Dorothy K. fund.

CLOSE

ANNOUNCER: For security reasons, certain names in the report of Dorothy K. Fund were changed. Each week the *Last Man Out* will expose a different phase of communism. Next

week Richard English will bring to our microphones the true story of another member of the Communist Party, documented and transcribed from the official files of United States government agencies. *Last Man Out* is an NBC Radio Network production by Richard English. Directed by Andrew C. Love and written by Richard George Pettichine. Our musical score is composed and conducted by Dimitri Tiomkin, Academy Award Winner. This is NBC, the National Broadcasting Company.
SOUND: NBC chimes. N-B-C.

221. Latitude Zero

Adventure serial about Craig MacKenzie (Lou Merrill), a submarine captain from a world beneath the sea called Latitude Zero. Sustaining. NBC, 1941.

OPEN

SOUND: Water gushing against the side of the submarine *Omega*.
VOICE: Longitude 180 degrees, 12 minutes.
VOICE: Latitude ... Zero.
VOICE: All hands at stations. Standby for dive.
SOUND: Submarine descending to the bottom of the sea.
ANNOUNCER: The National Broadcasting Company presents—
VOICE: Lat-i-tude Zerrrooooooo.
SOUND: Thunder cracking.
ANNOUNCER: *Latitude Zero*. Adventure fans, attention. Tonight begins the first episode of the most exciting and fabulous adventure story you've ever heard, *Latitude Zero*, especially written for radio by Ted Sherdeman. A story of five men against the world; heroic men with ideals and courage and strength to fight for them in—
SOUND: Thunder with lightning.
ANNOUNCER: *Latitude Zero*.
THEME MUSIC: Up full then out.

CLOSE

THEME MUSIC: Up full then under...
ANNOUNCER: Next week, same day, same time, don't miss the thrilling revelations of the mys-

terious Captain MacKenzie, builder of the *Omega*, the strange submarine from the unknown port. You'll find thrills, action and adventure on the next installment of—

VOICE: Lat-i-tude Zerrroooooo.

SOUND: A large gong.

ANNOUNCER: *Latitude Zero*, especially written for radio by Ted Sherdeman, originates in Hollywood's Radio City. This is the National Broadcasting Company.

SOUND: NBC chimes. N-B-C.

222. Leave It to Joan

Comedy with Joan Davis as a salesgirl at Wollock's Department Store. Sponsored by Roi-Tan Cigars and Half & Half Pipe Tobacco. CBS, 1949–1950.

OPEN

ANNOUNCER (Ken Niles): Well, as I live and breathe, it's got a hole in its head, it's a Roi-Tan Cigar.

JOAN DAVIS: I breathe too and they say I've got a hole in my head. I'm Joan Davis.

CHORUS: Leave It to Joan.

THEME MUSIC: Up full then under...

ANNOUNCER: Roi-Tan, the cigar that breathes, presents *Leave It to Joan* with the music of Lyn Murray and starring America's queen of comedy, Joan Davis, Roi-Tan's cigar store Indian. Man to man, smoke Roi-Tan, the cigar that breathes. Yes, breathes. The famous breathing channel in each Roi-Tan cigar makes it easy drawing. So breathe in that mellow richness, breathe in that fragrant aroma. Man to man, you're missing something until you smoke Roi-Tan, the cigar that breathes. Light up a Roi-Tan and—

CHORUS:
Leave It to Joan,
Leave It to Joan.

THEME MUSIC: Up full then out.

CLOSE

ANNOUNCER: Men, sit back, relax and light up a Roi-Tan, the cigar that breathes, the cigar that made cigar history because of its convenient hole in the head, its mellowed quality tobacco and its popular price.

THEME MUSIC: Up full then under...

ANNOUNCER: *Leave It to Joan* stars Joan Davis, Roi-Tan's cigar store Indian. Man to man, smoke Roi-Tan, the cigar that breathes. And, as I live and breathe, this is Ken Niles smoking a Roi-Tan.

THEME MUSIC: Up full then under...

ANNOUNCER: Mister, when you smoke Half & Half Pipe Tobacco, there's pleasure at both ends of your pipe.

GIRL: It smells swell.

ANNOUNCER: And it tastes great. You enjoy the wonderful flavor of Half & Half.

GIRL: And your better half shares the wonderful fragrance.

ANNOUNCER: You don't know the half of it until you smoke Half & Half, the perfect mixture of mild aromatic tobaccos that adds up to one perfect smoke.

GIRL (in sexy voice): If it's Half & Half you're smoking dear, just blow the smoke my way.

ANNOUNCER: Smoke Half & Half Pipe Tobacco for pleasure at both ends of your pipe.

THEME MUSIC: Up full then under...

ANNOUNCER: Joan Davis will be heard at this same time next week. Good night. This is CBS, the Columbia Broadcasting System.

THEME MUSIC: Up full then out.

223. Let George Do It

Crime drama about George Valentine, a private detective who places a personal newspaper ad to acquire clients. Various sponsors. Mutual (1946–1950), Syn. (1950–1954). Bob Bailey played George Valentine with Frances Robinson, Virginia Gregg and Shirley Mitchell as Clair Brooks, his assistant; Eddie Firestone, Jr. as Sonny, Clair's brother; and Joseph Kearns as Caleb, the elevator operator.

OPEN

VOICE: Personal notice. Danger is my stock and trade. If the job is too tough for you to handle, you've got a job for me, George Valentine. Write for full details.

THEME MUSIC: Up full then under...

ANNOUNCER (John Easton): The Mutual Broadcasting System presents *Let George Do It*, the story of a former police officer turned private detective who acquires danger and intrigue in a most unusual way: he advertises for it. Now with Bob Bailey starred as George Valentine, we present *Let George Do It*.

THEME MUSIC: Up full then out.

CLOSE

THEME MUSIC: Up full then under...

ANNOUNCER: Bob Bailey in *Let George Do It* also stars Virginia Gregg, Joseph Kearns and Eddie Firestone, Jr. Music is by Eddie Dunstedter. John Easton speaking. This is Mutual.

THEME MUSIC: Up full then out.

224. Let Yourself Go

Music and comedy coupled with the vaudeville-like humor of Milton Berle. Sponsored by Eversharp. CBS, 1944–1945.

OPEN

THEME MUSIC ("Buy Eversharp"): Up full then under...

ANNOUNCER (Ken Roberts): Eversharp invites you to *Let Yourself Go* and you'll always go right with Eversharp.

SONG:
> Buy Eversharp, buy Eversharp
> For writing pleasure.
> Buy Eversharp, buy Eversharp,
> They'll be forever.

ANNOUNCER: Yes, *Let Yourself Go*, starring Milton Berle, with Ray Bloch and his orchestra, Connie Russell and Joe Besser. Presented by Eversharp, world's leading manufacturer of fountain pens, repeater pencils, lead and desk sets. And now, here's the entertainment you've been waiting for, the fellow who let himself go and wound up becoming Ziegfeld's biggest folly, Milton Berle.

CLOSE

THEME MUSIC: Up full then under...

ANNOUNCER: You have been listening to *Let Yourself Go* with Milton Berle and presented by Eversharp.

SONG:
> Buy Eversharp, buy Eversharp,

For writing pleasure.
> Buy Eversharp, buy Eversharp,
> They'll be forever.

ANNOUNCER: For fountain pens, repeater pencils and lead and desk sets, trust Eversharp, the world's leading manufacturer. They're forever, they're Eversharp. This is Ken Roberts saying good night on behalf of Eversharp and reminding you to be with us again next Wednesday evening and *Let Yourself Go* with Milton Berle.

THEME MUSIC: Up full then under...

SONG: Buy Eversharp, buy Eversharp...

ANNOUNCER: This is CBS, the Columbia Broadcasting System.

225. Let's Pretend

Children's series that dramatized fairy tales as well as presenting original stories. Sponsored by Cream of Wheat (1943–1952). Sustaining at other times. CBS, 1934–1954.

OPEN (Cream of Wheat)

CHORUS:
> Cream of Wheat is so good to eat
> That we have it every day.
> We sing this song,
> It will make us strong
> And it makes us shout hooray.
> It's good for growing babies
> And grownups too to eat.
> For all the family's breakfast,
> You can't beat Cream of Wheat.

ANNOUNCER: Cream of Wheat, the great American family cereal, presents *Let's Pretend*. Well, hello audience, what is on your mind?

STUDIO AUDIENCE: We want *Let's Pretend*.

BILL ADAMS (as Uncle Bill): If you want *Let's Pretend*, you shall have *Let's Pretend*. And Gwen, what is today's story.

GWEN DAVIES (a regular): Oh, it's an exciting one, Uncle Bill, all about an old meanie called "The Yellow Dwarf."

CLOSE (Cream of Wheat)

UNCLE BILL: And next Saturday be sure to join us when Cream of Wheat will take us on another trip to the land of *Let's Pretend* to hear how an enchanted horse saves the life of a beautiful princess and brought dreadful punishment to a wicked woman. It's the story of "The Goose Girl." This is Bill Adams saying remember to eat Cream of Wheat, the great American family cereal. This is CBS, the Columbia Broadcasting System.

OPEN (sustaining)

CHORUS:

> Hello, hello, come on let's go
> It's time for *Let's Pretend*.
> The gang's all here
> And standing here
> Is Uncle Bill your friend.
> The story is exciting,
> It's fun right to the end.
> So young and old
> Do as you're told,
> Get set for *Let's Pretend*.

ANNOUNCER (Bill Lipton): Yes, it's radio's outstanding children's theater, *Let's Pretend*, created by Nila Mack.

BILL LIPTON (as Uncle Bill): Well, hello Pretenders.

KIDS: Hello, Uncle Bill.

BILL: Are you ready for a story?

KIDS: Let's go!

BILL: Let's go is right. Today, the story of "The Twelve Dancing Princesses."

CLOSE (sustaining)

THEME MUSIC: Up full then under…

ANNOUNCER: Be sure to be with us again next Saturday for another *Let's Pretend*, created by Nila Mack. This is Bill Lipton saying goodbye for *Let's Pretend*. This is CBS, the Columbia Broadcasting System.

226. A Life in Your Hands

Crime drama about Jonathan Kegg, a retired lawyer who offers his services as a friend of the court. Various sponsors (Raleigh and Heinz were frequent sponsors). NBC (1949–1951), ABC (1951–1952). Ned LeFevre, Lee Bowman and Carlton KaDell played Jonathan Kegg.

OPEN

THEME MUSIC: Up full then under…

ANNOUNCER (Myron Wallace): Raleigh Cigarettes presents Erle Stanley Gardner's *A Life in Your Hands*. Did you hear him threaten her? What was the position of the body? Was she still alive at 8:30? Listen while we place a life in your hands. You never know when you step from the safety of your home when you may witness a violent death and be called upon to testify as to what you saw and heard—and you suddenly find yourself with a life in your hands.

VOICE: Jonathan Kegg is a lawyer, a special lawyer, a friend of the court. He is a lawyer and expert who enters a case neither for the defendant nor the prosecutor. He acts impartially, seeking only the truth. He finds the truth by cross-examining witnesses. The truth can usually be learned and justice can be served. Jonathan never accepts a fee. He is financially secure and thus money will not tempt him. He has a passion to see justice done. He gathers the facts to fit them into a pattern—no matter which side it helps or hurts.

THEME MUSIC: Up full then out.

CLOSE

THEME MUSIC: Up full then under…

ANNOUNCER: This is Myron Wallace inviting you to be with us again next week when Raleigh Cigarettes, the pack with the coupon on the back, will again present *A Life in Your Hands*. This is NBC, the National Broadcasting Company.

THEME MUSIC: Up full then out.

SOUND: NBC chimes. N–B–C.

227. The Life of Riley

Comical incidents in the life of Chester A. Riley, a riveter for Stevenson Aircraft in Los Angeles. Sponsored by Dreft, Pabst Blue Ribbon Beer, Prell Shampoo and Teel Dentifrice. CBS (1941), ABC (1944–1945), NBC (1945–1951). Lionel Stander and William Bendix played Riley with Grace Coppin, Paula Winslow and Georgia Backus as his wife, Peg; Peggy Conklin, Sharon Douglas and Barbara Eiler as their daughter, Babs; and Jack Grimes, Scott Beckett,

Conrad Binyon, Bobby Ellis and Tommy Cook as their son, Junior.

OPEN (for Dreft)

THEME MUSIC: Up full then under…

ANNOUNCER (Ken Carpenter): Dreft, the sudsing miracle for silks, nylons, woolens and dishes, presents *The Life of Riley* with William Bendix as Riley.

THEME MUSIC: Up full then out.

CLOSE (for Dreft)

THEME MUSIC: Up full then under…

ANNOUNCER: Procter and Gamble, the makers of Dreft, the sudsing miracle for silks, nylons, woolens and dishes, invites you to be their guest next week to hear *The Life of Riley* with William Bendix as Riley. *The Life of Riley* is produced by Irving Brecher and is directed by Don Bernard. Music is by Lou Kosloff. This is Ken Carpenter inviting you to listen again next week to *The Life of Riley* and reminding you for faster, brighter, safer cleaning than any other previous suds in history, use Dreft. Don't get left, use Dreft. This is NBC, the National Broadcasting Company.

THEME MUSIC: Up full then out.

SOUND: NBC chimes. N-B-C.

OPEN (for Prell)

THEME MUSIC: Up full then under…

ANNOUNCER (Jimmy Wallington): Prell brings you *The Life of Riley*. Prell, the new emerald clear, radiant creme shampoo in the handy tube.

SONG:

> P-R-E-L-L, Prell Shampoo
> Leaves hair radiant, gleaming bright,
> Not a bit of dandruff in sight.
> Comes in a tube, handy too,
> P-R-E-L-L, Prell Shampoo.

ANNOUNCER: And now *The Life of Riley* with William Bendix as Riley.

CLOSE (for Prell)

GIRL VOCALIST:

> I'm Tallulah, the tube of Prell,
> And I'll make your hair look swell.
> It'll shine, it'll glow,

> For radiant hair, get a hold of me,
> Tallulah, the tube of Prell.

ANNOUNCER: Yes, try Prell. Listen again next week when Dreft, the sudsing miracle for silks, nylons, woolens and dishes, brings you *The Life of Riley*. Good night, this is NBC, The National Broadcasting Company.

SOUND: NBC chimes. N-B-C.

OPEN (for Teel)

THEME MUSIC: Up full then under…

ANNOUNCER (Ken Carpenter): Teel for a beautiful smile presents *The Life of Riley* for laughs.

THEME MUSIC: Up full then under…

ANNOUNCER: Teel, T-E-E-L, Teel, the amazing liquid dentifrice, brings you *The Life of Riley* with William Bendix as Riley.

SOUND: Applause.

ANNOUNCER: Remember friends, for a beautiful smile, it's T-E-E-L, Teel and just for laughs it's R-I-L-E-Y, and *The Life of Riley*.

THEME MUSIC: Up full then out.

ANNOUNCER: People used to be shocked when you told them they were grinding cavities into their own teeth by use of toothpaste and powders containing harsh abrasives. But now millions of people use Teel to avoid such damage. Millions of people know that Teel cleans teeth without abrasives; they realize the tremendous importance of this fact to the beauty and well-being of their teeth. But do you realize that importance? Teel alone of all leading dentifrices, contains no abrasives, cleans teeth safely and gently with a patented ingredient. The Teel way takes an extra minute a week to make teeth look their sparkling best, safely. Just follow the easy directions on the package. Everybody loves the tangy flavor of Teel and its refreshing aftertaste. Insist on T-E-E-L, Teel, the safe liquid dentifrice.

THEME MUSIC: Up full then under… (as the show begins).

CLOSE (for Teel)

THEME MUSIC: Up full then under…

ANNOUNCER: Procter and Gamble, the makers of Teel, the amazing liquid dentifrice, invite you to be their guest next week to hear *The Life of Riley* with William Bendix as Riley.

William Bendix appears by arrangement with Hal Roach. *The Life of Riley*, produced for Teel by Irving Brecher, is directed by Don Bernard. This is Ken Carpenter on behalf of Teel, inviting you to listen again next week and remember it's R-I-L-E-Y, Riley for laughs, and for a lovely smile it's T-E-E-L, Teel that amazing liquid dentifrice that protects teeth beautifully. Be sure to listen to *The Life of Riley*, same time next week brought to you by Teel. And now stay tuned to this station for *Truth or Consequences*. Good night.

THEME MUSIC: Up full then out.

ANNOUNCER: This is NBC, the National Broadcasting Company.

SOUND: NBC chimes. N-B-C.

228. Life with Luigi

Comedy about Luigi Basco (J. Carrol Naish), an Italian immigrant in Chicago's Little Italy. Sponsored by Wrigley's Chewing Gum (1951–1952); sustaining at other times. CBS, 1948–1953. Basis for the television series.

OPEN (from 1948)

THEME MUSIC ("Oh Marie"): Up full then under...

ANNOUNCER (Bob Lemond): As every American schoolchild knows—

GIRL: On October 12, 1492, an Italian explorer, Christopher Columbus, discovered America.

ANNOUNCER: On September 27, 1947, an Italian immigrant named Luigi Basco rediscovered America.

GIRL: Christopher Columbus arrived with three vessels.

ANNOUNCER: Luigi Basco arrived with three dollars.

GIRL: When Christopher Columbus landed in America he said, "I name thee San Salvadore."

ANNOUNCER: When Luigi Basco landed in New York he said—

LUIGI: Please, give-a me a ticket to Chicago.

MUSIC ("Chicago, My Kind of Town"): Up full then under...

ANNOUNCER: And so we invite you to Chicago's Little Italy for a new comedy, *Life with Luigi*, the story of an immigrant created by Cy Howard and starring J. Carrol Naish. From America, Christopher Columbus described his adventures to Queen Isabella in Spain. From Chicago, Luigi Basco describes his adventures to his Mama Basco in Italy.

THEME MUSIC ("Oh Marie"): Up full then under...

LUIGI: Dear Mama Mia, I make a promise to write, so I write... [His experiences would then comprise the story.]

CLOSE (from 1948)

THEME MUSIC: Up full then under...

ANNOUNCER: Be sure to listen next week at this same time for *Life with Luigi*, a Cy Howard production. This is CBS, the Columbia Broadcasting System.

OPEN (from 1952)

THEME MUSIC: Up full then under...

ANNOUNCER (Charles Lyon): The makers of Wrigley's Spearmint Chewing Gum invite you to enjoy life, *Life with Luigi*, a comedy starring that celebrated actor, Mr. J. Carrol Naish with Alan Reed as Pasquale.

THEME MUSIC: Up full then out.

ANNOUNCER: Friends, the makers of Wrigley's Spearmint Chewing Gum are glad to bring you *Life with Luigi* because they feel it is a friendly, good-natured show that offers you relaxation and enjoyment. And you know Wrigley's Spearmint Chewing Gum offers you relaxation and enjoyment too. So chew Wrigley's Spearmint Gum often, every day. Millions enjoy it and you will too. Now Wrigley's Spearmint Chewing Gum brings you Luigi as he writes another letter describing his adventures in America to his Mama Basco in Italy.

CLOSE (from 1952)

THEME MUSIC: Up full then under...

ANNOUNCER: The makers of Wrigley's Spearmint Chewing Gum invite you to listen next week at this same time when Luigi Basco writes another letter to Mama Basco in Italy. *Life with Luigi* is a Cy Howard production. This is CBS, the Columbia Broadcasting System.

THEME MUSIC: Up full then fade out.

229. The Lifebuoy Show

Music, songs and comedy featuring host Bob Burns as the Arkansas Traveler. Sponsored by Lifebuoy Soap. NBC, 1944–1946.

OPEN

CHORUS: Lifebuoy, the name of the soap is Lifebuoy.

ANNOUNCER (Doug Gorlay): From Hollywood, *The Lifebuoy Show* starring Lifebuoy's own Bob Burns with Bob's special guest for tonight, Cass Daley and ventriloquist Shirley Dinsdale and her mischievous little doll, Judy; that band that plays for fun, Spike Jones and His City Slickers; and here he is for Lifebuoy, America's great storyteller, philosopher, traveler and exponent of good old common sense, Bob Burns. [He would then begin the show with a joke-telling session.]

CLOSE

THEME MUSIC: Up full then under...

ANNOUNCER: You have been listening to *The Lifebuoy Show* with Lifebuoy's own Bob Burns, America's great storyteller. This is Doug Gorlay speaking for Lever Brothers Company, makers of Lifebuoy Soap. Be with us again next week at this same time for another session of *The Lifebuoy Show*. This is NBC, the National Broadcasting Company.

THEME MUSIC: Up full then out.

SOUND: NBC chimes. N-B-C.

230. Light of the World

Dramatizations based on stories from the Bible. Sponsored by General Mills. CBS, 1940–1950. Bret Morrison served as the narrator. The following excerpts are from the episode of June 6, 1944 (the date of the D-Day invasion). General Mills donated its commercial time for the war bond drive.

OPEN

THEME MUSIC: Up full then under...

ANNOUNCER (Ted Campbell): *The Light of the World*. The story of the Bible, an external beacon lighting man's way through the darkness of time. Brought to you by General Mills.

THEME MUSIC: Up full then out.

ANNOUNCER: You know now the invasion is actually under way. I don't believe there is one of us who doesn't feel a deep personal obligation to every man on the invasion front. We all feel that nothing is too much for us to do to back up our men, that nothing we could do could ever compare with what they're doing for us. Well, there are many things we can do, but one thing we must do right away is to put every dollar that we absolutely don't have to use for food or rent or doctor bills into war bonds. Yes, we must give our men over there all-out financial support right away. The greater the battle, the greater the need of our money for their equipment. And right now, they're engaged in the greatest battle in our history, the greatest battle in the history of the world. Yes, whatever we do, we must all dig deeply into our pockets and our savings accounts and put every dollar we can possibly spare into war bonds right away. It's now or never.

THEME MUSIC: Up full then under...

ANNOUNCER: On this critical day in our history our thoughts are with the valiant men who stormed the fortress of Europe and our hearts are united in a single prayer, a prayer that God will watch over the men we love, granting the victory for which they fight and the lasting peace which victory will bring. In the belief that the lessons on the pages of the Bible will bring comfort and inspiration at this time of conflict and crisis, we put aside our story today of Jezebel's daughter, Ethalia, to recall some of the immortal stories of man's faith in God and of God's mercy and goodness...

CLOSE

THEME MUSIC: Up full then under...

ANNOUNCER: Now with the invasion so much on our minds, naturally we're all talking about it. It's the most important thing in our lives. But please, when we talk, let's remember this—careless talk costs lives. Our enemy is clever, he hopes we aren't. He hopes we'll tell in a bus, or a restaurant, or to someone who'll repeat it, some little piece of information he wants. He hopes we'll talk about our letters from men in the service and repeat what they said. And those of us who are in war work— yes, he hopes we'll let out some of the things we know about our work. Well, let's fool him please. The enemy has big ears; he hopes we have big mouths. Let's show him he's wrong. Let's think before we speak. Let's remember that careless talk costs lives.

THEME MUSIC: Up full then under...

ANNOUNCER: *Light of the World*, the day-to-day story of the Bible, currently the story of Jezebel's daughter, Ethalia from the Second Book of Chronicles, will be continued tomorrow at this same time. This is Ted Campbell inviting you to be with us then.

THEME MUSIC: Up full then out.

ANNOUNCER: This is CBS, the Columbia Broadcasting System.

231. Lights Out

Suspense stories dealing with the occult and the supernatural. Various sponsors. NBC (1935–1939; 1945–1946), CBS (1942–1943), ABC (1947). The series was hosted by Wyllis Cooper (1934–1936), Arch Oboler (1936–1939; 1942–1946) and Boris Karloff (1947).

OPEN (early)

SOUND: Howling dogs, blowing wind.
THEME MUSIC: Up full then under...
ANNOUNCER (George Stone): This is the witching hour. It is the hour when dogs howl and evil is let loose on a sleeping world. Want to hear about it? Then turn out your lights!

CLOSE (early)

SOUND: Howling dogs, blowing wind.
THEME MUSIC: Up full then under...
ANNOUNCER: *Lights Out*, with your host, the writer and producer of these *Lights Out* stories, Wyllis Cooper, will return next week at this same time. Be with us then. This is the Red Network of the National Broadcasting Company.
THEME MUSIC: Up full then out.
SOUND: NBC chimes. N-B-C.

OPEN (later)

ANNOUNCER (Bob Lemond): Lights Out, everybody.
SOUND: A gong.
HOST (Arch Oboler): It ... Is ... Later ... Than ... You ... Think. This is Arch Oboler bringing you another in our series of stories of the unusual. And once again we caution you— these *Lights Out* stories are definitely not for the timid soul. So we tell you calmly and very sincerely, if you frighten easily, turn off your radio now. [Arch would then introduce the evening's story.]

CLOSE (later)

HOST: Our play has ended and may it always continue to be just that—a play. This is Arch Oboler inviting you to be with us again next week for another *Lights Out*. Until then, pleasant dreams.
THEME MUSIC: Up full then under...
ANNOUNCER: *Lights Out* with your host, the writer and producer of *Lights Out*, has come to you from our studios in New York. This is NBC, the National Broadcasting Company.
THEME MUSIC: Up full then out.
SOUND: NBC chimes. N-B-C.

232. The Line-Up

Crime drama that detailed the investigations of Lt. Ben Guthrie and Sgt. Matt Grebb of the San Francisco Police Department. Sustaining. CBS, 1950–1953. Bill Johnstone played Ben Guthrie; Joseph Kearns, Wally Maher then Santos Ortega played Matt Grebb.

OPEN

ANNOUNCER (Dan Cubberly): Ladies and gentlemen, we take you behind the scenes at a police headquarters in a great American city where, under glaring lights, will pass before us the innocent, the vagrant, the thief, the murderer. This is *The Line-Up*.
THEME MUSIC: Up full then out.

CLOSE

THEME MUSIC: Up full then under...

ANNOUNCER: *The Line-Up*, where before you passed the innocent, the vagrant, the thief, the murderer. Listen again next week when we bring you *The Line-Up*.

THEME MUSIC: Up full then under...

ANNOUNCER: *The Line-Up* starring Bill Johnstone as Lieutenant Ben Guthrie and Wally Maher as Sergeant Matt Grebb was written by E. Jack Neuman with music composed and conducted by Eddie Dunstedter. *The Line-Up* is produced and directed by Jaime Del Valle.

THEME MUSIC: Up full then under...

ANNOUNCER: All the best fun-making from Arthur Godfrey's daytime shows on CBS Radio. That's what you'll hear every Sunday afternoon on most of these same CBS stations when king Arthur Godfrey and his roundtable holds court. Dan Cubberly speaking; and remember, you'll enjoy *Grand Central Station* every Saturday in the daytime hours on the CBS Radio Network.

THEME MUSIC: Up full then fade out.

233. The Linit Bath Club Revue

Variety series hosted by Fred Allen that combined music and songs with jokes and skits. Sponsored by Linit Beauty Bath. CBS, 1932–1933. The opening and closing segments are from the broadcast of December 25, 1932.

OPEN

THEME MUSIC ("Hello, Evening Star"): Up full then under...

ANNOUNCER (Ken Roberts): Christmas greetings, ladies and gentlemen, from the makers of Linit, the bath way to a soft, smooth skin. Hope you've had a joyful holiday. Tonight we present for your entertainment, Fred Allen and his associate members of *The Linit Bath Club Revue*. An announcement of unusual importance to every woman in the radio audience will be made later in the program. Be sure to listen for it. And now on with the show. Presenting Fred Allen.

SOUND: Applause.

FRED: Thank you ladies and gentlemen, thank

you. [Following Fred's monologue, the announcer returns.]

ANNOUNCER: Here is the announcement you have been waiting to hear. After you have enjoyed the delightful luxury of the sensational Linit Beauty Bath, do not discard the Linit package for the top of every Linit package now has real value. If you will send it to us with ten cents to cover handling and postage, we will mail you an attractive perfume container. Avoid delay, order yours tonight and be the first one in your set to have one or more of these smart perfume containers. Here's all you have to do. Send the top flap of a Linit package together with ten cents to cover handling and postage to the makers of Linit. You will find the address printed on the Linit package. This premium offer is confined to the United States only.

CLOSE

THEME MUSIC: Up full then under...

FRED: Good night ladies and gentlemen and I hope you all enjoyed a real pleasant Christmas. And while it's a little early, I trust you will all have a happy and prosperous 1933. There's some consolation, though. No matter what other nations reject their war debts, America certainly got even with Turkey today. So don't forget, we'll all be looking for you next Sunday.

ANNOUNCER: This is Ken Roberts saying goodbye for Linit. this is the Columbia Broadcasting System.

Note: The program also featured Portland Hoffa and the Lou Katzman Orchestra.

234. The Little Man Inside

Comedy with Jack Webb as the voice of conscience inside the head of harassed businessman John Nelson. Sustaining. NBC Blue, 1941.

OPEN

THEME MUSIC: Up full then under...

ANNOUNCER: Presenting *The Little Man Inside*. The Blue Network introduces *The Little Man Inside*. It's the story of that peculiar character within us that dictates our thoughts and runs our machinery, sometimes so differently than the way we want them to run. Here is the story of everyday John Nelson and his thoughts; but there is nothing commonplace about his thoughts and through the medium of this program, we bring you John Nelson, his down-to-earth adventures, and his out-of-this world thoughts.

THEME MUSIC: Up full then out.

CLOSE

THEME MUSIC: Up full then under...

ANNOUNCER: And so closes another episode in the life of John Nelson and *The Little Man Inside*. Listen again tomorrow at this same time as John Nelson, with the help of *The Little Man Inside*, tries to solve the mystery of why his son punched the neighborhood boy in the left eye. And tune in every day at this same time for the unusual program, *The Little Man Inside*. This is the Blue Network.

THEME MUSIC: Up full then out.

235. Little Orphan Annie

Adventure serial about an orphan girl and her dog (Sandy), the wards of "Daddy" Oliver Warbucks. Sponsored by Ovaltine. Blue (1931–1936), NBC (1936–1940), Mutual (1940–1942). Shirley Bell and Janice Gilbert played Annie with Stanley Andrews, Henry Saxe and Boris Aplon as Daddy Warbucks.

OPEN

THEME MUSIC ("Little Orphan Annie"): Up full then under...

SONG:
> Who's that little chatterbox?
> The one with pretty auburn locks?
> Whom do you see,
> Little Orphan Annie.
> She and Sandy make a pair,
> They never seem to have a care.
> Cute little she,
> It's Little Orphan Annie.

ANNOUNCER (Pierre Andre): Well, here it is, 5:45 again, the time you hear *Little Orphan*

Annie before drinking your Ovaltine every night.

THEME MUSIC: Up full then under...

ANNOUNCER: Every time you treat yourself to Ovaltine, you're helping Annie too because that's the way you help to keep her adventures going on the radio. So if you haven't had your Ovaltine lately, ask your mother to get you a can at her drug or grocery store right away. And remember, it's especially important to get that Ovaltine now, because then you'll have a chance to get that beautiful Orphan Annie birthday ring we've been telling you about. Boys and girls everywhere are sending in for their rings now. And everybody who sees this ring wants one like it right away. They just can't get over what a beauty it is, with its genuine gold-plated finish and its beautiful big birthstone that sparkles and shines like everything. So you certainly want to get busy and send for your ring this very night. Be sure to keep listening after tonight's adventure is over because I'm going to tell you exactly how you can get your Orphan Annie birthday ring if you get busy right away. But now for our adventure...

CLOSE

ANNOUNCER: And now, if any of you boys and girls haven't sent in for your Orphan Annie ring yet, listen carefully because I'm going to tell you exactly how you can get this ring with your own special birthstone in it to make it your personal birthstone ring. You'll be surprised when you see how bright and shiny it is because it's a genuine gold-plated ring, finished in genuine 24-karat gold plate with a special rose-gold finish over that. And what's more, it's an automatic fitting ring, so it's sure to fit your finger exactly right where you wear it. And just wait until you see the birthstone that's set in this ring. It's a handmade simulated birthstone that we specially imported from Europe. And best of all, Annie sees that you get your own special birthstone in your ring. You know, we've seen some rings with imported, simulated birthstones like these selling for as much as two to four dollars in the stores. But you can't buy one of these Orphan Annie birthday rings anywhere because they were made especially for Annie's friends who drink Ovaltine and you can get one for only ten cents in coin and just one Ovaltine aluminum seal. Here's all you have to do. Just print your name and address plainly on a piece of paper. Next, put down your birthday month. Then send it all to Little Orphan Annie, Chicago, Illinois. That's all there is to it. Be sure to put down your exact birthday month so Annie will know what kind of birthstone to have put in your ring. And be sure to put in the Ovaltine seal and ten cents in coin when you send your letter to Annie. And then Annie will send you her gold-plated birthday ring as fast as she can. So get busy this very night. And be here right on the dot tomorrow at 5:45 because nobody wants to miss out on the fun of our next adventure with Annie. That will be tomorrow at 5:45 remember. Until then, goodbye.

THEME MUSIC: Up full then fade out.

236. The Lives of Harry Lime

Adventure about Harry Lime (Orson Welles), an international rogue and confidence man. Various sponsors. Syn., 1952–1953. Anton Karas composed "The Third Man Theme."

OPEN

ANNOUNCER: Presenting Orson Welles as *The Third Man.*

THEME MUSIC: Up full then under...

ANNOUNCER: *The Lives of Harry Lime*, the fabulous stories of the immortal character originally created in the motion picture *The Third Man* with zither music by Anton Karas.

SOUND: A gunshot.

HARRY LIME: That was the gunshot that killed Harry Lime. He died in a sewer beneath Vienna, as those of you know who saw the movie *The Third Man.* Yes, that was the end of Harry Lime, not the beginning. Harry Lime had many lives and I can recount all of them. How do I know? It's very simple, because my name is Harry Lime.

THEME MUSIC: Up full then out.

CLOSE

THEME MUSIC: Up full then under...

ANNOUNCER: *The Lives of Harry Lime* stars Orson Welles in the title role. Harry Alan Towers is the producer.

THEME MUSIC: Up full then out.

237. The Log of the Black Parrot

Audition program that was an attempt to revise *The Voyage of the Scarlet Queen* (*see* that entry) with Elliott Lewis as Matthew Kincaid, master of a schooner called the *Black Parrot.* The program was virtually identical with the prior series with only Lewis's character name being different. Sustaining. CBS, May 6, 1950. Ed Max recreated his role of Red Gallagher, the first mate.

OPEN

SOUND: Ocean waves; wind hitting a ship's sails.

THEME MUSIC: Up full then under...

KINCAID: Log entry, the schooner *Black Parrot*, Matthew Kincaid, master. Six, May, 1950. Position, 17 degrees, 5 minutes South; 147 degrees West. Course, 43 degrees. Fresh breeze, sky overcast; barometer, 310 and falling.

THEME MUSIC: Up full then under...

ANNOUNCER (Bob Stevenson): *The Log of the Black Parrot* with Elliott Lewis starred as Captain Matthew Kincaid and written by the masters of the sea story, Gil Dowd and Anthony Ellis.

THEME MUSIC: Up full then under...

ANNOUNCER: The passage of the black schooner sailing the southern oceans, sailing into adventures with the strange and restless man who is her master, as set down in *The Log of the Black Parrot.*

THEME MUSIC: Up full then under... (as the story would then begin.)

CLOSE

ANNOUNCER: You are listening to Elliott Lewis as Captain Matthew Kincaid in Gil Dowd and Anthony Ellis's story of the sea, *The Log of the Black Parrot.*

THEME MUSIC: Up full then under...

KINCAID: Log entry, the schooner *Black Parrot*,

5:30 P.M. Wind, fresh; sky, fair. Sea cresting with high cross swells. Ship secure for the night; signed, Matthew Kincaid, master.

THEME MUSIC: Up full then under...

ANNOUNCER: You're invited to sail into further adventures with *The Log of the Black Parrot* next week at this same time. Ed Max is heard as Red Gallagher. Music was conducted by Walter Schumann and composed by Nathan Scott. *The Black Parrot* was produced by El-liott Lewis and directed by Gil Dowd.

THEME MUSIC: Up full then out.

ANNOUNCER: Bob Stevenson speaking. This is CBS, the Columbia Broadcasting System.

238. The Lone Ranger

Western about the only survivor of a group of Texas Rangers who avenges crimes as the Lone Ranger. Various Sponsors (most often by Bond Bread, Cheerios Cereal and Silvercup Bread). Mutual (1933–1942), Blue/ABC (1942–1954).

John Reid, alias the Lone Ranger, was first played by George Seaton, then Jack Deeds and James Jewell (all in 1933). Earl Graser next played the Ranger (1933–1941) followed by Brace Beemer (1941–1954). Tonto, his faithful Indian friend, was played by John Todd. The first recorded program aired on January 17, 1938. Programs broadcast prior to this date were pre-sented live and are believed not to exist in recorded form. "The William Tell Overature" by Rossini was used as the theme.

OPEN (early)

THEME MUSIC: Up full then under...

SOUND: Horse galloping.

LONE RANGER: Hi-yo, Silver, away!

SOUND: Gunshots.

ANNOUNCER: A fiery horse with the speed of light, a cloud of dust and a hearty hi-yo, Sil-ver! *The Lone Ranger!*

THEME MUSIC: Up full then under...

ANNOUNCER: When the Western United States were first opened to settlers, the promise of easy wealth brought honest men and criminals to the new territory. Both found that wealth could only be purchased by hard work and

the criminals returned to their old habits. The Masked Rider of the plains fought them tire-lessly, however. Astride his great horse Silver, he rode the length and breath of seven states in the cause of justice and in time brought law and order to the lawless frontier. Return with us now to those thrilling days when the west was young and adventure lay at the end of every trail. The Lone Ranger rides again!

LONE RANGER: Come along Silver. Tonto is waiting on the trail ahead. Hi-yo, Silver, aaaaa-waaaaay.

THEME MUSIC: Up full then out.

OPEN (later)

THEME MUSIC: Up full then under...

SOUND: Horse galloping.

LONE RANGER: Hi-yo, Silver!

SOUND: gunshots, hoofbeats.

ANNOUNCER: A fiery horse with the speed of light, a cloud of dust, and a hearty hi-yo, Sil-ver. *The Lone Ranger!* With his faithful In-dian companion, Tonto, the daring and re-sourceful Masked Rider of the plains led the fight for law and order in the early western United States. Return with us now to those thrilling days of yesteryear. From out of the past come the thundering hoofbeats of the great horse Silver. The Lone Ranger rides again!

LONE RANGER: Come on Silver, let's go big fella! Hi-yo, Silver, aaaaawaaaaay!

THEME MUSIC: Up full then out.

CLOSE (typical)

BANKER: That's the man I saw in the Sheriff's office.

SHERIFF: Well, if it wasn't for him, the crooks would have made off with all the money in your bank.

BANKER: By gosh, I reckon you're right, Sheriff. Just who is he?

SHERIFF: By golly, don't you know? Why he's the Lone Ranger.

RANGER (riding off): Hi-yo, Silver, aaaaa-waaaaay!

THEME MUSIC: Up full then under...

ANNOUNCER: This is a feature of the Lone Ranger, Incorporated, created and produced by George W. Trendle, directed by Charles B.

Livingston and edited by Fran Stryker. The part of the Ranger is played by Brace Beemer. This is Fred Foy speaking.

THEME MUSIC: Up full then fade out.

239. The Lone Wolf

Crime drama about Michael Lanyard, a private detective who is known as the Lone Wolf. Various sponsors. Mutual, 1948–1949. Walter Coy and Gerald Mohr played Michael Lanyard.

OPEN

SOUND: Knocks on a door.

GIRL: Who is it?

VOICE: Michael Lanyard.

SOUND: Door opening.

GIRL: The Lone Wolf.

MICHAEL: May I come in?

THEME MUSIC: Up full then under…

ANNOUNCER (Bob Anderson): Michael Lanyard returns in the adventures of *The Lone Wolf*. Mutual presents the adventures of *The Lone Wolf*, based on the famous character from American fiction by Louis Joseph Vance and known the world over for more than a quarter of a century. And now Walter Coy as Michael Lanyard, the Lone Wolf.

THEME MUSIC: Up full then out.

CLOSE

THEME MUSIC: Up full then under…

ANNOUNCER: You have been listening to *The Lone Wolf*, based on the character created by Louis Joseph Vance and starring Walter Coy as Michael Lanyard. This is Bob Anderson reminding you to join us again next week, same time, same station for another adventure of *The Lone Wolf*. This program came to you from Hollywood and was heard in Canada through the facilities of the Canadian Broadcasting System. This is the Mutual Broadcasting System.

THEME MUSIC: Up full then out.

240. Lorenzo Jones

Lighthearted serial about a garage mechanic and amateur inventor. Sponsored by Bayer Aspirin, Hazel Bishop Cosmetics, Phillips Milk of Magnesia, and Procter and Gamble. NBC, 1937–1955. Karl Swenson played Lorenzo Jones with Betty Garde and Lucille Wall as his wife, Belle. The song "Funiculi, Funicula" was used as the theme.

OPEN

THEME MUSIC: Up full then under…

ANNOUNCER (George Putnam): Now smile awhile with Lorenzo Jones and his wife, Belle. We all know couples like lovable and practical Lorenzo Jones and his dedicated wife Belle. Lorenzo's inventions have made him a character to the town, but not to Belle who loves him. Their struggle for security is anybody's story, but somehow with Lorenzo it has made more smiles then tears.

THEME MUSIC: Up full then out.

ANNOUNCER: The makers of Phillips Milk of Magnesia Tablets present this program for your enjoyment and to introduce to you the convenient tablet form of Phillips Milk of Magnesia. Each little tablet contains the equivalent of a teaspoonful of liquid Phillips. Phillips Milk of Magnesia Tablets act rapidly in the stomach to bring you prompt relief from acid indigestion and other upsets arising from excess stomach acidity. You can get the flat, purse-size tin for only 25 cents at any drugstore.

THEME MUSIC: Up full then under…

ANNOUNCER: And now to our story of Lorenzo Jones and his wife, Belle…

CLOSE

THEME MUSIC: Up full then under…

ANNOUNCER: Listen in tomorrow at this same time for the next episode of the story of *Lorenzo Jones*. Your announcer, George Putnam.

THEME MUSIC: Up full then out.

ANNOUNCER: This is NBC, the National Broadcasting Company.

SOUND: NBC chimes. N-B-C.

241. Luke Slaughter of Tombstone

Western about Luke Slaughter, a cavalryman turned cattle rancher. Sustaining. CBS, 1958. Sam Buffington played Luke Slaughter with Junius Matthews as his sidekick, Wichita Bagby; Charles Seel as Sheriff Clint Wallace; and Vic Perrin in various roles.

OPEN

SOUND: A cattle drive.

LUKE: Slaughter's my name, Luke Slaughter. Cattle's my business. It's a tough business. I've got a big stake in it. There's no man west of the Rio Grande big enough to take it from me.

THEME MUSIC: Up full then under...

ANNOUNCER: *Luke Slaughter of Tombstone*. Civil War cavalryman turned Arizona cattleman. Across the territory from Yuma to Fort Defiance; from Flagstaff to the Wachukas and below the border from Chiwawa to Sonora, his name was respected and feared—depending which side of the law you were on. Man of vision, man of legend—*Luke Slaughter of Tombstone*.

THEME MUSIC: Up full then out.

CLOSE

ANNOUNCER: *Luke Slaughter of Tombstone* starring Sam Buffington is produced by William N. Robson. Supporting Mr. Buffington were Junius Matthews, Charles Seel and Vic Perrin with music composed and conducted by Wilbur Hatch.

THEME MUSIC: Up full then under...

ANNOUNCER: Next week at this time we return with—

LUKE: Slaughter's the name, Luke Slaughter. When we meet up again you can call me that. Luke Slaughter.

ANNOUNCER: This is the CBS Radio Network.

THEME MUSIC: Up full then out.

242. Lum and Abner

Comedy about Lum Edwards (Chester Lauck) and Abner Peabody (Norris Goff), friends who run the Jot 'Em Down General Store in Pine Ridge, Arkansas. Sponsored by Alka Seltzer, Ford, Frigidaire and Quaker Oats. NBC Red (1931–1933), Mutual (1934—1935),

NBC Blue (1935–1938; 1941–1944), CBS (1938–1940; 1947–1950), ABC (1944–1947; 1953–1954). Half-hour version of the 15-minute series was called "The New Lum and Abner Show" (CBS, 1947–1950).

OPEN (15 min.)

SOUND: Phone rings.

LUM: The phone's ringing Abner. I believe that's our ring.

ABNER: I believe you're right. Let's see.

SOUND: Abner picking up the phone.

ABNER: Hello, Jot "Em Down Store. This is Lum and Abner.

ANNOUNCER (Gene Hamilton): Now let's see what's going on in Pine Ridge...

CLOSE (15 min.)

ANNOUNCER: Be with us again next week everybody. This is the Columbia Broadcasting System.

OPEN (1948)

SOUND: Phone rings.

LUM: By grannies, Abner, I believe that's our ring.

ANNOUNCER (Wendell Niles): Frigidaire, a division of General Motors, presents *The New Lum and Abner Show*. Tonight, Frigidaire brings you a new kind of visit with those old characters down in Pine Ridge, Arkansas, with Clarence Hartzell as Ben Withers, the music of Felix Mills and starring your old favorites, *Lum and Abner*.

THEME MUSIC: Up full then under...

ANNOUNCER: America's number-one refrigerator is Frigidaire. Number one in popularity, number one in dependability. So when it comes to a new refrigerator for your home, remember Frigidaire, America's number-one refrigerator.

THEME MUSIC: Up full then under...

ANNOUNCER: As we look in on the little community of Pine Ridge we find Lum and Abner in their Jot 'Em Down Store...

CLOSE (1948)

THEME MUSIC: Up full then under...

ANNOUNCER: *The New Lum and Abner Show* is

brought to you each week with the best wishes of your Frigidaire dealer, a division of General Motors, manufacturers of a complete line of appliances, air conditioners and commercial refrigeration equipment. And until next Sunday night, same time, same station, this is Wendell Niles saying good night for Frigidaire, America's number-one refrigerator. This is CBS, the Columbia Broadcasting System.

THEME MUSIC: Up full then out.

OPEN (1950)

ANNOUNCER (Wendell Niles): *The Lum and Abner Show.*

THEME MUSIC ("Down the Old Party Line"): Up full then under…

ANNOUNCER: With your old friends Zasu Pitts, Andy Devine, Cliff Arquette, Jim Backus, music by Opie Cates and starring Lum and Abner.

THEME MUSIC: Up full then out.

ANNOUNCER: *Lum and Abner* will be with us in a minute, but first a word from the Ford dealers of America.

SPOKESMAN: People everywhere are talking about the economy of the 1950 Ford. Ford owners everywhere are finding out about the economy of the great new Ford. They're saving real money now because of Ford's low price and they'll be saving real money for years to come because of Ford's low operating and maintenance costs. Why not see for yourself. Stop by your neighborhood Ford dealer. Get the facts on Ford economy, take the wheel and test drive the big new Ford.

ANNOUNCER: And here they are, your old favorites, *Lum and Abner.*

CLOSE (1950)

THEME MUSIC: Up full then under…

ANNOUNCER: Be with us again next week everybody. This is CBS, the Columbia Broadcasting System.

THEME MUSIC: Up full then out.

243. Ma Perkins

Daily serial about Ma Perkins, the mother of three children (John, Evey and Fay) and the owner of a lumberyard in the town of Rushville. Sponsored by Oxydol. NBC/CBS, 1933–1960. Virginia Payne played Ma Perkins with Rita Ascott, Marjorie Hannon, Cheer Brenston, Laurette Fillbrandt and Margaret Draper as Fay; Dora Johnson, Laurette Fillbrandt and Kay Campbell as Evey; and Gilbert Faust as John. The theme, "Ma Perkins," was composed by Don Marcotte.

OPEN

ANNOUNCER: Seeing is believing. See an Oxydol wash. See how Oxydol washes clothes white for life.

THEME MUSIC: Up full then under…

ANNOUNCER (Charles Warren): Now, everybody ready for Oxydol's own *Ma Perkins*, America's mother of the air, brought to you by Procter and Gamble, makers of Oxydol Soap Flakes.

THEME MUSIC: Up full then out.

ANNOUNCER: Today, the big news is reaching everywhere. News that there is a great new Oxydol, a wonderful new kind of Oxydol that works such wonders that we want you to see them for yourself because seeing is believing. First, clothes wash to a new brilliant whiteness, a new kind of radiant whiteness in a single washing. And second, clothes keep a brilliant new whiteness for all the years you wash them. They stay white for life. That's why we call the new Oxydol lifetime Oxydol. Many thousands of women from coast to coast have already been witness to the wonders of this new lifetime Oxydol. Don't miss this marvelous soap discovery. Lifetime Oxydol puts new whiteness in your clothes the very first wash. Keeps them white for life. See it happen and seeing is believing. Let Oxydol keep your clothes white for life.

THEME MUSIC: Up full then under…

ANNOUNCER: And now for *Ma Perkins*…

CLOSE

THEME MUSIC: Up full then under…

ANNOUNCER: Now there's new hope for dingy yellow clothes. Now there's new life for your whitest towels and table linen because now there's a great new Oxydol, a great new Oxydol with a washing action so amazing that it makes a wonderful change in your first wash. It's a change so startling that you have to see it to believe it. One Oxydol washing does it and what's more amazing is that as long as you keep using new Oxydol, your clothes keep a brilliant new whiteness for the years you wash them. They stay white for life. That's why this new Oxydol is called lifetime Oxydol. You'll see it happen and seeing is believing. Let Oxydol keep your clothes white for life.

THEME MUSIC: Up full then under...

ANNOUNCER: For now, this is Charles Warren inviting you to listen again tomorrow to Oxydol's own *Ma Perkins*, same time, same station—

THEME MUSIC: Up full then out.

ANNOUNCER: And reminding you that seeing is believing.

SOUND: Musical sting.

ANNOUNCER: See an Oxydol wash, see how Oxydol washes clothes white, for life.

THEME MUSIC: Up full then fade out.

244. The Magic Key of RCA

Variety series featuring performances by outstanding guests, including artists who recorded for the RCA Victor record label. Sponsored by RCA. NBC, 1935–1939. Frank Black composed the theme, "You Are Music."

OPEN

ANNOUNCER (John Wald): The Radio Corporation of America presents *The Magic Key*.

THEME MUSIC: Up full then under...

ANNOUNCER: Through the universal services of the Radio Corporation of America, *The Magic Key of RCA* returns to bring you another hour of entertainment from Minneapolis, Chicago and New York City, featuring the Minneapolis Symphony Orchestra under the distinguished leadership of Eugene Ormandy, Cornelia Otis Skinner, internationally famous character actress, Mischa Lebitsky, one of the great masters of the piano, and the noted NBC news commentator John B. Kennedy.

CLOSE

ANNOUNCER: The weekly radio concerts of the Minneapolis Symphony Orchestra are among the many excellent programs which come to you every week, every day, every hour of the day over the facilities of the National Broadcasting Company. In entering your house as a member of your family circle, NBC performs with friendly efficiency one of the most responsible portions of the universal theater of the Radio Corporation of America. Ever mindful of the wide variety of American tastes, program schedules range all the way from trivial comedy to superb Saturday afternoon operatic broadcasts direct from the stage of the Metropolitan Opera Company in New York City. In all, about 50,000 network programs are broadcast each year involving some 500,000 individual appearances before the microphone. Are you prepared for their reception? Will you hear voices and music perfectly reproduced exactly as they were transmitted from the studio? The famous RCA Magic Brain Radio with the magic eye and RCA metal tubes were created by the same engineers who designed the same equipment transmitting NBC programs. That's your best assurance of best reception to you always.

THEME MUSIC: Up full then under...

ANNOUNCER: We cordially invite you to be with us next Sunday when *The Magic Key* will return again and members of the RCA family will present Lauritz Melchoir, Ruth Etting, Russ Morgan and his orchestra, a scene from the current Broadway success *Call It a Day*, John B. Kennedy in a special feature, and Frank Black conducting the NBC Symphony Orchestra. This is John Wald speaking for members of RCA through the National Broadcasting Company.

THEME MUSIC: Up full then out.

SOUND: NBC chimes. N-B-C.

245. The Magnificent Montague

Comedy about Edwin Montague, a washed-up Shakespearean actor who now hosts a radio serial called "Uncle Goodheart." Various sponsors. NBC, 1950–1951. Monty Woolley played Edwin Montague with Anne Seymour as his wife, Lily.

OPEN

THEME MUSIC: Up full then under…

ANNOUNCER (Don Pardo): *The Magnificent Montague* starring Monty Woolley as Edwin Montague. The Magnificent Montague, or, as he modestly puts it himself, the greatest living Shakespearean actor on the stage, is today a broken man. This paragon of the legitimate theater, this thespian rock who sneered at anything not connected with the theater—this man today is in radio, thanks to his wife Lily Boheme, his one-time leading lady. Montague, the King Lear, the Macbeth of yesteryear is today Uncle Goodheart, hero of an afternoon radio serial.

THEME MUSIC: Up full then out.

CLOSE

THEME MUSIC: Up full then under…

ANNOUNCER: Tune in next week and find out what happens when the Magnificent Montague and radio meet head on. Remember next week, same time, same station, it's *The Magnificent Montague* starring Monty Woolley, created and written by Nat Hiken. Also in the cast were Anne Seymour as Lily and Pert Kelton as Agnes the maid. Original music was composed and conducted by Jack Ward. Don Pardo speaking. This is NBC, the National Broadcasting Company.

SOUND: NBC chimes: N-B-C.

246. Mail Call

Variety series geared to the U.S. military personnel stationed overseas during (and after) World War II. Sustaining. AFRS, 1942–1950.

OPEN (wartime)

MUSIC: Mail call bugle sound.

CLERK: All right men, here it is, *Mail Call.* Taylor. Harris. Swenson. Clark. Worsoski…

SOLDIER: Hey clerk, don't I rate?

CLERK: Sure soldier, here you are; this is for you—a letter from home.

GUEST HOST (here, Jack Benny): Hi ya, folks, this is Jack Benny speaking for Ann Sheridan, Rosemary Lane, the Kingsmen and myself. This letter from us to you is the best way we know to say we're thinking of you. It's presented especially for you men serving overseas by the Special Services Division of the War Department in cooperation with the leading motion picture studios in Hollywood. If the next thirty minutes makes you feel a little closer to home, that's what we're aiming for.

ANNOUNCER (Bill Goodwin): The *Mail Call* brings you a letter from home… [A voice is then heard reading, for example, a letter from a mother to her son. Music, skits and songs are used to convey the contents of that letter.]

CLOSE

ANNOUNCER: For Jack Benny, Ann Sheridan, Rosemary Lane, the Kingsmen and yours truly, Bill Goodwin, and all the *Mail Call* cast, the best of luck and so long for now. Another letter from home will be coming your way the next time you hear the "mail call."

OPEN (postwar)

SOUND: Army mail call bugle.

ANNOUNCER (Chet Huntley): *Mail Call* from the United States of America.

THEME MUSIC: Up full then under…

ANNOUNCER: Stand by Americans, stand by fighting men of the United Nations, here's your special air mail delivery letter from the United States. It's *Mail Call*, an open letter to you from any American with anything worth saying, playing or singing. It's *Mail Call*, the biggest slice of America we can send you in one radio envelope. Okay America, start writing.

THEME MUSIC: Up full then out. (At this time, the episode's guest host would begin the show, and guests would entertain.)

CLOSE

THEME MUSIC: Up full then under…

ANNOUNCER: That's all of *Mail Call* for this trip. Down at the bottom of the letter you'll see some autographs you might like to keep—

Charles Laughton, Fibber McGee and Molly, Frances Langford, Art Tatum and His Swing Trio, Desi Arnaz, the Douglas Serenaders, the Mail Call Orchestra, and yours truly, Chet Huntley. This broadcast is arranged through the cooperation of the Hollywood Victor Committee. Another *Mail Call* will be coming your way next time when you hear—

SOUND: Army mail call bugle.

ANNOUNCER: *Mail Call* is produced for you men in the armed forces of the United Nations by the Special Service Division of the War Department of the United States of America. This program has been a part of our English language shortwave service.

THEME MUSIC: Up full then fade out.

247. The Majestic Master of Mystery

Mystery stories, presented in serial form, as told by the Majestic Master of Mystery, spokesman for the show's sponsor, Majestic Radios. Syn., 1933–1934. Maurice Joachim played the Majestic Master of Mystery.

OPEN

ANNOUNCER: In the majesty of motion, from the boundless everywhere, comes the magic name, Majestic, Mighty Monarch of the Air. In just a few seconds you'll hear the first episode of that thrilling story "The Phantom Spoilers," as related by Majestic's Master of Mystery. He is brought to you through the courtesy of the manufacturers of Majestic Radios, America's most trusted radio receiver. At the conclusion of this program, the Majestic Master of Mystery will tell you about the fantastic gift he has for you and how to get it. And now "The Phantom Spoilers," related by Majestic's Master of Mystery himself.

CLOSE

ANNOUNCER: And who was the murdered man? The veil of mystery will undoubtedly be lifted when Majestic's Master of Mystery returns to the air with the next episode of "The Phantom Spoilers." And now he will tell you about the free gift he has to offer.

MASTER: In the heart of the jungle in India there grows the sacred sandalwood tree. For hundreds of years the sandalwood itself has been carved out by devout Hindus into swastika charms—the oldest good-luck emblem known to man. When I left India, I brought along quite a number of these sacred swastikas carved out of sandalwood. I want you to have a swastika absolutely free. You will be proud to own it, proud to display it. Your announcer will tell you how you may secure one of these sacred sandalwood swastikas absolutely free.

ANNOUNCER: Here is something that is well to remember. Only the finest tubes can give you the utmost in all-around performance. If you are replacing a single tube or a complete set, Majestic tubes will make your old radio new or your new radio perfect. These new tubes assure perfect tone and the finest reception. And now to secure the sandalwood swastika. When you purchase a Majestic tube, cut off the top and bottom flaps from the carton. Mail these two pieces together with your name and address to Majestic's Master of Mystery in care of this station. Then you will receive the sacred emblem that is a symbol of good luck absolutely free. Be with us again for *The Majestic Master of Mystery*.

248. Major Hoople

Comedy centered around Amos Hoople, a military man who runs the Hoople Boarding House with his wife, Martha. Sustaining. Blue, 1942–1943. Arthur Q. Bryan played Amos Hoople with Patsy Moran as Martha and Mel Blanc as their boarder, Tiffany Twiggs.

OPEN

THEME MUSIC: Up full then under...

ANNOUNCER: He's not a sergeant; he's not a lieutenant; he's not a captain. He's a major! Yes, ladies and gentlemen, it's *Major Hoople*.

SOUND: Applause.

THEME MUSIC: Up full then under...

ANNOUNCER: From out of the comic strip and into your homes, we bring you that overstuffed philosopher, Major Amos Hoople, his ever-loving but not-too-trusting wife,

Martha, his precocious nephew, Little Alvin, and his star boarder and number one complainer, Tiffany Twiggs.

THEME MUSIC: Up full then out.

CLOSE

THEME MUSIC: Up full then under...

ANNOUNCER: *Major Hoople* is based on the comic strip *Our Boarding House* by Gene Ahern and stars Arthur Q. Bryan as Major Hoople. Original music was composed and conducted by Lou Bring. Major Hoople comes to you each week at this same time over most of these same stations. This program came to you from Hollywood. This is the Blue Network.

THEME MUSIC: Up full then fade out.

249. The Man Behind the Gun

Anthology series based on the experiences of servicemen and women during World War II. Sustaining. CBS, 1942–1944.

OPEN

THEME MUSIC: Up full then under...

ANNOUNCER: The Columbia Broadcasting System presents *The Man Behind the Gun*, dedicated to the fighting men of the United States and the United Nations and broadcast in the hope that these authentic accounts of men and women will bring you a better understanding of the job being done by our fighting forces everywhere in the world and the job we have to do to keep them fighting.

THEME MUSIC: Up full then out.

CLOSE

NARRATOR (Jackson Beck): The Army Medical Corps needs nurses; it needs two thousand nurses a month. Registered nurses are urgently requested to apply for commission to the Surgeon General of the United States at Washington, D.C., or at the Red Cross chapter in your city. This is indeed a matter of life and death. Women without previous nurses' training are wanted as volunteer nurses' aides

to fill the gaps this war has made in nursing facilities here at home. Your local Red Cross will tell you how you can serve at home and help release a registered nurse for duty at the war front.

THEME MUSIC: Up full then under...

ANNOUNCER: All the incidents broadcast were based on fact; the names used, however, are fictitious, and any similarity to actual individuals in our armed forces is purely coincidental. Tune in again next week at this same time when *The Man Behind the Gun* brings you another report of history in the making. And remember, you'll listen with a clearer conscience if you've already bought that extra war bond. This is CBS, the Columbia Broadcasting System.

THEME MUSIC: Up full then fade out.

250. The Man Called X

Adventure about Ken Thurston, an American intelligence agent who operates under the code name "X." Various sponsors (General Motors, Lockheed, and Pepsodent were frequent sponsors). CBS (1944; 1947–1948), Blue/ABC (1944–1945), NBC (1945–1946; 1950–1952). Herbert Marshall played Ken Thurston.

OPEN

THEME MUSIC: Up full then under...

ANNOUNCER (Jack Latham): Listen now as Herbert Marshall stars as *The Man Called X.*

THEME MUSIC: Up full then under...

ANNOUNCER: Wherever there is mystery, intrigue and romance in all the strange, dangerous places of the world, there you will find Ken Thurston, *The Man Called X.*

THEME MUSIC: Up full then under...

ANNOUNCER: Ken Thurston is a man who crosses the ocean as readily as you and I cross town. He is a man who fights today's war in his unique fashion so that tomorrow's peace will make the world a safe neighborhood for all of us. Now, listen to Herbert Marshall as Ken Thurston in *The Man Called X.*

THEME MUSIC: Up full then out.

CLOSE

THEME MUSIC: Up full then under...

MARSHALL: Join us, won't you, when next I return as *The Man Called X*. Good night.

THEME MUSIC: Up full then under…

ANNOUNCER: *The Man Called X* starring Herbert Marshall is a J. Richard Kennedy production. All characters and incidents in this program are fictitious and any resemblance of incidents is purely coincidental. So until next week, please consult your local papers for time and station. This is Jack Latham saying good night from *The Man Called X*.

THEME MUSIC: Up full then fade out.

251. The Man from Homicide

Crime drama about Lieutenant Dana (Dan Duryea) of the Homicide Squad. Various sponsors, ABC, 1951.

OPEN

THEME MUSIC: Up full then under…

ANNOUNCER (Orville Anderson): *The Man from Homicide*, a new dramatic series starring Dan Duryea as Lieutenant Dana.

VOICE: According to Webster's unabridged dictionary, homicide is the killing of one human being by another.

DANA: According to a man from homicide, that's just the beginning of a dirty, dangerous job that doesn't end until the killer is found. But I like it, maybe because I don't like killers.

ANNOUNCER: And now *The Man from Homicide* starring Dan Duryea as Lieutenant Dana.

THEME MUSIC: Up full then out.

CLOSE

THEME MUSIC: Up full then under…

ANNOUNCER: You have just heard *The Man from Homicide* starring Dan Duryea. The script was written by Louis Vittes and was produced and directed by Helen Mack. Music composed and conducted by Robert Armbruster. Orville Anderson speaking. This is ABC, the American Broadcasting Company.

252. The Manhattan Merry-Go-Round

Music and songs presented from imaginary night clubs in New York City. Various sponsors. Blue (1932–1933), NBC (1933–1949).

OPEN

THEME SONG ("Manhattan Merry-Go-Round"): Up full then under…

CHORUS:
Jump on the Manhattan Merry-Go-Round
We're touring alluring old New York town.
Broadway to Harlem, a musical show
The orchestra directs at your radio.
We're serving music, fun and laughter
Our happy hearts will follow after,
And we'd like to have you all with us
On the Manhattan Merry-Go-Round.

THEME MUSIC: Up full then under…

ANNOUNCER (Ford Bond): Here's *The Manhattan Merry-Go-Round* that brings you the bright side of life, that whirls you in the music to one of the big spots in New York town to hear the top songs of the week sung so clearly you can understand every word and sing them yourself.

THEME MUSIC: Up full then out.

ANNOUNCER: RCA Victor presents *The Manhattan Merry-Go-Round*. Friends of RCA will be interested to know that RCA Victor will soon have on display a new 1937 line of RCA Victor radios and 27 of these new 1937 RCA radios are priced under $100. These radios incorporate many new features and many new improvements built out of the Radio Corporation of America's engineering experience in operating the world's largest broadcasting and world-wide communication services. Those of you who are planning to buy a new radio or phonograph, we urge you to compare RCA Victor's beautiful cabinets, superb engineering features and higher fidelity tone than the offerings of other radio manufacturers. If you do, we are sure your choice will be the choice of an increasing number of people—RCA Victor. These new 1937 instruments will be on display in most RCA Victor dealers stores within the next ten days. They may be purchased on convenient terms of payment.

THEME MUSIC: Up full then under... (as the program begins).

CLOSE

THEME MUSIC: Up full then under...

ANNOUNCER: RCA Victor has presented *The Manhattan Merry-Go-Round* with songs sung so clearly you can understand every word and sing them yourself.

THEME MUSIC: Up full then under...

ANNOUNCER: Ten short years ago, the National Broadcasting Company first came into existence. This year, on its tenth anniversary, this broadcasting service of RCA is the largest in the world. And understandably, the most pungent medium ever devised for the dissemination of music, information and entertainment. The same is true in communication; what was scarcely dreamed of a few years back is now a business necessity. Forty-seven foreign countries and a dozen cities in the United States are linked to RCA by the fastest and most direct means of radio telegraph known. In the field of manufactured products came the earliest radio sets. The new 1937 RCA Victor radios, which feature Magic Brain and Magic Eye metal rubes, will soon be on display and you will be amazed at the progress made toward perfect tone reproduction. In recorded music and phonographs, in marine radio, in sound motion pictures, in every interrelated field, the Radio Corporation of America is making history.

THEME MUSIC: Up full then under...

ANNOUNCER: Featured on tonight's show were Marian McManus, Glenn Cross, Lucy Marlowe, Dennis Ryan, Thomas L. Thomas, the Men About Town and the music of Victor Arden and his Broadway Stage Band. *The Manhattan Merry-Go-Round* is produced by Frank and Anne Hummert and directed by Paul DuMont. Ford Bond speaking. This is NBC, the National Broadcasting Company.

THEME MUSIC: Up full then out.

SOUND: NBC chimes. N-B-C.

253. Manhunt

Crime drama about Bill Morton (Maurice

Tarplin), a homicide detective who teams with medical examiner Drew Stevens (Larry Haines) to solve crimes. Various sponsors. Syn., 1945.

OPEN

ANNOUNCER (after a teaser is played to establish a crime): Clever murderer, clever. You figured out a murder that no man could commit with a weapon that may never be found. Who will know where or how to look for you? Who will start the "manhunt"?

SOUND: Clash of symbols.

ANNOUNCER: *Manhunt* and "The Clue of the Telltale Trigger."

SOUND: Clash of symbols.

CLOSE

SOUND: Clash of symbols.

ANNOUNCER: *Manhunt* with Larry Haines and Maurice Tarplin.

SOUND: Clash of symbols.

ANNOUNCER: Be with us for the next *Manhunt*.

SOUND: Clash of symbols.

254. Mark Sabre

Crime drama about a chief homicide inspector with the L.A.P.D. Sponsored by Bayer Aspirin, Dr. Lyon's Tooth Powder, Molle Shaving Creme and Phillips Milk of Magnesia. ABC, 1952–1954. Bill Johnstone and Robert Carroll played Mark Sabre.

OPEN

THEME MUSIC: Up full then under...

ANNOUNCER (Roger Forster): Bayer Aspirin, for fast relief of headache pain, brings you *Mystery Theater* and *Mark Sabre*, Chief Inspector with the Los Angeles Police Department.

THEME MUSIC: Up full then under...

ANNOUNCER: If you suffer with ordinary headaches, remember this about genuine Bayer Aspirin: you needn't accept anybody's word for its quick-acting properties. Your own eyes will show you one reason why Bayer Aspirin means fast relief. Simply drop a Bayer Aspirin tablet in a glass of water and watch how quickly it acts. You'll see it start to disintegrate before it reaches the bottom of the glass. And that's what it does in your stomach; it begins to disintegrate almost instantly. This amazingly fast disintegrating action is one reason you can see why Bayer Aspirin tablets give you relief with astounding speed. Keep this in mind next time you have a headache and want fast relief. When you buy ask for it by name—Bayer Aspirin, not just aspirin alone. Get the 100 tablet bottle and you get aspirin tablets for less than a penny apiece.

THEME MUSIC: Up full then under...

ANNOUNCER: Now to tonight's *Mark Sabre* story.

CLOSE

THEME MUSIC: Up full then under...

ANNOUNCER: Bayer Aspirin has just brought you transcribed Inspector Mark Sabre on *Mystery Theater*.

THEME MUSIC: Up full then under...

ANNOUNCER: If your teeth have gradually lost their old-time whiteness and brightness, perhaps it's because you've changed your way of cleaning teeth, so try using a dentifrice that whitens and brightens teeth, makes them really clean. And remember no dentifrice cleans teeth like powder. Try Dr. Lyon's Tooth Powder and if you don't agree it gets your teeth cleaner than your present dentifrice, return the package and your money will be refunded. Get regular or ammoniated Dr. Lyon's Tooth Powder.

THEME MUSIC: Up full then under...

ANNOUNCER: Inspector Sabre is played by Robert Carroll. Sergeant Tim Maloney is James Westerfield. The orchestra is conducted by Clark Whipple. The names of all characters in tonight's dramatization are fictitious and any resemblance to living persons is purely coincidental. Listen again next week to *Mystery Theater* and *Mark Sabre* of the Homicide Squad. Roger Forster speaking. This program has come to you from New York. America is sold on ABC, the American Broadcasting Company.

THEME MUSIC: Up full then fade out.

255. Mark Trail

Adventure series about Mark Trail, a con-

servationist who protects Nature from man. Mutual (1950–1951; sponsored by Kellogg's), ABC (1951–1953; sustaining). Matt Crowley, John Larkin and Staats Cotsworth played Mark Trail; with Ben Cooper and Ronald Liss as Scotty; and Joyce Gordon and Amy Sidell as Cherry, Mark's young friends.

OPEN

ANNOUNCER (Jackson Beck): Kellogg's Pep, the build-up wheat cereal with a prize in every package, invites you to share another thrilling adventure with Maaark Traaaaaail!

SOUND: Forest burning.

ANNOUNCER: Battling the raging elements!

SOUND: Wolf howl.

ANNOUNCER: Fighting the savage wilderness!

SOUND: Horse hoofbeats.

ANNOUNCER: Striking at the enemies of man and nature!

SOUND: Musical sting.

ANNOUNCER: One man's name resounds from snow-capped mountains to down across the sun-baked plains. Maaaark Traaaaaail!

SOUND: Musical sting.

ANNOUNCER: Guardian of the forests!

SOUND: Musical sting.

ANNOUNCER: Protector of wildlife!

SOUND: Musical sting.

ANNOUNCER: Champion of man and nature!

SOUND: Musical sting.

ANNOUNCER: Maaaark Traaaaaail!

CLOSE

ANNOUNCER: For more punch till lunch it's Kellogg's Corn Flakes and for more thrilling adventures in the great outdoors, it's *Mark Trail*.

THEME MUSIC: Up full then under...

ANNOUNCER: *Mark Trail* is based on the character created by Ed Dodd. Matt Crowley is heard as Mark Trail with Ben Cooper as Scotty and Joyce Gordon as Cherry. Jackson Beck speaking. This is the Mutual Broadcasting System.

THEME MUSIC: Up full then out.

256. The Marriage

Comedy-drama about incidents in the lives

of the Marriott family: parents Ben and Liz (Hume Cronyn, Jessica Tandy) and their children, Emily and Peter (Denise Alexander, David Pfeffer). Sustaining. NBC, 1953–1954. Basis for the television series.

OPEN

THEME MUSIC: Up full then under...

ANNOUNCER (Bob Denton): Jessica Tandy and Hume Cronyn in *The Marriage*. With a conviction that marriage remains the most popular domestic arrangement between friendly people, NBC takes pleasure in presenting one of the most distinguished couples in the American theater, Jessica Tandy and Hume Cronyn, transcribed, as Liz and Ben Marriott, bringing you the love and laughter of *The Marriage*.

THEME MUSIC: Up full then out.

CLOSE

THEME MUSIC: Up full then under...

ANNOUNCER: Let us extend an invitation to all of you to drop by next week at this same time for another half-hour observation of *The Marriage*. *The Marriage* is transcribed and written by Ernest Kinoy with Denise Alexander heard as Emily and David Pfeffer as Pete. *The Marriage* is an NBC Radio production directed by Edward King. This is Bob Denton speaking. This program came to you from our Radio City studios in New York. Let a kitchen radio fill your day with wonderful music on the NBC Radio Network.

THEME MUSIC: Up full then out.

SOUND: NBC chimes. N-B-C.

257. The Marx Brothers Show

Comedy that revolved around brothers Groucho and Chico Marx as the owners of a theatrical agency called the Square Deal Amusement Company. Sustaining. CBS, 1937–1938. The program featured singer Hollis Shore and the music of the Raymond Paige Orchestra.

OPEN

THEME MUSIC: Up full then under...

ANNOUNCER: From Hollywood, California, *The Marx Brothers Show*.

GROUCHO: Good evening, ladies and gentlemen. This is Groucho Marx speaking. Tonight, Chico and myself, with the help of that grand musical director Raymond Paige, bring you a slice of life in that crazy world they call Hollywood. As we drop into your home every Friday night, we're going to try to show you the unsung heroes of the motion picture business—the Hollywood agents.

THEME MUSIC: Up full then out.

CLOSE

THEME MUSIC: Up full then under...

GROUCHO: Ladies and gentlemen, this is Groucho Marx hoping that you liked the program and will be with us again next Friday evening. And so, my friends, for Raymond Paige and myself, I say good night. Say good night, Chico.

CHICO: Good night, Chico.

ANNOUNCER: This is the Columbia Broadcasting System.

THEME MUSIC: Up full then fade out.

258. Mary Foster, the Editor's Daughter

Daily serial about Mary Foster (Joan Banks), a reporter for the *Sentinel*, a small-town newspaper. Sponsored by Kroger's Baked Goods. Mutual, 1941–1948.

OPEN

ANNOUNCER: Kroger's, the store that gives you better value, better baked foods, presents *Mary Foster, the Editor's Daughter*.

CHORUS:
> Kroger's, Kroger's, Kroger's.
> Everything from bread to cake
> Is better if it's Kroger baked.
> Money-saving value too,
> Kroger's is the store for you.
> Kroger's, Kroger's, Kroger's.

ANNOUNCER: Yes friends, Kroger's is famous for fine baked foods, better baked food. You'll agree when you taste Kroger bread, the bread that has finer texture, better taste and longer-lasting freshness. Without a doubt it's the best bread that Kroger ever baked. Yes lady, if you want a bread that's velvet smooth, that stays fresh longer, then you want Kroger bread. Try it, enjoy the best bread that Kroger ever baked. And now *Mary Foster, the Editor's Daughter.*

CLOSE

ANNOUNCER: Kroger's, the store that gives you better value, better baked foods, has presented *Mary Foster, the Editor's Daughter.*

CHORUS:

> Kroger's, Kroger's, Kroger's.
> Everything from bread to cake
> Is better if it's Kroger baked.
> Money-saving value too,
> Kroger's is the store for you.
> Kroger's, Kroger's, Kroger's.

ANNOUNCER: That's right friends, you'll find the value of the week at your Kroger store, and this week it's Kroger Pineapple Fudge Golden Layer Cake, another oven treasure from the famous Kroger bakery. Two feather-light layers baked to a golden richness, filled with a delicate vanilla cream filling, then iced all over with pineapple preserves fudge icing. Kroger's Pineapple Fudge Golden Layer Cake is Kroger baked as only master bakers can bake it. It's the cake of the week, the value of the week for only 59 cents. So visit your neighborhood Kroger store, the only place you'll find Kroger's Pineapple Fudge Golden Layer Cake, feather light and oven fresh, only 59 cents. Another value of the week from Kroger's, the store that gives you better values, better baked goods.

THEME MUSIC: Up full then under...

ANNOUNCER: Tune in again tomorrow at this same time for another dramatic, transcribed chapter of *Mary Foster, the Editor's Daughter.* Joan Banks is heard as Mary Foster with Parker Fennelly as Henry Foster. This is the Mutual Broadcasting System.

THEME MUSIC: Up full then out.

259. Maxwell House Coffee Time

Comedy about incidents in the hectic lives of comedian George Burns and his wife Gracie Allen. Sponsored by Maxwell House Coffee. NBC, 1945–1950.

OPEN

GRACIE: Another cup of Maxwell House Coffee, George?

GEORGE: Sure, pour me another cup, Gracie.

GRACIE: You know, Maxwell House is always good to the last drop.

GEORGE: And that drop's good too.

THEME MUSIC ("Love Nest"): Up full then under...

ANNOUNCER (Toby Reed): Yes, it's *Maxwell House Coffee Time* starring George Burns and Gracie Allen with our special guest tonight, Bing Crosby, yours truly Toby Reed, Gale Gordon, Hans Conried, Henry Blair, Meredith Willson and the Maxwell House Orchestra, and Bill Goodwin. For America's Thursday night comedy enjoyment it's George and Gracie. And for America's everyday coffee drinking enjoyment, it's Maxwell House, always good to the last drop. And here they are, George Burns and Gracie Allen...

CLOSE

ANNOUNCER: Mmmmmm! So good to the last drop. Ask anybody what product is known by those words and their answer is certain to be Maxwell House Coffee. For generations those words have stood for coffee that's especially rich, mellow and full-bodied. More people buy Maxwell House than any other brand of coffee in the world because it's truly good to the last drop.

THEME MUSIC: Up full then under...

ANNOUNCER: Join us again next Thursday when we'll be back. George Burns, Gracie Allen, Bill Goodwin, Meredith Willson and the Maxwell House Orchestra, and yours truly Toby Reed. And now, here are our stars:

GEORGE: Good night everyone.

GRACIE: Until next Thursday, good night.

ANNOUNCER: Until next Thursday when Jane

Wyman will be our guest, good night and good luck from the makers of Maxwell House, America's favorite brand of coffee, always good to the last drop. This is NBC, the National Broadcasting Company.

SOUND: NBC chimes. N-B-C.

260. The Maxwell House Show Boat

Variety series that presented music, songs and comedy set on a Mississippi show boat. Sponsored by Maxwell House Coffee. NBC (1932–1937; 1940–1941).

OPEN

SOUND: People chatting as a show boat approaches shore and sounds its horn.

ANNOUNCER (John Stephenson): Ladies and gentlemen, here she comes, Maxwell House presents *The Maxwell House Show Boat*. Here you are, one solid hour of entertainment with Frank McIntire as Captain Henry, Louise Massey and the Westerners, Bob Hope, Sonny Childs, Ross Graham, Willie Morris, the famous Maxwell House Singers, Gus Haenschen and that Show Boat Band. The Mississippi's favorite show boat is puffing right down into Casco Bay tonight. Stand by for that landing folks.

CHORUS:
    Here comes the show boat,
    Here comes the show boat,
    Puff, puff, puff, puff,
    Puff, puff, puffing aaaa-loooong.

ANNOUNCER: And there on the bridge waving is Captain Henry himself.

CAPTAIN HENRY: Howdy, Howdy folks, come up the gangplank, everybody's welcome. Your ticket of admission is just your enjoyment of Maxwell House Coffee… [The program then begins.]

CLOSE

SOUND: People chatting as they disembark.

ANNOUNCER: The show's over and the show boat is departing but Captain Henry and *The Maxwell House Show Boat* will return next

Thursday at this same time. John Stephenson speaking for the makers of Maxwell House, America's largest-selling coffee. This is the NBC Radio Network.

SOUND: NBC chimes. N-B-C.

261. Mayor of the Town

Comedy about a kindly mayor in the town of Springdale. Sponsored by Mutual, Noxzema and Rinso. NBC (1941–1942), CBS (1942–1947), ABC (1947–1948), Mutual (1949). Lionel Barrymore, who played the Mayor, also composed the theme, "Mayor of the Town." Agnes Moorehead played his housekeeper, Marilly, and Conrad Binyon was his nephew, Butch.

OPEN

THEME MUSIC: Up full then under…

ANNOUNCER (Frank Martin): Noxzema presents *Mayor of the Town* starring Lionel Barrymore with Agnes Moorehead as Marilly and Conrad Binyon as Butch.

THEME MUSIC: Up full then under…

ANNOUNCER: Remember Mark Twain's famous comment "Everybody talks about the weather but nobody does anything about it?" Well, I'd like to add a postscript. You can do something about what the weather does to you. You don't just have to put up with a chapped, wind-burned face, rough red hands or the overall discomfort of winter skin. Reach for Noxzema Medicated Skin Cream. See how it soothes and softens dry skin, makes hands look white, more appealing. Get a jar of Noxzema tomorrow. The big ten-ounce economy size is being featured at your druggist now. And now to Springdale and the *Mayor of the Town* starring Lionel Barrymore.

THEME MUSIC: Up full then out.

CLOSE

THEME MUSIC: Up full then under…

ANNOUNCER: Be sure to be with us next week at this same time when the makers of Noxzema again present the *Mayor of the Town*. The original *Mayor of the Town* theme was composed by Lionel Barrymore. Mr. Barrymore appeared by arrangement with Metro-Gold-

wyn-Mayer. And now this is Frank Martin wishing you all a very pleasant good night from Noxzema. This is ABC, the American Broadcasting Company.
THEME MUSIC: Up full then fade out.

262. The McCoy

Crime drama about Mike McCoy (Howard Duff), a Hollywood-based private detective. Sustaining. NBC, 1951. Walter Schumann composed the theme.

OPEN

VOICE: This is *The McCoy*.
THEME MUSIC: Up full then under...
ANNOUNCER: The National Broadcasting Company presents *The McCoy* starring Howard Duff as Mike McCoy.
THEME MUSIC: Up full then under...
MIKE (typing): For the file, Mike McCoy, Criminal Investigator. File 354, twenty-second of April, 1951, Los Angeles, California... [As Mike continued to type, his report would be presented as the story.]

CLOSE

CLOSING THEME ("I'll Be Seeing You"): Up full then under...
ANNOUNCER: *The McCoy* starring Howard Duff is written, directed and produced by David Friedkin and Morton Fine with music composed and conducted by Walter Schumann. This has been an NBC Hollywood Program Department production.
THEME MUSIC: Up full then out.
SOUND: NBC chimes. N-B-C.

263. McGarry and His Mouse

Comedy about Dan McGarry, a trouble-prone rookie detective, and his "Mouse," Kitty Archer, the girlfriend who looks out for him. Various sponsors. NBC (1946), Mutual (1947). Roger Pryor, Wendell Corey and Ted de Corsia played Dan McGarry with Shirley Mitchell,

Peggy Conklin and Patsy Campbell as Kitty Archer.

OPEN

VOICE: Calling all cars. Calling all cars. Has anybody seen Detective McGarry?
McGARRY: Yea Sarge, I have.
SARGE: Who are you?
McGARRY: Detective McGarry.
THEME MUSIC: Up full then under...
ANNOUNCER (Bert Parks): Yes friends, it's *McGarry and His Mouse* starring Wendell Corey with Peggy Conklin. The misadventures of rookie detective McGarry have been made famous by Matt Taylor in the pages of *This Week* magazine. And now here he is, Dan McGarry himself. Handsome as ever, brave as ever and confused as ever.
THEME MUSIC: Up full then out.

CLOSE

THEME MUSIC: Up full then under...
ANNOUNCER: *McGarry and His Mouse* with Wendell Corey as Detective Dan McGarry and Peggy Conklin as his mouse, Kitty Archer, is based on characters created by Matt Taylor for *This Week* magazine. Be with us again next week for another *McGarry and His Mouse*. Bert Parks speaking, this is NBC, the National Broadcasting Company.
THEME MUSIC: Up full then out.
SOUND: NBC chimes. N-B-C.

264. Me and Janie

Humorous events in the life of George O'Hanlon (himself), his wife Janie (Lurene Tuttle) and their son Tommy (Jeffrey Silver). Sponsored by Tums. NBC, 1949.

OPEN

GEORGE: Hi folks, it's *Me and Janie*.
THEME MUSIC: Up full then under...
ANNOUNCER (Don Wilson): Yes friends, it's the Tums show, *Me and Janie* starring George O'Hanlon, the guy next door who is always trying to get out from behind the eight ball. And this is Don Wilson, ladies and gentlemen,

to tell you that if your favorite foods like coffee or steak smothered in onions give you heartburn or acid indigestion, listen. Now you can enjoy steak, onions, coffee and other foods you like without suffering acid indigestion. Simply take a couple of Tums after eating. Almost instantly Tums neutralizes excess acid and settles and soothes your stomach. You feel better fast. So to enjoy the foods you like, get Tums tonight. Only ten cents a roll, three roll box a quarter, at all drug stores. Tums—T-U-M-S—Tums for the tummy. And now *Me and Janie*, another adventure in the lives of George and Jane O'Hanlon.

THEME MUSIC: Up full then out.

CLOSE

THEME MUSIC: Up full then under...

ANNOUNCER: Be with us again next Tuesday when Tums, for relief of acid indigestion brings you *Me and Janie*. *Me and Janie* starred George O'Hanlon with Lurene Tuttle as Janie and Jeffrey Silver as Tommy. Original music was composed and conducted by Johnny Duffy. Don Wilson speaking for NBC, the National Broadcasting Company.

THEME MUSIC: Up full then out.

SOUND: NBC chimes. N-B-C.

265. Meet Corliss Archer

Comical events in the life of Corliss Archer, a 16-year-old high school girl. Various sponsors (Anchor Hocking Glass, Campbell Soup, Pepsodent and Toni were frequent sponsors). CBS (1943–1952; 1954–1956), ABC (1952–1953). Janet Waldo, Priscilla Lyon and Lugene Saunders played Corliss Archer with Fred Shields, Frank Martin and Bob Bailey as her father, Harry; and Irene Tedrow, Mary Jane Croft and Helen Mack as her mother, Janet. Basis for the television series.

OPEN

THEME MUSIC: Up full then under...

ANNOUNCER (Ken Carpenter): Transcribed from Hollywood, we invite you to *Meet Corliss Archer*, America's teenage sweetheart, featur-ing Fred Shields, Helen Mack and starring Janet Waldo as Corliss Archer.

THEME MUSIC: Up full then under...

ANNOUNCER: *Meet Corliss Archer* is brought to you by the Campbell Soup Company, makers of delicious Campbell's Tomato Soup.

THEME MUSIC: Up full then out.

ANNOUNCER: Campbell Tomato Soup is superb; its flavor is unmatched. Campbell uses only tomatoes grown under their supervision; tomatoes that are extra luscious, heavy with fine flavor and deep in color. Campbell takes these specially grown tomatoes and smoothly blends them with golden table butter and adds delicate seasonings to bring out the fresh, rich tomato flavor. This has been a great year for tomatoes and you'll enjoy more than ever the taste these fine tomatoes give to Campbell's Tomato Soup. So, won't you take this friendly reminder. For the rare, good eating that awaits you in a steamy plate full of Campbell's Tomato Soup, put Campbell's Tomato Soup on your grocery list right now. You'll be glad you did.

THEME MUSIC: Up full then under...

ANNOUNCER: And now to 32 Oak Street, the home of the Archer family, as we prepare to *Meet Corliss Archer*.

CLOSE

THEME MUSIC: Up full then under...

ANNOUNCER: *Meet Corliss Archer* starring Janet Waldo is based on characters created by F. Hugh Herbert. It is a James L. Sasser Production directed by Steven Hayden. *Meet Corliss Archer* has been presented by the Campbell Soup Company, makers of delicious Campbell's Tomato Soup. Ken Carpenter speaking. This is CBS, the Columbia Broadcasting System.

THEME MUSIC: Up full then fade out.

266. Meet Me at Parky's

Variety series that mixed music and songs with the comedy of Harry Einstein as Nick "Parky" Parkyakarkas, the owner of Parky's a Greek restaurant. Various sponsors. NBC (1945–1947), Mutual (1947–1948).

OPEN

ANNOUNCER: *Meet Me at Parky's.*

THEME MUSIC: Up full then under...

ANNOUNCER: Well, come along to Parky's Restaurant and say hello to Betty Rhodes, Sheldon Leonard, Wally Maher, Opie Cates, his clarinet and his orchestra, and our genial host, the star of our show, Parkyakarkas.

THEME MUSIC: Up full then out.

CLOSE

THEME MUSIC: Up full then under...

ANNOUNCER: *Meet Me at Parky's* starred Harry Einstein as Parky with Betty Jane Rhodes, Opie Cates, Sheldon Leonard and Wally Maher. Be with us again next week for *Meet Me at Parky's* starring Harry Einstein. Art Gilmore speaking.

THEME MUSIC: Up full then out.

267. Meet Millie

Comedy about Millie Bronson, a secretary who is secretly in love with her boss, investment counselor Johnny Boone, Jr. Various sponsors. CBS, 1951–1953. Basis for the television series. Audrey Totter and Elena Verdugo played Millie with Bea Benaderet and Florence Halop as her mother, "Mama"; Marvin Kaplan as their friend, Alfred; and John Tracy and Rye Billsbury as Johnny.

OPEN (Audrey Totter)

THEME MUSIC: Up full then under...

ANNOUNCER (Bob Lemond): And now, *Meet Millie*, created and transcribed by Frank Galen and starring Audrey Totter. Yes, we're about to say hello to Mama, played by Bea Benaderet, and Alfred, played by Marvin Kaplan, as once again we *Meet Millie*.

THEME MUSIC: Up full then out.

CLOSE (Audrey Totter)

THEME MUSIC: Up full then under...

ANNOUNCER: Don't forget next week at this same time when you have another date to *Meet Millie*. Music is composed and conducted by Irving Miller. *Meet Millie* is produced by Frank Galen and directed by Bill Manhoff. Bob Lemond speaking. This is the CBS Radio Network.

THEME MUSIC: Up full then out.

OPEN (Elena Verdugo)

ANNOUNCER (Roy Rowan): Arrid Creme Deodorant, America's largest-selling deodorant, presents *Meet Millie.*

THEME MUSIC: Up full then under...

ANNOUNCER: *Meet Millie*, created by Frank Galen. Starring Florence Halop as Mama, Marvin Kaplan as Alfred and Elena Verdugo as Millie.

THEME MUSIC: Up full then under...

ANNOUNCER: A gay comedy about the life and loves of a Manhattan secretary.

THEME MUSIC: Up full then out.

ANNOUNCER: Man, it's here, an utterly new kind of shave, a 24-hour shave. It's Rise, the self-rising lather, America's number one speed shave; now keeps you looking close-shaved and clean-shaved all day and all night. Unlike any other lather or brushless, Rise is super pressurized, creates millions of tiny bubbles, millions more than any other shaving creme. Its self-rising lather makes your whiskers stand up straight, soaks them soft down to the face so your razor actually cuts them off at the skin line, smoothly, comfortably. And here's the big bonus. Only Rise gives you built-in after-shave comfort. Combats razor sting and burn, leaves your skin feeling smooth and comfortable. Enjoy this new exciting 24-hour shave. Look close-shaved, clean-shaved all day, all night. Get Rise, America's number one shave, only 69 cents.

THEME MUSIC: Up full then under...

ANNOUNCER: And now to Elena Verdugo in *Meet Millie...*

CLOSE (Elena Verdugo)

WOMAN: Women, don't let perspiration stains ruin your dresses, use Arrid creme deodorant, the vanishing creme deodorant that now contains the magic ingredient Perstop. Use daily, new Arrid with Perstop gives more protection than the leading deodorant. Perstop in Arrid makes Arrid a real vanishing creme deodorant. So don't be half-safe, be completely safe, use Arrid to be sure.

THEME MUSIC: Up full then under…
ANNOUNCER: You have been listening to *Meet Millie* with Elena Verdugo as Millie, Florence Halop as Mama and Marvin Kaplan as Alfred. *Meet Millie* is created by Frank Galen and is produced and directed by Lester Vail. Music is under the direction of Irving Miller. Be sure to tune in again next week over most of these same stations when once again we *Meet Millie*. This is Roy Rowan speaking. *Meet Millie* is a CBS Radio Network production.
THEME MUSIC: Up full then fade out.

268. Meet Miss Sherlock

Crime drama about Jane Sherlock, a buyer for Blossom's Department Store, who helps her boyfriend, lawyer Peter Blossom, solve crimes. Various sponsors. CBS, 1946–1947. Sandra Gair, Betty Moran and Monte Margetts played Jane Sherlock with David Vale as Peter Blossom.

OPEN

THEME MUSIC: Up full then under…
ANNOUNCER (Murray Wagner): Jane Sherlock is not your average girl. She works for a department store and her last name is the first name of that great detective Sherlock Holmes. Jane feels that she too should be a detective and sets about helping her lawyer boyfriend, heir to the Blossom Department Store fortune, and the police solve crimes. Yes, it's time to *Meet Miss Sherlock*, a smart little gal who stumbles across real-live clues.
THEME MUSIC: Up full then out.

CLOSE

THEME MUSIC: Up full then under…
ANNOUNCER: Be with us again at this same time next week to *Meet Miss Sherlock*. Betty Moran appears as Jane with David Vale as Peter and Bill Conrad as Captain Dingle.
THEME MUSIC: Up full then under…
ANNOUNCER: *Meet Miss Sherlock*, produced by Dave Baer with original music by Milton Charles, is presented from Columbia Square in Hollywood. Murray Wagner speaking. This is the Columbia Broadcasting System.
THEME MUSIC: Up full then fade out.

269. Meet the Meeks

Comical incidents in the lives of Mortimer Meek (Forrest Lewis), his wife Agatha (Beryl Vaughn) and their daughter Peggy (Fran Allison). Sponsored by Swift and Company. NBC, 1947–1949.

OPEN

ANNOUNCER (John Weigel): Say, it's time for—
WOMAN: All Sweet.
MAN: Did you hear what the lady said?
WOMAN: I said All Sweet. All Sweet is the margarine with the delicate, natural flavor.
ANNOUNCER: Yes, friends, that's what all the ladies are saying. All Sweet, the margarine with the delicate, natural flavor. Swift's All Sweet Margarine invites you to the little white house with the green shutters on Elm Street to *Meet the Meeks* with Forrest Lewis as Mortimer Meek, whom we laughingly refer to as the head of the family.

CLOSE

ANNOUNCER: For spreading bread from crust to crust, All Sweet Margarine is a must. For giving recipes special flavor, creamy All Sweet wins your favor. No, ladies, I haven't turned poet; I'm just giving you the facts. The facts are mighty important to you flavor-wise, nutrition-wise and economy-wise. And say, speaking of being wise, you'll be wise to pick up some lickin' good All Sweet today. Whether you buy yellow All Sweet, as you may do if you live in one of the states whose laws permit the sale of colored margarine, or the regular white All Sweet, always insist on All Sweet, the margarine with the delicate, natural flavor.
THEME MUSIC: Up full then under…
ANNOUNCER: *Meet the Meeks* stars Forrest Lewis with Beryl Vaughn as Agatha and Fran Allison as Peggy. Be sure to join us over these same stations next Saturday when All Sweet, the margarine with the delicate, natural flavor, again invites you to *Meet the Meeks*. This is John Weigel speaking. This is NBC, the National Broadcasting Company.
THEME MUSIC: Up full then out.
SOUND: NBC chimes. N-B-C.

270. The Mel Blanc Show

Comedy that centers on Mel Blanc as the owner of Mel Blanc's Fix-It-Shop. Sponsored by Colgate. CBS, 1946–1947. Mel Blanc plays himself and Zookie, his dim-witted, Porky Pig–like talking assistant. Mary Jane Croft is Betty Colby, Mel's girlfriend and Joseph Kerns is Betty's father.

OPEN

THEME MUSIC: Up full then under...
ANNOUNCER (Bud Easton): From Hollywood, Colgate Tooth Powder presents *The Mel Blanc Show* with Mary Jane Croft, Joe Kearns, Hans Conreid, Earle Ross, the Sportsmen, Victor Miller and his orchestra and starring the creator of the voice of Bugs Bunny—
MEL: Ahhh, what's up Doc?
ANNOUNCER: Yes, Colgate Tooth Powder for a breath that's sweet and teeth that sparkle brings you *The Mel Blanc Show* with Mel playing his new character Zookie and starring himself in person, Mel Blanc.
MEL: Hi folks. Ugga ugga boo, ugga boo boo ugga.
SOUND: Applause over theme music as the show beings.

CLOSE

CHORUS:
Use Colgate Tooth Powder
Keep Smilin' just right.
Use it each morning
and use it each night.
Don't take a chance
With your romance
Use Colgate Tooth Powder.
MEL: This is Mel Blanc saying thanks for listening. Good night and tha-tha-tha-tha-that's all folks.
ANNOUNCER: This is Bud Easton reminding you that Colgate Tooth Powder for a breath that's sweet and teeth that sparkle brings you *The Mel Blanc Show* every Tuesday at this time. Be sure to join us again next Tuesday night with Mel and the people you'll meet at Mel Blanc's Fix-It-Shop. This is CBS, the Columbia Broadcasting System.

Note: Mel is a member of a lodge called the Loyal Order of Benevolent Zebras and "ugga ugga boo, ugga boo boo ugga" is the secret password.

271. Melody and Madness

Variety program of music, songs and light comedy hosted by Robert Benchley. Sponsored by Old Gold Cigarettes. CBS, 1938–1939.

OPEN

ANNOUNCER (Del Sharbutt): Will somebody please wake up Benchley.
CHORUS:
Will somebody wake up Benchley,
Will somebody wake up Benchley.
Better get him up,
Will somebody please wake up Benchley.
ROBERT BENCHLEY (yawning): I'm up!
THEME MUSIC: Up full then under...
ANNOUNCER: Old Gold presents Robert Benchley in *Melody and Madness*. The Steve Allard Company, makers of those double mellow Old Gold Cigarettes, welcomes you to another Sunday night program featuring the music of Artie Shaw and his orchestra. And starring radio's leading lobbyist for lucid lunacy, Robert Benchley.

CLOSE

THEME MUSIC: Up full then under...
ANNOUNCER: This is Del Sharbutt inviting you to be with us again next Sunday night when the Steve Allard Company, makers of those double mellow Old Gold Cigarettes, presents another session of lunacy with Robert Benchley. This program has come to you from New York. This is CBS, the Columbia Broadcasting System.
THEME MUSIC: Up full then fade out.

272. The Mercury Theater on the Air

Dramatic adaptations of stories by famous authors. Sustaining. CBS, 1938. Orson Welles served as the host. The first movement from Tchaikovsky's *First Piano Concerto* was used as the theme. The segments that follow are from the episode of October 30, 1938 ("The War of the Worlds").

ANNOUNCER: The Columbia Broadcasting System and its affiliated stations present Orson Welles and *The Mercury Theater on the Air* in "The War of the Worlds" by H.G. Wells.

THEME MUSIC: Up full then under...

ANNOUNCER: Ladies and gentlemen, the director of the Mercury Theater and star of these broadcasts, Orson Welles. [Orson would then begin the drama with a prologue of events to come; here, the story of a Martian invasion of Earth.]

CLOSE

THEME MUSIC: Up full then under...

ORSON: This is Orson Welles, ladies and gentlemen, out of character to assure you that "The War of the Worlds" has no further significance than the holiday offering it was intended to be. It was our version of dressing up in a sheet and saying boo. Starting now, we couldn't soap all your windows and steal all your garden gates by tomorrow night so we did the next best thing; we annihilated the world before your very ears and utterly destroyed the CBS. You'll be relieved, I hope, to learn that we didn't mean it and that both institutions are open for business. So goodbye, everybody, and remember please, for the next day or so, the terrible lesson you learned tonight: that grinning, glowing, globular invader of your living room is an inhabitant of the pumpkin patch and if your doorbell rings and nobody is there, that was no Martian, it's Halloween.

THEME MUSIC: Up full then under...

ANNOUNCER: Tonight the Columbia Broadcasting System and its affiliated stations from coast to coast has brought you "The War of the Worlds" by H.G. Wells, the 17th in its weekly series of dramatic broadcasts featuring Orson Welles and *The Mercury Theater on the Air*. Next week we present a dramatization of three famous short stories. This is the Columbia Broadcasting System.

THEME MUSIC: Up full then fade out.

273. Michael Shayne

Crime drama about a tough private detective named Michael Shayne. In the first version of the series, *Michael Shayne, Private Detective* (Mutual, 1944–1946), Wally Maher (then Louis Arthur) played Michael Shayne. Phyllis Knight, his secretary and girlfriend, was played by Cathy Lewis. The second version of the series, *The New Adventures of Michael Shayne* (ABC, 1948–1950), starred Jeff Chandler in the title role (Phyllis was not a part of the format). The final version, *The Adventures of Michael Shayne* (ABC, 1952–1953), starred Robert Sterling as Michael Shayne and Judith Parrish as Phyllis Knight. Various sponsors.

OPEN (Michael Shayne, Private Detective)

THEME MUSIC: Up full then under...

ANNOUNCER: *Michael Shayne, Private Detective* starring Wally Maher and Cathy Lewis in a series of mystery stories based on the fictional detective created by Brett Halliday. And now, with Wally Maher starred, we present *Michael Shayne, Private Detective*.

THEME MUSIC: Up full then out.

CLOSE (Michael Shayne, Private Detective)

THEME MUSIC: Up full then under...

ANNOUNCER: You have been listening to *Michael Shayne, Private Detective*. Our program stars Wally Maher as Michael Shayne with Cathy Lewis as Phyllis Knight. All names used in tonight's story are fictitious; any resemblance to actual persons is purely coincidental. Michael Shayne is based on the character created by Brett Halliday. Be with us again next week for another *Michael Shayne, Private Detective*. This is Mutual.

THEME MUSIC: Up full then out.

OPEN (The New Adventures of Michael Shayne)

THEME MUSIC: Up full then under...

ANNOUNCER (Bill Russo): *The New Adventures of Michael Shayne* starring Jeff Chandler. Michael Shayne is back in his old haunts in New Orleans. This is your director, Bill Russo, inviting you to listen to another transcribed adventure from the files of Michael Shayne, private detective.

THEME MUSIC: Up full then out.

CLOSE (The New Adventures of Michael Shayne)

THEME MUSIC: Up full then under…

ANNOUNCER: *The New Adventures of Michael Shayne* starring Jeff Chandler has come to you, transcribed, from Hollywood. This is your director, Bill Russo, inviting you to be with us again next week for another transcribed adventure from the files of Michael Shayne, private detective. The character of Michael Shayne is based on the stories by Brett Halliday. All names used are fictional; any resemblance to real persons is unintentional. This is ABC, the American Broadcasting Company.

THEME MUSIC: Up full then out.

OPEN (The Adventures of Michael Shayne)

THEME MUSIC: Up full then under…

ANNOUNCER: The American Broadcasting Company takes pride in presenting a new series based on Michael Shayne, a fictional detective created by Brett Halliday and starring Robert Sterling in *The Adventures of Michael Shayne*.

THEME MUSIC: Up full and out.

CLOSE (The Adventures of Michael Shayne)

THEME MUSIC: Up full then under…

ANNOUNCER: The American Broadcasting Company has just presented, transcribed, another episode in a new series based on the character created by Brett Halliday. Robert Sterling stars as Michael Shayne with Judith Parrish as Phyllis Knight. Original music is composed and conducted by John Duffy. All names and places used in tonight's story are fictional; any resemblance to real persons and places is unintentional. Be with us again next week when the American Broadcasting Company will again present *The Adventures of Michael Shayne*.

THEME MUSIC: Up full then out.

274. The Milton Berle Show

Variety series mixing skits and jokes with music and songs. Sponsored by Philip Morris Cigarettes. NBC, 1947–1948. Philip Morris is represented by its trademark, Johnny the Bellboy (Johnny Roventini).

OPEN

ANNOUNCER (Frank Gallop): *The Milton Berle Show*.

SPONSOR'S THEME ("On the Trail"): Up full then under…

JOHNNY: Call for Philip Mor-rees, call for Philip Mor-rees.

ANNOUNCER: Make no mistake. Of all leading cigarettes, Philip Morris and only Philip Morris is recognized by eminent nose and throat specialists as definitely less irritating. No other cigarette can make that statement. So take a tip from Johnny and—

JOHNNY: Call for Philip Mor-rees.

MILTON BERLE SHOW THEME: Up full then under…

ANNOUNCER: From Radio City in New York, here is *The Milton Berle Show*, with Pert Kelton, Jack Albertson, Johnny Gibson, Mary Shipp, Charles Irving, Billy Sands, Roger DeKoven, our singing star Dick Carney, Ray Bloch and his orchestra, and yours truly Frank Gallop.

THEME MUSIC: Up full then out.

ANNOUNCER: Ladies and gentlemen, here he is, Milton Berle.

SOUND: Applause… (after which Milton begins the show with jokes).

CLOSE

JOHNNY: This is Johnny again, returning now to the thousands of store windows and counters all over America. Look for me. I'll be waiting for you. Come in and—Call for Philip Mor-rees.

SPONSOR'S THEME: Up full then under…

ANNOUNCER: Yes, if every smoker knew what Philip Morris smokers know, they'd all change to Philip Morris, America's finest cigarette.

JOHNNY: Call for Philip Mor-rees.

ANNOUNCER: *The Milton Berle Show* was written by Nat Hiken and Aaron Ruben. This is Frank Gallop saying good night from Philip Morris.

MILTON: And this is Milton Berle, good night.

ANNOUNCER: This is NBC, the National Broadcasting Company.

SOUND: NBC chimes. N-B-C.

275. Miss Pinkerton, Inc.

Crime drama about Mary Vance (Joan

Blondell), a law student who inherits the Vance Detective Agency from a late uncle, and Dennis Murray (Dick Powell), the police lieutenant she helps solve crimes. Sustaining. NBC, 1941.

OPEN

SOUND: Police whistles, car sirens.

THEME MUSIC: Up full then under...

ANNOUNCER (Art Gilmore): *Miss Pinkerton, Inc.* starring Joan Blondell and Dick Powell.

THEME MUSIC: Up full then under...

ANNOUNCER: We present a new series of half-hour comedy-detective dramas complete in each episode yet featuring the same principal characters in situations of adventure, thrills and romance.

THEME MUSIC: Up full then under...

ANNOUNCER: *Miss Pinkerton, Inc.* with Joan Blondell as Mary Vance, a law student with a nose for murder, and Dick Powell as Dennis Murray, the police lieutenant who finds Mary attractive but wishes she'd poke her pretty nose into someone else's business. *Miss Pinkerton, Inc.* now begins its story for tonight...

CLOSE

THEME MUSIC: Up full then under...

ANNOUNCER: *Miss Pinkerton, Inc.* was conceived and produced by J. Donald Wilson. This is Art Gilmore speaking. Listen in next week to *Miss Pinkerton, Inc.* starring Joan Blondell and Dick Powell. This is NBC, the National Broadcasting Company.

THEME MUSIC: Up full then out.

SOUND: NBC chimes. N-B-C.

Note: Pinkerton in the title refers to a private detective (a term made famous when the first private detective organization, the Pinkerton Detective Agency, was formed and operatives were called "Pinkerton's").

276. Mr. Ace and Jane

Incidents in the lives of Goodman Ace, an advertising executive, and his scatterbrained wife, Jane. Sustaining. CBS, 1948.

OPEN

THEME MUSIC ("Manhattan Serenade"): Up full then under...

ANNOUNCER (Ken Roberts): From New York City comes the *Mr. Ace and Jane* program, a weekly half-hour comedy series starring radio's original comedy couple, the Aces.

THEME MUSIC: Up full then out.

ANNOUNCER: Once again the strains of "Manhattan Serenade" introduce the story of Mr. Ace and his wife Jane. *Mr. Ace and Jane*, starring Goodman Ace and his wife, Jane.

CLOSE

THEME MUSIC: Up full then under...

ANNOUNCER: Tune in again next week for another chapter in the lives of *Mr. Ace and Jane.* Good night.

GOODMAN: Good night.

JANE: Good night.

ANNOUNCER: This is CBS, the Columbia Broadcasting System.

THEME MUSIC: Up full then fade out.

277. Mr. Aladdin

Crime drama about Robert Aladdin, a private detective who advertises himself as the "man who can do anything." Sustaining. CBS, 1951. Paul Frees starred as Robert Aladdin with Sylvia Sims as his secretary, Jeannie Mobley. The song "Bewitched, Bothered and Bewildered" was used as the theme.

OPEN

THEME MUSIC: Up full then under...

ANNOUNCER (Bill Anders): Once upon a time, the year being 1951, a young man walked down the streets of an island, the island called Manhattan, and if some of the feats he performed have the feeling of magic, is that surprising? His name was Aladdin.

THEME MUSIC: Up full then under...

ANNOUNCER: *Mr. Aladdin*, a wonderful, new adventure series starring Paul Frees.

THEME MUSIC: Up full then out.

CLOSE

THEME MUSIC: Up full then under...

ANNOUNCER: *Mr. Aladdin* was produced and directed by Elliott Lewis with music composed and conducted by Marlin Skiles. Tonight's transcribed minor miracle was constructed by Richard Paul. Paul Frees is starred as Mr. Aladdin with Sylvia Sims as Jeannie Mobley. *Mr. Aladdin* was suggested by a book by Carlos Drake. Bill Anders speaking. And remember, your news is always accurately reported when it comes from the CBS Radio Network.

THEME MUSIC: Up full then fade out.

278. Mr. and Mrs. Blandings

Comedy about Jim Blandings (Cary Grant), a harassed New York advertising executive who moves his wife, Muriel (Betsy Drake), and children, Susan and Joan (Anne Whitfield, Patricia Ianola), to Connecticut to find a quieter life. Sponsored by TWA. NBC, 1951.

OPEN

THEME MUSIC: Up full then under...

ANNOUNCER (Don Stanley): Flying's the way to travel and the way to fly is TWA, Trans World Airlines. Presenting Cary Grant and Betsy Drake as Mr. and Mrs. Blandings in a new series based on Eric Hodgins' best-selling novels *Mr. Blandings Builds His Dream House* and *Blandings Way*.

THEME MUSIC: Up full then out.

ANNOUNCER: Did you know that TWA offers the only one-airline service from coast to coast in the United States and all the way to Europe, Africa or Asia?

CHORUS:
> You love to fly
> High up in the sky.
> You ride the airways
> To starry stairways.
> Smoother and quicker,
> Flying's the way
> And the best way to fly—TWA.

ANNOUNCER: *Mr. and Mrs. Blandings* starring Cary Grant and Betsy Drake with Gale Gordon as Bill Cole in a series about a man's efforts to find a dream life away from the hassles of the big city.

CLOSE

THEME MUSIC: Up full then under...

ANNOUNCER: Tune in next week, same time, same station for *Mr. and Mrs. Blandings* starring Cary Grant and Betsy Drake and brought to you by Trans World Airlines. Across the U.S. and overseas, you can depend on TWA. Betsy Drake appeared through the courtesy of RKO Pictures and David O. Selznick. Watch for the next Selznick release, *Gypsy Blood* starring Jennifer Jones and produced in Technicolor. Gale Gordon appeared as Bill Cole with Anne Whitfield as Susan and Patricia Ianola as Joan. Don Stanley speaking. Next it's Tallulah's *Big Show*. Three chimes mean good times on NBC.

SOUND: NBC chimes. N-B-C.

279. Mr. and Mrs. North

Crime drama about Jerry and Pamela North, a married couple who solve crimes (mostly those that Pamela stumbles across). Carl Eastman and Peggy Conklin first played the roles. They were followed by Joseph Curtin and Alice Frost and finally by Richard Denning and Barbara Britton. Sponsored by Colgate, Halo, Palmolive and Woodbury. CBS (1941–1942), NBC (1942–1950), CBS (1950–1955). Basis for the television series.

OPEN (1944)

ANNOUNCER (Ben Grauer): Woodbury Facial Soap, the beauty soap for the skin you love to touch.

SONG:
> You're lovely,
> Never, never change.
> Keep that breathless charm,
> Won't you please arrange it,
> 'Cause you're lovely,
> Just the way you look tonight.

ANNOUNCER: The makers of Woodbury Facial Soap, the beauty soap made for the skin alone, present the adventures of *Mr. and Mrs. North* with Joseph Curtin and Alice Frost—*Mr. and Mrs. North*.

CLOSE (1944)

THEME MUSIC: Up full then under...

ANNOUNCER: Starting today your bookseller has

a sale on the latest *Mr. and Mrs. North* mystery novel. It's titled *Killing the Goose*. Get a copy of *Killing the Goose* tonight. Next Wednesday evening, another radio adventure of *Mr. and Mrs. North* starring Alice Frost and Joseph Curtin. For thrills and laughs, be sure to listen, won't you. This is Ben Grauer saying good night for Woodbury Facial Soap, the beauty soap for the skin you love to touch. This is NBC, the National Broadcasting Company.

THEME MUSIC: Up full then out.

SOUND: NBC chimes. N-B-C.

OPEN (1952)

SOUND: Pamela and Jerry at their apartment door. Pamela opens the door.

PAMELA (startled): Jerry!

JERRY (yelling): The lights!

PAMELA (flicking on the light switch with no results): A fuse must have blown.

JERRY: Or someone pulled the master switch; and in that case, the murderer is still in the house!

THEME MUSIC: Up full then under...

ANNOUNCER (Joseph King): *Mr. and Mrs. North*, transcribed, starring Richard Denning and Barbara Britton as Mr. and Mrs. North. Listen as Pam and Jerry solve the mystery "Deadly Innocent."

THEME MUSIC: Up full then out.

CLOSE (1952)

THEME MUSIC: Up full then under...

ANNOUNCER: Pam and Jerry are sure to have more exciting adventures next week. Listen in, won't you? There's always mystery well sprinkled with humor on *Mr. and Mrs. North*. This is CBS, the Columbia Broadcasting System.

THEME MUSIC: Up full then fade out.

280. Mr. Chameleon

Crime Drama about a man, known only as Mr. Chameleon (Karl Swenson), who uses disguises to solve crimes. Various sponsors (with Bayer Aspirin, General Foods and Wrigley's Chewing Gum frequently sponsoring). CBS, 1948–1952.

OPEN

THEME MUSIC: Up full then under...

ANNOUNCER (George Byron): Tonight, we again present the famous *Mr. Chameleon* of Central Police Headquarters in another of his celebrated cases of crime and murder. Mr. Chameleon, as you know, is the dreaded detective who frequently uses a disguise to track down a killer—a disguise which at all times is easily recognized by the audience. And now, *Mr. Chameleon*.

THEME MUSIC: Up full then out.

CLOSE

THEME MUSIC: Up full then under...

ANNOUNCER: The part of *Mr. Chameleon* is played by Karl Swenson, written by Gene Carroll and based on the original story by Frank and Anne Hummert. Directed by Henry Howard with music selected by Victor Arden.

THEME MUSIC: Up full then under...

ANNOUNCER: Listen next Friday evening at this same time for *Mr. Chameleon*, the man of many faces, in another murder-mystery. Tomorrow's daytime listening on the CBS Radio Network features John Reed King's lively *Give and Take* quiz show and the merry competition of Arlene Francis, Bill Cullen and their opposing teams on *Fun for All*. Every Saturday at the stars address the riots on CBS Radio with *Give and Take* and *Fun for All* over most of these same stations. Don't miss a minute of these two delightful daytimers tomorrow.

THEME MUSIC: Up full then under...

ANNOUNCER: Listen for *Mr. Chameleon*, the man of many faces, at this same time next week. And remember, *Gangbusters* go into action on Saturday nights on the CBS Radio Network.

THEME MUSIC: Up full then fade out.

281. Mr. District Attorney

Crime drama based on the files of various district attorneys' offices. Various sponsors (Pepsodent Tooth Powder and Vitalis Hair Tonic were frequent sponsors). NBC (1939; 1940–1951), Blue/ABC (1939–1940; 1951–1952), Syn.

(1952–1953). Mr. District Attorney was played by Raymond Edward Johnson, Dwight Weist, Jay Jostyn and David Brian.

OPEN (original)

ANNOUNCER: Citizens of America, *Mr. District Attorney*. Mr. District Attorney, champion of the people and defender of truth. Starring Raymond Edward Johnson as Mr. District Attorney.
THEME MUSIC: Up full then out.

CLOSE (original)

THEME MUSIC: Up full then under...
ANNOUNCER: You have just heard *Mr. District Attorney*, dramatized by Phillips H. Lord from facts furnished from public prosecutors throughout the entire nation. Ladies and gentlemen, *Mr. District Attorney* will be with you again tomorrow night. This was a program of the National Broadcasting Company, RCA Building, Radio City, New York.
SOUND: NBC chimes. N-B-C.

OPEN (revised)

ANNOUNCER: Mr. District Attorney, champion of the people, defender of truth, guardian of our fundamental rights to life, liberty and the pursuit of happiness.
THEME MUSIC: Up full then under...
MR. D.A.: And it shall be my duty as district attorney not only to prosecute to the limit of the law all persons accused of crimes perpetrated within this county but to defend with equal vigor the rights and privileges of all its citizens.
THEME MUSIC: Up full then out.

CLOSE (revised)

THEME MUSIC: Up full then under...
MR. D.A.: This is David Brian. I hope you enjoyed this case from the files of *Mr. District Attorney*. Join us when we present our next case based on the facts of crime from the files of *Mr. District Attorney*.
THEME MUSIC: Up full then out.

282. Mister Feathers

Comedy about an elderly man, known as Mister Feathers, who owns the Pike City Pharmacy. Sustaining. Mutual, 1949–1950. Parker Fennelly played Mister Feathers with Elinor Phelps as his wife, Bunny.

OPEN

THEME MUSIC: Up full then under...
ANNOUNCER (Bob Emerick): Mutual presents Parker Fennelly as *Mister Feathers*. Mister Feathers, a man not quite like any neighbor you ever had. Mister Feathers at grips with his life in the untroubled and quiet untypical town of Pike City.
THEME MUSIC: Up full then out.

CLOSE

THEME MUSIC: Up full then under...
ANNOUNCER: You've been visiting with *Mister Feathers* starring Parker Fennelly and written by Gerald Holland. Produced by Herbert Rice with original music composed and conducted by Ben Ludlow. This is Bob Emerick speaking. Join us next week at this time for another visit with *Mister Feathers*, heard in Canada through the facilities of the Canadian Broadcasting System. This is the Mutual Broadcasting System.
THEME MUSIC: Up full then fade out.

283. Mr. Keen, Tracer of Lost Persons

Originally, a crime drama about a kind and understanding private detective (Mr. Keen) and his assistant, Mike Clancy, who specialized in locating missing people. After five years, the format changed to focus on Mr. Keen and Mike as homicide detectives (even though the title remained the same). Various sponsors. Blue (1937–1942), CBS (1942–1951; 1952–1953), NBC (1951–1952). Bennett Kilpack, Phil Clarke and Arthur Hughes played Mr. Keen with Jim Kelly as Mike Clancy. The song "Someday I'll Find You" was used as the theme.

OPEN

THEME MUSIC: Up full then under...

ANNOUNCER (Larry Elliott): *Mr. Keen, Tracer of Lost Persons* is on the air.

THEME MUSIC: Up full then under...

ANNOUNCER: *Mr. Keen, Tracer of Lost Persons* is one of the most famous characters of American fiction and one of radio's most thrilling dramas. Tonight and every Thursday night from 7:30 to eight, Eastern War Time, the famous old investigator will take from his files and bring to us one of his most celebrated missing persons cases. Now, *Mr. Keen, Tracer of Lost Persons*.

THEME MUSIC: Up full then out.

CLOSE

THEME MUSIC: Up full then under...

ANNOUNCER: You have been listening to *Mr. Keen, Tracer of Lost Persons*, now on the air at a new time, every Thursday night at 7:30 to eight, Eastern War Time, over this network. Don't miss *Mr. Keen* next Thursday night. This is Larry Elliott saying good night.

THEME MUSIC: Up full then out.

Note: Many episodes have the following simplified opening:

THEME MUSIC: Up full then under...

ANNOUNCER: *Mr. Keen, Tracer of Lost Persons*, is based on the book *Mr. Keen*.

THEME MUSIC: Up full then out.

284. Mr. Moto

Crime drama about I.A. Moto (James Monks), a Japanese-born American citizen who works as both a private detective and as an agent for the U.S. government. Sustaining. NBC, 1951.

OPEN

I.A. MOTO: This is Mr. Moto.

THEME MUSIC: Up full then under...

ANNOUNCER: NBC presents the world's greatest international detective-philosopher. Mr. I.A. Moto, a man of mystery, of culture and sensitivity, a man who, while hating violence, fights Communism ruthlessly both at home and abroad with his courage, his brains and his fabulous knowledge of international persons, places and things.

THEME MUSIC: Up full then out.

CLOSE

THEME MUSIC: Up full then under...

ANNOUNCER: James Monks starred as *Mr. Moto*. It was written and directed by Harry W. Junkin. The music was transcribed.

THEME MUSIC: Up full then out.

285. Mr. President

Dramatizations based on little-known incidents in the lives of U.S. presidents. Sustaining. ABC, 1947–1953.

OPEN

THEME MUSIC: Up full then under...

ANNOUNCER: *Mr. President* starring Edward Arnold. Mr. President, the man in the White House, chosen by his fellow citizens as the First Citizen. We invite you to now become better acquainted with one of America's greatest men. These are transcribed stories of the men who have lived in the White House. Dramatic, exciting, but little-known events in their lives which you and I so rarely hear. True, human stories of *Mr. President*.

THEME MUSIC: Up full then out.

CLOSE

THEME MUSIC: Up full then under...

ANNOUNCER: You have been listening to Edward Arnold as *Mr. President*. Next week more true but little-known incidents in the life of America's greatest men. Be sure to listen. This is ABC, the American Broadcasting Company.

THEME MUSIC: Up full then fade out.

286. The Modern Adventures of Casanova

Adventure about Christopher Casanova

(Errol Flynn), an agent for the World Criminal Police Commission who is also a descendant of the famous Italian lover. Sponsored by Charles Antell, Inc. Mutual, 1951–1952.

OPEN

ANNOUNCER: Charles Antell, creators of Formula 9, and Natural Health Aid present *The Modern Adventures of Casanova.*
THEME MUSIC: Up full then under…
GIRL: Darling, why darling, no one has made me feel this way before. But darling, I don't even know your name.
MAN: My name, oh, didn't I tell you, darling? It's Casanova.
ANNOUNCER: *The Modern Adventures of Casanova*, starring Errol Flynn as Christopher Casanova, direct descendant of the fabulous Italian diplomat, author and soldier of fortune, a brave spirit and a free one, whose sensible fault was not that he kissed, but that he told. Today's Casanova is often embarrassed at the implications of his name, though he carries it proudly through the drawing rooms of international society and few know that this modern Casanova has another identity—agent for World Pol, the World Criminal Police Commission. It is from his experiences we bring you *The Modern Adventures of Casanova.*
THEME MUSIC: Up full then out.
ANNOUNCER: So you may enjoy a full half-hour of entertainment by transcription, there will be no commercial messages throughout the program itself. This is at the request of our sponsor, National Health Aid, the makers of Fast Tabs, the safe, sure way to take off weight, and Charles Antell, the creator of Formula 9 for beautiful hair. And now *The Modern Adventures of Casanova.*

CLOSE

ANNOUNCER: Ladies and gentlemen, we have been giving you pure entertainment for 27 minutes, now we're going to give you a lucky number. For those of you who have dry hair, hair that's burned from permanents and quick-drying machines, wouldn't you like to have a beautiful head of hair again? Then take my advice and put back the natural oils. You see, 90 percent of all hair trouble is a lack of natural oil. You take the oil out and as a result you have dry hair, dull, lifeless hair. But when you put the oil back, once again Mother Nature can give you healthy, beautiful hair. Now I'm going to give you your lucky number. Your lucky number is 9, Charles Antell Formula 9, the full-strength lanolin formula that has taken the country by storm. Formula 9 will give your hair plenty of natural body and elasticity without a trace of grease or oil. Formula 9 is food and nourishment. All you need, man, woman or child, is Formula 9 to have really healthy, well-groomed hair. This has been a transcribed presentation of Charles Antell, Inc.
THEME MUSIC: Up full then under…
ANNOUNCER: You have just heard *The Modern Adventures of Casanova* based upon an idea by and starring Errol Flynn. This program was directed by William N. Robson. Original music composed and conducted by Walter Schumann. Charles Antell, the creators of Formula 9, has presented *The Modern Adventures of Casanova* by arrangement with Metro-Goldwyn-Mayer. This is the Mutual Broadcasting System.
THEME MUSIC: Up full then fade out.

287. Molle Mystery Theater

Mystery and detective fiction stories sponsored by Molle Shaving Creme. NBC, 1943–1948. Bernard Lenrow played the host, Geoffrey Barnes.

OPEN

THEME MUSIC: Up full then under…
ANNOUNCER (Dan Seymour): Molle, M-O-L-L-E, Molle, the brushless shaving creme with a special protective film that guards your face, presents the *Molle Mystery Theater.* Tonight, Molle, the brushless shaving creme which puts face protection first, brings you another in the series of programs which puts mystery and excitement first. Each Tuesday night at this time you hear one of the great mystery stories selected either from the famous classics or from the best of the moderns by Mr. Geoffrey Barnes. Mr. Barnes, having made a life study

of mystery fiction, is a connoisseur of fine detective stories. Mr. Barnes.

BARNES: Good evening and welcome to the *Molle Mystery Theater*... [He would then introduce the evening's story.]

CLOSE

ANNOUNCER: Even a man with tough whiskers or tender skin can enjoy a clean, comfortable shave. How? Just use Molle, the heavier, brushless shaving creme, because—

SONG:
> It's smooth, so smooth,
> It's slick, so slick.
> It's a smooth, smooth,
> Slick, slick shave you get
> With M-O-L-L-E, Molle.

ANNOUNCER: The heavier brushless shaving creme for tough whiskers or tender skin. Enjoy a Molle shave tomorrow.

THEME MUSIC: Up full then under...

ANNOUNCER: Be with us next week when the *Molle Mystery Theater* will present another story taken from the great mystery stories of literature. This is NBC, the National Broadcasting Company

THEME MUSIC: Up full then out.

SOUND: NBC chimes. N-B-C.

288. Murder and Mr. Malone

Crime drama centering on John J. Malone, a criminal attorney working out of Chicago. Various sponsors. ABC, 1947–1948. Frank Lovejoy played John J. Malone. See also *The Amazing Mr. Malone.*

OPEN

THEME MUSIC: Up full then under...

ANNOUNCER (Dresser Dahlstead): The American Broadcasting Company presents *Murder and Mr. Malone,* an exciting half-hour mystery created by Craig Rice and starring Frank Lovejoy. Our locale is the city of Chicago. The time is the present and the hero of these weekly adventures is the amazing Mr. Malone.

THEME MUSIC: Up full then out.

CLOSE

THEME MUSIC: Up full then under...

ANNOUNCER: You have been listening to *Murder and Mr. Malone* with Frank Lovejoy starred as John J. Malone. All names and places mentioned in tonight's story are fictional. *Murder and Mr. Malone* is produced by Bernard L. Schubert with music by Rex Koury. Dresser Dahlstead speaking. This is ABC, the American Broadcasting Company.

THEME MUSIC: Up full then fade out.

289. Murder by Experts

Dramatizations of crime stories chosen by leading mystery writers. Sustaining. Mutual, 1949–1951. The series was hosted by (in order): John Dickson Carr, Alfred Hitchcock and Brett Halliday.

OPEN

THEME MUSIC: Up full then under...

ANNOUNCER (Phil Tonkin): *Murder by Experts.*

THEME MUSIC: Up full then under...

ANNOUNCER: The Mutual Broadcasting System presents *Murder by Experts* with your host and narrator, Mr. John Dickson Carr, world-famous mystery novelist and author of the recently published best-seller *The Life of Sir Arthur Conan Doyle.*

HOST: This is John Dickson Carr. Each weekday at this time, *Murder by Experts* brings you a story of crime and mystery which has been chosen for your personal approval by one of the world's leading detective writers, those who are themselves masters of the art of murder and can hold tensity at its highest. [He would then introduce the evening's story.]

CLOSE

THEME MUSIC: Up full then under...

ANNOUNCER: *Murder by Experts* with your host, John Dickson Carr, is produced by Robert Arthur and David Cogan. Music is composed and conducted by Emerson Buckley. This is Phil Tonkin reminding you to be with us again next Sunday evening for another story of crime on *Murder by Experts*. This is Mutual.

THEME MUSIC: Up full then fade out.

290. Murder Clinic

Adaptations of detective fiction stories hosted by Frank Knight. Sustaining. Mutual, 1942–1943.

OPEN

THEME MUSIC: Up full then under...

ANNOUNCER: *Murder Clinic*, stories of the world's greatest detectives of fiction—men against murder. Each week at this time, WOR-Mutual turns the spotlight on one of these great hunters of men and brings you the story of his most exciting case. Tonight is Frederick Irving Anderson's famous detective Police Deputy Paar, that visitor from a Vermont farm, often called the "man with a nose for murder."

THEME MUSIC: Up full then out.

HOST (Frank Knight): Good evening Deputy Paar, you're going to tell us the story called "Gulf Stream Green." Now why have you chosen that particular story?

PAAR (Mark Smith): Well it illustrates, rather perfectly, a pet theory of mine: that the egotism of murderers is quite enormous... [He would then begin the story; here about a girl who is killed when she is mistaken for the killer's real target—an opera singer.]

CLOSE

THEME MUSIC: Up full then under...

ANNOUNCER: You have been listening to *Murder Clinic*. *Murder Clinic*, the WOR-Mutual series which brings you each week an exciting case [from] one member from the select band of the world's great detectives. Next week we're especially privileged to bring you G.K. Chesterton's monumental creation the great detective priest Father Brown. The story he will tell is that world-famous masterpiece "The Oracle of the Dog," in which Father Brown reveals that like St. Francis, he also understands the unspoken language of all

God's creatures. Tonight's detective was Police Deputy Paar, Frederick Irving Anderson's famous detective played by Mark Smith. This program was an international exchange feature over the coast-to-coast network of the Canadian Broadcasting System. Original music was composed and conducted by Ralph Barnhart and conducted by Bob Stanley. Tales told on *Murder Clinic* are adapted by authors Lee Wright and John A. Bassett. *Murder Clinic* is produced under the direction of Alvin Flannigan. Frank Knight speaking. This is Mutual.

THEME MUSIC: Up full then fade out.

291. My Favorite Husband

Comical events in the lives of marrieds George and Liz Cooper. Sponsored by General Foods. CBS, 1948–1951. Lucille Ball played Liz Cooper with Lee Bowman and Richard Denning as George Cooper.

OPEN

THEME MUSIC: Up full then under...

ANNOUNCER (Bob Lemond): It's time for *My Favorite Husband* starring Lucille Ball. Yes, the gay family series starring Lucille Ball with Richard Denning, transcribed, is brought to you by the Jell-O family of red-letter deserts.

SONG:
> Oh, the big red letters
> Stand for the Jell-O family,
> That's Jell-O, yum, yum, yum.
> Jell-O Puddings, yum, yum, yum,
> Jell-O tap-i-o-ca puddings,
> Yes sir-reeee.

ANNOUNCER: And now to 321 Bundy Avenue in Los Angeles, the home of Liz and George Cooper...

CLOSE

ANNOUNCER: The new, delicious Jell-O Puddings are here. They have that real old-fashioned goodness; they're creamy, smooth, full-flavored and tempting. There's three delicious Jell-O Puddings to choose from: rich chocolate, mellow butterscotch, and creamy, delicate vanilla. You'll like all these new Jell-O

Puddings; they're real old-fashioned puddings made a new-fashioned way. Try some tomorrow.

THEME MUSIC: Up full then under…

ANNOUNCER: General Foods, makers of Jell-O Puddings and gelatin desserts, has presented Lucille Ball and Richard Denning as Liz and George Cooper in *My Favorite Husband*. Also appearing in tonight's story were Gale Gordon, Bea Benaderet and Ruth Perrot. Original music was composed and conducted by Wilbur Hatch. This is Bob Lemond speaking for the Jell-O family and reminding you to be with us again next Friday evening for another visit with George and Liz Cooper. Till then, good night. This is CBS, the Columbia Broadcasting System.

THEME MUSIC: Up full then fade out.

292. My Friend Irma

Comical incidents in the lives of Irma Peterson, a dizzy blonde secretary, and her level-headed roommate, Jane Stacy (also a secretary). Various sponsors (Camel Cigarettes and Pepsodent Toothpaste were frequent sponsors). CBS, 1947–1954. Marie Wilson played Irma with Cathy Lewis as Jane and John Brown as Al, Irma's boyfriend. Basis for the television series. The song "Friendship" by Cole Porter was used as the theme (replaced later by "Street Scene" by Alfred Newman).

OPEN

ANNOUNCER: The Columbia Broadcasting System presents—

JANE: *My Friend Irma.*

THEME MUSIC: Up full then under…

ANNOUNCER: Starring Marie Wilson as Irma and Cathy Lewis as Jane with John Brown as Al.

CHORUS:
Friendship, friendship,
Just the perfect blendship.
When other friendships have been forgot,
Theirs will still be hot.

THEME MUSIC: Up full then under…

JANE (speech varies by episode): Sure, it's something to sing about and they can sing about it maybe because they haven't got any friends.

But I'm singing the blues about it because I've got a friend, *My Friend Irma*. Now, don't get me wrong, I love that girl, most people do. It's just that Mother Nature gave some girls brains, intelligence and cleverness; but with Irma, well Mother Nature slipped her a Mickey… [Jane's speech would then lead into the story.]

CLOSE

CATHY: Well, that's *My Friend Irma*. Good night.

THEME MUSIC: Up full then under…

ANNOUNCER: *My Friend Irma* starring Marie Wilson with Cathy Lewis and John Brown is a Cy Howard production. Original music is composed and conducted by Lud Gluskin with vocals by the Sportsmen. This is Frank Bingham speaking for CBS, the Columbia Broadcasting System.

THEME MUSIC: Up full then fade out.

293. My Little Margie

Comical incidents in the lives of 21-year-old Margie Albright (Gale Storm) and her 50-year-old father, Vern (Charles Farrell). Various sponsors. CBS (1952–1955), Mutual (1953–1954). The program also starred Gil Stratton, Jr. as Freddie Wilson, Margie's boyfriend, and Verna Felton as Margie's neighbor, Mrs. Odetts. Basis for the television series. Alexander Laszlo composed the theme, "My Little Margie."

OPEN

THEME MUSIC: Up full then under…

ANNOUNCER (Roy Rowan): *My Little Margie* starring Gale Storm as Margie and Charles Farrell as Vern. *My Little Margie*, the story of a 21-year-old girl with a problem—her father; and the story of a 50-year-old father with a problem—his daughter. Margie's problem is a father who won't settle down; Vern's problem is a daughter who won't listen. What happens when both try to teach the other a lesson? Let's find out as we meet *My Little Margie* starring Gale Storm and Charles Farrell.

THEME MUSIC: Up full then out.

CLOSE

VERN (after story ends): Well, that's *My Little Margie.*

THEME MUSIC: Up full then under...

ANNOUNCER: *My Little Margie* starring Gale Storm and Charles Farrell is based on characters created by Frank Fox and is produced, directed and transcribed by Gordon P. Hughes for Hal Roach, Jr. and Rolland Reed. Verna Felton is Mrs. Odetts and Gil Stratton, Jr. is Freddie. I'm Roy Rowan. Be with us again next week for another episode of *My Little Margie.* Bing Crosby sings Monday through Friday nights on the CBS Radio Network.

THEME MUSIC: Up full then fade out.

294. My Mother's Husband

Life in turn-of-the-century St. Louis as seen through the eyes of 18-year-old Virginia Brickel (Sharon Douglas), the daughter of Harvey and Dorothy Brickel (William Powell, Sarah Selby). Various sponsors. NBC, 1950.

OPEN

THEME MUSIC: Up full then under...

ANNOUNCER (Jack McCoy): William Powell in *My Mother's Husband.*

CHORUS:
> Oh backward, turn backward
> Oh time in thy flight,
> When a bike built for two
> Was a courtship divine.

ANNOUNCER: Ladies and gentlemen, we introduce *My Mother's Husband* starring William Powell.

CHORUS:
> When ladies wore blushes
> And gents the moustache,
> And an actress in tights
> Was a barbershop smash.

ANNOUNCER: A new program about a gentleman of the old school in those grand and fabulous days when we and the century were very young.

CHORUS:
> Oh days that we treasure
> With memories a-glow,

> When we sat on the front porch
> And sang soft and low.

VIRGINIA: Visitors to St. Louis will tell you that the most awe-inspiring sights in this growing metropolis are the great Union Station, the gigantic Gage Bridge and my mother's husband, Harvey Jefferson Brickel. Yes, and proud tourists often boast that they not only witnessed the four o'clock feeding of the man-eating lion at Forest Park Zoo, but they also saw the six o'clock homecoming of my mother's husband to Vander Veller Place for supper...

CLOSE

CHORUS:
> Good night ladies,
> Good night ladies.

ANNOUNCER: Featured in tonight's cast were Sarah Selby as Dorothy and Sharon Douglas as Virginia. Jack McCoy speaking. This program was created and written by Charles Tazwell. Music composed and conducted by Jeff Alexander. The entire production was under the direction of Joe Rines. The star of *My Mother's Husband* is William Powell.

CHORUS:
> Good night ladies.

HARVEY: Good night, Dorothy, good night, Virginia, good night, everyone.

CHORUS:
> Good night ladies,
> We're going to sleep toooo-niiiiight.

ANNOUNCER: This is NBC, the National Broadcasting Company.

SOUND: NBC chimes. N–B–C.

295. Myrt and Marge

Daily serial about Myrt Spear and Marge Minter, show-business girls (chick chick dancers) in the Broadway musical "Hayfield's Pleasures." Various sponsors. CBS, 1931–1942. The series also ran on Mutual in 1939. Myrtle Vail and Alice Yourman played Myrt; Donna Damerel Fick, Helen Mack and Alice Goodkin played Marge. "Dream Waltz" and "Poor Butterfly" were used as the theme songs.

OPEN

ANNOUNCER (Andre Baruch): The story of *Myrt and Marge*.

THEME MUSIC: Up full then under...

ANNOUNCER: It's time once again to visit ever glamorous Broadway for the story of two chorus girls and their exciting lives on the Gay White Way.

THEME MUSIC: Up full then under...

ANNOUNCER: The house lights go down, the footlights go on. The curtain rises on the next chapter in the story of *Myrt and Marge*.

THEME MUSIC: Up full then out.

CLOSE

THEME MUSIC: Up full then under...

ANNOUNCER: There's a lot bound to happen in the next thrilling chapter of the story of *Myrt and Marge*. This is Andre Baruch speaking.

THEME MUSIC: Up full then out.

296. The Mysterious Traveler

Supernatural-based stories hosted by a man (a doctor by profession) who rides a train and invites listeners to join him for a story. Sustaining. Mutual, 1934–1952. Maurice Tarplin plays the Mysterious Traveler.

OPEN

THEME MUSIC: Up full then under...

ANNOUNCER (Jimmy Wallington): Mutual presents *The Mysterious Traveler*.

SOUND: Train in motion.

TRAVELER: This is the Mysterious Traveler inviting you to join me for another journey into the realm of the strange and terrifying. I hope you will enjoy the trip and it will thrill you a little and chill you a little. So, settle back, get a good grip on your nerves and be comfortable, if you can... [He would then begin the evening's story.]

CLOSE

SOUND: Train in motion.

TRAVELER: This is the Mysterious Traveler again. Did you enjoy our little trip?

SOUND: Train stopping.

TRAVELER: You're getting off here? Perhaps we'll meet again soon. I take this train every week at this time.

THEME MUSIC: Up full then under...

ANNOUNCER: You have just heard *The Mysterious Traveler*, a series of dramas of the strange and terrifying. Maurice Tarplin is heard as the Mysterious Traveler with music under the direction of Henry Sylvern. The entire production is under the supervision of Jock MacGregor. Jimmy Wallington speaking. This is Mutual.

THEME MUSIC: Up full then fade out.

297. Mystery Award Theater

Adaptations of mystery stories from various literary sources. Various sponsors. Syn., 1949.

OPEN

THEME MUSIC: Up full then under...

ANNOUNCER: *Mystery Award Theater* with D.E. McHenry, associate professor of political science and dean of the division of social sciences, University of California in Los Angeles, mentor of *Mystery Award Theater*. Dr. McHenry.

MCHENRY: Ladies and gentlemen, your good sponsor has asked me to select for you each week the very best mystery stories my associates and I find in our searches in that popular and instructive literary field. The Mystery Writers of America, the national association of the most famous authors in this field, have made it possible for us to dramatize these selections for you each week.

CLOSE

THEME MUSIC: Up full then under...

MCHENRY: Join us again at this same time next week on *Mystery Award Theater*. *Mystery Award Theater* is produced by Lee Crosby and George L. Fogel. Good night.

THEME MUSIC: Up full then fade out.

298. Mystery House [1946]

Anthology-like series about a publishing

house, owned by Dan and Barbara Glenn, that dramatizes its manuscripts before it publishes them. Various sponsors. Syn., 1946. Forrest Lewis and Nanette Sargent played Dan and Barbara Glenn.

OPEN

THEME MUSIC: Up full then under...
ANNOUNCER: *Mystery House* with Forrest Lewis and Nanette Sargent as Dan and Barbara Glenn, owners of that strange publishing company *Mystery House.*
THEME MUSIC: Up full then under...
ANNOUNCER: *Mystery House*, that strange publishing firm run by Dan and Barbara Glenn, where each new novel is acted out by the Mystery House staff before it is accepted for publication. *Mystery House.*
THEME MUSIC: Up full then out.

CLOSE

THEME MUSIC: Up full then under...
ANNOUNCER: Each week, a new dramatization for radio as Dan and Barbara Glenn and their staff act out a novel on *Mystery House*. Forrest Lewis and Nanette Sargent are starred.
THEME MUSIC: Up full then out.

Note: Forrest Lewis and Nanette Sargent portrayed the leads in all stories with guests appearing as their staff (the supporting players).

299. Mystery House [1951]

Tales of suspense and the supernatural hosted by (and starring) Bela Lugosi. Sustaining. Mutual, 1951.

OPEN

THEME MUSIC: Up full then under...
HOST: This is Bela Lugosi welcoming you to *Mystery House.*
THEME MUSIC: Up full then under...
ANNOUNCER (Ken Carpenter): *Mystery House* starring Bela Lugosi. *Mystery House* where lives again the greatest mystery theater the world has ever known. *Mystery House*, where tonight, the distinguished actor Mr. John Carradine joins Bela Lugosi in presenting "The Thirsty Death."

THEME MUSIC: Up full then under...
ANNOUNCER: And now the curtain rises on "The Thirsty Death" starring Bela Lugosi and his guest at *Mystery House*, John Carradine. [Story of a doctor's efforts to seek revenge when he believes his wife is having an affair.]

CLOSE

ANNOUNCER: Ladies and gentlemen, that was "The Thirsty Death" starring Bela Lugosi and John Carradine with Lurene Tuttle.
BELA: What's the matter, Ken, we didn't frighten you, did we?
ANNOUNCER: Well, I'm afraid you did, Bela; that was pretty scary.
BELA: Oh, that was nothing.
ANNOUNCER: Nothing?
BELA: No, wait until you hear next week's story, a play about a woman who was buried alive. And my guest will be the beautiful and charming Simone Simon. I hope you and the audience will join me next week for *Mystery House.*
THEME MUSIC: Up full then under...
ANNOUNCER: Bela Lugosi is currently being starred in a series of *Mystery House* pictures for Universal Studios. You'll find *Mystery House* novels on sale at your local bookstore. John Carradine will be seen in the title role of *Bluebeard.* This is Ken Carpenter.
THEME MUSIC: Up full then fade out.

300. Mystery in the Air

Murder-mystery stories with host Peter Lorre as the lead in each adaptation. Sponsored by Camel Cigarettes. NBC, 1947.

OPEN

THEME MUSIC: Up full then under...
ANNOUNCER (Harry Morgan): Camel Cigarettes present *Mystery in the Air* starring Peter Lorre. Each week at this hour, Peter Lorre brings us the excitement of the great stories of the strange and unusual, of dark and compelling mysteries culled from the four corners of world literature. Tonight, "The Lodger" by Jack London.

THEME MUSIC: Up full then out.

SPOKESMAN: *Mystery in the Air* starring Peter Lorre is brought to you by Camel Cigarettes. Experience the best teacher, try a Camel. Let your own experience tell you why more people are smoking Camels than ever before. And the best place for that experience is right in your own T-zone. That's T for taste and T for throat. Find out what your taste has to say about the rich full flavor of Camel's superb blend of choice tobaccos. Find out how your throat reacts to Camel's cool, cool mildness. You, like millions of delighted smokers may well find yourself saying Camel suits my T-zone to a T.

THEME MUSIC: Up then under (as the story begins; here a retelling of the Jack the Ripper legend).

CLOSE

THEME MUSIC: Up full then under…

ANNOUNCER: Next week, *Mystery in the Air* starring Peter Lorre brings you another adaptation of one of the great masterpieces culled from the four corners of world literature. This is Harry Morgan inviting you to be with us next week for another *Mystery in the Air*. This is NBC, the National Broadcasting Company.

THEME MUSIC: Up full then out.

SOUND: NBC chimes. N-B-C.

301. Mystery Is My Hobby

Crime drama about Barton Drake (Glenn Langan), a mystery novelist who helps the police solve crimes. Various sponsors. Syn., 1949–1951.

OPEN

THEME MUSIC: Up full then under…

DRAKE: *Mystery Is My Hobby*. Ladies and gentlemen, Barton Drake speaking.

SOUND: Applause.

DRAKE: For this week's drama I've selected Case History 127 from my book, *Mystery Is My Hobby*. I call it "Death Is a Grain of Sand."

ANNOUNCER: And now to Glenn Langan as Barton Drake in the first act of—

DRAKE: *Mystery Is My Hobby*.

CLOSE

THEME MUSIC: Up full then under…

ANNOUNCER: And here's Glenn Langan with a word about next week's story.

SOUND: Applause.

GLENN: Thank you Bruce Buell and thank you ladies and gentlemen for being with us. Next week plan to be with us when I bring you Case History Number 128. It's a story of murder and a famous necklace. I call it "Death Is a Jewell." Until then, this is Glenn Langan saying adios.

THEME MUSIC AND APPLAUSE: Up full then fade out.

302. Mystery Playhouse

Anthology series geared to the military that rebroadcast mystery episodes from other programs. Sustaining. AFRS, 1944–1947. The example used is a World War II episode (August 10, 1944) featuring *The Adventures of the Thin Man*. Howard Duff played the host, Sergeant X.

OPEN

THEME MUSIC: Up full then under…

HOST: Good evening, this is Sergeant X. Of all the countless characters created by the pen, comparatively few are destined for a long, public life. However, Dashiell Hammett, the mystery writer, created a couple of characters named Nick and Nora Charles about 10 or more years ago. Well, Nora and Nick are still around and still doing fine as you'll hear tonight in the *Mystery Playhouse*.

THEME MUSIC: Up full then under…

HOST: Yes, tonight, the *Mystery Playhouse* is host to Nick and Nora Charles as they appear in another episode from *The Adventures of the Thin Man*.

THEME MUSIC: Up full then out.

CLOSE

HOST: Thank you Nick and Nora Charles for another chapter in *The Adventures of the Thin Man*, tonight's presentation in the *Mystery*

Playhouse. Before taking our usual trip to the green room, let's discuss three ways we can all help lengthen the war. Here they are. First, throw away all your extra equipment. Second, don't take care of the equipment and ordnances you have left. Third, waste your field rations; only eat the parts you like. Well, that's only three ways, but if each and every man and woman in the service indulged in just those three consistently, V-Day would be a far cry indeed. Of course no one would act like that on purpose. Unfortunately, we all tend to treat G.I. material a little bit like a stepsister. And when you multiply your carelessness and wastage a million or more times, it's no longer funny. So let's not help lengthen the war, let's shorten it by conserving everything we have.

THEME MUSIC: Up full then under…

HOST: And to the green room and a preview performance of our next *Mystery Playhouse* attraction … Follow me please … Come.

SOUND: A scene from the next episode (in this case, from *Ellery Queen*).

HOST: Well, there's the beginning of our next *Mystery Playhouse* production featuring the master detective Ellery Queen. So come with your thinking caps on next time as Ellery Queen turns his attention to "The Adventure of the Dark Secret." This is Sergeant X closing the door to the *Mystery Playhouse*. Good night, sleep tight.

THEME MUSIC: Up full then fade out.

303. The NBC Story Shop

Anthology series that brings to life fictional characters from books, cartoons, comic strips and mythology. Sustaining. NBC, 1947.

OPEN

THEME MUSIC: Up full then under…

ANNOUNCER (Charles F. McCarthy): Presenting *The NBC Story Shop* with stories for young people as told by Craig McDonnell.

CLOSE

CRAIG: This is your storyteller, Craig McDonnell, saying goodbye until next time fellows and girls.

THEME MUSIC: Up full then under…

ANNOUNCER: *The NBC Story Shop* was produced in Radio City, New York, by Art Richards and, as always, your storyteller was Craig McDonnell. And don't forget, boys and girls, next week Craig McDonnell will tell you another wonderful story. That's next Saturday at this very same time over this very same station on *The NBC Story Shop*. This is NBC, the National Broadcasting Company.

THEME MUSIC: Up full then out.

SOUND: NBC chimes. N-B-C.

304. NBC University Theater

Anthology series that presents top-name stars in adaptations of works by famous authors. Sustaining. NBC, 1948.

OPEN

THEME MUSIC: Up full then under…

ANNOUNCER: *The NBC University Theater* brings you Boris Karloff in "The History of Mr. Polley" by H.G. Wells, the fourth in our series of full hour dramatizations of outstanding works in modern British and American fiction.

THEME MUSIC: Up full then out.

CLOSE

THEME MUSIC: Up full then under…

ANNOUNCER: Productions of the *NBC University Theater* are used in conjunction with a course in Anglo-American fiction at the University of Louisville under a national college-by-radio plan, which permits listeners to profit from self-advancement or to earn credits toward a college degree by means of radio and supplementary study.

THEME MUSIC: Up full then fade out.

305. The Nebbs

Humorous incidents in the lives of marrieds Rudy and Fanny Nebbs (Gene Lockhart, Kathleen Lockhart). Sponsored by Cystex. Mutual, 1945–1946.

OPEN

THEME MUSIC: Up full then under...
ANNOUNCER (Tom Dixon): Cystex presents *The Nebbs* starring Gene Lockhart and Kathleen Lockhart as Rudy and Fanny Nebbs.
SOUND: Applause.
ANNOUNCER: *The Nebbs*, straight from America's famous comic strip with Junior, Obie Slider and all the others you laughed, worried and adventured with for 22 years. We'll return with *The Nebbs* in just a moment.
SPOKESMAN: Ask your doctor and he's likely to tell you a high percentage of people do not drink enough water. So here's a health tip. Drink a glass of cool, pure water after every meal and at the same time take two tasteless, sugar-coated little tablets of Cystex. The Cystex, you see, goes right along with the water to help nature clear away the acids, which if too concentrated and allowed to accumulate, may cause loss of energy, make you nervous and what is of prime importance, may interrupt your sleep. So if you're run down and tired and old before your time, why don't you try taking Cystex—C-Y-S-T-E-X—with a full glass of water after each meal. Cystex must satisfy you in every way, do far more for you than you expect, or you simply return the empty package and your money back is guaranteed. So get money back guarantee Cystex from your druggist today. Take it with a glass of water every day and see how it makes you feel like new again.
ANNOUNCER: And now back to our story with Gene Lockhart and Kathleen Lockhart as Rudy and Fanny Nebbs.

CLOSE

THEME MUSIC: Up full then under...
ANNOUNCER: Join us next Sunday at this same time when Cystex again presents Gene Lockhart and Kathleen Lockhart as *The Nebbs*. If you would like to attend one of our broadcasts and see Gene and Kathleen Lockhart in person, write to radio station KHJ, Los Angeles, 38, for tickets. This is Tom Dixon saying good night for Cystex. This is the Mutual Broadcasting System.

306. Ned Jordan, Secret Agent

Adventure series about Ned Jordan (Jack McCarthy), a U.S. government agent who works undercover as an insurance investigator for the Consolidated American Railroad. Various sponsors. Mutual, 1940–1942. Also in the cast were Shirley Squires as Judy Medwick, Ned's girlfriend; and Dick Osgood as Agent Proctor.

OPEN

SOUND: Train roaring down the tracks.
ANNOUNCER (Bob Hite): Speeding from coast to coast, the Federal Express thunders through the night. Adventure, thrills, romance. Ride the rails with *Ned Jordan, Secret Agent*.
SOUND: Train whistle blowing.
ANNOUNCER: Under the guise of settling labor and accident claims for the Consolidated American Railroad, Ned Jordan secretly investigates the activities of foreign agents and other federal enemies—missions known only to J.B. Medwick, president of the railroad. Government agents act on the information gathered by Jordan, who steps quietly out of the picture.
SOUND: Train entering a station (at which time the story begins).

CLOSE

SOUND: Train bells.
CONDUCTOR: All aboard! All aboard!
SOUND: Train pulling out of a station.
ANNOUNCER: You have just heard *Ned Jordan, Secret Agent*, which came to you from the studios of WXYZ, Detroit, and are sent to you each Tuesday night at this same time. Jack McCarthy is heard as Ned Jordan with Shirley Squires as Judy Medwick and Dick Osgood as Agent Proctor. These stories are a copyright feature of Ned Jordan, Secret Agent, Incorporated. All characters, names and incidents used in this drama are purely fictitious. Bob Hite speaking. This is the Mutual Broadcasting System.

307. Nero Wolfe

Mystery series about Nero Wolfe, an overweight, New York-based private detective who solves crimes from the comfort of his home (at 601 West 35th Street) through the legwork of his investigator, Archie Goodwin. Various sponsors. Originally aired as *The Adventures of Nero Wolfe* (Blue/ABC, 1943–1944; Mutual, 1945–1946) with J.B. Williams, Santos Ortega, Luis Van Rooten and Francis X. Bushman as Nero Wolfe; and Joseph Julian, Louis Vittes and Elliott Lewis as Archie Goodwin. Revised as *The New Adventures of Nero Wolfe* (NBC, 1950–1951) with Sydney Greenstreet as Nero Wolfe; and Wally Maher, Lamont Johnson, Larry Dobkin and Harry Bartell as Archie Goodwin.

OPEN (original)

THEME MUSIC: Up full then under…

ANNOUNCER (Jim Bannon): *The Adventures of Nero Wolfe.* Jergens, the makers of Jergens Lotion for soft, smooth, romantic hands, presents *The Adventures of Nero Wolfe* starring Francis X. Bushman as Nero Wolfe, the celebrated criminologist created by Rex Stout, with Elliott Lewis as Archie Goodwin.

THEME MUSIC: Up full then out.

CLOSE (original)

THEME MUSIC: Up full then under…

ANNOUNCER: Jergens, the lotion for smooth, romantic hands has presented *The Adventures of Nero Wolfe* with Francis X. Bushman and Elliott Lewis. The characters of Nero Wolfe and Archie Goodwin were created by Rex Stout. *The Adventures of Nero Wolfe* is produced by Travis Wells with music by Lew White. This is Jim Bannon saying good night for Jergens Lotion, the lotion for soft, smooth, romantic hands. This is the Mutual-Don Lee Broadcasting System.

OPEN (revised)

SOUND: Phone ringing.

ANNOUNCER (Don Stanley): Ladies and gentlemen, the ringing of that phone bell brings you mystery, adventure.

ARCHIE (picking up receiver): Nero Wolfe's office. Archie Goodwin speaking.

THEME MUSIC: Up full then under…

ANNOUNCER: Ladies and gentlemen, it's that renowned genius who is the bulkiest, balkiest,

most ponderous and most brilliant detective in the world. Yes, none other than that chairborne mass of unpredictable intellect, Nero Wolfe, created by Rex Stout and brought to you in a new series of adventures over the NBC network in the person of Mr. Sydney Greenstreet.

THEME MUSIC: Up full then out.

CLOSE (revised)

THEME MUSIC: Up full then under…

ANNOUNCER: You have been listening to *The New Adventures of Nero Wolfe* starring Sydney Greenstreet with Harry Bartell as Archie Goodwin. Tonight's transcribed story was based on the characters created by Rex Stout. Don Stanley speaking. This is NBC, the National Broadcasting Company.

THEME MUSIC: Up full then out.

ANNOUNCER: Three chimes mean good times on NBC. Sunday on NBC means fun with Cary Grant and Betsy Drake as they star as Mr. and Mrs. Blandings, the proud but bewildered owners of the famous dream house. The chimes are your invitation every Sunday to *Mr. and Mrs. Blandings.* Tomorrow, for excitement, hear Herbert Marshall as *The Man Called X* on NBC.

SOUND: NBC chimes. N–B–C.

308. Nick Carter, Master Detective

Crime drama about the investigations of private detective Nick Carter. Various sponsors. Mutual, 1943–1953. Lon Clark plays Nick Carter with Helen Choate and Charlotte Manson as his secretary, Patsy Brown. See also *Chick Carter, Boy Detective.*

OPEN

SOUND: Knocks and bangs at a door.

GIRL: What's the matter? What is it?

MAN: Another case for Nick Carter, master detective.

THEME MUSIC: Up full then under…

ANNOUNCER (Hugh Sanders): Yes, another case for that most famous of all manhunters, the detective whose ability at solving crime is unequaled in the history of detective fiction, Nick Carter, master detective.

THEME MUSIC: Up full then out.

CLOSE

ANNOUNCER: Say Nick, how about giving us a few of the ingredients that make up your story for next week.

NICK: Why sure, Hugh. Take a beautiful young girl who is positive she's going crazy, just as her mother did before her.

PATSY: Then add a boyfriend who refused to believe she was losing her mind in spite of the evidence to the contrary.

NICK: Mix them together and add a country doctor who alone knows the secret behind it all.

PATSY: And you have the tense and unbelievable situation with which Nick was faced.

ANNOUNCER: And what do you call this witch's brew, Nick?

NICK: We call it "The Case of the Demented Daughter."

ANNOUNCER: Featured stories of Nick Carter appear in every issue of *The Shadow* comic. Lon Clark is starred as Nick Carter with Charlotte Manson as Patsy and Ed Latimer as Matty. Music is by George Wright. Any resemblance in these programs to persons living or dead or to actual places is purely coincidental. *Nick Carter, Master Detective* is presented on most of these Mutual stations each week at this same time. This is Hugh Sanders saying so long until next week.

THEME MUSIC: Up full then fade out.

309. Night Beat

Crime drama about Randy Stone, a newspaper reporter who covers the night beat for the *Chicago Star*. Sustaining (Pabst Blue Ribbon Beer and Wheaties sponsored for a short time). NBC, 1950–1952. Frank Lovejoy played Randy Stone. Frank Worth composed the "Night Beat" theme.

OPEN

THEME MUSIC: Up full then under...

ANNOUNCER (Donald Rickles): *Night Beat*.

THEME MUSIC: Up full then under...

RANDY: Hi, this is Randy Stone, I cover the night beat for the *Chicago Star*.

ANNOUNCER: *Night Beat* starring Frank Lovejoy as Randy Stone.

THEME MUSIC: Up full then out.

CLOSE

THEME MUSIC: Up full then under...

ANNOUNCER: You have been listening to *Night Beat* starring Frank Lovejoy as Randy Stone. *Night Beat* is produced by Warren Lewis with original music composed and conducted by Frank Worth. All names used in tonight's story are fictitious; any similarity to persons living or dead is purely coincidental. Donald Rickles speaking. Join us again next week, same time, same station for *Night Beat*.

THEME MUSIC: Up full then out.

ANNOUNCER: This is NBC, the National Broadcasting Company.

SOUND: NBC chimes. N-B-C.

310. Night Watch

Reality series that recorded the actual cases of police cars on patrol. Sustaining. CBS, 1954–1955.

OPEN

VOICE: Five-four in service. Starting mileage 6428, that's six-four-two-eight. Detectives Perkins and Walters with police recorder Don Reed. Central District Patrol, tour of duty, six P.M. to two A.M. on the night watch.

VOICE: Check. Five-four. Mileage 6428, patrolling district; 6:04 P.M., starting night watch.

SOUND: Background street noises.

DON REED: This is Don Reed, I'm a police recorder. The sounds you are listening to are real. This is a police car reporting in service for night duty. You will actually ride with this detective unit and follow the activities of the police officers in this car. You'll watch and listen with me as the cases unfold. And, as you listen, remember the people you hear are not actors and all the voices and sounds are authentic. For this is *Night Watch.*

ANNOUNCER: *Night Watch.* For the first time through the medium of network radio, the actual on-the-scene report of your police force in action. There are no actors; there is no script. The investigations are recorded as they actually occurred. *Night Watch*, presented with the cooperation of the police department of Culver City, California, W.N. Hildebrand, chief. We switch you to car five-four, now on patrol, and police recorder Don Reed.

CLOSE

DON: This is Don Reed, police recorder. The sounds you heard in this program were real, there were no actors and no script. Be with us again next week when I report for another *Night Watch.*

ANNOUNCER: *Night Watch* with Don Reed is a CBS Radio Network production and is produced in cooperation with the Culver City Police Department, W.N. Hildebrand, chief. This is CBS, the Columbia Broadcasting System.

311. Nightmare

Stories that depict the plight of people faced with unexpected situations. Various sponsors. Mutual, 1953–1954. Hosted by Peter Lorre.

OPEN

THEME MUSIC: Up full then under…

ANNOUNCER: In the dark of night, from the shadows of the senses comes fits of fantasy and fear—*Nightmare*, starring as your exciting guide to terror, Peter Lorre.

SOUND: Peter Lorre introducing the evening's story.

ANNOUNCER: You are listening to Peter Lorre tell you of "Coincidence," another transcribed story of *Nightmare.*

SOUND: Peter continuing with the story… (here, about a man who finds a gun and is mistaken for a killer).

CLOSE

PETER (following the story): I do hope you will

sleep well tonight, I know I will. Thanks for listening tonight. By the way, what makes you afraid?

THEME MUSIC: Up full then under…

ANNOUNCER: Join Peter Lorre next week for another transcribed story of *Nightmare.* This is Mutual.

THEME MUSIC: Up full then fade out.

312. The Notorious Tarique

Crime drama about François Tarique (Turhan Bey), a Frenchman who collects rare and valuable objects. Various sponsors. ABC, 1947.

OPEN

THEME MUSIC: Up full then under…

TARIQUE: Mine is a strange business. No time clocks, no office, no title. My work may take an hour or a year. It may lead me across the street or around the world. You see, I find and collect things. Things of great rarity and value. And wherever there are such things, wherever the stakes are high, there are sure to be scoundrels who search and plunder and often it seems, for one reason or another, there also am I. Oh, yes, my name is François Tarique.

ANNOUNCER: And who is the Notorious Tarique? He is many things to many men— and women. To some his name strikes terror, to others it spells enchantment, to you it means adventure, intrigue and romance. Ladies and gentlemen, the American Broadcasting Company is proud to present *The Notorious Tarique*, written by Milton Merlin and starring that celebrated actor Turhan Bey.

THEME MUSIC: Up full then out.

CLOSE

ANNOUNCER: You have just heard the first in a new series of romantic adventures starring Turhan Bey as the Notorious Tarique.

THEME MUSIC: Up full then under…

ANNOUNCER: This is a presentation of the American Broadcasting Company, written and produced by Milton Merlin and directed by Dwight Houser. Music composed and conducted by Basil Adlam.

THEME MUSIC: Up full then out.
ANNOUNCER: This is ABC, the American Broadcasting Company.

313. Official Detective

Crime drama that takes a behind-the-scenes look at a police department as seen through the cases of Detective Lieutenant Dan Britt. Various sponsors. Mutual, 1946–1957. Ed Begley, then Craig McDonnell played Dan Britt.

OPEN

ANNOUNCER (Jack Irish): *Official Detective*, dedicated to the men who guard your safety and protect your home—your police department.
THEME MUSIC: Up full then under...
ANNOUNCER: *Official Detective*, presented by the Mutual Broadcasting System in cooperation with *Official Detective Stories* magazine and starring Craig McDonnell as Detective Lieutenant Dan Britt.
THEME MUSIC: Up full then out.

CLOSE

THEME MUSIC: Up full then under...
ANNOUNCER: *Official Detective* starring Craig McDonnell as Detective Lieutenant Dan Britt is based on stories appearing in *Official Detective Stories* magazine. All names and places used in tonight's story are fictitious; any similarity to persons living or dead or real places is purely coincidental. Be with us again next week for another *Official Detective*. Jack Irish speaking. This is Mutual.
THEME MUSIC: Up full then fade out.

314. O'Hara

Crime drama about Bob O'Hara (Jack Moyles), a freelance journalist "in the far places of the world." Sustaining. CBS, 1951.

OPEN

THEME MUSIC: Up full then under...

ANNOUNCER (Art Gilmore): *O'Hara*.
THEME MUSIC: Up full then under...
O'HARA: O'Hara, Hong Kong, to Trans World News, San Francisco. I'm forwarding herewith the most unusual story I've run across in 15 years of reporting. You may think it belongs in the Sunday supplement; I think it deserves the front page. Details to follow. Signed, O'Hara.
ANNOUNCER: CBS brings you *O'Hara* starring Jack Moyles, the adventures of a freelance foreign correspondent in the far places of the world.
THEME MUSIC: Up full then out.

CLOSE

THEME MUSIC: Up full then under...
ANNOUNCER: *O'Hara* stars Jack Moyles in the title role with Byron Kane as Commissioner Phelps.
THEME MUSIC: Up full then under...
ANNOUNCER: *O'Hara* is produced and directed each Sunday night at 8:30 by Tommy Tomlinson and Sterling Tracy for CBS, the Columbia Broadcasting System.
THEME MUSIC: Up full then fade out.

315. The Old Hag's Hour Glass

Anthology series that presented three to four horror vignettes per episode. Sustaining. Syn., 1930s. Noreen DeMille played the Old Hag (the host) and all female roles.

OPEN

THEME MUSIC: Up full then under...
ANNOUNCER: Presenting Noreen DeMille in *The Old Hag's Hour Glass*. Miss DeMille plays all female characters.
SOUND: Old Hag laughing menacingly.
OLD HAG: Gather around folks, I've got some pretty tales to tell ya, pictures from my hour glass of life. The first is a choice bit from over the Canadian border. A pretty French-Canadian gal and her lover, a mounted policeman, is talking together deep in the woods... [This is a strange story about a girl who kills the

man who murdered her mother then tells her lover of the deed. He refuses to arrest her—until she tells him "You are Canadian Mounted Police, but I give you up because I love you."]

CLOSE

THEME MUSIC: Up full then under…

OLD HAG: How'd you like 'em? Right pretty stories weren't they? Well my hour glass is empty and it's time to tell ya goodbye. Goodbye.

ANNOUNCER: We have presented Noreen De-Mille in *The Old Hag's Hour Glass*. Miss De-Mille played all female characters.

THEME MUSIC: Up full then fade out.

316. One Man's Family

Dramatic serial about incidents in the lives of the Barbour family of San Francisco. Blue Bonnett Margarine, Chase and Sanborn Coffee, Miles Laboratories, Royal Puddings and Gelatin, Tender Leaf Tea, Toni Home Permanents and Wesson Oil were frequent sponsors. NBC, 1932–1959. Episodes were presented as a chapter followed by a book (for example, Chapter 12, Book 72) then a title ("A Touch of Christmas Spirit"). There were 3,256 episodes (134 books) and just as many different openings and closings, although each was similar in nature. J. Henry Smythe played the father, Henry Barbour, and his wife, Frances, was played by Minetta Ellen and Mary Adams. Their children were Paul (Michael Raffeto, Russell Thorson), Hazel (Bernice Berwin), Claudia (Kathleen Wilson, Floy Margaret Hughes, Barbara Fuller, Laurette Fillbrandt), Clifford (Barton Yarborough) and Jack (Page Gilman). "Destiny Waltz" by Sydney Barnes was the original theme (1932–1941); "Patricia" by Paul Carson was used as the theme 1941–1959.

OPEN

THEME MUSIC ("Patricia"): Up full then under…

ANNOUNCER: *One Man's Family*, brought to you by the makers of Chase and Sanborn Coffee and Blue Bonnett Margarine. *One Man's*

Family is dedicated to the mothers and fathers of the younger generation and to their bewildering offspring. Today we present the opening chapter of Book 65 entitled "The Dying Fires of Europe." And now the author has a personal word for you. It will be given by Paul.

PAUL BARBOUR: There is a custom of long standing on *One Man's Family* of giving an introductory preface for the beginning of each new book. This is not only the launching of a new volume, Book 65, but the beginning of a new year. And just as 1948 is a continuation of events which had their beginnings in 1947, so this new book of the family is a continuation of events that had their roots in previous volumes… [A recap would follow before the new story began.]

CLOSE

ANNOUNCER: You have just heard Chapter One of Book 65 of *One Man's Family*, written and produced under the direction of Carlton E. Morse for the makers of Chase and Sanborn Coffee and Blue Bonnett Margarine. Chapter Two, entitled "Teddy Barbour After Two Years," will come to you next week at this same hour. *One Man's Family* comes to you from California. This is NBC, the National Broadcasting Company.

THEME MUSIC: Up full then out.

SOUND: NBC chimes. N-B-C.

317. The Open Door

Drama about Erik Hansen, dean of students at Vernon University, who helps those who come through his open office door. Sponsored by Royal Puddings and Gelatin. CBS, 1943–1944. Dr. Alfred T. Dorf played Eric Hansen.

OPEN

ANNOUNCER (Arnold Moss): Welcome, friends, you've come to *The Open Door* and the makers of Royal Puddings and Royal Gelatin invite you to enter and meet Dr. Hansen.

HANSEN: Come in, come in, the door is open.

THEME MUSIC: Up full then out.

ANNOUNCER: Here comes Mary Woods of the Royal kitchens with a paper bag. Something good for me, Miss Woods?

MARY: Something good, period, Arnold. I'm taking home some macaroons for dinner tonight.

ARNOLD: I'll bet you're gonna snuggle them up to Royal Pudding.

MARY: I'm going to put them on Royal Pudding for a nice crunchy taste that I know will make a hit. I hope all our listeners will try this easy dessert soon. First, make Royal Butterscotch Pudding just as the package says in that astonishingly quick way. When you're ready to serve it, crush a few macaroons and sprinkle them over the top and that's all. Royal desserts, all four kinds, are awfully good just as is, but you'll like thinking up variations, like this macaroon idea for butterscotch pudding. One thing I want you to insist on though, is always getting Royal Puddings. There just isn't any substitute for it.

THEME MUSIC: Up full then under...

ANNOUNCER: And now to *The Open Door*.

CLOSE

ANNOUNCER: You know that's true what Mary Woods said about keeping Royal Puddings on hand in an assortment of flavors. There's delicate Royal Vanilla Pudding, rich Royal Chocolate, golden Royal Butterscotch and the tapioca member, Royal Vanilla Tapioca Pudding. All so easy, all so good.

MARY: And while we're stocking the pantry, let's not forget Royal Gelatin desserts with their wonderful fruity flavors. They're different from all the others and they're flavor-sealed.

ANNOUNCER: That's right, Royal Pudding and Royal Gelatin desserts. That's the way to have better meals without fuss.

THEME MUSIC: Up full then under...

ANNOUNCER: Be sure to listen again tomorrow to *The Open Door*. Your narrator for *The Open Door*, Arnold Moss.

THEME MUSIC: Up full then out.

ANNOUNCER: This is CBS, the Columbia Broadcasting System.

318. Our Gal Sunday

Daily serial drama about an orphan girl (Sunday) who marries a titled Englishman (Lord Henry Brinthrope). Various sponsors. CBS, 1937–1959. Dorothy Lovell and Virginia Smolen played Sunday; Karl Swenson and Alistair Duncan were Henry.

OPEN

THEME MUSIC ("Red River Valley"): Up full then under...

ANNOUNCER (Ed Fleming): Once again we present *Our Gal Sunday*, the story of an orphan girl named Sunday from the little mining town of Silver Creek, Colorado, who in young womanhood married England's richest, most handsome lord, Lord Henry Brinthrope. The story that asks the question, "Can this girl, from a little mining town in the west, find happiness as the wife of a wealthy and titled Englishman?"

THEME MUSIC: Up full then out.

ANNOUNCER: It is true that thousands of people were first introduced to Anacin through their own physicians and dentists. These people know how incredibly fast Anacin brings relief for the pain of headache, neuritis and neuralgia. There is an important reason why Anacin relieves pain so promptly. It's the reason you'll want to remember for pain. Anacin is like a doctor's prescription; that is, it is not comprised of just one but a combination of medically proven ingredients in easy to take tablet form. Next time you suffer from the sudden pain of headache don't wait for relief. Try Anacin and you'll be delighted with the incredibly fast, effective action. Use only as directed. If pain persists or is unusually severe, see you doctor. Ask for Anacin, spelled A-N-A-C-I-N, at your drug store today.

THEME MUSIC: Up full then under...

ANNOUNCER: And now, *Our Gal Sunday*.

CLOSE

THEME MUSIC: Up full then under...

ANNOUNCER: As a high quality floor wax, Old English is rated tops, yet what a money saver it is. A full pint costs only 49 cents; 10 cents in savings over other top quality waxes. Self-polishing. You just spread Old English—no rubbing wax on floors or linoleum—and it polishes itself to a super shine that's longer lasting too. So remember, always insist on Old English for a super shine at a super saving.

THEME MUSIC: Up full then under…

ANNOUNCER: *Our Gal Sunday* will be on the air at this same time tomorrow.

THEME MUSIC: Up full then out.

ANNOUNCER: This is CBS, the Columbia Broadcasting System.

319. Our Miss Brooks

Comedy that revolved around Connie Brooks, an English teacher at Madison High School. Sponsored by American Home Products, the Colgate-Palmolive Company and Toni Home Permanents. CBS, 1948–1957. Eve Arden played Connie. Jeff Chandler then Robert Rockwell played biology teacher Philip Boynton; Gale Gordon was Principal Osgood Conklin; and Dick Crenna was student Walter Denton.

OPEN

THEME MUSIC: Up full then under…

ANNOUNCER (Roy Rowan): Lustre Creme Shampoo, for soft, glamorous, caressable hair, and Palmolive Soap, your beauty hope, bring you Eve Arden as *Our Miss Brooks*.

SOUND: Applause.

ANNOUNCER: And now let's see what's happening in the life of Connie Brooks, English teacher at Madison High School…

CLOSE

THEME MUSIC: Up full then under…

ANNOUNCER: Tune in again next week for another *Our Miss Brooks* show. *Our Miss Brooks* is brought to you by the Colgate-Palmolive Company, makers of Lustre Creme Shampoo for soft, glamorous, caressable hair, and Palmolive Soap, your beauty hope. *Our Miss Brooks* starring Eve Arden is produced by Larry Berns, written and directed by Al Lewis with music by Wilbur Hatch. Also in the cast were Robert Rockwell, Gale Gordon and Dick Crenna. America listens most to the CBS Radio Network.

THEME MUSIC: Up full then fade out.

320. Out of the Deep

Adventure series about the life of Gunnar Carlisle, deep-sea diver and captain of the cargo ship *Blue Falcon*. Various sponsors. NBC, 1945–1946. Wally Maher, then Ted Maxwell, played Gunnar; Ed Max was his first mate, Charlie Bartlett.

OPEN

VOICE: All hands, stand by for adventure.

THEME MUSIC: Up full then under…

VOICE (echo effect): *Out of the Deep.*

ANNOUNCER (Don Stanley): *Out of the Deep*, strange stories based on the true-life adventures of Captain Gunnar Carlisle, noted deep-sea diver and soldier of fortune.

THEME MUSIC: Up full then out.

GUNNAR: This is Gunnar Carlisle, skipper of the *Blue Falcon*, at anchor at home port in Santa Monica, California… [He would then begin the story.]

CLOSE

ANNOUNCER: From *Out of the Deep* has come another strange story based on the true-life adventures of Captain Gunnar Carlisle, noted deep-sea diver and soldier of fortune.

THEME MUSIC: Up full then under…

ANNOUNCER: *Out of the Deep* is produced and directed by Warren Lewis. Ted Maxwell played Gunnar Carlisle with Ed Max as Charlie Bartlett. This is a presentation of the NBC Hollywood Program Department.

THEME MUSIC: Up full then out.

SOUND: NBC chimes. N–B–C.

321. Passport for Adams

Drama about a newspaper editor (Doug Adams) and a photojournalist (Perry Quisinberry) who work as foreign correspondents for the Consolidated Syndicate. Various sponsors. CBS, 1943. Robert Young then Myron McCormick played Doug; Dane Clark, then Paul Mann, was Perry. Lucien Marowick composed the "Passport for Adams" theme.

OPEN

THEME MUSIC: Up full then under...

ANNOUNCER: The Columbia Broadcasting System presents *Passport for Adams*, the sixth of a series of programs starring Robert Young as Doug Adams, the country editor who has been sent on a trip around the world to visit the cities and talk to the people of the United Nations. Tonight's program, written and directed by Norman Corwin, takes Adams to the important war city of Tel Aviv, Palestine.

THEME MUSIC: Up full then out.

CLOSE

THEME MUSIC: Up full then under...

ANNOUNCER: You have been listening to *Passport for Adams* starring Metro-Goldwyn-Mayer's distinguished Robert Young. Tonight's passport was written, directed and produced by Norman Corwin. The original musical score was composed by Lucien Marowick and conducted by Lud Gluskin. Paul Mann is heard as Perry Quisinberry. Next week at this time, Columbia's *Passport for Adams* takes war correspondent Doug Adams to Moscow, the capital city of our great fighting ally, the Union of Soviet Socialist Republics. This is CBS, the Columbia Broadcasting System.

THEME MUSIC: Up full then fade out.

322. Pat Novak for Hire

Crime drama about a tough private detective who will take any job for money. Sponsored by Gallen Kamp Shoes. ABC, 1946–1947; 1949. Ben Morris, then Jack Webb, played Pat Novak.

OPEN

ANNOUNCER (George Fenneman): The American Broadcasting Company brings to its entire network one of radio's most unusual programs, *Pat Novak for Hire*, presented by Gallen Kamp.

SONG:

> Cinderella lost a shoe
> And so she got a mate.
> With lovely shoes
> A girl can't lose.
> In Gallen Kamps she'll rate.

ANNOUNCER: More miles to a Gallen Kamps. Yes, Gallen Kamps, the family shoe stores with the yellow front, the largest store chain in the west with stores from Canada to Mexico, Gallen Kamps presents—

THEME MUSIC: Up full then under...

ANNOUNCER: *Pat Novak for Hire.*

SOUND: Foghorns, waterfront activity.

PAT: Sure, I'm Pat Novak for hire. That's what the sign on the front of my shop says—Pat Novak for Hire... [At this point Pat would begin the evening's story about his troubles; for example: "Down here on the San Francisco docks you gotta rob a few graves if you want cigarette money. Sometimes, during a good week, you can duck trouble three or four days in a row—and then it creeps up on you like an old charge account. Well, I should have known that when I went to the bank...."]

CLOSE

SONG:

> Cinderella lost a shoe
> And so she got a mate.
> With lovely shoes
> A girl can't lose,
> In Gallen Kamps she'll rate.

ANNOUNCER: What girl hasn't dreamed a Cinderella dream of her own and wished for a fairy godmother to make those dreams come true? Here's what the newest Cinderella, Marilyn Buford, Miss America, says.

MARILYN: The modern girl doesn't waste time dreaming. She makes her dreams come true and she needs no fairy godmother to give her lovely shoes. She doesn't, that is, if she's discovered my favorite shoe store, Gallen Kamps.

ANNOUNCER: Yes, Marilyn, for graceful, lovely shoes, flattering and in the latest fashion, wise girls go to Gallen Kamps. Gallen Kamps are shoe style leaders.

MARILYN: And so amazingly priced, a girl can afford to have all the shoes she needs.

ANNOUNCER: And here's extra good news of a Thanksgiving shoe sale. Yes, prices are actually going down on many of the up-to-the-minute shoe styles tomorrow at Gallen Kamps. So shop this sale at the Gallen Kamps store near you tomorrow to step assured in the exciting holiday activities ahead. Look lovely in Gallen Kamps.

THEME MUSIC: Up full then under...

ANNOUNCER: The American Broadcasting Company has brought you *Pat Novak for Hire* starring Jack Webb. This is George Fenneman reminding you to be with us again next week at this same time, same station for radio's newest show, *Pat Novak for Hire*. And don't forget the store with the yellow front, the Gallen Kamps store. Gallen Kamps shoes are good shoes, there's something about them you'll like. This program came to you from Hollywood. This is ABC, the American Broadcasting Company.

THEME MUSIC: Up full then fade out.

323. The Paul Winchell– Jerry Mahoney Show

Comedy-variety series focusing on the antics of Jerry Mahoney, the mischievous wooden dummy of ventriloquist Paul Winchell. Sustaining. Mutual, 1943–1944.

OPEN

THEME MUSIC: Up full then under...

ANNOUNCER: Yes, it's *The Paul Winchell-Jerry Mahoney Show* featuring that lovely young singing star Vera Barton, and Bob Stanley and his orchestra. And here he is, that talented young ventriloquist, Paul Winchell and his little wooden dummy pal, Jerry Mahoney.

SOUND: Applause (at which time Paul and Jerry begin the show.)

CLOSE

THEME MUSIC: Up full then under...

ANNOUNCER: Well, that's our show for tonight. Here is Paul Winchell to say—

PAUL: Good night folks, hope to see you next week.

ANNOUNCER: And here's Jerry to say—

JERRY: Good night folks.

ANNOUNCER: Be with us again next week at 9:30 P.M. Eastern War Time for another *Paul Winchell and Jerry Mahoney Show*. The *Paul Winchell-Jerry Mahoney Show* stars Paul Winchell with Vera Barton and the orchestra of Bob Stanley; Roger Bower is the producer.

This program came to you from the Mutual Theater in New York. You are listening to the Mutual Broadcasting System.

THEME MUSIC: Up full then fade out.

324. The Penny Singleton Show

Comedy about Penny Williamson, the widowed mother of two children, as she struggles to run a business and provide for her daughters, Sue and D.G. Various sponsors, NBC, 1950. Penny Singleton played Penny; Sheila James was Sue and Marylee Robb D.G.

OPEN

THEME MUSIC: Up full then under...

ANNOUNCER (Frank Martin): On stage from Hollywood, another of NBC's outstanding half-hour presentations, *The Penny Singleton Show*.

PENNY: Hello, happy you're listening.

SOUND: Applause.

THEME MUSIC: Up full then under...

ANNOUNCER: Penny Singleton stars in our story of Penny Williamson, a young widow and the mother of D.G. and Sue. Penny supports her family and home by selling real estate in the firm of Williamson and Wiggins.

THEME MUSIC: Up full then out.

CLOSE

THEME MUSIC: Up full then under...

ANNOUNCER: *The Penny Singleton Show* featured Jim Backus as Penny's partner, Horace Wiggins; Marylee Robb as D.G., Sheila James as Sue; and Bea Benaderet as Margaret, the cook. Music was composed and conducted by Von Dexter. *The Penny Singleton Show*, written and produced by Robert Sotoberg, stars Penny Singleton.

PENNY: Good night, keep well.

THEME MUSIC: Up full then under...

ANNOUNCER: Frank Martin speaking. This is NBC, the National Broadcasting Company.

THEME MUSIC: Up full then out.

SOUND: NBC chimes. N-B-C.

325. People Are Funny

Game show in which people perform stunts for prizes. Sponsored by Mars Candies, Raleigh Cigarettes and Toni Home Permanents. NBC, 1942–1960. Hosted by Art Baker then Art Linkletter. Basis for the television series.

OPEN

THEME MUSIC: Up full then under…

ANNOUNCER (Rod O'Connor): Toni, Toni Home Permanents presents *People Are Funny*. Yes, tonight from Hollywood, John Guedel's production of *People Are Funny*, brought to you by Toni Home Permanents. And now here he is, the man who sets out to prove people are funny, Art Linkletter.

SOUND: Applause… (after which Art begins the show).

CLOSE

THEME MUSIC: Up full then under…

ANNOUNCER: Toni Home Permanents has presented *People Are Funny* with Art Linkletter. *People Are Funny* is produced by John Guedel and came to you from Hollywood. Be sure to see *People Are Funny* on NBC television. Rod O'Connor speaking. This is NBC, the National Broadcasting Company.

THEME MUSIC: Up full then out.

SOUND: NBC chimes. N-B-C.

326. The Pet Milk Show

Variety series hosted by singer Vic Damone. Sponsored by Pet Milk. NBC, 1948–1950. The song "You and the Night and the Music" was used as the theme.

OPEN

THEME MUSIC: Up full then under…

VIC (singing):

> You and the night
> And the music
> Fill me with flaming desire
> Setting my being
> Completely on fire.

ANNOUNCER (Warren Sweeney): Pet Milk, the original evaporated milk, presents *The Pet Milk Show* with Kay Armen, the Emily Coty Serenaders, Gus Haenschen and the Pet Milk Orchestra and starring Vic Damone.

VIC (singing):

> After the night
> And the music die
> Will I have you?

SOUND: Applause… (the show begins with Vic singing a song).

CLOSE

ANNOUNCER: It is a known fact that wholesome food is essential to our feeling better, working better and living happier. No food is more important than milk, long recognized as the most nearly perfect food. Whole milk is one of the essentials of an adequate, properly balanced diet. One of the surest ways to get this milk into the diet is to use Pet Evaporated Milk in the preparation of everyday foods. Pet Milk is concentrated to double richness. Puts into foods extra wholesomeness, supplies more of the protective whole milk substances. Yet, surprising as it may seem, costs less than ordinary milk. So if you want to give your family meals they like which are at the same time good to eat, serve nourishing, wholesome meals made with Pet Milk, the original evaporated milk.

THEME MUSIC: Up full then under…

ANNOUNCER: This is Warren Sweeney, your host for Pet Milk, the original evaporated milk, wishing you good luck and good night. This is NBC, the National Broadcasting Company.

THEME MUSIC: Up full then out.

SOUND: NBC chimes. N-B-C.

327. Pete Kelly's Blues

Crime drama about Pete Kelly (Jack Webb), a jazz musician of the 1920s who plays cornet at Lupo's, a speakeasy at 417 Cherry Street in Kansas City. Various sponsors. NBC, 1951. Dick Cathcart composed the theme, "Pete Kelly's Blues."

OPEN

THEME MUSIC: Up full then under…

ANNOUNCER: This one's about Pete Kelly. It's about the world he goes around in. It's about the big music and the big trouble in the big twenties. So when they ask you, tell them this one's about the blues, *Pete Kelly's Blues.*

THEME MUSIC: Up full then under...

ANNOUNCER: *Pete Kelly's Blues* starring Jack Webb with story by Jim Mosher and music by Dick Cathcart.

PETE (speech varies by episode): Number 417 Cherry Street is a standard speakeasy. Their help is paid in cash; the books are burnt at the end of the month. Every week we use 30 cases of booze and a pound of coffee and after salaries, there's gas and lights and payoffs to the prohibition boys. In Kansas City, the price is good: for a hundred bucks they steer in the drunks and make one raid a year. The place is run by George Lupo; he's a quiet little guy who wouldn't give you the sweat off an ice pitcher. The beer is green and the gin is as young as yesterday; and the music is loud. I'm Pete Kelly, I play cornet. We start every night about ten o'clock and we play till they sweep out the broken glass. We don't draw any customers, we don't chase any away. The music is straight New Orleans. It started in the funeral parlors of Storyville and drifted up North. Some of it laid over in Chicago. That's where I got on and rode it out here with a piano player named Augie... [Pete would then begin the story.]

CLOSE

THEME MUSIC: Up full then under...

ANNOUNCER: *Pete Kelly's Blues* starring Jack Webb with story by Jim Mosher and music by Dick Cathcart; scoring by Matty Matlock. *Pete Kelly's Blues* is based on characters created by Richard L. Greene. This is NBC, the National Broadcasting Company.

THEME MUSIC: Up full then out.

SOUND: NBC chimes. N-B-C.

328. The Phil Harris–Alice Faye Show

Comedy-variety series that mixed music and songs with humorous events in the life of bandleader Phil Harris (himself), his wife, Alice Faye (herself), and their children, Little Alice (Jeanine Roos) and Phyllis (Anne Whitfield). Elliott Lewis played band member Frankie Remley and Walter Tetley was Julius Abbruzio, the annoying delivery boy. Sponsored by Rexall and RCA. NBC, 1948–1954.

OPEN

ANNOUNCER (Bill Forman): Good health to all from Rexall.

THEME MUSIC: Up full then under...

ANNOUNCER: Yes, it's Sunday, time for *The Phil Harris-Alice Faye Show,* presented by the makers of Rexall drug products and ten thousand independent Rexall family druggists.

THEME MUSIC: Up full then out.

REXALL SPOKESMAN: Good evening, this is your Rexall family druggist taking a little time from behind the prescription counter this Sunday evening to speak for all 10,000 of us, the 10,000 independent druggists who have added Rexall to their own store name. You can always tell us by the orange and blue Rexall sign on our windows. The sign means we carry the 2,000 or more drug products made by the Rexall Drug Company. They range all the way from aspirin to penicillin, and they're as fine and pure and dependable as science can make them. We independent druggists recommend them to our customers because we know you can depend on any drug product that bears the name Rexall.

THEME MUSIC: Up full then under...

ANNOUNCER: And now your Rexall family druggist brings you *The Phil Harris-Alice Faye Show* written by Dick Singer and Ray Chevillat, with Elliott Lewis, Walter Tetley, Jeanine Roos, Anne Whitfield, Walter Scharf and his music, yours truly, Bill Forman, and starring Phil Harris and Alice Faye.

THEME MUSIC: Up full then out.

CLOSE

THEME MUSIC: Up full then under...

ANNOUNCER: Be sure to be with us again next Sunday when the makers of Rexall drug products and your friendly neighborhood Rexall Drugstores present *The Phil Harris-Alice Faye*

Show. Bill Forman speaking. This is NBC, the National Broadcasting Company.
SOUND: NBC chimes. N-B-C.

329. Philco Radio Time

Variety series hosted by singer-actor Bing Crosby. Sponsored by Philco Electronics. ABC, 1946–1949.

OPEN

THEME MUSIC ("Where the Blue of the Night"): Up full then under...
BING (singing):
> Where the Blue of the Night
> Meets the gold of the day
> Someone waits for me.

THEME MUSIC: Under...
ANNOUNCER: This is Ken Carpenter welcoming you to *Philco Radio Time*, produced and transcribed in Hollywood with John Scott Trotter and his orchestra, Jud Conlan's Rhythmaires and Bing's guests, Edgar Bergen, Charlie McCarthy and Mortimer Snerd.
THEME MUSIC: Up full then under...
ANNOUNCER: Folks, you can walk into your Philco dealer tomorrow and bend an ear to the greatest invention of our times in recorded music, Philco's new phonograph that plays the forty-five-minute record. What's more, you can take it with you because your Philco dealer is ready to make immediate delivery on a variety of new models that play both kinds of records, long-playing and standard. These new Philco's set a standard that leaves conventional phonographs as dead as the Dodo bird. Seeing is believing, but listening is better still. Get a demonstration now of the newest thing in radio phonographs from Philco, the leader.
THEME MUSIC: Up full then under (as Bing begins the show with a song).

CLOSE

BING: Folks, don't forget your community chest. Everybody benefits, everybody gives. Good night and thanks.
THEME MUSIC: Up full then under...

ANNOUNCER: This program was produced and transcribed in Hollywood. Tune into *Philco Radio Time* next week to hear Bing Crosby, John Scott Trotter and his orchestra, the Rhythmaires and Bing's guests Oscar Levant and Peggy Lee. And remember, keep your eye on your Philco dealer now for the newest thing in radio phonographs from Philco, the leader. This is ABC, the American Broadcasting Company.
THEME MUSIC: Up full then fade out.

330. The Philip Morris Playhouse

Anthology series that presented stories of crime, mystery and suspense. Sponsored by Philip Morris Cigarettes. CBS, 1941–1943; 1948–1949; 1951. Philip Morris was represented by its trademark, Johnny the Bellboy (Johnny Roventini).

OPEN

ANNOUNCER (Art Ballinger): Johnny presents *The Philip Morris Playhouse*, produced, edited and directed by William Spier. Tonight's star—Howard Duff.
SPONSOR'S THEME ("On the Trail"): Up full then under...
JOHNNY: Call for Philip Mor-rees. Call for Philip Mor-rees.
ANNOUNCER: It's a wonderful, wonderful feeling to wake up fresh with no cigarette hangover. Yes, you'll be glad tomorrow if you smoke Philip Morris today.
JOHNNY: Call for Philip Mor-rees.
ANNOUNCER: And now, with Howard Duff as our star, we bring you "Four Hours to Kill," tonight's production transcribed in *The Philip Morris Playhouse*. [The story of a man who accidentally kills his brother during an argument then tries to cover up the deed.]

CLOSE

ANNOUNCER: Tonight, *The Philip Morris Playhouse* has presented "Four Hours to Kill," produced, edited and directed by William Spier. Our star, Howard Duff, will be back in a moment for a curtain call. In the meantime, it's a wonderful, wonderful feeling to wake up fresh with no cigarette hangover. Yes, that's something more and more smokers who have changed to Philip Morris are discovering every day. Millions of new smokers now enjoy in Philip Morris, a milder smoke, a fresher, cleaner smoke then they have ever known before. Yes, join the millions and see what a difference it makes, what a pleasure it is to smoke America's finest cigarette. Next time you step up to a cigarette counter, call for Philip Morris—and remember you'll be glad tomorrow you smoked Philip Morris today.

HOWARD: What have you lined up for next week, Johnny?

JOHNNY: Next week, *The Philip Morris Playhouse* will present Chester Morris in an exciting script called "Papa Turns Green." But before you go, may I present you with this carton of Philip Morris cigarettes and thank you for being with us.

HOWARD: Thank you, Johnny. Good night.

JOHNNY: Good night, Mr. Duff.

ANNOUNCER: And now good-bye Johnny, see you next Friday, same time, same station when once again we present transcribed, *The Philip Morris Playhouse* starring Chester Morris. Until then—

JOHNNY: Call for Philip Mor-rees.

THEME MUSIC: Up full then under...

ANNOUNCER: Pick a number from one to ten.

VOICE: I'll take five.

ANNOUNCER: That's the winner, that's Revelation, a blend of five great tobaccos cut five different ways. Revelation is a great pipe tobacco that is smooth burning and fragrant. Only 15 cents for the pocket tin. Revelation.

THEME MUSIC: Up full then under...

ANNOUNCER: Tonight's original radio play was by Howard Swanton. Music for *The Philip Morris Playhouse* is under the direction of Lud Gluskin. All names and characters used on this program are fictitious. Any similarity to persons living or dead is purely coincidental. This is Art Ballinger saying good night for Philip Morris.

THEME MUSIC: Up full and out.

ANNOUNCER: This is CBS, the Columbia Broadcasting System.

331. Philo Vance

Crime drama about a private detective who solves baffling crimes. Various sponsors. NBC (1945), Syn., (1948–1950). Jose Ferrer and Jackson Beck played Philo Vance; Joan Alexander and Frances Farras played his secretary, Ellen Deering.

OPEN

THEME MUSIC: Up full then under...

ANNOUNCER: A baffling crime; a mysterious murder. When the police are puzzled they turn to Philo Vance, the confidential investigator with a skill for unraveling mysteries. *Philo Vance*, starring Jackson Beck with Frances Farras as Ellen, the secretary almost as shrewd as her boss.

THEME MUSIC: Up full then out.

CLOSE

THEME MUSIC: Up full then under...

ANNOUNCER: You have just heard another adventure from the files of *Philo Vance*, private investigator. Jackson Beck is heard as Philo Vance with Frances Farras as Ellen. All names used in tonight's story are fictitious. *Philo Vance* is a Frederic W. Ziv production.

THEME MUSIC: Up full then fade out.

332. The Player

Anthology series featuring Paul Frees playing all the roles in various dramatizations. Sustaining. Syn., 1948–1949.

OPEN

THEME MUSIC: Up full then under...

SOUND: A brief scene from the particular episode.

ANNOUNCER (Gary Goodwin): And thus we begin another story by the Player, starring America's most versatile actor, Mr. Paul Frees. And here's the Player, Mr. Paul Frees.

PAUL: How do you do, ladies and gentlemen? This is the Player, welcoming you to our presentation of "First Citizen of the Bowery."

CLOSE

THEME MUSIC: Up full then under…

ANNOUNCER: And now Paul Frees, your one-man theater who portrays all of the parts.

PAUL: "First Citizen of the Bowery" was written by Ben Pearson and produced by Sam Kierner with music composed and performed by Ramey Idris. Special effects by Gary Cole. Your announcer was Gary Goodwin. Won't you join us again when we present another exciting story for your entertainment. This is the Player, Paul Frees, saying goodbye until next we meet.

THEME MUSIC: Up full then fade out.

333. Popeye the Sailor

Comedy about the adventures of Popeye the Sailor Man, his girlfriend, Olive Oyl, and Bluto, Popeye's rival for Olive's affections. Unlike the theatrical cartoon, radio's Popeye derives his strength from the sponsor's product, Wheatena. NBC (1935–1936), CBS (1936–1938). Det Poppen, Floyd Buckley and Jack Mercer played Popeye; Olive La Moy and Mae Questel were Olive Oyl; and Jackson Beck was Bluto.

OPEN

VOICE: All hands on deck, here's Popeye.

SOUND: Ship's bells ringing.

THEME MUSIC ("Popeye the Sailor Man"): Up full then under…

POPEYE (singing):
> I'm Popeye the Sailor Man,
> I'm Popeye the Sailor Man.
> I am what I am
> 'Cause I am what I am,
> I'm Popeye the Sailor Man.

THEME MUSIC: Up full then under…

ANNOUNCER (Kelvin Keech): Wheatena's his diet. He asks you try it with *Popeye the Sailor Man*.

THEME MUSIC: Up full then out.

FEMALE VOICE: Jimmy, Janet, time to get up.

ANNOUNCER: Well that's the signal for old man stomach to get busy. He phones up to your brain and says "Hello brain, it's been a long time since supper. Now how about sending down some food." Boys and girls want to know how to please old man stomach an awful lot. Send him down some nice hot brown Wheatena. Yes sir, that will make him happy and contented. It tastes great going down and the minute it gets there, it makes you feel good all over because your tummy doesn't keep all that Wheatena for itself. No sir. Popeye's favorite cereal goes right to work, making muscles and putting zip and go into those arms and legs of yours. When your brain gets that phone call tomorrow morning, you know the answer don't you? One dish of Wheatena coming down.

THEME MUSIC: Up full then under (as the show begins).

CLOSE

ANNOUNCER: Say, did you ever sniff hot brown Wheatena bubbling in the saucepan? I don't care whether you're six or sixty, there's something to make you hungry clear down to your toes. Why, just one whiff of that toasty fragrance and your next stop is the breakfast table. And Wheatena tastes just as good as it smells. Wheatena has a flavor like no other cereal you ever tasted. Say, here's a sporting proposition. Try Wheatena just once. And if it isn't the best-tasting cereal you ever ate, well, forget Wheatena from then on. So what do you say, is that a go?

THEME MUSIC: Up full then under…

ANNOUNCER: *Popeye the Sailor* is based on the characters created by E.C. Seegar and features the voice of Jack Mercer as Popeye. Kelvin Keech speaking.

THEME MUSIC: Up full then fade out.

334. The Private Files of Rex Saunders

Crime drama about a sophisticated British private detective based in New York City. Sponsored by RCA. NBC, 1951. Rex Harrison played Rex Saunders.

OPEN

THEME MUSIC: Up full then under…

ANNOUNCER (Kenneth Banghart): RCA Victor and its thousands of dealers present Rex Harrison starring in another intriguing adventure, transcribed from *The Private Files of Rex Saunders.*

OPEN

THEME MUSIC: Up full then under...

ANNOUNCER: RCA Victor, world leader in radio, first in recorded music and first in television, brings you a new series of exciting detective adventures with Rex Harrison, brilliant international star of stage and screen. It's good company anywhere, yes anywhere, anytime. There's fun at your fingertips with an RCA portable radio, at home or away from home, on your bedside table or at the beach; it's great to own this pick of the portables, an RCA Victor. You'll enjoy the extra range; you'll rave about the tone, thanks to RCA's Golden Throat Tone System. Yet your RCA boasts a compactness and lightness you never dreamed possible. Most of all, you get the strongest reception ever received on battery operation because RCA's radio batteries are engineered for top performance and extra listening hours. Yes, on every count, an RCA Victor portable radio is great company anywhere. Take your pick of the many beautifully styled models at your RCA Victor dealer. Remember to insist on RCA Victor.

THEME MUSIC: Up full then under...

ANNOUNCER: and now *The Private Files of Rex Saunders.*

CLOSE

ANNOUNCER: Here's an album that belongs in your record library, the magnificent new RCA Victor Red Seal of Mario Lanza singing eight of the arias included in his new M-G-M hit, *The Great Caruso.* Now, the full, rich voice of America's most sensational singing discovery is captured in all its beauty on RCA Victor Red Seal records. Yours not only to enjoy once, but over and over again through the years. Available now at your RCA record dealers in all three speeds: 78, long play and 45. Stop in tomorrow and get your copy of the RCA Victor Red Seal album featuring Mario Lanza in selections from *The Great Caruso.*

THEME MUSIC: Up full then under...

ANNOUNCER: Remember, whether you're buying a television set, a radio, a Victrola phonograph or records, put your faith in the cornerstone of American home entertainment for three generations, RCA Victor. RCA Victor and its dealers have brought you *The Private Files of Rex Saunders.* The entire production was under the direction of Himan Brown. This is Kenneth Banghart speaking for RCA Victor. This is NBC, the National Broadcasting Company.

THEME MUSIC: Up full then out.

SOUND: NBC chimes. N-B-C.

335. The Private Lives of Ethel and Albert

Comedy about incidents in the everyday lives of marrieds Ethel and Albert Arbuckle (Peg Lynch and Alan Bunce), residents of the small town of Sandy Harbor. Sustaining. ABC, 1948–1950. Peg Lynch and Alan Bunce were previously the stars of *Ethel and Albert* (ABC, 1944–1948), a 15-minute comedy dialogue program that evolved into *The Private Lives of Ethel and Albert.*

OPEN

THEME MUSIC: Up full then under...

ANNOUNCER: *The Private Lives of Ethel and Albert* starring Peg Lynch and Alan Bunce. The small things in everyday life are pretty much the same in every family. We're all familiar with the trivial incidents in the daily routine and it's these very things that make up *The Private Lives of Ethel and Albert.*

THEME MUSIC: Up full then out.

CLOSE

THEME MUSIC: Up full then under...

ANNOUNCER: *The Private Lives of Ethel and Al-*

bert comes to you each weekday at this time. The show is written by Peg Lynch who plays the part of Ethel. Albert is played by Alan Bunce. The program is produced by Bob Cotton. This is ABC, the American Broadcasting Company.

THEME MUSIC: Up full then fade out.

336. The Private Practice of Dr. Dana

Drama that centered on Steve Dana (Jeff Chandler), a private-practice doctor who also works at Hayes General Hospital. Various sponsors. CBS, 1947–1948.

OPEN

THEME MUSIC: Up full then under…

ANNOUNCER: *The Private Practice of Dr. Dana* starring Jeff Chandler and brought to you each Sunday afternoon at this same time. And now, with Jeff Chandler starred, we bring you another story from the colorful career of the private practice of Steve Dana, M.D.

THEME MUSIC: Up full then out.

CLOSE

THEME MUSIC: Up full then under…

ANNOUNCER: And there you have *The Private Practice of Dr. Dana* starring Jeff Chandler. Betty Lou Gerson was heard as Dr. Carol Tracy and Mary Lansing as Nurse Gorcey. *The Private Practice of Dr. Dana* is produced by Sterling Tracy with original music composed and conducted by Eddie Dunstedter. Be with us again next Sunday for another colorful story from *The Private Practice of Dr. Dana*. This is CBS, the Columbia Broadcasting System.

THEME MUSIC: Up full then fade out.

337. Pursuit

Crime drama about Peter Black, a British police inspector who relentlessly pursues criminals. Sponsored by Dr. Lyon's Tooth Powder, Ford Motor Company, Molle Shaving Creme and Wrigley's Chewing Gum. CBS, 1949–1952. Ted de Corsia, then Ben Wright, played Peter Black.

OPEN

ANNOUNCER (Bob Stevenson): And now *Pursuit*.

SOUND: London's Big Ben tolling.

ANNOUNCER: A criminal strikes and fades quietly back into the shadows of his own dark world. And then the man from Scotland Yard, the famous Inspector Peter Black, and the dangerous, relentless pursuit—when man hunts man.

THEME MUSIC ("Pursuit"): Up full then under…

ANNOUNCER: In just a moment, tonight's story.

SPOKESMAN: One thing *you* may not notice, that other people do, is a gradual loss of whiteness and brightness in your teeth and you of your charm. If your winning smile has faded, start using a dentifrice that whitens and brightens your teeth, try Dr. Lyon's Tooth Powder. Dr. Lyon's Tooth Powder gets your teeth cleaner than the dentifrice you're now using, whitens and brightens your teeth in a way that it makes your smile gleam with all its old luster and brilliance. You can buy regular Dr. Lyon's Tooth Powder; or if you want the best of the ammoniated tooth powders, buy ammoniated Dr. Lyon's. Remember, be sure to get Dr. Lyon's and get back your winning smile.

THEME MUSIC: Up full then under…

ANNOUNCER: And now with Ben Wright starred as the famous Peter Black of Scotland Yard, we bring you tonight's story of *Pursuit*.

THEME MUSIC: Up full then out.

CLOSE

THEME MUSIC: Up full then under…

ANNOUNCER: You have been listening to *Pursuit* with Ben Wright starred as the famous Peter Black of Scotland Yard. *Pursuit* is under the supervision of Elliott Lewis and features the music of Eddie Dunstedter. Bob Stevenson speaking. This is CBS, the Columbia Broadcasting System.

THEME MUSIC: Up full then fade out.

338. Quiet Please

Mystery stories that place people in a hazy dreamworld where things are not always as they seem. Sustaining. Mutual (1947–1948), ABC (1948–1949). Ernest Chappell served as the host and narrator. The "Second Movement" from Franck's *Symphony in D Minor* was used as the theme.

OPEN

THEME MUSIC: Up full then under…
ANNOUNCER (Ed Michael): Quiet please. Quiet please. The Mutual Broadcasting System presents *Quiet Please*, written and directed by Wyllis Cooper and featuring Ernest Chappell.
THEME MUSIC: Up full then out.

CLOSE

THEME MUSIC: Up full then under…
ANNOUNCER: You have listened to *Quiet Please*, which is written and directed by Wyllis Cooper. The man who spoke to you was Ernest Chappell.
HOST: Until next week at this time, I am quietly yours, Ernest Chappell.
ANNOUNCER: *Quiet Please* came to you from New York. Ed Michael speaking. This is the Mutual Broadcasting System.
THEME MUSIC: Up full then fade out.

339. The Quiz Kids

Game show in which children answered questions put to them by quiz-master Joe Kelly. Various sponsors (Alka-Seltzer was a frequent sponsor). NBC (1940; 1946–1951), Blue/ABC (1940–1946), ABC (1952–1953).

OPEN

THEME MUSIC ("School Days"): Up full then under…
ANNOUNCER (Robert Murphy): *The Quiz Kids*, brought to you by the makers of Alka-Seltzer for headache. Alka-Seltzer for acid indigestion. Alka-Seltzer for cold distress. Yes, when these occasional ailments make you miserable, take Alka-Seltzer for really fast, really effective relief.

SOUND: Bell ringing.
HOST: Well, there's the bell calling the class to order. *Quiz Kids*. And listen, here's today's first question: "If Dewey is elected, what is it that he will wear into the White House that no other president has had and for how many years?"
ANNOUNCER: Yes, that's our first brain teaser this afternoon. You listeners have a few seconds to think it over while the youngsters here in our classroom get ready for roll call. And here they are, the quiz kids and the chief quizzer himself, Joe Kelly.
JOE: Thank you Bob Murphy and welcome everyone. Well here we go with another competitive question session in radio's famous classroom of the air. And competing in this 425th *Quiz Kids* broadcast are—
KIDS (IN THEIR OWN VOICES): Michael Mullin, Rene Templeton, Joel Cooperman, Claire Frye, Ira Leigh. [The program then begins.]

CLOSE

JOE: We'll be calling roll at this same time next Sunday. Until then, this is Joe Kelly dismissing "the quiz kids." Goodbye kids.
ANNOUNCER: Alka-Seltzer has presented *The Quiz Kids* starring Joe Kelly. Robert Murphy speaking. This is NBC, the National Broadcasting Company.
SOUND: NBC chimes. N-B-C.

Note: Answer to the question used in the open: a moustache (last worn by Taft 35 years before in 1913).

340. Radio City Playhouse

Anthology series featuring adaptations of works by noted authors. Stories are referred to as "Attractions." Sustaining. NBC, 1948–1950.

OPEN

THEME MUSIC: Up full then under…
ANNOUNCER (Robert Warren): The National Broadcasting Company presents *Radio City Playhouse*, Attraction Two. Tonight's play is titled "Ground Floor Window." It was written by an extremely talented young author, Ernest Kinoy, with Bill Redford starring as

Danny and directed by Harry W. Junkin. Here is *Radio City Playhouse*, Attraction Two, "Ground Floor Window."

CLOSE

ANNOUNCER: That was "Ground Floor Window," Attraction Two, *Radio City Playhouse*, as written by Ernest Kinoy and directed by Harry W. Junkin. Next week the *Radio City Playhouse* presents "Of Unsound Mind," written by our director, Harry W. Junkin. It is the story of Myra, beautiful, gracious and charming—and without a soul. We sincerely hope you will be with us next Saturday when we bring you "Of Unsound Mind" by Harry W. Junkin, Attraction Three, *Radio City Playhouse*. Robert Warren speaking. This is NBC, the National Broadcasting Company.

THEME MUSIC: Up full then out.

SOUND: NBC chimes: N-B-C.

341. Raffles

Crime drama about A.J. Raffles (Horace Braham), a reformed burglar turned private detective. Sustaining. NBC (1949–1950), ABC (1950–1953).

OPEN

ANNOUNCER: There's danger; there's mystery; there's action on the way with *Raffles*.

THEME MUSIC: Up full then under...

ANNOUNCER: Raffles, formerly gentleman cracksman, gentleman adventurer, ace of knaves. Raffles, now reformed, matches wits with the underworld; devotes his time and talent to upholding law and order, even though his methods are highly unconventional and would never be found in the police manual.

THEME MUSIC: Up full then out.

CLOSE

THEME MUSIC: Up full then under...

ANNOUNCER: The radio mysteries of *Raffles* starring Horace Braham, are heard over this station every week at this same time. The entire production was under the direction of Jock MacGregor. Be with us again next week when there's danger, there's mystery, there's action on the way with *Raffles*.

THEME MUSIC: Up full then fade out.

342. The Raleigh Room

Variety session hosted by singer Hildegarde. Sponsored by Raleigh Cigarettes. NBC, 1944–1945.

OPEN

ANNOUNCER: Does your cigarette taste different lately? Not if you smoke Raleigh. They're blended with fully aged, fully mellowed tobacco.

THEME MUSIC: Up full then under...

ANNOUNCER: Raleigh Cigarettes invites you to the beautiful *Raleigh Room*, to the music of Harry Sosnik and his orchestra. There go the spotlights and here she is, our vivacious star, the incomparable Hildegarde.

HILDEGARDE: Thank you, thank you and good evening ladies and gentlemen. Once again welcome to the informal *Raleigh Room*... [Hildegarde would then begin the show with a song.]

CLOSE

THEME MUSIC: Up full then under...

ANNOUNCER: Raleigh Cigarettes, the cigarette that is fully aged and fully mellowed, has presented *The Raleigh Room* with the incomparable Hildegarde. Be with us again next week when Raleigh Cigarettes will present *The Raleigh Room*. This is NBC, the National Broadcasting Company.

THEME MUSIC: Up full then out.

SOUND: NBC chimes. N-B-C.

343. Renfrew of the Mounted

Adventure series about Douglas Renfrew, a Royal Canadian Mounted Policeman. CBS (1936–1937; sponsored by Wonder Bread), Blue (1937–1940; Sustaining). House Jameson played Inspector Renfrew.

OPEN

SOUND: Howling wind; howling dogs.
VOICE: Renfrew, Renfrew of the Mounted!
RENFREW: Renfrew reporting, ready for action.
ANNOUNCER (Bert Parks): Once again we bring you *Renfrew of the Mounted*, another story of the famous inspector of the Royal Canadian Mounted Police. Known to thousands of admirers through the books and stories of Laurie Yorke Erskine and adapted to radio by George Ludlum.

CLOSE

ANNOUNCER: So we close another adventure of *Renfrew of the Mounted*, famous inspector of the Royal Canadian Mounted Police, known to thousands of young Americans and Canadians through the books and stories of Laurie Yorke Erskine and specially adapted for radio by George Ludlum. House Jameson is Renfrew. *Renfrew of the Mounted* is a program of the National Broadcasting Company.
SOUND: NBC chimes. N-B-C.

344. Results, Inc.

Crime drama about Johnny Strange and Teresa "Terry" Travers, partners in a detective agency called Results, Inc. Sustaining. Mutual, 1944. Lloyd Nolan played Johnny with Claire Trevor as Terry.

OPEN

THEME MUSIC: Up full then under…
ANNOUNCER (Bob O'Connor): Presenting Lloyd Nolan and Claire Trevor in a new radio series, *Results, Incorporated*.
THEME MUSIC: Up full then under…
LLOYD: *Results, Incorporated*. Your problem is our problem. Where others fail, we succeed. Contact Johnny Strange, Room 201, Security Building.
THEME MUSIC: Up full then out.

CLOSE

ANNOUNCER: Lloyd and Claire, you certainly had us worried there for a minute. Say, what have you on tab for next week? Another comedy-mystery?
CLAIRE: You see, in our next story, Johnny Strange has a most amazing adventure.
LLOYD: Yea, it all starts out when a guy named Trazona hires us to locate his brother.
CLAIRE: Johnny can't resist a late afternoon cocktail, so he stops in a local pub.
LLOYD: And the next thing I know, I'm on the floor, the place is deserted, a gun is in my hand and a dead policeman is lying beside me.
CLAIRE: And solving the mystery proves to be one of the most exciting experiences ever encountered by Results, Incorporated.
THEME MUSIC: Up full then under…
ANNOUNCER: The mystery-comedy series, *Results, Inc.*, has starred Lloyd Nolan as Johnny Strange and Claire Trevor as the irrepressible Teresa Travers. Miss Trevor appeared through the courtesy of RKO Studios and Mr. Nolan through the courtesy of 20th Century-Fox. Tonight's script by Sol Stein and Martin Worth was based on characters created by Lawrence Edmond Taylor. Music by Russ Trump. Our thanks for listening. Bob O'Connor speaking. This is Mutual.
THEME MUSIC: Up full then fade out.

345. Richard Diamond, Private Detective

Crime drama about a former police officer turned private detective. Various sponsors (Camel Cigarettes and Rexall Drugs were frequent sponsors). NBC (1949–1950), ABC (1951–1953). Dick Powell played Richard Diamond; Virginia Gregg was his girlfriend, Helen Asher; and Ed Begley was Lt. Walt Levinson. Basis for the television series.

OPEN

ANNOUNCER (Eddie King): The makers of Rexall drug products and your friendly neighborhood Rexall Drugstores present—
SOUND: Richard Diamond whistling.
ANNOUNCER: Here's Dick Powell as *Richard Diamond, Private Detective*.
THEME MUSIC: Up full then under…
ANNOUNCER: Richard Diamond will begin in

just a moment, but first, here's your Rexall druggist.

DRUGGIST: Recently, a customer asked me for an example of Rexall quality that she could see with her own eyes. I told her one example like that is the label on the Rexall drug product and she came back with—

WOMAN: But every drug product has a label.

DRUGGIST: Yes, ma'am, that's true, but let's take a look at this Rexall label for a minute. See these three different sets of numbers?

WOMAN: Yes.

DRUGGIST: Each one means that certain important steps in the preparation of this product have been carefully done and thoroughly checked.

WOMAN: And I've looked on a label as just a piece of paper with the name of the product.

DRUGGIST: Well, ma'am, those pieces of paper are handled like currency in a bank. They're kept in a locked room until the labeling process begins. Then a certain amount is counted out very carefully and after the labeling run, everyone of them is counted again and checked against the number of bottles or packages labeled. Naturally, the two have to balance.

WOMAN: Well, that is evidence I can see for myself.

DRUGGIST: Yes ma'am, evidence of the painstaking care and accuracy that go into the preparation of all of the more than 2,000 or more [sic] drug products made by the Rexall Drug Company. When you remember things like this you understand why some 10,000 independent Rexall druggists tell you, you can depend on any drug product that bears the name Rexall.

THEME MUSIC: Up full then under...

ANNOUNCER: And now, here's Dick Powell as *Richard Diamond, Private Detective.*

CLOSE

THEME MUSIC: Up full then under...

ANNOUNCER: Rexall, the name that stands for quality and its drugstores from coast to coast, have presented Dick Powell as *Richard Diamond, Private Detective.* Ed Begley appeared as Levinson with Virginia Gregg as Helen. Music is by Frank Worth. Be with us again next week for *Richard Diamond, Private Detective.* Eddie King speaking. This is NBC, the National Broadcasting Company.

THEME MUSIC: Up full then out.

SOUND: NBC chimes. N-B-C.

346. The Right to Happiness

Daily serial about events in the life of Carolyn Kramer. Sponsored by CBS Radio and Procter and Gamble (Crisco and Ivory Soap). Blue (1939–1940), CBS (1940–1941), NBC (1941–1960). Eloise Kummer and Claudia Morgan played Carolyn Kramer. "Song of the Soul" by Joseph Breil was used as the theme.

OPEN

THEME MUSIC: Up full then under...

ANNOUNCER (Ron Rawson): This is *The Right to Happiness,* brought to you by Procter and Gamble, makers of Crisco. Happiness is the sum total of many things—of health, security, friends and loved ones. But most important is a desire to be happy and the will to help others find their right to happiness as well.

THEME MUSIC: Up full then under...

ANNOUNCER: *The Right to Happiness*—a very human story.

THEME MUSIC: Up full then under... (as the story begins).

CLOSE

ANNOUNCER: Say ladies, are you cooking with Crisco? It's all vegetable, it's digestible and it makes the most amazing cakes. Try the new Crisco cake. They're better on every account—lighter, better texture, moister, richer too, way ahead of cakes made the old-fashioned way. Remember, for really gorgeous cakes, try new Crisco cake; recipes are on the can.

THEME MUSIC: Up full then under...

ANNOUNCER: Procter and Gamble, the makers of Crisco—it's all vegetable, it's digestible—has presented *The Right to Happiness.* Be with us again tomorrow for *The Right to Happiness.* This is NBC, the National Broadcasting Company.

THEME MUSIC: Up full then out.

SOUND: NBC chimes, N-B-C.

347. Road of Life

Daily serial about Jim Brent, a doctor in the town of Merrimack. Sponsored by Procter and Gamble. NBC (1937–1954), CBS (1952–1959). It appeared on CBS and NBC 1952–1954. Ken Griffin, Matt Crowley, Don MacLaughlin, David Ellis and Howard Teichmann played Dr. Brent. The "First Movement" of Tschaikowsky's *Sixth Symphony* is used as the theme.

OPEN

GIRL SINGER:
> D-U-Z, D-U-Z.
> I put DUZ in my washing machine,
> See how clothes come out so clean.
> When I DUZ my wash I sing
> DUZ does everything.

THEME MUSIC: Up full then under...

ANNOUNCER: (Clayton Collyer): Yes, it's the DUZ program, *Road of Life*.

THEME MUSIC: Up full then under...

ANNOUNCER: Let's stop in at the Duzins house. Well, there's young Davie, just coming in the door and looking very pleased.

DAVIE (to her mother): Mom, you'll never guess, but I just won a title.

MOTHER: A what?

DAVIE: A title. I've just been awarded the Best Dressed Young Woman to Shop at Penny Packer's Candy Store on Third Street. And Mom, I owe it all to DUZ and to you, my own sweet mother.

MOTHER: Thank you, Davie.

DAVIE: And to DUZ, that wonderful, heavenly new kind of soap that does everything in the world.

MOTHER: You're sure right, Davie. DUZ deserves credit for keeping all our clothes so nice.

THEME MUSIC: Up full then under...

ANNOUNCER: And now DUZ invites you to listen to *The Road of Life*.

CLOSE

THEME MUSIC: Up full then under...

ANNOUNCER: You know most of us have certain favorite songs that mean something pretty special to us. Take this little song for instance.

GIRL SINGER:
> When I DUZ my wash I sing
> D-U-Z does everything.

ANNOUNCER: When it comes to tossing everything in your washbasket, DUZ is a whiz. It just can't be beat by any soap. DUZ gets the grimiest work clothes clean easy; it gives your towels true whiteness and it's safer for the colored rayons you wash; safer than any other leading packaged soap sold for washday. Yes, the soap to remember on washday is DUZ and the song to remember is—

GIRL SINGER: D-U-Z does everything.

THEME MUSIC: Up full then under...

ANNOUNCER: Be sure to listen again to another absorbing episode on *Road of Life*.

DUZ MUSIC THEME: Up full then under...

GIRL SINGER:
> D-U-Z, D-U-Z.
> I put DUZ in my washing machine,
> D-U-Z does everything.

THEME MUSIC: Up full then under...

ANNOUNCER: This is Clayton Collyer wishing you a good day. The shortage of fats and oil is critical; it's world-wide. So won't you help. Everybody, everyday, save every drop of used fat. This is NBC, the National Broadcasting Company.

THEME MUSIC: Up full then out.

SOUND: NBC chimes. N-B-C.

348. The Road to Danger

Adventure about Stumpy and Cottonseed, U.S. Army truckers during World War II. Sustaining. NBC, 1942–1945. Curley Bradley played Stumpy with Clarence Hartzell as Cottonseed.

OPEN

COTTONSEED: Stumpy, what in tarnation are we waitin' on now?

STUMPY: Not a darn thing I can see, Cottonseed, let's go!

SOUND: Truck engine starting, then moving out.

THEME MUSIC: Up full then under...

ANNOUNCER: The National Broadcasting Company presents *The Road to Danger*, the story of two American truck drivers on the un-

marked highways of the world. Right this minute they're ready to shake, rattle and roll up to the lines where the air is filled with flying steel; they're set for another long haul along the highway that is *The Road to Danger.*
THEME MUSIC: Up full then out.

CLOSE

THEME MUSIC: Up full then under…
ANNOUNCER: You have just heard another in NBC's series *The Road to Danger.* Curley Bradley is Stumpy and Clarence Hartzell is Cottonseed. Romelle Fay was at the organ. Next week, same time, same station, be sure to join us again on *The Road to Danger* when you'll hear—
COTTONSEED: Stumpy, what are we waitin' on?
STUMPY: Not a darn thing, Cottonseed, let's go!
SOUND: Truck speeding off.
ANNOUNCER: This is the National Broadcasting Company.
THEME MUSIC: Up full then out.
SOUND: NBC chimes. N-B-C.

349. Rocky Fortune

Crime drama about a tough private detective who will take whatever jobs he can find to make money. Sustaining. NBC, 1953–1954. Frank Sinatra played Rocky Fortune with Barney Phillips as Sergeant Hamilton J. Finger.

OPEN

THEME MUSIC: Up full then under…
ANNOUNCER (Eddie King): And now, Frank Sinatra, transcribed, as Rocky Fortune. NBC presents Frank Sinatra starring as that footloose and fancy-free young gentleman Rocky Fortune.
THEME MUSIC: Up full then under…
ROCKY: Hi there, I'm Rocky Fortune… [Rocky would then talk about an incident which would be presented in a flashback story.]

CLOSE

THEME MUSIC: Up full then under…
ANNOUNCER: NBC has presented Frank Sinatra

as that footloose and fancy-free young gentleman Rocky Fortune. Also in the cast was Barney Phillips as Sergeant Finger. All names and places used in tonight's story were fictional. Eddie King speaking. This is NBC, the National Broadcasting Company.
THEME MUSIC: Up full then out.
SOUND: NBC chimes. N-B-C.

350. Rocky Jordan

Adventure about Rocky Jordan, owner of the Cafe Tambourine in Cairo, Egypt. Various Sponsors. CBS, 1948–1950 (with Jack Moyles as Rocky); 1951 (with George Raft as Rocky).

OPEN (Jack Moyles)

ANNOUNCER (Larry Dobkin): Time now for *Rocky Jordan.*
THEME MUSIC: Up full then under…
ANNOUNCER: Again we bring you a story of adventure with a man named Rocky Jordan, proprietor of the Cafe Tambourine in Cairo. Cairo, gateway to the ancient East where modern life unfolds against the backdrop of antiquity. *Rocky Jordan* starring Jack Moyles.
THEME MUSIC: Up full then out.

CLOSE (Jack Moyles)

THEME MUSIC: Up full then under…
ANNOUNCER: Remember this same time each Sunday night for *Rocky Jordan. Rocky Jordan* is produced by Cliff Powell with original music composed and conducted by Milton Charles. *Rocky Jordan* is produced from Columbia Square in Hollywood and stars Jack Moyles in the title role. Larry Dobkin speaking. This is CBS, the Columbia Broadcasting System.
THEME MUSIC: Up full then out.

OPEN (George Raft)

THEME MUSIC: Up full then under…
ANNOUNCER (Joe Walters): Now starring George Raft we bring you a world of adventure with *Rocky Jordan.*
THEME MUSIC: Up full then under…
ANNOUNCER: The Cafe Tambourine, crowded

with tourists, camel drivers, women, sheiks, forgotten men down on their luck, the lonely and the lost. For this is Cairo, gateway to the ancient East where modern adventure and intrigue unfold against the backdrop of antiquity. *Rocky Jordan.*

THEME MUSIC: Up full then out.

CLOSE (George Raft)

THEME MUSIC: Up full then under...

ROCKY: Hope to see you at the Cafe Tambourine again next week. Until then, sieta (goodbye).

ANNOUNCER: *Rocky Jordan* stars Mr. George Raft. Our original music is composed and conducted by Richard Aurandt. Joe Walters speaking. This transcribed program came to you over the CBS Radio Network.

THEME MUSIC: Up full then out.

351. Roger Kilgore, Public Defender

Crime drama about a public defender of indigent clients. Various sponsors. Mutual, 1948. Raymond Edward Johnson, then Santos Ortega, played Roger Kilgore.

OPEN

ANNOUNCER: The Mutual Broadcasting System presents *Roger Kilgore, Public Defender.*

THEME MUSIC: Up full then under...

VOICE: We hold these truths to be self-evident that all men are created equal. That they are endowed by their creator with certain inalienable rights. That among these are life, liberty and the pursuit of happiness.

ROGER: I'm Roger Kilgore, Public Defender, a paid servant of the public. It's my duty to defend any person accused of a crime who is unable to pay for his own defense.

THEME MUSIC: Up full then out.

CLOSE

THEME MUSIC: Up full then under...

ANNOUNCER: *Roger Kilgore, Public Defender,* produced and directed by Jock McGregor, featured Santos Ortega as the public defender

and Staats Cotsworth as the District Attorney. Original music was played by Milton Kane. All names, places and dates used in this program were, for obvious reasons, fictitious. Remember that justice, equal justice, is the sacred right of all people in a democracy. Carl Caruso speaking. This is the Mutual Broadcasting System.

THEME MUSIC: Up full then fade out.

352. Rogers of the Gazette

Comical incidents in the life of Will Rogers, Jr. (himself), editor of the *Gazette,* newspaper of the town of Olearia. Various sponsors. CBS, 1953–1954. Also in the cast was Georgia Ellis as Will's assistant, Maggie Button.

OPEN

MAGGIE: Ladies and gentlemen, the editor of the Olearia *Weekly Gazette,* Mr. Will Rogers, Jr.

WILL: Thank you. You know, some newspapers claim they print all the news that's fit to print and some others, who won't admit it, just print the news that fits.

THEME MUSIC: Up full then under...

ANNOUNCER (Bob Lemond): Tonight the makers of Wrigley's Spearmint Chewing Gum bring you *Rogers of the Gazette,* the transcribed, heart-warming story of a country newspaper and its friendly editor. *Rogers of the Gazette* starring Will Rogers, Jr., is brought to you by Wrigley's Spearmint Chewing Gum.

THEME MUSIC: Up full then out.

ANNOUNCER: For refreshment while you work, for enjoyment anytime, chew a stick of Wrigley's Spearmint Gum. The delicious, long-lasting real mint flavor of Wrigley's spearmint cools your mouth and freshens your taste. The good, smooth chewing helps keep you fresh and alert, adds enjoyment to whatever you are doing. So indoors, outdoors, whether at work or play, enjoy chewing Wrigley's Spearmint Gum. Wrigley's Spearmint, refreshing and delicious.

THEME MUSIC: Up full then under...

ANNOUNCER: And now to the little town of Olearia and to the offices of the *Weekly Gazette...*

CLOSE

THEME MUSIC: Up full then under...

ANNOUNCER: Next week Wrigley's, the chewing treat enjoyed by millions, will bring you another *Rogers of the Gazette* starring Will Rogers, Jr. Georgia Ellis was heard as Maggie. Tonight's story was produced and transcribed by Mr. Norman MacDonnell. The special music was composed by Rene Garrigan and conducted by Wilbur Hatch. Tomorrow night don't miss *Cathy and Elliott Lewis on Stage* on most of these CBS stations. Bob Lemond speaking. All summer long enjoy refreshing dramas on *The Thursday Theater* on the CBS Radio Network.

THEME MUSIC: Up full then fade out.

353. Rogue's Gallery

Crime drama about Richard Rogue, a tough private detective who takes whatever cases will make him money. Sponsored by Fitch Shampoo and Easy Cut Electric Lawn Mowers. Mutual (1945–1946), NBC (1946–1947), ABC (1950–1951). Dick Powell, Barry Sullivan and Paul Stewart played Richard Rogue with Peter Leeds as Eugor, "the nasty little spook" Rogue meets when he drifts to Cloud Eight after getting knocked out.

OPEN

ANNOUNCER: *Rogue's Gallery* starring Paul Stewart as Richard Rogue.

THEME MUSIC: Up full then under...

ROGUE: Some people collect old violins, some people collect rare china, some people collect old coins; but I collect murders.

SOUND: Gunshots.

THEME MUSIC: Up full then under...

ANNOUNCER: *Rogue's Gallery*, the thrilling, spine-tingling adventures of Richard Rogue, private investigator, is presented each week at this time by your local dealer who services and sells the Easy Cut Electric Mower. That's the dealer that's making an unheard of offer that you can't afford to miss. There's no strings, no gimmicks, no small type to this offer. Just try an Easy Cut Electric Mower in your yard for ten days. Give the Easy Cut a full tryout.

Then, if for any reason, or no reason at all, you don't want to keep it, your dealer will refund every penny of your money. Yes, try the Easy Cut Electric Mower. Compare its many advantages. Notice the larger rear coaster for easier handling. Notice the flat switch for effortless starting. Notice the rubber tire ball-bearing wheels. Notice the powerful one-third horsepower motor. Yes, compare and you'll buy an Easy Cut Electric Mower. See it tomorrow at your dealers.

THEME MUSIC: Up full then under...

ANNOUNCER: And now *Rogue's Gallery* with Paul Stewart as private investigator Richard Rogue.

CLOSE

ANNOUNCER: You can't lose on the offer now being made by your Easy Cut Electric Lawn Mower dealer. All you do is take the easy-to-operate East Cut Electric Mower home. Try it for ten days. After you try it for ten full days and, if for any reason you don't want to keep it, return it to your dealer and he'll refund your full purchase price without any questions asked. You couldn't ask for a better deal. See your Easy Cut dealer right away. Remember, the solution to easier, faster grass cutting is an Easy Cut Electric Powered Mower. Now to remind you to listen next week at this same time to *Rogue's Gallery*, presented by your Easy Cut Electric Mower dealer, is Richard Rogue.

THEME MUSIC: Up full then under...

ROGUE: We hope you enjoyed tonight's story in this new series and we will be back as usual next week. And we hope too that you'll be around and hang another portrait in *Rogue's Gallery*.

THEME MUSIC: Up full then out.

ANNOUNCER: This program was transcribed and came to you from New York. This is ABC, the American Broadcasting Company.

354. Romance

Anthology series featuring stories of romance and adventure. Sustaining (Colgate, 1944–1946; Wrigley's, 1950; and Jergens, 1952–1953, sponsored as indicated). CBS, 1943–1957.

ANNOUNCER: Now from Hollywood, *Romance*.
THEME MUSIC: Up full then under...
ANNOUNCER: *Romance*, bringing you the finest stories of the world's greatest authors. Stories of the courage, the devotion, the adventure of love, all strung on the bright thread of romance. Tonight we take you to the wild mountains of Portugal where two lovers invite terror and death in order to achieve their freedom as Kenneth Bennett tells it in his exciting tale "To Live Again." [Story about a peasant girl who risks her life to help her boyfriend, a wanted killer, escape from the police.]
THEME MUSIC: Up full then out.

THEME MUSIC: Up full then under...
ANNOUNCER: *Romance*, under the direction of Norman MacDonnell, brings you the greatest love stories of today and yesterday. Tonight you heard Ken Bennett's unusual story "To Live Again" starring Bill Conrad and Georgia Ellis. If you're an employer you might have mixed feelings about having a stenographer like Millie around the office. Audrey Totter stars as Millie in CBS's new Monday night comedy series on most of these same stations. Take a tip from us and [listen to] *Meet Millie*, which follows immediately over most of these same CBS stations. This is CBS, the star's address, the Columbia Broadcasting System.
THEME MUSIC: Up full then out.

ANNOUNCER (Dan Cubberly): Now from Hollywood, *Romance*.
THEME MUSIC: Up full then under...
ANNOUNCER: *Romance*, transcribed stories of love and adventure, of comedy and crisis, of conflict and human emotion. Today an unusual and dramatic account of superstition and hate in bayous of Louisiana as we bring you William Froug's terrifying story "The Lu-Garu." [Story about a stranger who moves to the bayou and is believed to be a Lu-Garu— a werewolf—by the locals after a baby mysteriously dies.]
THEME MUSIC: Up full then out.

THEME MUSIC: Up full then under...
ANNOUNCER: *Romance* is produced and directed by William Froug. "The Lu-Garu" was written by Mr. Froug. Featured in the cast were Sam Edwards, Lillian Vief, Barney Phillips, Herb Butterfield, Joseph Kearns, Parley Baer, Jack Edwards and Jack Kruschen. Music is supervised by Jerry Goldsmith. This is Dan Cubberly inviting you to hear *Romance*, transcribed, next week at this same time. Law and order needed a helping hand in the early days of Dodge City. And a helping hand is just what Marshal Matt Dillon had to offer. For some really wild, really western thrills, hear what happens when the marshal's good friend Doc gets into a tight situation and needs some help to get out of it. It's yours right now for *Gunsmoke* follows immediately on most of these same stations.
THEME MUSIC: Up full then fade out.

355. The Romance of Helen Trent

Daily serial about Helen Trent, chief gown designer at Parafilm Studios, as she struggles to find a true love. Various sponsors. CBS, 1933–1960. Virginia Clark, Betty Ruth Smith and Julie Stevens played Helen Trent. Stanley Davis (later Lawrence Salerno) hummed the theme, "Juanita."

ANNOUNCER (Fielden Farrington): And now *The Romance of Helen Trent*.
THEME MUSIC: Up full then under...
ANNOUNCER: Once again the makers of Benefax Multi Vitamins presents *The Romance of Helen Trent*, the story of a woman who found that when life seemed finished, over, she could still recapture romance at 35 and even beyond.
THEME MUSIC: Up full then out.

THEME MUSIC: Up full then under...
ANNOUNCER: Be sure to listen again tomorrow

for the real-life drama of Helen Trent and her struggles to prove that because a woman is 35 or more, romance in life need not be over, that romance can begin at 35.

THEME MUSIC: Up full then under...

ANNOUNCER: *The Romance of Helen Trent* is produced by Frank and Anne Hummert; Betty Ruth Smith is heard as Helen Trent. This is Fielden Farrington speaking. This is CBS, the Columbia Broadcasting System.

THEME MUSIC: Up full then fade out.

356. The Roy Rogers Show

Western adventures set in modern times with Roy Rogers, "King of the Cowboys," and his wife, Dale Evans, "Queen of the West." Sponsored by Dodge Autos, Miles Laboratories, Post Cereals and Quaker Oats. Mutual (1944–1945; 1948–1950), NBC (1946–1947; 1951–1955).

OPEN (early)

THEME MUSIC: Up full then under...

ANNOUNCER (Lou Crosby): *The Roy Rogers Radio Show*. Yes, folks, it's *The Roy Rogers Radio Show* for the whole family. Adventure! Suspense! Mystery! and music. Starring Roy Rogers, King of the Cowboys, and Dale Evans, Queen of the West, with the Mello Men and an all-star cast. And now here to greet you with a song and a story are Roy and Dale.

ROY: Well good evening folks, greetings again to the whole family... [Roy would then begin a story about his and Dale's adventures.]

CLOSE (early)

ROY: That's all for now folks. This is Roy Rogers saying to all of you from all of us, goodbye, good luck and may the Good Lord take a liking to you. See you next week.

THEME MUSIC: Up full then out.

OPEN (later)

CHORUS: P-O-S-T.

ANNOUNCER: Post, the cereals you like the most, brings you *The Roy Rogers Show* starring the King of the Cowboys himself, Roy Rogers.

CHORUS:
It's round-up time
On the Double-R-Bar,
Saddle your horse,
'Cause we're gonna ride far.

ANNOUNCER: The Double-R-Bar Ranch, transcribed stories and songs of the real west, with the Whippoorwills, the wisest trail scout of them all, Jonah Wild, played by Forrest Lewis, the Queen of the West, Dale Evans, and in person, the King of the Cowboys, Roy Rogers.

ROY: Well howdy folks, this is Roy Rogers. If you want to do Mom a favor, remind her to keep Post cereals on the shelf all the time. Buckaroos, remind her tomorrow before she does her shopping. You can count on anything bearing the brand name Post. [Roy would then begin a story recounting his and Dale's adventures.]

CLOSE (later)

ROY: That's all for now folks. Remember, buckaroos, to have Post cereal for breakfast every morning. This is Roy Rogers saying goodbye, good luck and may the Good Lord bless you. See you next week.

THEME MUSIC: Up full then out.

357. The Royal Gelatin Hour

Music and songs coupled with comedy and dramatic skits with singer Rudy Vallee as the host. Sponsored by Royal Gelatin. NBC, 1936–1939.

OPEN

THEME MUSIC: Up full then under...

ANNOUNCER: Rudy Vallee requests your attention for *The Royal Gelatin Hour* with guests Fanny Brice, Tallulah Bankhead and Joe Laurie, Jr.

RUDY: Hi ho, everybody, this is Rudy Vallee and company. Tonight, Fanny Brice brings her little hellcat Baby Snooks to an eastern microphone for the last time before leaving for Hollywood in a new screen contract; Tallulah Bankhead will be heard in a new play by Dorothy Parker; and Joe Laurie, Jr., continues on his novel way for the fourth consecutive week… (Rudy would then begin the show.)

CLOSE

RUDY (singing):
>   Goodbye girls, it's through.
>   Each girl that I have met
>   I say goodbye to you
>   Without the least regret.

RUDY (speaking): This is Rudy Vallee saying good night.

THEME MUSIC: Up full then under…

ANNOUNCER: Be with us again next week at this same time when the makers of Royal Gelatin will again present Rudy Vallee in *The Royal Gelatin Hour*. This is NBC, the National Broadcasting Company.

THEME MUSIC: Up full then out.

SOUND: NBC chimes. N-B-C.

358. The Saint

Adventures of Simon Templar, alias the Saint, a wealthy, devil-may-care modern-day Robin Hood who helps people in trouble. Both sustaining and sponsored (by Bromo Seltzer, Campbell Soup, Ford Motor Company). NBC (1945; 1950–1951), CBS (1945; 1947–1948), Mutual (1949–1950). Edgar Barrier, Brian Aherne, Vincent Price, Tom Conway and Barry Sullivan played the Saint.

OPEN

THEME MUSIC ("The Saint"): Up full then under…

ANNOUNCER: The adventures of *The Saint*, starring Vincent Price. The Saint, based on characters created by Leslie Charteris and known to millions from books, magazines and motion pictures. The Robin Hood of modern crime now comes to radio starring Hollywood's brilliant and talented actor, Vincent Price, *The Saint*.

THEME MUSIC: Up full then out.

CLOSE

THEME MUSIC: Up full then under…

ANNOUNCER: You have been listening to another transcribed adventure of *The Saint*, the Robin Hood of modern crime. And now here is our star, Vincent Price.

PRICE: This is Vincent Price inviting you to join us again next week at this same time for another exciting adventure of *The Saint*. Good night.

ANNOUNCER: *The Saint*, based on characters created by Leslie Charteris, has starred Vincent Price in the title role. Be with us again next week when the Robin Hood of modern crime returns in another adventure of *The Saint*. This is CBS, the Columbia Broadcasting System.

THEME MUSIC: Up full then fade out.

359. Sara's Private Caper

Comedy about Sara Berner (herself), a police department secretary who takes matters into her own hands to solve crimes. Sponsored by Wheaties. NBC, 1950.

OPEN

THEME MUSIC: Up full then under…

ANNOUNCER (Frank Martin): Wheaties presents Sara Berner in *Sara's Private Caper*. On stage tonight from Hollywood, Sara Berner, the police secretary with the mind of a detective, in *Sara's Private Caper*, brought to you by Wheaties.

THEME MUSIC: Up full then out.

ANNOUNCER: It's a wonderful morning when you've had your Wheaties, breakfast of champions. Now look, you don't have to be a champion to eat Wheaties. Whatever you do, Wheaties is for you too. You need vitamins and minerals, just like anyone else. Tomorrow, get yourself a box of Wheaties, the big box; they taste so good they won't last long. Pour them in the bowl, slice in the fruit, pour on the milk, pick up the spoon and enjoy yourself. Wheaties, breakfast of champions; it's a wonderful morning when you've had your Wheaties.

THEME MUSIC: Up full then under…

ANNOUNCER: And now back to Sara Berner and *Sara's Private Caper*.

CLOSE

ANNOUNCER: Congratulations on your brand-new radio program, it's fun.

SARA: Oh thank you Frank, it's fun to do it. I'm certainly looking forward to a summer full of Wheaties.

FRANK: Sara, so am I. You know about Wheaties, I take it, whole wheat flakes, crisp, tempting.

SARA: Know about them? Frank, I love Wheaties. They're practically part of the family.

FRANK: Fine, fine, and we're happy to have you as part of the Wheaties family, Sara. See you next Thursday night for *Sara's Private Caper* on these same NBC stations.

SARA: Oh thank you Frank, and get your Wheaties, everybody. Good night.

THEME MUSIC: Up full then under...

ANNOUNCER: Sara Berner in *Sara's Private Caper* is produced and directed by Joe Parker. Original music was composed and conducted by Robert Armbruster. And this is the Wheaties man, Frank Martin, inviting you to listen next Monday night to Frank Lovejoy in *Night Beat* on the Wheaties Big Parade. See you then. This is NBC, the National Broadcasting Company.

THEME MUSIC: Up full then out.

SOUND: NBC chimes. N-B-C.

360. The Saturday Night Swing Club

Variety series featuring swing music with Paul Douglas (then Ted Husing) as the host. Sustaining. CBS, 1936–1939.

OPEN

THEME MUSIC: Up full then under...

ANNOUNCER (Mel Allen): *The Saturday Night Swing Club* is now in session. And as we herald in [*sic*] the first anniversary session of *The Saturday Night Swing Club*, making a full year of a series of programs devoted by the Columbia network to that thing called swing. And here's your swing commentator, Paul Douglas. Swing it, Mr. Douglas.

SOUND: Applause.

PAUL: Thank you very much and thank you Mel Allen and greetings brothers and sisters of *The Saturday Night Swing Club*. Throughout the nation and to our shortwave listeners all over the world, it's Saturday swing time.

CLOSE

THEME MUSIC: Up full then under...

ANNOUNCER: So ends another session of *The Saturday Night Swing Club*. Your old swing conductor Paul Douglas will return next week with another session of *The Saturday Night Swing Club*. The Raymond Scott Quintet and Leith Stevens and his orchestra were heard on tonight's program. This is Mel Allen inviting you to be with us again next Saturday evening. This is CBS, the Columbia Broadcasting System.

THEME MUSIC: Up full then fade out.

361. Saunders of the Circle X

Western about "Singapore" Bill Saunders, foreman of the Circle X Ranch. Sustaining. Blue, 1941–1942. John Cubbertson played Bill Saunders. Bill's horse was named Pony.

OPEN

SOUND: Horses galloping.

ANNOUNCER: *Saunders of the Circle X.*

THEME MUSIC: Up full then under...

ANNOUNCER: We bring you a new story of the western range, *Saunders of the Circle X*, the story of "Singapore" Bill Saunders, foreman of the Circle X Ranch, as he battles the unscrupulous characters who inhabit the lawless West of a century ago. This is *Saunders of the Circle X* with John Cubbertson as Bill Saunders, the seafaring man turned foreman nicknamed "Singapore" for his world travels.

THEME MUSIC: Up full then out.

CLOSE

THEME MUSIC: Up full then under...

ANNOUNCER: You have just heard another story in Samuel Dickson's story of the western range, *Saunders of the Circle X*. Listen this same time next Thursday evening over most of these stations when we learn the fate of "Singapore" Bill Saunders in another exciting episode of—

SOUND: Horse galloping.

ANNOUNCER: *Saunders of the Circle X.*

THEME MUSIC: Up full then out.

ANNOUNCER: This is the Blue Network of the National Broadcasting Company.

SOUND: NBC chimes. N-B-C.

362. Scattergood Baines

Lighthearted drama about the philosophical owner of a hardware store in the town of Cold River. Sustaining. Mutual, 1949. Wendell Holmes played Scattergood Baines; Leora Thatcher was his wife, Mandy: and Parker Fennelly was his friend, Hannibal Gibbey.

OPEN

ANNOUNCER (Bob Emerick): Mutual brings you your old friend Scattergood Baines.

THEME MUSIC: Up full then under…

ANNOUNCER: Yes, it's Clarence Buddington Kelland's famous character Scattergood Baines, brought to life in a new series of fast-moving adventures. But he's the same old Scattergood you all know—the shrewd and jovial hardware merchant who usually finds himself drawn into just about everything that happens around him. Scattergood Baines, the best-loved, most cussed-at and by all odds, the fattest man in the bustling town of Cold River.

THEME MUSIC: Up full then out.

CLOSE

ANNOUNCER: This has been another adventure of *Scattergood Baines*, based on the famous character created by Clarence Buddington Kelland. *Scattergood Baines* is written for radio by Jerry Holland and produced by Herbert Rice with original music composed and conducted by Ben Ludlow.

THEME MUSIC: Up full then under…

ANNOUNCER: Wendell Holmes is Scattergood Baines. Hannibal Gibbey is played by Parker Fennelly. This is Bob Emerick speaking. Be

with us next week at this time for another adventure with *Scattergood Baines*. This program was heard in Canada through the facilities of the Canadian Broadcasting Corporation. This is the Mutual Broadcasting System.

THEME MUSIC: Up full then fade out.

363. The Sealed Book

Eerie tales told by the Keeper of the Sealed Book (Philip Clarke). Various sponsors. Mutual, 1945.

OPEN

SOUND: Sinister laughing.

KEEPER: *The Sealed Book.*

SOUND: A large gong.

ANNOUNCER (Jimmy Wallington): Once again, the Keeper of the Sealed Book is ready to unlock the ponderous volume in which are recorded all the secrets and mysteries of mankind throughout the ages. All the lore and learning of the ancients, all the strange and mystifying stories of the past, the present and the future.

SOUND: A large gong.

THEME MUSIC: Up full then under…

ANNOUNCER: Keeper of the Book, what tale will you tell us this time?

KEEPER: First I must unlock the great padlock which keeps the Sealed Book safe from prying eyes.

SOUND: Book opening.

KEEPER: Now, what story shall I tell you? I have here tales of every kind, tales of murder, of madness, of dark deeds and events strange beyond all belief. Let me see.

SOUND: Keeper flipping through the pages.

KEEPER: Yes, here's a tale for you, a dark story of two brothers, one of them killed because he could not help himself. The other one was interested in murder too—but in a very different way. The title of the tale is—

SOUND: A large gong, followed by a musical sting.

KEEPER: "The Hands of Death." Here is the tale as it is written in *The Sealed Book*. [Weird story about a man with deformed hands who kills people who find him grotesque.]

CLOSE

SOUND: A large gong.

KEEPER: The sound of the Great Gong tells me I must lock the book once again.

ANNOUNCER: One moment, Keeper of the Book. What story from *The Sealed Book* will you tell us next time?

KEEPER: Next time? Are you sure you want to know? Perhaps my next story will be about you. For I have here all the stories that ever happened and many that have yet to come to pass, but I'll find one for you in just a moment.

THEME MUSIC: Up full then under...

ANNOUNCER: And now, Keeper of the Book, have you found the story that you will tell us next time?

KEEPER: Yes, I've found one. It's a story about a man who found the secret of immortality, of life everlasting, and how he tried to make himself master of the Earth. The title of the tale is "The King of the World."

SOUND: A large gong.

ANNOUNCER: Be sure to be with us next time when the Great Gong heralds another strange and exciting story from—

KEEPER: *The Sealed Book.*

ANNOUNCER: *The Sealed Book*, written by Bob Arthur and David Kogan, is produced and directed by Jock McGregor. This is Mutual.

THEME MUSIC: Up full then fade out.

364. Second Husband

Serial about Brenda Cummings, a woman who marries for the second time. Sponsored by Bayer Aspirin and Dr. Lyon's Tooth Powder. Blue (1936–1937; 1942), NBC (1937), CBS (1937–1946). Helen Menken and Cathleen Cordell played Brenda Cummings, with Joseph Curtin and Richard Waring as her husband, Grant Cummings. The songs "Diane" and "I Love Were All" were used as the themes.

OPEN

THEME MUSIC: Up full then under...

ANNOUNCER (Andre Baruch): Time now for *Second Husband* starring Helen Menken as Brenda Cummings. *Second Husband* is pre-

sented by the makers of Dr. Lyon's Tooth Powder.

THEME MUSIC: Up full then out.

ANNOUNCER: Have your teeth lost their old-time whiteness and brightness? Try using a dentifrice that whitens and brightens teeth and makes them really clean. Try Dr. Lyon's Tooth Powder; it cleans like no other dentifrice. If you don't agree that Dr. Lyon's Tooth Powder doesn't get [*sic*] your teeth cleaner than your present dentifrice, simply return the package and your money will be refunded.

THEME MUSIC: Up full then under...

ANNOUNCER: And now to our story of *Second Husband.*

CLOSE

THEME MUSIC: Up full then under...

ANNOUNCER: *Second Husband* starring Helen Menken as Brenda Cummings will be back on the air at this same time tomorrow. *Second Husband* is produced by Frank and Anne Hummert. Andre Baruch speaking. This is CBS, the Columbia Broadcasting System.

THEME MUSIC: Up full then fade out.

365. The Secrets of Scotland Yard

Crime dramas based on the official files of Scotland Yard. Various sponsors. Mutual, 1957–1958. Hosted by Clive Brook.

OPEN

THEME MUSIC: Up full then under...

ANNOUNCER (Sanford Marshall): The Mutual Broadcasting System presents *The Secrets of Scotland Yard* with your host and narrator Clive Brook. Brought to you by the Mutual Broadcasting System in cooperation with Ex-Lax, America's largest selling laxative; the Vitamin Consumer Service; Harrison Home Products, introducing in America from West Germany, the world's smallest precision adding machine; and Reader's Digest and the Reader's Digest Book Club. And now *The Secrets of Scotland Yard* and your host Clive Brook. [He would then introduce a dramatization based on a case file from Scotland Yard.]

CLOSE

THEME MUSIC: Up full then under...

ANNOUNCER: The Mutual Broadcasting System has presented *The Secrets of Scotland Yard* with your host and narrator Clive Brook in cooperation with chocolated Ex-Lax, America's largest-selling laxative; VCS, the Vitamin Consumer Service; Reader's Digest; and Harrison Home Products. This is Sanford Marshall inviting you to return next week when we again reveal *The Secrets of Scotland Yard.*

THEME MUSIC: Up full then fade out.

366. Sergeant Preston of the Yukon

Adventure series about Sergeant William Preston of the Canadian Northwest Mounted Police, and his dog, Yukon King, as they uphold the law. Sponsored by the Quaker Oats Company. Mutual, 1951–1955. Paul Sutton, Jay Michael and Brace Beemer played Sgt. Preston. See also *Challenge of the Yukon.*

OPEN

SOUND: Howling winds.

ANNOUNCER (Jay Michael): Now, as howling winds echo across the snow-covered reaches of the wild Northwest, the Quaker Oats Company, makers of Quaker Puffed Wheat and Quaker Puffed Rice, the delicious cereal shot from guns, presents *Sergeant Preston of the Yukon.*

SOUND: Dog barking.

ANNOUNCER: It's Yukon King, swiftest and strongest lead dog of the Northwest, breaking the trail for Sergeant Preston of the Northwest Mounted Police in the relentless pursuit of lawbreakers.

PRESTON: On King; on you huskies.

SOUND: Dogs barking.

ANNOUNCER: The adventures of Sergeant Preston and his dog Yukon King as they meet the challenge of the Yukon.

THEME MUSIC ("The Donna Diana Overture"): Up full then out.

CLOSE

THEME MUSIC: Up full then under...

ANNOUNCER: These *Sergeant Preston of the Yukon* adventures are brought to you Monday through Friday at this time by the Quaker Oats Company by special recording in cooperation with the Mutual Broadcasting System. They are a copyright feature of Sergeant Preston of the Yukon, Inc. Created by George W. Trendle, produced by Trendell-Campbell-Muir, Inc. and directed by Fred Flowerday. The part of Sergeant Preston is played by Paul Sutton. This is Jay Michael wishing you good luck and good health for Quaker Puffed Wheat and Quaker Puffed Rice. So long. This is Mutual, radio network for all America.

THEME MUSIC: Up full then fade out.

367. Sez Who?

Game in which players have to identify well-known celebrities by their voices. Sustaining. CBS, 1957–1958. Hosted by Henry Morgan.

OPEN

THEME MUSIC: Up full then under...

ANNOUNCER (John Cameron Swayze): In the next half-hour you will hear the voices of some of the world's best-known personalities on radio's newest, most exciting fun game, *Sez Who?* Yes, it's time for *Sez Who?* and here's the star of *Sez Who?*, Henry Morgan.

SOUND: Applause... [Henry would then begin the show by playing a recorded voice and asking a panel to identify it.]

CLOSE

THEME MUSIC: Up full then under...

ANNOUNCER: So ends another session of *Sez Who?* Be with us again next week for another session of radio's most exciting fun game show. Until then, this is John Cameron Swayze for *Sez Who?* This is CBS, the Columbia Broadcasting System.

THEME MUSIC: Up full then fade out.

368. The Shadow

Mystery series that ran on CBS (1930–1932), NBC (1932–1935) and Mutual (1937–1954). Prior to being titled *The Shadow*, in which Lamont Cranston fought evil as the mysterious Shadow, the series featured a character called the "Shadow," who narrated mystery stories. The series was originally titled *Detective Story Hour* then *Detective Story Program, Blue Coal Radio Revue, Love Story Drama, Love Story Hour* and finally *The Shadow* (in 1937). James La Curto originally played the Shadow (1930) with Frank Readick, Jr. in the role from 1931 to 1937. On September 26, 1937, the format changed to reflect Lamont Cranston as a crime fighter. His "lovely aid and traveling companion, Margot Lane" was also introduced at this time. The following is a listing of the Lamont and Margot pairings: Orson Welles and Agnes Moorehead (1937–1938); Orson Welles and Margot Stevenson (1938); Bill Johnstone and Agnes Moorehead (1938–1939); Bill Johnstone and Marjorie Anderson (1939–1940); Bill Johnstone and Jeanette Nolan (1940–1943); Bret Morrison and Marjorie Anderson (1943–1944); John Archer and Judith Allen (1944–1945); Steve Courtleigh and Laura Mae Carpenter (1945); Bret Morrison and Lesley Woods (1945–1946); Bret Morrison and Grace Matthews (1946–1949); Bret Morrison and Gertrude Warner (1949–1954). Blue Coal was the principal sponsor and featured John Barclay as the Blue Coal Heating Expert in commercials (played by Tim Frawley, then Paul Huber). Opening and closing signatures varied through the years. Four examples are listed, beginning with the very first *Shadow* episode (September 26, 1937) with Orson Welles and Agnes Moorehead. As is typical with this series, cast and credits are not given in the opening or closing theme. The theme for all versions is "Omphale's Spinning Wheel" from *Le Rouet d'Omphale*, "Opus 31" by Camille Saint-Saëns.

OPEN (1937)

THEME MUSIC: Up full then under...
SOUND: The Shadow laughing menacingly.
SHADOW: Who knows what evil lurks in the hearts of men? The Shadow knows.
ANNOUNCER: Blue Coal presents *The Shadow*, a man of mystery who strikes terror in the very souls of sharpsters, lawbreakers and criminals.
THEME MUSIC: Up full then out.
ANNOUNCER: All signs point to a severe winter. Be prepared. If you want to be sure of even, dependable, healthful heat in any kind of weather, insist on Blue Coal, America's finest anthracite mined from the fields in northern Pennsylvania, the coal that's colored the harmless blue at the mines for your protection.
THEME MUSIC: Up full then under (as the show would then begin).

CLOSE (1937)

ANNOUNCER: Before another episode of *The Shadow* draws to a close, John Barclay, Blue Coal's heating expert, would like to say a few words. Mr. Barclay.
BARCLAY: Good evening friends. If you're interested in having a more comfortable home this winter, be sure to call your local Blue Coal dealer for he's more than just a fuel dealer; he's an authority on modern home heating. You see, for more than six years, I've trained servicemen for these Blue Coal dealers. These men, known as John Barclay Servicemen, have made thousands of families, like yours, able to enjoy a greater degree of comfort and save heating dollars too. I thank you.
ANNOUNCER: The story you have just heard is copyrighted by *The Shadow* magazine. Real names are never used in these *Shadow* stories.
THEME MUSIC: Up full then under...
SOUND: Shadow laughing menacingly.
SHADOW: The weed of crime bears bitter fruit. Crime does not pay. The Shadow knows. [Laugh continues.]
VOICE (PAPERBOY YELLING): Extra, Extra, next week at this same time, *The Shadow* returns. Extra, Extra, Extra.
THEME MUSIC: Up full then out.

OPEN (1941)

THEME MUSIC: Up full then under...
SOUND: Shadow laughing menacingly.
SHADOW: Who knows what evil lurks in the hearts of men? The Shadow knows. [Laugh continues.]
THEME MUSIC: Up full then under...

ANNOUNCER (Jean Paul King): The thrilling adventures of *The Shadow* are on the air, brought to you each week by the Blue Coal dealers of America. These dramatizations are designed to demonstrate forcibly to old and young alike that crime does not pay.

THEME MUSIC: Up full then out.

BARCLAY: While they set the stage for today's *Shadow* drama, let me ask you a brief but vital question. Have you heard about the new easy three-way plan for better home heating? It's the Blue Coal plan, with the accent on convenience, economy and comfort. Blue Coal in your furnace means a steady-burning, longer-lasting fire that heats your home comfortably from cellar to attic. Next time you order fuel, insist upon Blue Coal. Your neighborhood Blue Coal dealer will be glad to explain his three-way plan for better home heating. Phone him tomorrow, won't you?

THEME MUSIC: Up full then under…

ANNOUNCER: The Shadow, mysterious character who aids the forces of law and order, is, in reality Lamont Cranston, wealthy young man about town. As the Shadow, Cranston is gifted with hypnotic powers to cloud men's minds so that they cannot see him. Cranston's friend and companion, the lovely Margot Lane, is the only other person who knows to whom the voice of the invisible Shadow belongs. Today's story, "The Shadow Challenged."

THEME MUSIC: Up full then under as the story begins [here, about Lamont's efforts to find a copycat Shadow who is killing scientists].

CLOSE (1941)

THEME MUSIC: Up full then under…

ANNOUNCER: Today's program is based on the story copyrighted by *The Shadow* magazine. The characters, names, places and plots are fictitious; any similarity to persons living or dead is purely coincidental.

THEME MUSIC: Up full then under…

SOUND: Shadow laughing menacingly.

SHADOW: The weed of crime bears bitter fruit. Crime does not pay. The Shadow knows. [Laugh continues.]

THEME MUSIC: Up full then under…

ANNOUNCER: Next week, same time, same station, the Blue Coal dealers of America will bring you an adventure of *The Shadow* that will amaze you with its breath-taking thrills. So be sure to listen. And be sure to phone your friendly Blue Coal dealer for greater heating comfort at less cost. This is Jean Paul King saying keep the home fires burning with Blue Coal.

THEME MUSIC: Up full then out.

OPEN (1943)

THEME MUSIC: Up full then under…

SOUND: Shadow laughing menacingly.

SHADOW: Who knows what evil lurks in the hearts of men? The Shadow knows. [Laugh continued.]

ANNOUNCER: The Shadow, Lamont Cranston, a man of wealth, a student of science, and a master of other people's minds, devotes his life to righting wrongs, protecting the innocent and using advanced methods that may ultimately become available to all law enforcement agencies. Cranston is known to the underworld as the Shadow—never seen, only heard. Haunting to superstitious minds as a ghost, as inevitable as a guilty conscience, the Shadow's true identity is known only to his constant friend and aide, Margot Lane. The thrilling adventures of *The Shadow* are on the air, brought to you each week at this time by the Blue Coal dealers of America. These dramatizations are designed to demonstrate to the old and young alike that crime does not pay.

THEME MUSIC: Up full then out (as the episode would then begin).

CLOSE (1943)

BARCLAY: Are you running your home on a budget plan? If you are, then every penny counts and you can save not only pennies, but dollars by heating your home with Blue Coal. Yes, any way you look at it, Blue Coal gives you more for your money. It burns better, lasts longer, distributes dependable, healthy heat that will cut down your heating costs. And no wonder. You see Blue Coal is America's hardest blue coal. It comes from the heart of the northern Pennsylvania anthracite fields, thousands of feet below the surface, where only the choicest hard coal is mined. What's more, with every order of Blue Coal, you enjoy the extra home heating service and free advice of your neighborhood Blue Coal dealer. Call him tomorrow.

THEME MUSIC: Up full then under...

ANNOUNCER: You have been listening to a dramatized version of one of the many copyrighted stories which appear in *The Shadow* magazine.

THEME MUSIC: Up full then under...

SOUND: Shadow laughing menacingly.

SHADOW: The weed of crime bears bitter fruit. Crime does not pay. The Shadow knows. [Laugh continued.]

THEME MUSIC: Up full then out.

OPEN (1949)

THEME MUSIC: Up full then under...

SOUND: Shadow laughing menacingly.

SHADOW: Who knows what evil lurks in the hearts of men? The Shadow knows. [Laugh continued.]

ANNOUNCER: Once again we bring you the thrilling adventures of *The Shadow*—the hard and relentless fight of one man against the forces of evil. The Shadow, mysterious character who aids the forces of law and order, is, in reality, Lamont Cranston, wealthy man about town. Several years ago in the Orient, Cranston learned a strange and mysterious secret—the hypnotic power to cloud men's minds so they cannot see him. Cranston's friend and companion the lovely Margot Lane is the only person who knows to whom the voice of the invisible Shadow belongs.

THEME MUSIC: Up full then under (as the episode then begins).

CLOSE (1949)

THEME MUSIC: Up full then under...

ANNOUNCER: *The Shadow* program is based on stories copyrighted by Street and Smith Publications. The characters, names, places and plot are fictitious. Any similarity to persons living or dead is purely coincidental. Again next week *The Shadow* will demonstrate that—

SHADOW: The weed of crime bares bitter fruit. Crime does not pay. The Shadow knows.

SOUND: Shadow laughing menacingly.

THEME MUSIC: Up full then out.

369. Sherlock Holmes

Crime drama about a brilliant detective who solves crimes through deductive reasoning. NBC (1930–1935; 1936–1942; 1955), Mutual (1936; 1943–1946; 1947–1949), ABC (1946–1947; 1949–1950; 1956). also titled *The Adventures of Sherlock Holmes* and *The New Adventures of Sherlock Holmes*. Following is a breakdown of the performers who played Sherlock Holmes and his associate Dr. Watson: Richard Gordon and Leigh Lovel (1930–1933); Luis Hector and Leigh Lovel (1934–1935); Richard Gordon and Harry West (1936); Basil Rathbone and Nigel Bruce (1939–1945); Tom Conway and Nigel Bruce (1946–1947); John Stanley and Alfred Shirley (1947–1948); John Stanley and Ian Martin (1948–1949); Ben Wright and Eric Snowden (1949–1950); John Gielgud and Ralph Richardson (1955–1956). Based on a sampling of the relatively few shows that are in circulation, the opening and closing signatures are basically the same: a mention of the title and the particular stars. Sponsored programs have added dialogue promoting the particular product. The following sponsored the series: George Washington Coffee (1930–1935), Household Finance (1936), Bromo Quinine (1939–1942), Petri Wine (1943–1946; 1949–1950), the Semler Company (1946–1947), Clipper Craft Clothes (1947–1949); various sponsors (1955–1956).

OPEN (1943)

THEME MUSIC ("March of the Ancestors"): Up full then under...

ANNOUNCER (Harry Bartell): Petri Wines brings you Basil Rathbone and Nigel Bruce in *The New Adventures of Sherlock Holmes*. The Petri family, the family that took time to bring you good wine, invites you to listen to Dr. Watson tell us another exciting adventure he shared with his old friend, that master detective, Sherlock Holmes. And I'd like to tell you about something Dr. Watson shared with me the other night, some Petri California Sherry. Did you ever have a glass of Petri Sherry before dinner? Well, that's a swell time for it because that Petri Sherry is the best beginning a good meal ever had. What a wine. You don't have to serve it in a fancy wine glass either, not Petri Sherry; that wine would taste wonderful if you drank it out of a water glass. It's a good idea to always have Petri Sherry in the house because it's just the thing to serve when company catches you unexpected and believe me, you can serve that Petri Sherry proudly because it's a fact that the name Petri is the proudest name in the history of American wine.

THEME MUSIC: Up full then under...

ANNOUNCER: And now let's visit with our good friend Dr. Watson. I know he's expecting us.

SOUND: Knock at door.

DR. WATSON: Come in, come in.

SOUND: Door opens.

DR. WATSON: Ah, good evening Mr. Bartell.

HARRY: Good evening Doctor... [Harry and Dr. Watson would exchange a bit of conversation after which Dr. Watson would tell Harry about an adventure he shared with Sherlock Holmes.]

CLOSE (1943)

THEME MUSIC: Up full then under...

ANNOUNCER: The Petri family, the family that took time to bring you good wine, has presented *The New Adventures of Sherlock Holmes* with Basil Rathbone and Nigel Bruce. Be with us next week when Dr. Watson will tell us another of the exciting adventures he shared with his good friend master detective Sherlock Holmes. And remember Petri for good wine. This is Mutual.

OPEN (1947)

THEME MUSIC: Up full then under...

ANNOUNCER: From New York City, the makers of Clipper Craft Clothes for men and 1,036 leading retail stores from coast to coast present the world's most famous detective, *Sherlock Holmes.*

THEME MUSIC: Up full then out.

CLOSE (1947)

THEME MUSIC: Up full then under...

ANNOUNCER: Clipper Craft Clothes for men and its 1,036 leading retail stores from coast to coast have presented *Sherlock Holmes*. This is Cy Harrice inviting you to be with us again next week when Clipper Craft will present an-

other Sherlock Holmes mystery. This is Mutual.

THEME MUSIC: Up full then out.

OPEN (1955)

THEME MUSIC: Up full then under...

ANNOUNCER: *The Adventures of Sherlock Holmes*, immortal stories of Sir Arthur Conan Doyle, dramatized anew with Sir Ralph Richardson as Dr. Watson and Sir John Gielgud in the role of Sherlock Holmes. And now *The Adventures of Sherlock Holmes* with Sir John Gielgud as Sherlock Holmes and Sir Ralph Richardson as our storyteller, Dr. James Watson.

THEME MUSIC: Up full then out.

CLOSE (1955)

THEME MUSIC: Up full then under...

ANNOUNCER: You have just heard *The Adventures of Sherlock Holmes* with Sir John Gielgud as Sherlock Holmes and Sir Ralph Richardson as Dr. James Watson. Be with us again next week for another mystery based on the immortal stories of Sir Arthur Conan Doyle.

THEME MUSIC: Up full then out.

370. Shorty Bell

Comical misadventures of a young newspaper reporter. Various sponsors. CBS, 1948. Mickey Rooney played Shorty Bell with Jeanne Bates as his girlfriend, Joan.

OPEN

THEME MUSIC: Up full then under...

ANNOUNCER: The Columbia Broadcasting System proudly presents *Shorty Bell*, cub reporter and young man about town. Shorty Bell, produced and directed by William N. Robson, stars Mickey Rooney in the title role. And now to Capitol City and the newsroom of the *Daily Times* for another comical adventure with John Marshall Bell, Jr., better known as Shorty Bell.

THEME MUSIC: Up full then out.

CLOSE

THEME MUSIC: Up full then under...

ANNOUNCER: *Shorty Bell*, written by Samuel W. Taylor, is produced and directed by William N. Robson. Music is conceived and conducted by Cy Feurer. Next week, Mickey Rooney returns in the role of Shorty Bell. Until this same time next week then, good night. This is the Columbia Broadcasting System.
THEME MUSIC: Up full then fade out.

371. The Silver Eagle

Adventure about Jim West, a Canadian Northwest Mounted Policeman who uses a bow and arrow and is called the Silver Eagle (after his trademark of eagle feather arrows). Various sponsors (General Mills was a frequent sponsor). ABC, 1951–1955. Jim Ameche played Jim West.

OPEN

ANNOUNCER (Ed Cooper): *The Silver Eagle!*
SOUND: Wolf cry followed by a horse galloping.
ANNOUNCER: A cry of the wild, a trail of danger, a scarlet rider of the Northwest Mounted serving justice with the swiftness of an arrow.
SOUND: Arrow being released from a bow.
ANNOUNCER: *The Silver Eagle!*
THEME MUSIC: Up full then under…
SOUND: Blizzard, followed by the barking of a dog team.
ANNOUNCER: The untamed North, frontier of adventure and peril. The lone, mysterious North where one man, dedicated to the motto of the Canadian Northwest Mounted Police, faces danger and death to bring in the lawless and maintain the right of the most famous Mountie of them all—the Silver Eagle.
THEME MUSIC: Up full then out.

CLOSE

THEME MUSIC: Up full then under…
ANNOUNCER: You have been listening to *The Silver Eagle*, created, produced and written by James Jewell. Jim Ameche is heard as Jim West, alias the Silver Eagle. Music is under the direction of Richard Dix. Ed Cooper speaking. This is ABC, the American Broadcasting Company.
THEME MUSIC: Up full then fade out.

372. The Singing Lady

Songs and stories for children with singer-actress Ireene Wicker. Sponsored by Kellogg's Cereals. Blue (1932–1938; 1940–1941), NBC (1938–1939), ABC (1945). A variation of the song "Little Boy Blue" was used as the theme.

OPEN

THEME MUSIC: Up full then under…
IREENE (singing):
> Little Boy Blue
> Come blow your horn,
> Call all of the funny folk
> Out of the corn.
> Little Miss Muffet,
> Little Jack Horner,
> Leave your toys
> And sing awhile.
> Then to supper,
> My how you'll smile.
> Good Rice Krispies
> In a big bowl,
> We'll all be as
> Merry as Old King Cole.

ANNOUNCER (Bob Brown): Hello, boys and girls, you all know what that song means, don't you? The Kellogg Singing Lady is here, sent to you by the Kellogg Company of Battle Creek, Michigan, and London, Ontario, the makers of Kellogg's Rice Krispies and all of those other delicious cereals. Kellogg's Rice Krispies are the lightest, crunchiest, most delicious little bubbles of crisp rice that you've ever tasted. And they're so bubbly and fresh that they actually sing a little song of their own when you pour milk or cream over them; right, Singing Lady?
IREENE: That's right, Mr. Brown. Kellogg's Rice Krispies really are a singing cereal and I want all of you boys and girls to hear that Rice Krispies song just as soon as you can. Tell mother that you want Kellogg's Rice Krispies for supper tonight. And when you pour the milk over them, listen to the way those little Rice Krispies sing—Snap, Crackle, Pop. Now it's time for us to begin our show for today…

CLOSE

ANNOUNCER: Thank you Singing Lady, that was

a beautiful story. And now, boys and girls, get out your paper and pencil and ask your mother to help you send for one of these wonderful Singing Lady sunsuits. The Singing Lady herself will be very happy when you get your sunsuit and so will you. Are you ready now? Then write which size you want—2-, 4- or 6-year-old; then tell us if you want the boys' suit or the girls' and which color you like best. The boys' suits come in blue or green and the girls' in pink or yellow. Now, remember to print your name and address very clearly and enclose 15 cents in coin together with two package tops from any of our Kellogg's cereals. Send your request to the Singing Lady in care of the Kellogg Company, Battle Creek, Michigan, or if you live in Canada, write to the Singing Lady in care of the Kellogg Company, London, Ontario, and your suit will be sent to you at once. Remember, two Kellogg package tops, 15 cents in coin and don't forget to tell her the size you want: 2-, 4- or 6-year-old and whether it's for a boy or a girl.

THEME MUSIC: Up full then under…

IREENE (singing):

> Little Boy Blue
> Put your horn away,
> We've come to the
> End of another day.
> Tell Jack and Jill
> And old Pussycat,
> Little Miss Muffet,
> Old Jack Sprat.
> Now good night,
> It's time to eat
> Good Rice Krispies,
> My, what a treat.
> Then we'll fly
> Through the soft moon beams
> Until we come to
> The Land of Dreams.

THEME MUSIC: Up full then under…

IREENE (talking): Remember, Kellogg's Rice Krispies are the singing cereal. I hope you'll all have them for supper tonight or for breakfast tomorrow morning. And now good night boys and girls and pleasant dreams.

ANNOUNCER: And Kellogg's *Singing Lady* will be on the air tomorrow afternoon at this same time. Bob Brown speaking for the Kellogg Company from our Chicago studios. This is the National Broadcasting Company.

THEME MUSIC: Up full then out.

SOUND: NBC chimes. N-B-C.

373. The Six Shooter

Compelling western about Britt Poncett, a legendary gunman known as the Six Shooter. Various sponsors. NBC, 1953–1954. James Stewart played Britt Poncett.

OPEN

THEME MUSIC ("Highland Lament"): Up full then under…

SOUND: Horse trotting.

ANNOUNCER (Hal Gibney): The man in the saddle is angular and long-legged. His skin is sun-dyed brown; the gun in his holster is gray steel and Rainbow mother-of-pearl. The handle, unmarked. The gun has killed and the man has killed. People call them both the Six Shooter. Presenting one of the screen's favorite stars, Mr. James Stewart … [in] *The Six Shooter*, the transcribed series of radio dramas based on the life of Britt Poncett, the Texas plainsman who wandered through the Western territories leaving behind a trail of still-remembered legends.

THEME MUSIC: Up full then out.

CLOSE

THEME MUSIC: Up full then under…

ANNOUNCER: The National Broadcasting Company has presented James Stewart as the Six Shooter. Mr. Stewart may currently be seen in the Universal-International picture *Thunder Bay. The Six Shooter* is an NBC Radio Network production in association with Revue Productions and is based on the character created by Frank Burke. Special music was by Basil Adlam. The entire production is under the direction of Jack Johnstone. All characters and incidents were fictitious and any resemblance to actual characters or incidents is purely coincidental. Hal Gibney speaking. This is NBC, the National Broadcasting Company.

THEME MUSIC: Up full then out.
SOUND: NBC chimes. N-B-C.

374. Smilin' Ed and His Buster Brown Gang

Children's program of comedy, stories and songs hosted by Smilin' Ed McConnell. Sponsored by Buster Brown Shoes. NBC, 1944–1953. See also *The Buster Brown Gang.*

OPEN

ED: Hi kids, you better come a runnin', it's old *Smilin' Ed and His Buster Brown Gang.*
SONG:
The happy gang of Buster Brown is on the air,
The happy gang of Buster Brown is on the air.
We frolic, we sing and play,
Come on and shout hooray,
Buster Brown is on the air.
ED: Hello, kids, hello Mother, hello Daddy, hello Grandmother, hello Granddad, this is your buddy Smilin' Ed and all his gang here in Hollywood for a good old Saturday hoop 'em up. [Ed would then begin the show with a story from Ed's Story Book.]

CLOSE

ED: Now kids, don't forget to be on hand next Saturday at this same time. Don't forget church and Sunday school and be listening next Saturday for our little tune from Hollywood. When you hear it, come a-runnin'.
SONG:
The happy gang of Buster Brown
now leaves the air,
The happy gang of Buster Brown
now leaves the air...
ED: So watch us, buddies, next Saturday when we return with a bang, hip-hooray, Buster Brown is on the air.
ANNOUNCER: This is NBC, the National Broadcasting Company.
SOUND: NBC chimes. N-B-C.

375. The Smiths of Hollywood

Comedy about Sir Cecil Smythe (Arthur Treacher), a destitute Englishman who moves to Hollywood, California, and into the home of his nephew, Bill Smith (Harry Von Zell), his wife, Nancy (Brenda Marshall) and their daughter, Shirley (Jan Ford), nicknamed "Bumps." Various sponsors. Mutual, 1947.

OPEN

THEME MUSIC: Up full then under...
HARRY VON ZELL: From Hollywood, California, we bring you *The Smiths of Hollywood.* Bill Smith, that's me Harry Von Zell. Nancy Smith—
BRENDA MARSHALL: That's me, Brenda Marshall.
HARRY: Our charming little daughter, Bumps Smith—
JAN FORD: That's me, Jan Ford.
HARRY: And our uncle, Sir Cecil Smythe—
ARTHUR TREACHER: That is I, Arthur Treacher.
HARRY: *The Smiths of Hollywood.*
ANNOUNCER (Tyler McVey): Yes, ladies and gentlemen, it's *The Smiths of Hollywood,* with Arthur Treacher, Brenda Marshall, Harry Von Zell, Carl Hoff's orchestra and a distinguished supporting cast from screen and radio. And now here's Bill Smith.
BILL: Hello. Hollywood is the home of many moving picture stars. It's also the home of Bill and Nancy Smith. You never heard of them? Well, let's get acquainted... [The episode would then begin.]

CLOSE

BILL: Don't forget next week, same time, same station, it's a date at our house. See you then.
THEME MUSIC: Up full then under...
ANNOUNCER: *The Smiths of Hollywood* is produced by Andrew Hickox. Tyler McVey speaking. This is Mutual.
THEME MUSIC: Up full then fade out.

376. Songs by Sinatra

Music and songs with singer-actor Frank Sinatra as the host. Sponsored by Old Gold Cigarettes. CBS, 1945–1947.

OPEN

ANNOUNCER (Jerry Lawrence): Old Gold presents—

THEME MUSIC: Up full then under…

ANNOUNCER: *Songs by Sinatra.* Old Gold invites you to another informal session in which there'll be songs by Sinatra and the Bobby Tucker Chorus with the music of Axel Stordahl and his orchestra.

THEME MUSIC: Up full then out.

ANNOUNCER: Why be irritated? Light up an Old Gold. Especially today there is nothing like the comfort and pleasure of a fine cigarette. Other smokers, you won't get that comfort and pleasure if your cigarette is harsh, hot and dry. So, to help prevent cigarette dryness, Old Gold's fine tobaccos are finely conditioned with apple honey. This special conditioning process helps hold in the natural moisture, helps guard your smoking enjoyment. Yes, extra flavor, plus extra protection to prevent cigarette dryness, that's Old Gold. Try a pack just as soon as you can.

THEME MUSIC: Up full then under. (Frank would then begin the show.)

CLOSE

ANNOUNCER: Don't let little annoyances get you down. Why be irritated? Light up an Old Gold. Its tobaccos are specially conditioned to help guard against cigarette dryness to give you more smoking pleasure.

THEME MUSIC: Up full then under…

ANNOUNCER: Old Gold has presented *Songs by Sinatra* with Frank Sinatra, the Bobby Tucker Chorus and the orchestra of Axel Stordahl. Be with us again next Wednesday when Old Gold will present another informal session of *Songs by Sinatra.* Jerry Lawrence speaking. This is CBS, the Columbia Broadcasting System.

THEME MUSIC: Up full then fade out.

377. Space Patrol

Science-fiction adventure about Buzz Corry, commander in chief of the Space Patrol, a 30th century organization responsible for the safety of the United Planets. Sponsored by Nestlé's Cocoa and chocolate bars and Ralston Chex Cereals. ABC, 1950–1955. Ed Kemmer played Buzz Corry with Lyn Osborn as Cadet Happy, Virginia Hewitt as Carol Carlisle (daughter of the Secretary General of the United Planets) and Nina Bara as Tonga, the alien ally. Based on the television series.

OPEN

THEME MUSIC: Up full then under…

ANNOUNCER (Dick Tufeld): *Space Patrol!* High adventures in the wild, vast reaches of space. Missions of daring in the name of interplanetary justice. Travel into the future with Buzz Corry, commander in chief of the Space Patrol.

THEME MUSIC: Up full then under…

ANNOUNCER: *Space Patrol* is presented by Nestlé's Eveready Cocoa in the bright red can and those terrific Nestlé's chocolate bars. Stand by for exciting action on *Space Patrol.*

THEME MUSIC: Up full then out.

ANNOUNCER: Space Patrollers, have you sent for your Rocket Cockpit? Imagine, you can have an exact, fully equipped model of the XR-C. You can fly with us into the vast reaches of outer space. Up, up, forty, fifty, one hundred thousand miles an hour. Past the moon, above Mars, through the star-studded rings of Saturn, even to the barrier of time itself. Say, what fun you and your pals will have with these sensational rocket cockpits. Now, don't wait another minute to get your rocket cockpit. Here's what you do. Send your name and address and 25 cents in coin together with a lid from a can of Nestlé's Eveready Cocoa or a tracing of the front of the label to Nestlé's, Box 54, St. Louis, Missouri. Send today.

SOUND: Swoosh of wind.

ANNOUNCER: And now back to *Space Patrol.*

CLOSE

ANNOUNCER: In just a moment a preview of next week's exciting *Space Patrol* adventure, but first a word from Wheat Chex and Rice Chex, the bite-size breakfast cereal in the bright red and white checkerboard package. Space Patrollers, in each swell-tasting Chex, you don't get just one power-packed grain of wheat and rice, but you get more than ten grams of power in every Chex and Chex even spells fun. C—crispness; Chex are as crisp as an ice cream cone. H—the happiest tasting cereal ever. E—easy eatin'; the size that's just right for a kid's bite. And X—extra fun when you mix Rice Chex with Wheat Chex in your breakfast bowl. So, for more fun power, charge up with Chex.

ANNOUNCER (Following preview): Be sure to see what happens when Buzz and Happy find themselves in the middle of a situation involving the Space Patrol, the army and the atomic bomb, next week on *Space Patrol.* *Space Patrol* is created by Mike Mosser and written by Norman Jolley. Ed Kemmer stars as Buzz Corry with Lyn Osborn as Cadet Happy, Nina Bara as Tonga and Virginia Hewitt as Carol Carlisle.

THEME MUSIC: Up full then under...

ANNOUNCER: *Space Patrol* was brought to you by Nestlé's Eveready, the instant cocoa, and famous Nestlé's chocolate bars. Remember N-E-S-T-L-É'-S, Nestlé's makes the very best chocolate. Be sure to see *Space Patrol* on ABC television every Saturday. Consult newspaper for time and station. Dick Tufeld speaking. This is ABC, the American Broadcasting Company.

THEME MUSIC: Up full then out.

378. Special Assignment

Adventure series based on the experiences of the newsreel cameramen who risk their lives to record the news as it happens. Sustaining. Mutual, 1946–1947. Jeff (Jeff Haggerty) is head of the International Newsreel Service; Richard (Richard Arlen) is his top cameraman; and Linda (Linda Hayes) is the radio broadcaster.

OPEN

VOICE: *Special Assignment.*

ANNOUNCER: Fire, floods, war, disaster. Every day, every moment, somewhere on the Earth, there is news in the making, electrifying events that change the destinies of men and nations. Wherever and whenever that news is made, there are too the men behind the cameras, the newsreel men of the world, dauntless, unfearing men, ofttimes sacrificing life itself to bring to the silver screen the shadows of major events. To these men of the cameras

and to their courage do we humbly dedicate *Special Assignment* starring Richard Arlen and Linda Hayes.

CLOSE

SOUND: Telegraph signals.

ANNOUNCER: Flash! Mr. Jeff Haggerty, editor in chief of the International Newsreel Service, announces that next week he is assigning Richard Arlen to a special assignment that promises to be the most exciting of Arlen's career. Listen to this station, same time next week for all the details.

THEME MUSIC: Up full then under...

VOICE: *Special Assignment.*

THEME MUSIC: Up full then out.

379. The Spike Jones Show

Variety session hosted by bandleader Spike Jones. Sponsored by Coca-Cola. CBS, 1947–1948.

OPEN

THEME MUSIC: Up full then under...

ANNOUNCER (Michael Roy): Coca-Cola presents *The Spike Jones Show* with Spike and the City Slickers, including Doodles Weaver as Professor Feedlebaum, George Rock, Dick and Freddie Morgan, Sir Frederick Gass, Dr. Horatio Q. Birdbath, and our special guest, Boris Karloff. And here he is, Spike Jones... [who would then begin the show with a song from his band, the City Slickers.]

CLOSE

THEME MUSIC: Up full then under...

ANNOUNCER: Coca-Cola has presented *The Spike Jones Show* with Spike Jones and the City Slickers. Be with us again next week, same time, same station for another *Spike Jones Show* presented by the makers of Coca-Cola. Michael Roy speaking. This is CBS, the Columbia Broadcasting System.

THEME MUSIC: Up full then out.

Note: Some episodes are titled *Spotlight Revue* and open and close as follows.

OPEN

THEME MUSIC: Up full then under...

ANNOUNCER (Dick Joy): The Coca-Cola company presents *Spotlight Revue* starring Spike Jones and the City Slickers and Dorothy Shay, the Park Avenue hillbilly, and Doodles Weaver as Professor Feedlebaum with George Rock and our special guest for tonight, the eminent screen star Peter Lorre. And here are Spike Jones and Dorothy Shay... [who would begin the show with an exchange of jokes].

CLOSE

THEME MUSIC: Up full then under...

ANNOUNCER: Be with us again next week when the Coca-Cola company presents Spike Jones in *Spotlight Revue* with Dorothy Shay, the Park Avenue hillbilly. This is Dick Joy for CBS, the Columbia Broadcasting System.

THEME MUSIC: Up full then out.

380. The Stan Freberg Show

Satirical comedy skit show hosted by Stan Freberg. Sustaining. CBS, 1957.

OPEN

THEME MUSIC: Up full then under...

CHORUS:
> This is the third show
> Of the series,
> Of a brand new radio series.

ANNOUNCER (Peter Leeds): From Hollywood, we present *The Stan Freberg Show*.

CHORUS: With the music of Billy May—

ANNOUNCER: With Daws Butler, June Foray, Peter Leeds and Jud Conlan and the Rhythmaires.

CHORUS:
> You may not find us on your TV
> Because, in case you didn't know,
> We're being brought to you on
> R-A-D-I-O.

THEME MUSIC: Up full then out.

CLOSE

STAN: Until next week, this is Stan Freberg say-

ing thanks for listening. God bless you and good night.

THEME MUSIC: Up full then under...

ANNOUNCER: Be with us again next week at this same time for episode four of *The Stan Freberg Show*. Peter Leeds speaking. This is CBS, the Columbia Broadcasting System.

THEME MUSIC: Up full then out.

381. Stand By for Crime

Crime drama about Chuck Morgan, a news commentator for radio station KOP who reports on the crime scene. Various sponsors. Syn., 1953. Glenn Langan played Chuck Morgan with Adele Jergens as his secretary, Carol Curtis (whom he calls "Glamour Puss").

OPEN

THEME MUSIC: Up full then under...

ANNOUNCER: *Stand By for Crime.*

THEME MUSIC: Up full then under...

ANNOUNCER: *Stand By for Crime* with Glenn Langan as Chuck Morgan, news commentator, crime reporter, the man who sticks his nose into other people's business to bust the rackets and bring criminals to justice.

CHUCK: Hi, I'm Chuck Morgan. Maybe you've heard some of my news commentary over radio station KOP in Los Angeles. Yea, that's right, I'm the guy who's always sticking his nose into somebody else's crimes. I'm the sucker for busting up some dirty racket then blabbing into a microphone about it in the hope you folks out there will write to your congressman or something... [At this point, Chuck would relate a story about one of his broadcasts.]

CLOSE

CHUCK: Well, that about winds it up for now. Until next time, good night.

THEME MUSIC: Up full then under...

ANNOUNCER: All persons and situations portrayed in this program were entirely fictitious as is radio station KOP, and any similarity to actual persons living or dead is wholly coincidental.

THEME MUSIC: Up full then under...

ANNOUNCER: *Stand By for Crime* stars Glenn Langan and Adele Jergens and can be heard at this same time next week over this same station.

THEME MUSIC: Up full then fade out.

382. Stella Dallas

Daily serial about Stella Dallas, a seamstress, her husband, Stephen, and their daughter, Laurel. Various sponsors (Phillips Milk of Magnesia Tablets and Tetley Tea were frequent sponsors). CBS, 1938–1955. Anne Elstner played Stella with Frederic Tozere as Stephen and Joy Hathaway and Virginia Smolen as Laurel.

OPEN

THEME MUSIC ("Memories"): Up full then under...

CHORUS:
> Memories, memories,
> Dreams of love so true.

ANNOUNCER (Howard Claney): And now, *Stella Dallas*, the true-to-life sequel as written by us, to the world-famous drama of mother love and sacrifice.

CHORUS: For my beautiful memories.

ANNOUNCER: And now for our sequel to *Stella Dallas*, in which Stella saw her own beloved daughter, Laurel, marry into wealth and society and, realizing the differences in their worlds, went out of Laurel's life. These episodes in the later life of Stella Dallas are based on the novel by Olive Higgins Prouty and written by Frank and Anne Hummert.

THEME MUSIC: Up full then out.

CLOSE

THEME MUSIC: Up full then under...

ANNOUNCER: Don't miss tomorrow's dramatic developments in this sequel to *Stella Dallas*. This chapter in the later life of Stella Dallas is written by Frank and Anne Hummert and is based on the famous character created by Olive Higgins Prouty. This is Howard Claney speaking. This is CBS, the Columbia Broadcasting System.

THEME MUSIC: Up full then fade out.

383. The Steve Allen Show

Daily variety series of jokes, music, skits and songs hosted by Steve Allen. Various sponsors. CBS, 1950.

OPEN

THEME MUSIC: Up full then under...

ANNOUNCER (Johnny Jacobs): Colgate Dental Creme, to clean your breath while you clean your teeth, and Palmolive Soap for a lovelier complexion, bring you *The Steve Allen Show*.

STEVE (singing): Just driftin' along...

ANNOUNCER: Featuring Marian Morgan, Don Burke, the music of Ivan Ditmars, yours truly, Johnny Jacobs, and starring America's fastest rising comedian, Steve Allen... [Steve would then begin the show with a series of jokes.]

CLOSE

THEME MUSIC: Up full then under...

ANNOUNCER: You have been listening to *The Steve Allen Show*. *The Steve Allen Show* is produced by Gordon Hughes and brought to you by the Colgate-Palmolive Company, makers of Colgate Dental Creme for clean breath, and Palmolive Soap for a lovelier complexion. Be with us again tomorrow for more laughs with America's fastest-rising comedian, Steve Allen. Johnny Jacobs speaking. This is the Columbia Broadcasting System.

THEME MUSIC: Up full then fade out.

384. Steve Canyon

The adventures of Steve Canyon (Barry Sullivan), a former pilot with the Army Air Transport Corps, turned cargo pilot of a C-54 who charges a dollar a mile for his services. Sustaining. CBS, 1948. Richard Aurandt composed "The Steve Canyon Theme."

OPEN

THEME MUSIC: Up full then under...

ANNOUNCER: Take off time for *Steve Canyon*, colorful hero of Milton Caniff's exciting newspaper adventure strip, brought to the air by Canyon's wartime flying buddy, the gallant leader of America's first flying commando unit in Burma, the original Phil Cochran himself, Colonel Philip G. Cochran.

PHIL: This is Phil Cochran. You know, a guy doesn't bring many good things out of a war; the one good thing I was lucky enough to hang onto was the friendship of a lean, rangy rascal named Steve Canyon—pardon me, Captain Steve Canyon of the Air Transport Command. When the powers-that-be stopped World War II, somehow they just plum forgot to turn off old Steve; he's still out there, flying all over the place in a big surplus C-54. Destination, the nearest available dollar. And the dollars have been coming few and far between. Maybe he's not the best businessman, but he's sure a good correspondent; he loves to write. I get a letter from him every week, and this being another week, here's another letter postmarked August 27th, Rangoon, Burma. It starts "Dear Phil…" [At this point the story would begin based on Steven's letter.]

Close

PHIL (reading the end of Steve's letter): "… I didn't make up a word of it, honor bright. Pass this letter to any of my friends you might bump into and I'll be shooting you another one next week. As usual, Steve Canyon." Well, that's it, there's no telling what postmark next week's letter from Steve will be wearing. One thing we do know, it will be a half-hour long. Rendezvous point for next week is this same time, this same station. Until then, this is Phil Cochran saying good night to you and to Steve Canyon out there wherever you are. Long runways and happy landings.

THEME MUSIC: Up full then under…

ANNOUNCER: CBS has presented Barry Sullivan as *Steve Canyon*, colorful hero of Milton Caniff's exciting newspaper adventure strip, brought to the air by Canyon's wartime flying buddy, the gallant leader of America's first flying unit in Burma, Colonel Philip "Flip" Cochran. Music scored and conducted by Richard Aurandt. Special effects and technical advice by the United States Air Force. This is CBS, the Columbia Broadcasting System.

THEME MUSIC: Up full then fade out.

385. The Story of Dr. Kildare

Medical drama that centered on the work of James Kildare, a doctor at Blair General Hospital. Various sponsors. Syn., 1950–1952. Lew Ayres played Dr. James Kildare with Lionel Barrymore as his mentor, Dr. Leonard Gillespie.

Open

THEME MUSIC: Up full then under…

ANNOUNCER (Dick Joy): *The Story of Dr. Kildare.*

KILDARE: Whatsoever house I enter, there I will go for the benefit of the sick. And whatsoever things I see and hear concerning the life of men, I will keep silence thereon, counting such things to be held as sacred trusts.

THEME MUSIC: Up full then under…

ANNOUNCER: *The Story of Dr. Kildare* starring Lew Ayres and Lionel Barrymore. Metro-Goldwyn-Mayer brought you those famous motion pictures; now this exciting, heartwarming series is heard on radio. And now, *The Story of Dr. Kildare.*

Close

THEME MUSIC: Up full then under…

ANNOUNCER: You have just heard *The Story of Dr. Kildare* starring Lew Ayres and Lionel Barrymore. *Dr. Kildare* is presented by arrangement with Metro-Goldwyn-Mayer. Original music was composed and conducted by Walter Schumann. Dick Joy speaking.

THEME MUSIC: Up full then fade out.

386. Straight Arrow

Western about Steve Adams, owner of the Broken Bow Ranch, who battles crime as the mysterious Straight Arrow. Sponsored by Nabisco. Mutual, 1948–1951. Howard Culver played Steve Adams.

Open

THEME MUSIC: Up full then under…

SONG:

N-A-B-I-S-C-O

Nabisco is the name to know.
For a breakfast you can't beat
Try Nabisco Shredded Wheat.

THEME MUSIC: Up full then under…

ANNOUNCER (Fred Cole): Keen eyes fixed on a flying target. A gleaming arrow set against a rawhide string. A strong bow bent almost to the breaking point. And then—

SOUND: Bowstring being released then arrow reaching its target.

ANNOUNCER: *Straight Arrow.* Nabisco Shredded Wheat presents *Straight Arrow*, a new, thrilling adventure story from the exciting days of the Old West. To friends and neighbors alike, Steve Adams appeared to be nothing more than the young owner of the Broken Bow cattle spread. But when danger threatened innocent people and when evildoers plotted against justice, then Steve Adams, rancher, disappeared, and in his place came a mysterious stalwart Indian wearing the dress and war paint of a Commanche, riding his great golden Palomino, Fury. Galloping out of the darkness to take up the cause of law and order throughout the West comes the legendary figure of Straight Arrow.

THEME MUSIC: Up full then out.

CLOSE

THEME MUSIC: Up full then under…

ANNOUNCER: For thrilling adventures of the Old West, ride with Straight Arrow and remember—

SONG:

N-A-B-I-S-C-O
Nabisco is the name to know.
For a breakfast you can't beat
Try Nabisco Shredded Wheat.

ANNOUNCER: Listen again, Tuesday and Thursday at five o-clock over most of these stations for another adventure with Straight Arrow. This is the Mutual Broadcasting System.

THEME MUSIC: Up full then fade out.

387. The Strange Romance of Evelyn Winters

Daily serial about Gary Bennett, a Broadway playwright who becomes the guardian of Evelyn Winters, a 23-year-old woman, follow-
ing the death of her father, Gary's former Army commander. Sponsored by Sweetheart Soap. CBS, 1944–1948. Toni Darnay played Evelyn; Karl Weber and Martin Blaine were Gary.

OPEN

THEME MUSIC ("Sweetheart"): Up full then under…

ANNOUNCER (Larry Elliott): We now present *The Strange Romance of Evelyn Winters.*

THEME MUSIC: Up full then under…

ANNOUNCER: It's thrilling news, Sweetheart Soap's actual guarantee of loveliness to every woman who will change from inadequate care with wrong soap to more thorough beauty care with Sweetheart, the soap that agrees with your skin. Accept this promise of a fresher, clearer, brighter complexion. You see, for generations, lovely women have known the value of soft water for complexion care. You know this yourself. Soap lathers more abundantly in soft water, gives that deep cleansing lather you want. And Sweetheart Soap gives you this effect of soft water with ordinary water right in your own home. Yes, Sweetheart gives you extra lather, more lather than with the average soap. Prove it with this revealing test. Turn a cake of Sweetheart Soap a few times in your hands and just compare. Massage Sweetheart's mild, gentle lather on your face. See how wonderful its creamy mounds of extra lather feel. Notice how quickly the Sweetheart lather rinses completely off. Yes, you'll say this is almost like having soft water for complexion care right in my own home. And here's our guarantee. Get Sweetheart Soap today. Try it in place of wrong soap and haphazard beauty care. Then either you look lovelier or mail us the wrapper and get your money back plus postage. Get Sweetheart Soap today and this amazing guarantee.

THEME MUSIC: Up full then under…

ANNOUNCER: *The Strange Romance of Evelyn Winters.* The story of Gary Bennett, playwright, who suddenly and unexpectedly finds himself the guardian of lovely Evelyn Winters… [The story would then begin.]

CLOSE

THEME MUSIC: Up full then under…

ANNOUNCER: Be sure to listen tomorrow to the following chapter of *The Strange Romance of Evelyn Winters.* Till then, this is Larry Elliott saying goodbye for Sweetheart Soap, the soap that agrees with your skin.

THEME MUSIC: Up full then out.

ANNOUNCER: This is CBS, the Columbia Broadcasting System.

388. Suspense

Anthology series of mystery and suspense plays. Various sponsors (with Roma Wines, 1943–1947, and Auto Lite, 1949–1953, as frequent sponsors). CBS, 1942–1962.

OPEN (1943)

SOUND: Eerie chimes.

THEME MUSIC: Up full then under...

ANNOUNCER (Truman Bradley): *Suspense.*

HOST (Ted Osborne): This is the Man in Black, here again to introduce Columbia's program *Suspense.* Our star tonight is one of the most compelling actresses in America today, Miss Agnes Moorehead. Miss Moorehead returns to our stage to appear in a new study in terror by Lucille Fletcher called "Sorry, Wrong Number." This story of a woman who accidentally overhears a conversation with death and who ... [strives] frantically to prevent murder from claiming an innocent victim is tonight's tale of *Suspense.* If you have been with us these Tuesday nights, you will know *Suspense* is compounded of mystery and suspicion and dangerous adventure. In this series are tales calculated to intrigue you, stir your nerves; to offer you a precarious situation and then withhold the solution to the last possible moment. And so it is with "Sorry, Wrong Number" and the performance of Agnes Moorehead, we again hope to keep you in *Suspense.*

THEME MUSIC: Up full then out.

CLOSE (1943)

SOUND: Eerie chimes.

HOST: And so closes "Sorry, Wrong Number" starring Agnes Moorehead, tonight's tale of *Suspense.* This is your narrator, the Man in Black, who conveys to you Columbia's invitation to spend this half-hour in *Suspense* with us again next Tuesday when Mr. Donald Crisp and Mr. John Loder will star in the *Suspense* play called "The Extra Guests." Producer of these broadcasts is William Spier who, with Ted Bliss, the director, Lud Gluskin, the musical director and Lucille Fletcher, the author, collaborated on tonight's *Suspense.* This is the Columbia Broadcasting System.

THEME MUSIC: Up full then out.

OPEN (1947)

SOUND: Eerie chimes.

THEME MUSIC: Up full then under...

ANNOUNCER (Bob Stevenson): *Suspense.* Presented by Roma Wines. R-O-M-A, made in California for enjoyment throughout the world. Roma Wines presents *Suspense.* Tonight, Roma Wines brings you Mr. Sheldon Leonard and Mr. Elliott Reed in "Feast of the Furies," a *Suspense* play produced, edited and directed for Roma Wines by William Spier. *Suspense,* radio's outstanding theater of thrills, is presented for your enjoyment by Roma Wines, those excellent California wines that add so much pleasantness to the way you live. Yes, right now, a full glass would be very pleasant as Roma Wines brings you Sheldon Leonard and Elliott Reed in a remarkable tale of *Suspense.*

THEME MUSIC: Up full then out.

CLOSE (1947)

THEME MUSIC: Up full then under...

ANNOUNCER: *Suspense,* presented by Roma Wines, R-O-M-A, made in California for enjoyment throughout the world. Sheldon Leonard will be seen in the Frank Capra production *It's a Wonderful Life;* Elliott Reed appeared through the courtesy of Paramount Pictures, producers of *To Each His Own.* Next Thursday, same time, Roma Wines will bring you Mr. Michael O'Shea as star of *Suspense,* radio's outstanding theater of thrills, produced by the Roma Wine Company of Fresno, California. This is CBS, the Columbia Broadcasting System.

THEME MUSIC: Up full then out.

OPEN (1950)

THEME MUSIC: Up full then under...

ANNOUNCER (Harlow Wilcox): Auto Lite and its 96,000 dealers present—

THEME MUSIC: Up full then under...

ANNOUNCER: *Suspense.*

THEME MUSIC: Up full then under...

ANNOUNCER: Tonight Auto Lite brings you "Rave Notice," a *Suspense* play starring Mr. Milton Berle.

THEME MUSIC: Up full then out.

ANNOUNCER: In just a moment Mr. Milton Berle in the first act of "Rave Notice," but first—

VOICE: Wilcox, I say Wilcox, I hear you're a campaign manager.

HARLOW WILCOX: You bet Senator, and my candidate is a cinch to win.

SENATOR: What's his name?

WILCOX: He's the famous Auto Lite Stay Full Battery. My candidate is so well known that every valiant voter wants his valor and veracity.

SENATOR: What's his platform?

WILCOX: Why the famous Auto Lite Stay Full Battery needs water only three times a year in normal car use and he's running on a platform to give longer life—70 percent longer life in fact as proved in tests conducted by the Society of Automotive Engineers. Every plate of the Auto Lite Stay Full Battery is protected with a fiberglass retaining matt to help reduce flaking and shedding. So friends, join the crowd voting for the Auto Lite Stay Full Battery, the battery that needs water only three times a year in normal car use. See your neighborhood Auto Lite battery dealer. Remember, you're always right with Auto Lite.

THEME MUSIC: Up full then under...

ANNOUNCER: And now with "Rave Notice" and the performance of Mr. Milton Berle, Auto Lite hopes once again to keep you in *Suspense.*

THEME MUSIC: Up full then out.

CLOSE (1950)

THEME MUSIC: Up full then under...

ANNOUNCER: *Suspense,* presented by Auto Lite. Tonight's star, Mr. Milton Berle.

VOICE: Well Wilcox, did your candidate win?

HARLOW WILCOX: Win? Why Senator, the Auto Lite Stay Full Battery is the winningest candidate the polls have ever produced. And this leader is only one of over 400 Auto Lite winners for cars, trucks, planes and boats made by Auto Lite in 28 plants from coast to coast. These include complete electrical systems, spark plugs, batteries, generators, coils, distributors, electric windshield wipers, starting motors—all engineered to fit perfectly because they're a perfect team. So friends, ask for and insist on Auto Lite original factory parts at your neighborhood service station, car dealer, garage or repair shop. Remember, you're always right with Auto Lite.

THEME MUSIC: Up full then under...

ANNOUNCER: Next week on *Suspense,* Miss Barbara Stanwyck as a woman who gambled and the stake was death in "The Wages of Sin," a tale well calculated to keep you in *Suspense.*

THEME MUSIC: Up full then under...

ANNOUNCER: Tonight's *Suspense* play was produced and directed by Elliott Lewis with music composed by Lucien Morawick and conducted by Lud Gluskin. Parts of this program were transcribed. Milton Berle appeared through the courtesy of Texaco and remember next week on *Suspense,* Miss Barbara Stanwyck in "The Wages of Sin."

THEME MUSIC: Up full then out.

SOUND: Phone ringing; then receiver being picked up.

GIRL: You can buy Auto Lite Stay Full Batteries, Auto Lite Standard or Resistor Spark Plugs, Auto Lite electrical parts at your neighborhood Auto Lite dealers. Switch to Auto Lite. Good night.

THEME MUSIC: Up full then under...

ANNOUNCER: This is CBS, the Columbia Broadcasting System.

THEME MUSIC: Up full then fade out.

OPEN (1955)

THEME MUSIC: Up full then under...

ANNOUNCER: And now tonight's presentation of radio's outstanding theater of thrills, *Suspense.*

THEME MUSIC: Up full then under...

ANNOUNCER: Tonight we bring you a story of Christmas shopping and a present that went astray. We call it "A Present for Benny." And now, starring Jack Kruschen, here is tonight's *Suspense* play, "A Present for Benny" [about two small-time hoods who plan a big Christmas surprise for Machine Gun Benny, a mobster who is threatening their territory].

CLOSE (1955)

ANNOUNCER: Let's look ahead to 1966 and there you are in your beautiful home. You've got automatic gadgets everywhere. There's a sparkling new dream car in your garage and the youngsters are in a fine college. All's right with the world. Is this just an idle dream? No, this is a real future that you can start building right now with United States savings bonds. In 10 years you'll get back four dollars for every three dollars you've invested. Join the payroll savings plan where you work or buy bonds where you bank. Start in 1956 to make 1966 the beginning of the golden years.

THEME MUSIC: Up full then under...

ANNOUNCER: *Suspense*, in which Jack Kruschen starred in tonight's presentation of "A Present for Benny." Next week a charming fantasy about a small boy who discovered a new world and lived forever in its enchantment. We call it "The Cave." That's next week on *Suspense*.

THEME MUSIC: Up full then under...

ANNOUNCER: *Suspense* is produced and directed by Anthony Ellis who also wrote tonight's script. Music was composed by Rene Garrigan and conducted by Wilbur Hatch.

THEME MUSIC: Up full then out.

ANNOUNCER: Time is growing short for the youngsters to write to Bing Crosby; the deadline for post-marked letters is Thursday, December 15th at midnight. All your youngster has to do is write a letter to Bing telling "what Christmas means to me." Then mail it to Bing Crosby, CBS Radio, Hollywood 28, California. The winner will read his letter in person when "America Sings with Bing" on Christmas Eve on CBS Radio. All youngsters 12 years of age and under are eligible. Stay tuned now for five minutes of CBS Radio news to be followed over most of these same stations by *The Jack Carson Show*.

THEME MUSIC: Up full then under...

ANNOUNCER: Thrill to *Gunsmoke*, every Saturday and Sunday on the CBS Radio Network.

THEME MUSIC: Up full then fade out.

389. The Sweeney and March Program

Comedy centering on Bob Sweeney and Hal March as comedians who host their own radio program. Sustaining. CBS, 1946–1948. Lud Gluskin composed the theme, "Sweeney and March."

OPEN

THEME MUSIC: Up full then under...

ANNOUNCER (Bob Lemond): From Hollywood, *The Sweeney and March Program*.

SOUND: Applause.

ANNOUNCER: The Columbia Broadcasting System and its affiliated stations present *The Sweeney and March Program*, starring the young comedy stylists Bob Sweeney and Hal March, and featuring the music of Lud Gluskin and his orchestra and the songs of the Sweeney and March Choral Society. I'm Bob Lemond.

THEME MUSIC: Up full then out.

CLOSE

THEME MUSIC: Up full then under...

ANNOUNCER: Next week, same time, same station, CBS will present *The Sweeney and March Program* with Lud Gluskin and his orchestra and the Sweeney and March Choral Society.

THEME MUSIC: Up full then under...

ANNOUNCER: This is CBS, the Columbia Broadcasting System.

THEME MUSIC: Up full then fade out.

390. Tailspin Tommy

The adventures of aviation hero Thomas "Tailspin Tommy" Tompkins (Mark Williams) and his friends Skeets Milligan (Milburn Stone) and Betty Lou Barnes (Marjorie Reynolds). Sustaining. CBS, 1941–1942.

OPEN

SOUND: Airplane in flight.

ANNOUNCER: *Tailspin Tommy* is on the air.

THEME MUSIC: Up full then under...

ANNOUNCER: Here he is again, ladies and gentlemen, come to tell you another thrilling story, that lovable, exciting aviation hero, Tailspin Tommy with his flying pals Skeets and Betty Lou. Stepping out of newspapers from coast to coast and jumping down from the motion picture screen, Tailspin visits you now each week over the radio. So join us for another exciting half-hour with that ace of the skies, Tailspin Tommy.

TOMMY: Good afternoon, folks; well, it's nice to be here again with Skeets and Betty Lou to tell you about another of our adventures…

CLOSE

TOMMY: I'll be with you again next Sunday afternoon to tell you another thrilling story. So until then, good afternoon, all.

THEME MUSIC: Up full then under…

ANNOUNCER: Be with us again next week at this same time when Tailspin Tommy will be heard in the story, "The Ghost Room," another in the adventures of *Tailspin Tommy*.

SOUND: Airplane in flight.

ANNOUNCER: Tune in every week at this time for that daring hero of the skies and his pals Skeets and Betty Lou straight from pictures and newspapers, created by Hal Forrest— *Tailspin Tommy*. This is CBS, the Columbia Broadcasting System.

THEME MUSIC: Up full then fade out.

391. Take It or Leave It

Game in which players attempt to double their money by answering questions of increasing difficulty. Sponsored by Eversharp. CBS (1940–1947), NBC (1947–1950). Bob Hawk, Phil Baker, Garry Moore, Eddie Cantor and Jack Paar served as the hosts. Became *The $64.00 Question* in 1950; served as the basis for *The $64,000 Question* on television.

OPEN

ANNOUNCER: Eversharp presents *Take It or Leave It*. Time to sharpen your wits with Eversharp.

THEME MUSIC: Up full then under…

ANNOUNCER: Yes, it's *Take It or Leave It*, pre-

sented by Eversharp, manufacturers of Eversharp precision writing instruments and Eversharp Schick injector razor blades. *Take It or Leave It*, the most exciting game ever played. The game that doubles in interest with every question asked. The game with a great jackpot race. And so I give you the man with the sixty-four dollar question, Eversharp's distinguished pay master of ceremonies, here he is, Phil Baker.

SOUND: Applause.

PHIL: Thank you, thank you ladies and gentlemen and welcome again to *Take It or Leave It*…

CLOSE

ANNOUNCER: Men, shave with an Eversharp Schick injector razor and you eliminate four biggest shaving nuisances forever. Listen. End nuisance number one—no time wasted. Nationwide tests prove Eversharp razors at least 50 percent faster. End nuisance number two: it's safer. Patented guard bars help prevent skin irritation. End nuisance number three: nothing to take apart. Cleans instantly. Just rinse, shake, put away. End nuisance number four: no blade to unwrap. Just push, pull, click, click. Eversharp Schick, the only razor with automatic blade changer locks clean new blades in position instantly. For the world's quickest, cleanest, easiest shave, buy an Eversharp Schick injector razor—a $1.75 value, special now only $1.25 complete with 20 blades.

THEME MUSIC: Up full then under…

PHIL: We hope all of you listening have enjoyed *Take It or Leave It* as much as Eversharp has enjoyed bringing it to you. We'll meet you all again next week at this same time, so let's make a date. This is Phil Baker reminding you to sharpen your wits with Eversharp. Bye bye, buy Eversharp.

THEME MUSIC: Up full then under…

ANNOUNCER: This is Jay Stewart saying good night for Eversharp. This is CBS, the Columbia Broadcasting System.

THEME MUSIC: Up full then fade out.

392. Tales of Fatima

Basil Rathbone plays himself, a renowned

stage actor famous for playing Sherlock Holmes, who has a keen interest in solving crimes. He draws inspiration by dreaming of Princess Fatima, a sultry woman who speaks to him and provides inspiration. Sponsored by Fatima Cigarettes. CBS, 1949. Also in the cast were Agnes Young as Lavender, Basil's wardrobe woman and assistant. Jack Miller composed "Fatima's Theme."

OPEN

BASIL: Hello there, this is Basil Rathbone. I'm so glad you can be with Fatima and me tonight.

THEME MUSIC: Up full then under…

ANNOUNCER (Michael Fitzmaurice): The *Tales of Fatima*, a new series of exciting mystery stories starring that distinguished actor Mr. Basil Rathbone.

THEME MUSIC: Up full then out.

BASIL: Before we begin tonight's tale, I've got something to say to you. If you smoke a long cigarette, smoke the new long Fatima. You see, the name Fatima has stood for the best in cigarette quality for 30 years, and now the new Fatima is the best of long cigarettes. Ladies and gentlemen, if you smoke a long cigarette, smoke the best of the long cigarettes, smoke Fatima.

THEME MUSIC: Up full then under…

BASIL: Our author for tonight, Gail Ingram, has written an astonishing mystery especially for me. I didn't know the solution until I recalled the words of Fatima.

FATIMA: In the words of Fatima, habit is law; we are, all of us, slaves to a habit.

BASIL: Those words are the key to tonight's *Tale of Fatima*. And here it is "A Much Expected Murder."

THEME MUSIC: Up full then out.

CLOSE

ANNOUNCER: Join us again next week when we'll have another exciting *Tale of Fatima*. Right, Mr. Rathbone?

BASIL: Yes indeed. Fatima helps me solve an amazing tale that started on a darkened street with a chase and reached its climax in a darkened room with a shot. See you than, everyone. Good night.

THEME MUSIC: Up full then under…

ANNOUNCER: The *Tales of Fatima* stars Basil Rathbone with original music by Jack Miller. Agnes Young was Lavender and Francis DeSales was Lieutenant Farrell. The entire production is under the direction of Harry Ingels. Michael Fitzmaurice speaking. This is CBS, the Columbia Broadcasting System.

THEME MUSIC: Up full then out.

393. Tales of the Texas Rangers

Dramatizations based on the files of the Texas Rangers, the oldest law enforcement organization in the U.S. Various sponsors. NBC, 1950–1952. Joel McCrea plays Ranger Jace Pearson.

OPEN

THEME MUSIC ("Texas Ranger March"): Up full then under…

ANNOUNCER (Hal Gibney): NBC presents *Tales of the Texas Rangers* starring Joel McCrea as Ranger Jace Pearson.

THEME MUSIC: Up full then under…

ANNOUNCER: Texas, more than 260,000 square miles and 50 men who make up the most famous and oldest law enforcement body in North America. Now, from the files of the Texas Rangers, come these stories based on fact. Only names, dates and places are fictitious for obvious reasons; the events themselves are a matter of record.

THEME MUSIC: Up full then out.

CLOSE

THEME MUSIC: Up full then under…

ANNOUNCER: Next week hear Joel McCrea as Texas Ranger Jace Pearson in another authentic reenactment of a thrilling case from the files of the Texas Rangers. Hal Gibney speaking for *Tales of the Texas Rangers*. This is NBC, the National Broadcasting Company.

THEME MUSIC: Up full then out.

SOUND: NBC chimes. N-B-C.

394. The Ted Lewis Show

Music and songs with orchestra leader Ted Lewis. Sustaining. Syn., 1934–1935; 1947–1948. The song "When My Baby Smiles at Me" was used as Ted's theme. (Introduced in 1921, it is believed to be radio's first theme song.)

OPEN

THEME MUSIC: Up full then under...
ANNOUNCER: "When My Baby Smiles at Me." What a familiar, tuneful radio signature and need I tell you, ladies and gentlemen, this melody heralds the approach to the microphone of that lovable, high-rated tragedian of song Ted Lewis.
THEME MUSIC: Up full then under...
TED: Good evening, ladies and gentlemen. Yes sir, is everybody happy... [Ted would then begin the show.]

CLOSE

THEME MUSIC: Up full then under...
ANNOUNCER: You have been listening to *The Ted Lewis Show* with the vocal stylings of Geraldine DuBois and the music of Paul Arnold and his orchestra. Be sure to be with us next week when that familiar radio signature "When My Baby Smiles at Me" heralds the return to the microphone of that lovable tragedian of song, Ted Lewis. Good night.
THEME MUSIC: Up full then out.

395. Texaco Star Theater

Variety session of music, songs and comedy hosted by comedian Fred Allen. Sponsored by Texaco. CBS, 1940–1944.

OPEN

THEME MUSIC: Up full then under...
ANNOUNCER (Arthur Godfrey): It's Texaco time with Fred Allen, Portland Hoffa and Al Goodman and his orchestra. This is Arthur Godfrey saying "you're welcome" from Texaco dealers from coast to coast. Welcome to the *Texaco Star Theater* and the Texaco dealers whole-hearted help in keeping that car of yours going for the transportation you've got to have. And now, ladies and gentlemen, there's only one comedian in radio you can tune in to during a blackout who isn't bright enough to violate the law, and here he is, Fred Allen in person.
FRED: Thank you and good evening ladies and gentlemen... [Fred would then begin the show with a series of jokes.]

CLOSE

FRED: Next Sunday night, ladies and gentlemen, our guest will be Orson Welles. And now Arthur, have you anything to add?
ARTHUR: Just a scrap, Fred. The scrap pile in every city mounts higher and higher but more is needed. You see, practically everything we need to win this war is made from scrap metal. Tanks, planes, aircraft carriers, everything. So throw your scrap into the fight.
FRED: And thank you, Arthur. This is Fred Allen speaking for Texaco dealers from coast to coast reminding you to drive under 35 miles per hour to save rubber and to drive into your Texaco dealer regularly to have your tires checked. Remember, you're welcome. Good night.
THEME MUSIC: Up full then under...
ANNOUNCER: This is the Columbia Broadcasting System.

396. Texaco Town

Eddie Cantor as the host of a series of comedy and music. Sponsored by Texaco Fire Chief Gasoline. CBS, 1937–1938.

OPEN

THEME MUSIC: Up full then under...
ANNOUNCER (Jimmy Wallington): Jacques Renard's orchestra is playing "Welcome to Texaco Town" and you are welcome. Lights, curtain, music.
THEME MUSIC: Up full then under...
ANNOUNCER: Once again, the 45,000 dealers who serve you with Fire Chief Gasoline and other Texaco products present your master of ceremonies, the Mayor of Texaco Town, Eddie Cantor.
EDDIE: Good evening ladies and gentlemen...

CLOSE

THEME MUSIC: Up full then under…

ANNOUNCER: Texaco invites you to be with us again next week when the curtain rises on another edition of *Texaco Town*, brought to you by the 45,000 dealers who serve Fire Chief Gasoline. This is Jimmy Wallington for Texaco. Good night. This is CBS, the Columbia Broadcasting System.

THEME MUSIC: Up full then fade out.

397. That Brewster Boy

Comedy that revolved around the antics of Joey Brewster, the mischievous son of Jim and Jane Brewster. Sponsored by the Quaker Oats Company. NBC (1941–1942), CBS (1942–1945). Eddie Firestone, Jr., Arnold Stang and Dick York played Joey, with Hugh Studebaker as Jim and Constance Crowder as Jane. Nancy, Joey's sister, was played by Louise Fitch and Patricia Dunlap.

OPEN

THEME MUSIC: Up full then under…

ANNOUNCER (Marvin Miller): *That Brewster Boy*. Quaker Oats, truly America's super breakfast, brings you *That Brewster Boy*, written by Pauline Hopkins and starring Eddie Firestone, Jr. This is the story of an average American family, the Brewsters. Of course, when we say average, we're talking about Mom, Dad and Nancy. We can't quite reconcile the word average with Joey Brewster… [The episode would then begin.]

CLOSE

ANNOUNCER: Did you have your Quaker Oats today? It's an economical breakfast; it still costs less than half a cent a serving. Serve your family delicious, healthful Quaker Oats, America's super breakfast regularly. So tomorrow ask your grocer for Mother's Oats or Quaker Oats.

THEME MUSIC: Up full then under…

ANNOUNCER: Be sure to tune in again next Monday at this same time for another enjoyable evening with *That Brewster Boy*. Mean-

while, be sure to ask your grocer for Quaker Oats, truly America's super breakfast. The original music on this program was created and conducted by Glenn Welding. This is Marvin Miller speaking for the Quaker Oats Company. This is the Red Network of the National Broadcasting Company.

THEME MUSIC: Up full then out.

SOUND: NBC chimes. N-B-C.

398. That Hammer Guy

Crime drama based on Mickey Spillane's famous fictional detective Mike Hammer. Various sponsors. Mutual, 1952–1953. Ted de Corsia, then Larry Haines, played Mike Hammer.

OPEN

ANNOUNCER: Here is Larry Haines in the Mickey Spillane mystery *That Hammer Guy*.

THEME MUSIC: Up full then under…

ANNOUNCER: The setting is New York City. The character is that tough private detective with an eye for the ladies and a nose for trouble. It's *That Hammer Guy*—Mike Hammer, private investigator.

THEME MUSIC: Up full then out.

CLOSE

THEME MUSIC: Up full then under…

ANNOUNCER: *That Hammer Guy* is based on the fictional character created by Mickey Spillane and stars Larry Haines in the title role. Be with us again next week for another mystery-adventure with Mickey Spillane's Mike Hammer on *That Hammer Guy*.

THEME MUSIC: Up full then fade out.

399. That's Rich

Comical events in the life of Rich Wilk, a hopeful actor and struggling songwriter in Hollywood. Various sponsors. CBS, 1954. Stan Freberg played Rich with Alan Reed as Jonathan Wilk, his uncle.

OPEN

THEME MUSIC: Up full then under…

ANNOUNCER (Bill Anders): From Hollywood, transcribed, CBS radio brings you a gay new comedy series, *That's Rich*, starring Stan Freberg as Richard E. Wilk, the hopeful actor and songwriter better known as Rich to his friends.

THEME MUSIC: Up full then under... (The episode then begins.)

CLOSE

THEME MUSIC: Up full then under...

ANNOUNCER: This has been *That's Rich*, transcribed, starring Stan Freberg as Rich and Alan Reed as Uncle Jonathan. Music by George Fields; Bill Anders speaking. *That's Rich* is produced and directed by Al Schwartz.

THEME MUSIC: Up full then out.

ANNOUNCER: This is CBS, the Columbia Broadcasting System.

400. Theater Guild on the Air

Dramatizations drawn from books, films and stage. Sponsored by U.S. Steel. CBS (1943–1944), ABC (1945–1949), NBC (1949–1953). The program is also known as *The U.S. Steel Hour*.

OPEN

THEME MUSIC: Up full then under...

ANNOUNCER (Norman Brokenshire): United States Steel—U.S.S., the industrial family that serves the nation—presents *The Theater Guild on the Air*. Our stars, Clifton Webb, Leonard Corbett and Mildred Natwick. Our play, *Blithe Spirit* by Noel Coward. Produced on the air tonight by the Theater Guild, one of America's foremost theatrical producers. Everyday, everywhere, you are served by products of steel. In your home, in your business, when you travel, the trademark of United States Steel—U.S.S.—on any steel product is your guarantee of quality steel. And now, direct from the stage of the Vanderbilt Theater in New York, the United States Steel Corporation brings you *Blithe Spirit* by Noel Coward.

THEME MUSIC: Up full then out.

CLOSE

ANNOUNCER: United States Steel—U.S.S., the industrial family that serves the nation—has presented the *Theater Guild on the Air*'s production of *Blithe Spirit* by Noel Coward. Theresa Helburn and Lawrence Langner are the producers with music by Harold Levy. The *Theater Guild on the Air* is brought to you each week at this time by United States Steel. Norman Brokenshire speaking. This is ABC, the American Broadcasting Company.

THEME MUSIC: Up full then fade out.

401. The Thin Man

Lighthearted crime drama about Nick Charles, a former private detective turned mystery editor, and his wealthy wife, Nora, as they attempt to solve mysteries. Sponsored by Heinz, Pabst Blue Ribbon Beer, Post Cereals, Sanka Coffee, Woodbury Soap. NBC (1941–1942; 1948), CBS (1943–1947), Mutual (1948–1949), ABC (1950). Claudia Morgan played Nora with Les Damon, Les Tremayne, Joseph Curtin, David Gothard and Bill Smith as Nick Charles. The series was originally titled *The Adventures of the Thin Man* (1941–1947) then *The New Adventures of the Thin Man* (1948–1950).

OPEN (original)

THEME MUSIC: Up full then under...

ANNOUNCER (Tom Shirley): Presenting radio's most popular mystery-comedy, *The Adventures of the Thin Man*, starring Claudia Morgan as Nora and David Gothard as Nick and brought to you by Post, makers of Post Toasties, the bubbly light, crisper corn flake.

CHORUS:
> We toast 'em crisp,
> We toast 'em light.
> You can tell by the taste
> We toast 'em right.
> They're a tasty treat,
> So good to eat.
> Delicious and light,
> Post Toasties, Post Toasties.

ANNOUNCER: And now Post Toasties presents Claudia Morgan as Nora and David Gothard as Nick in *The Adventures of the Thin Man*.

CLOSE (original)

ANNOUNCER: Have you tried Post Toasties lately? With Post Toasties you enjoy delicate toasted flakes that are packed with grand sunny flavor and you will find that each delicious spoonful is bubbly light and crunchy right to the last tempting bite. So for real refreshment, buy golden brown Post Toasties. Serve them often, you'll like them.

THEME MUSIC: Up full then under...

ANNOUNCER: Be sure to listen next Friday night when Post again brings you another exciting *Thin Man* adventure with Claudia Morgan and David Gothard. This is Tom Shirley saying good night and best wishes from Post, makers of Post Toasties.

CHORUS:
> We toast 'em crisp,
> We toast 'em light.
> They're a tasty treat,
> So good to eat.
> Delicious and light,
> Post Toastie, Post Toastie.

VOICE: And we like 'em.

THEME MUSIC: Up full then out.

VOICE: This is CBS, the Columbia Broadcasting System.

OPEN (revised)

SOUND: Nick Charles attempting to play the sponsor's tune, Pabst Blue Ribbon Beer, on a piano.

NORA: No Nicky, darling, that's not it.

NICK: It isn't, Nora?

NORA: No, it goes like this—

NORA (at the piano and singing):
> Thirty-three fine brews
> Blended into one great beer.

SPONSOR'S THEME MUSIC: Up full then under...

ANNOUNCER (Ed Herlihy): Pabst Blue Ribbon Beer presents *The New Adventures of the Thin Man*, with Nick and Nora Charles, the happiest, merriest married couple in radio.

THEME MUSIC: Up full then under...

ANNOUNCER: Tonight and every Tuesday night at this same time, that international favorite Pabst Blue Ribbon Beer proudly presents the finest in summer entertainment. So sit back, relax and pour yourself a tall, foaming glass full of blended splendid Pabst Blue Ribbon while you listen to the stars of our show, Claudia Morgan as Nora and Les Tremayne as Nick, in tonight's adventure of the *Thin Man*.

THEME MUSIC: Up full then out.

CLOSE (revised)

ANNOUNCER (following the story): Now if Nicky and Nora are smart, they'll go home and have themselves a cold, refreshing bottle of that blended splendid Pabst Blue Ribbon, the beer with the fresh, clean, sparkling flavor. Your Pabst Blue Ribbon is quite a favorite with happily married couples; just to mention a few, there is Mr. and Mrs. Gregory Peck and Mr. and Mrs. Bob Hope. Now, these people can certainly afford the best of everything and the fact that Pabst Blue Ribbon is served in their homes is a tribute to its quality. I could tell you about Pabst's 104 years of leadership in the art of brewing and explain how Pabst developed the science of blending. Yes, blending 33 fine brews to keep the same identical Blue Ribbon flavor and quality in bottle after bottle, year after year. But I'd rather you simply taste it yourself. By tasting, by comparing, you'll understand why millions the world over have settled down to blended splendid Pabst Blue Ribbon.

THEME MUSIC: Up full then under...

ANNOUNCER: Be sure to listen next Tuesday night when Pabst Blue Ribbon Beer brings you another happy, exciting *Thin Man* adventure with Les Tremayne and Claudia Morgan. The adventures of the *Thin Man* are brought to you by the Pabst Brewing Company of Milwaukee, Wisconsin, Newark, New Jersey, and Peoria, Illinois. And this is Ed Herlihy saying good night with the best wishes of Pabst Blue Ribbon dealers from coast to coast.

THEME MUSIC: Up full then under...

ANNOUNCER: And friends, now that summertime is really here to stay for a while, you'll be planning more and more hot weather meals. You know, an appetizing platter of cold cuts, sliced ham, turkey, corned beef, potato salad, and of course plenty of Pabst Blue Ribbon, nicely chilled in cans or bottles. Better order a good supply today just so you'll have it in your refrigerator when you get that thirsty feeling. Be sure it's Pabst Blue Ribbon, blended splendid Pabst Blue Ribbon.

THEME MUSIC: Up full then out.

ANNOUNCER: This is NBC, the National Broadcasting Company.

SOUND: NBC chimes. N-B-C.

402. Think

Suspense tales designed to make the listener think about the story being broadcast. Sustaining. ABC, 1953. Dave Ballard served as the host.

OPEN

ANNOUNCER (Bill Essen): To make you think … think … think … think.

HOST: *Think*. You live in a world made by you. *Think*. A world of fact and fantasy. *Think*. But where does [sic] fact and fantasy begin? *Think*. This is a program designed to make you think … think … think.

THEME MUSIC: Up full then out.

CLOSE

THEME MUSIC: Up full then under…

ANNOUNCER: This is a program to make you think … think … think. Bill Essen speaking. America is sold on ABC, the American Broadcasting Company.

THEME MUSIC: Up full then fade out.

403. Thirty Minutes in Hollywood

George Jessel as the host of a variety series sponsored by Gaffers and Sadler Appliances. Mutual, 1937–1938.

OPEN

THEME MUSIC ("California Here I Come"): Up full then under…

ANNOUNCER: Gaffers and Sadlers presents *Thirty Minutes in Hollywood* starring George Jessel and our special guest Miss Norma Talmadge, who will be interviewed by Ernest Schrapp,

well-known fashion creator for Hal Roach Pictures. The cast also includes Dorothy McNulty, Tommy Tucker and his orchestra, Amy Arnell and an added guest surprise that will tickle your ribs and touch your heart, those beloved comedians for over 50 years, Weber and Fields. We are now in George Jessel's office in Hollywood where Tommy Tucker and his band play the title song from the show *High Wide and Handsome*… [The show then begins.]

CLOSE

ANNOUNCER: Gaffers and Sadler is artistically styled to please the most fastidious housewife. The new Gaffers and Sadler gas ranges embody every modern innovation and improvement. So complete are they in perfection, a child can operate them and even the poorest cook can produce dishes cooked just right. Built for economy, precision, efficiency and convenience, the new Gaffers and Sadler gas ranges are made expressly for the fine homes of California. Go to your nearest dealer tomorrow and ask for a demonstration of the new Gaffers and Sadler gas range and the new Gaffers and Sadler electric refrigerators.

THEME MUSIC: Up full then under…

GEORGE: Good night everybody.

ANNOUNCER: Gaffers and Sadler has presented *Thirty Minutes in Hollywood* with George Jessel, Amy Arnell and Tommy Tucker and his orchestra. This is Mutual.

THEME MUSIC: Up full then fade out.

404. This Is Hollywood

Radio adaptations of motion pictures. Sponsored by Procter and Gamble. CBS, 1946–1947. Hosted by Hedda Hopper.

OPEN

THEME MUSIC: Up full then under…

ANNOUNCER (Bernard Dudley): Camay, the soap of beautiful women, presents *This Is Hollywood*, a brand new radio program bringing you each week the Hollywood screen stars and screenplays now being shown or soon to be seen in movie theaters throughout the country.

And here to tell you about tonight's show is Hollywood's own Hedda Hopper.

HEDDA: Thank you and hello everybody, welcome to Camay's new program, *This Is Hollywood*. Tonight we begin a series of Universal-International Pictures, all of which are currently being shown or about to be released. The series will include *So Goes My Love*, *The Stranger*, *The Egg and I*, *White Tie and Tails*, *The Magnificent Doll* and *The Dark Mirror* and in all of them we will bring you the stars who played in those pictures. Tonight we have *Notorious Gentlemen* starring those fine English actors who have so endeared themselves to us: Rex Harrison as Vivian Kenway; Lili Palmer as Ricki Crasner; and Heather Angel as Jenny Calthrop.

CLOSE

HEDDA: Thank you Rex Harrison, Lili Palmer and Heather Angel for your grand performances in *Notorious Gentlemen*. So long until next week.

THEME MUSIC: Up full then under…

ANNOUNCER: *This Is Hollywood* is presented each week at this time by Camay, the soap of beautiful women. Tonight's program was directed by Frank Woodruff and written by Bill Hampton. J. Arthur Rank is the producer and music is composed and conducted by Adolph Deutsch. Bernard Dudley speaking. This is CBS, the Columbia Broadcasting System.

THEME MUSIC: Up full then fade out.

405. This Is My Best

Adaptations of well-known stories and books. Sponsored by Cresta Blanca Wines. CBS, 1944–1946. Edward Arnold, Don Clark and Orson Welles hosted. (The signatures that follow are from the episode of March 13, 1945, the beginning of Orson Welles' run as host.) Bernard Katz composed the theme, "This Is My Best."

OPEN

HOST: Good evening, this is Orson Welles inviting you to listen now to "The Heart of Dark-

ness" by Joseph Conrad on Cresta Blanca's *This Is My Best*.

THEME MUSIC: Up full then under…

ANNOUNCER (John McIntire): *This Is My Best*, America's greatest stars in the world's best stories, presented each week by Shindley's Cresta Blanca Wine. Wine of a friendly nature, symbol of hospitality, compliments to honored guests, a wine to serve proudly, saying this is my best, this is Cresta Blanca. C-R-E-S-T-A … B-L-A-N-C-A … Cresta … Blanca, Cresta Blanca.

HOST: Orson Welles again. I can't tell you how truly pleased and proud I am to join the Cresta Blanca program *This Is My Best*, and I'm glad to start off with an old favorite, a show the Mercury Theater brought you first, the story we came to Hollywood to make a movie of; we never did, maybe someday we will, but I think it's particularly well suited for radio. Here it is, one of the best regarded and most typical of the works of Joseph Conrad, "The Heart of Darkness," could be described as a deliberate masterpiece or a downright incantation. Almost, we are persuaded that there's something after all, something essential waiting for us all in the dark areas of the world; aboriginally loathsome, immeasurable and certainly nameless.

THEME MUSIC: Up full then under… [The story begins; here about a navigator who journeys to a strange, dark land to find the missing fiancé of a girl.]

CLOSE

SOUND: Applause.

ANNOUNCER: Shindley's Cresta Blanca Wine joins our audience here in Hollywood in applauding Orson Welles for his production of "Heart of Darkness." In a few moments Mr. Welles will be back to tell you about next week.

THEME MUSIC: Up full then under…

ANNOUNCER: If there is one thing above all else that gives a charming woman a grand lift of her spirits it is to have a friend speak of her as the perfect hostess. And today, the perfect hostess usually serves a fine wine with her dinners. A wine like Cresta Blanca. For Cresta Blanca Wine has a way of saying to her guests, "Welcome, we're glad you're here." Cresta

Blanca adds a gay note of festivity to the feast. And remember, the service of wine is a simple thing. Just choose the Cresta Blanca table wine you like best and serve it well chilled. To a simple family meal or when company comes, Cresta Blanca Wine is a crowning touch, the crest of quality wine since 1889. Now, Mr. Orson Welles.

HOST: Thank you, thank you very much. Before I tell you about next week's show, here is an announcement from the Office of War Information. This year tens of thousands of deferred farm workers are scheduled to be called into the armed services. No longer a patriotic hobby but a vital war necessity for all who have garden plots to grow Victory Gardens in 1945. You can get expert advice by writing to Victory Gardens, Washington, 25, D.C. And now about next week's show. It's a comedy by the man who wrote "Mr. Winkle Goes to War." One of my favorite people, Ann Sothern, will be the star. The title is "Miss Dilly Says No" and need I say more. I sincerely hope you'll be with us next week. Until then I remain, as always, obediently yours,

THEME MUSIC: Up full then under...

ANNOUNCER: Our musical score was composed and conducted by Bernard Katz. Don't forget next week when Ann Sothern will star in a radio adaptation of Theodore Pratt's story "Miss Dilly Says No." and remember, whenever you dine, dine with wine and make it the best wine, C-R-E-S-T-A ... B-L-A-N-C-A ... Cresta ... Blanca, Cresta Blanca.

THEME MUSIC: Up full then under...

ANNOUNCER: *This Is My Best* is a presentation of the Cresta Blanca Company of Livermoore, California, and comes to you from Columbia's playhouse in Hollywood. John McIntire speaking. This is CBS, the Columbia Broadcasting System.

THEME MUSIC: Up full then fade out.

406. This Is Your FBI

Crime dramas based on the files of the Federal Bureau of Investigation as seen through the cases of agent Jim Taylor (Stacy Harris). Various sponsors, ABC, 1945–1953.

OPEN

ANNOUNCER (Larry Keating): To your FBI you look for national security and to your Equitable Society for financial security. These two great institutions are dedicated to the protection of you, your home and your country.

THEME MUSIC: Up full then under...

ANNOUNCER: *This Is Your FBI*, the official broadcast from the files of the Federal Bureau of Investigation... [The subject and title of the evening's story would then be given.]

CLOSE

THEME MUSIC: Up full then under...

ANNOUNCER: The incidents used in tonight's broadcast are adapted from the files of the Federal Bureau of Investigation. However, all names used are fictitious and any similarity thereof, to the names, persons or places, living or dead is accidental. *This Is Your FBI* is a Jerry Devine production. This is ABC, the American Broadcasting Company.

THEME MUSIC: Up full then fade out.

407. Those Websters

Comical incidents in the lives of the Websters: parents George and Jane and their children, Liz and Billy. Sponsored by Quaker Oats. CBS (1945–1946), Mutual (1946–1948). Willard Waterman starred as George Webster with Constance Crowder as Jane, Joan Alt as Liz and Gil Stratton, Jr. as Billy.

OPEN

SOUND: Phone ringing.

WOMAN (picking up receiver): Hello.

VOICE: Are you listening to your radio, ma'am?

WOMAN: Yes.

VOICE: To what program are you listening, please?

WOMAN: *Those Websters*.

VOICE: Can you tell me what's advertised?

WOMAN: Of course, everybody knows that. Delicious Quaker Oats.

THEME MUSIC: Up full then under...

ANNOUNCER (Charles Lyon): *Those Websters*, the Quaker Oats program, each week reminds you that families are fun. Now, in just a moment, we'll take you to 46 River Road to see what's doing at the home of *Those Websters*. But first, now let Quaker Oats cut breakfast costs. Quaker Oats is one of the world's finest foods. Great for growing children, great for working adults, yet this delicious growth and energy food costs less than one cent a serving. Everybody loves the natural nut-toasty flavor of Quaker Oats. Upgrade your breakfast, serve the whole family generous bowls of delicious Quaker Oats regularly. It's one of the world's finest foods yet it costs less than one cent a serving.

THEME MUSIC: Up full then under…

ANNOUNCER: We take you now to *Those Websters* for our weekly reminder that families are fun.

CLOSE

THEME MUSIC: Up full then under…

ANNOUNCER: *Those Websters*, starring Willard Waterman as George, features Constance Crowder, Joan Alt and Gil Stratton, Jr. *Those Websters* is presented by the Quaker Oats Company, makers of Quaker Oats, the delicious growth and energy food that costs less than one cent a serving. This is Charles Lyon inviting you to be with us again next week for more family fun on *Those Websters*. This Mutual.

THEME MUSIC: Up full then fade out.

408. Time for Love

Drama that revolved around the mysterious Dianne LaVolte and her lover, Michael Victor, as they battle the enemies of the free world. Sponsored by Jergens Hand Lotion (excluding sustaining episodes broadcast from January through May 1953). CBS, 1953–1954. Marlene Dietrich played Dianne with Robert Readick as Michael. Alec Wilder composed the "Time for Love" theme.

OPEN

THEME MUSIC: Up full then under…

ANNOUNCER (Lee Vines): The Columbia Broadcasting System presents Marlene Dietrich as the sultry Dianne LaVolte in *Time for Love*.

THEME MUSIC: Up full then under…

ANNOUNCER: *Time for Love*, a story of romance, a story of intrigue, a story of mystery as one woman battles the forces that threaten our society. *Time for Love* starring Marlene Dietrich.

THEME MUSIC: Up full then out.

CLOSE

THEME MUSIC: Up full then under…

ANNOUNCER: Marlene Dietrich will star in *Time for Love* again next week at this same time. *Time for Love* is produced by Marlene Dietrich with original music composed and conducted by Alec Wilder. Robert Readick is heard as our narrator, reporter Michael Victor. Lee Vines speaking. This is CBS, the Columbia Broadcasting System.

THEME MUSIC: Up full then fade out.

409. Time to Shine

Musical variety series hosted by bandleader Hal Kemp. Sponsored by Griffin Shoe Polish. CBS, 1938–1939.

OPEN

ANNOUNCER: Hal Kemp is on the air for Griffin.

CHORUS:
> It's time to shine.
> Shine your shoes
> And you'll wear a smile.
> Shine your shoes
> And you'll be in style.
> Sun shines east,
> Sun shines west.
> Griffin polish
> Shines the best.
> So keep your shoes shined
> With Griffin all the time.

SOUND: Bells sounding "It's Time to Shine"

CHORUS:
> It's time to shine,
> Everybody get set,
> It's time to shine.

ANNOUNCER: Griffin now presents the host of

our program, Hal Kemp... [at which time Hal begins the show].

CLOSE

THEME MUSIC: Up full then under...
ANNOUNCER: Griffin Shoe Polish has presented Hal Kemp and his orchestra in *Time to Shine*, a presentation of the Columbia Broadcasting System.
THEME MUSIC: Up full then fade out.

410. T-Man

Dramatizations based on the files of the U.S. Treasury Department. Various sponsors. CBS, 1950. Dennis O'Keefe stars as Agent Steve Larsen.

OPEN

THEME MUSIC: Up full then under...
ANNOUNCER (Bob Lemond): *T-Man* starring Dennis O'Keefe. T-Man, the law enforcement agent of the Treasury Department, skilled fighter against crime, relentless enemy of the underworld. Now, *T-Man* with Dennis O'Keefe as Treasury Agent Steve Larsen.
THEME MUSIC: Up full and out.

CLOSE

THEME MUSIC: Up full then under...
ANNOUNCER: *T-Man* with Dennis O'Keefe as Treasury Agent Steve Larsen is a transcribed story based on the files of the Treasury Department. Be with us next week when CBS radio brings you another transcribed story on *T-Man*. All names and places used in tonight's story are fictitious; any similarity to persons living or dead is coincidental. Bob Lemond speaking. This is CBS, the Columbia Broadcasting System.
THEME MUSIC: Up full then fade out.

411. Today's Children

Dramatic incidents in the lives of the Moran family: Mother Moran (Irna Phillips) and her children, Eileen (Fran Carlon, Ireene

Wicker), Kathryn (Helen Kane), Fran (Bess Johnson, Sunda Love) and Terry (Fred Von Ammon). Sponsored by General Mills and Pillsbury. NBC, 1933–1937 (for Pillsbury), 1943–1950 (for General Mills). "Aphrodite" and "Tales from the Vienna Woods" were used as the theme.

OPEN

THEME MUSIC: Up full then under...
ANNOUNCER (Louis Rowan): *Today's Children*, presented by the Pillsbury Flour Mills Company, makers of Pillsbury's Best Flour, Sno-Sheen Cake Flour, Farina and Wheat Bran.
THEME MUSIC: Up full then under...
ANNOUNCER: And now, *Today's Children*, the joys, the sorrows, the triumphs and tragedies of the Moran family.

CLOSE

THEME MUSIC: Up full then under...
ANNOUNCER: And so concludes this episode of *Today's Children*. The Pillsbury Flour Mills Company sincerely hopes you have enjoyed it. *Today's Children* has come to you as a presentation of the Pillsbury Flour Mills Company and will again be heard tomorrow morning at this same time. Your announcer is Louis Rowan speaking from our studios in Chicago. This is NBC, the National Broadcasting Company.
THEME MUSIC: Up full then out.
SOUND: NBC chimes. N-B-C.

412. Tom Corbett, Space Cadet

Radio adaptation of the television series about Tom Corbett, a cadet at Space Academy, U.S.A. Sponsored by Kellogg's Pep Cereal. ABC, 1951. Frankie Thomas plays Tom Corbett with Al Markim as Astro and Jan Merlin as Cadet Roger Manning.

OPEN

VOICE: Stand by to raise ship. Blast off minus five ... four ... three ... two ... one ... zero!

SOUND: Rocket ship blasting off.

THEME MUSIC: Up full then under…

ANNOUNCER (Jackson Beck): Kellogg's Pep, the build-up wheat cereal, invites you to rocket into the future with *Tom Corbett, Space Cadet*. As roaring rockets blast off to distant planets and far-flung stars, we take you to the age of the conquest of space with *Tom Corbett, Space Cadet*.

THEME MUSIC: Up full then out.

CLOSE

THEME MUSIC: Up full then under…

ANNOUNCER: Kellogg's Pep, the build-up wheat cereal has presented *Tom Corbett, Space Cadet*. Frankie Thomas is starred as Tom Corbett. Also in the cast are Al Markim, Jan Merlin and Patricia Ferris. Be sure to watch Tom Corbett on ABC television. Check local newspaper for time and channel. This is Jackson Beck inviting you to blast off again with *Tom Corbett, Space Cadet* when we return on Thursday with another episode. This is ABC, the American Broadcasting Company.

THEME MUSIC: Up full then out.

413. The Tom Mix Ralston Straight Shooters

Western that centered on Tom Mix, owner of the TM-Bar Ranch near Dobie, Texas. Sponsored by Ralston. NBC (1933–1937), Blue (1937–1942), Mutual (1944–1951). Artells Dickson, Russell Thorson, Jack Holden and Curley Bradley played Tom Mix. Tom's horse was named Tony. The song "When the Bloom Is on the Sage" was used as the theme.

OPEN

THEME MUSIC: Up full then under…

SONG:
> Shredded Ralston for your breakfast
> Starts a day off shining bright.
> Gives you lots of cowboy energy,
> With a flavor that's just right.
> It's delicious and nutritious,
> Bite size and ready to eat.
> Take a tip from Tom,

> Go tell Mom,
> Shredded Ralston can't be beat.

THEME MUSIC: Up full then under…

ANNOUNCER (Les Griffith): *The Tom Mix Ralston Straight Shooters* brings you action, mystery and mile-a-minute thrills in radio's biggest western detective program.

THEME MUSIC: Up full then out.

ANNOUNCER: *The Tom Mix Ralston Straight Shooters* is presented by the makers of Shredded Ralston. If you're like Tom, you'll want to keep in top condition. And the best way I know how to do this is to saddle up every morning with a hot dish of good old Ralston. It's packed with cowboy energy—just what you need to keep in top condition. Why not tell Mom tonight to get you the famous red and white checkerboard package of good old Ralston tomorrow. Be like Tom, eat Ralston for cowboy energy.

THEME MUSIC: Up full then under…

ANNOUNCER: And now come up to the Rio Grande country as we begin a thrilling, action-packed adventure with Tom Mix, owner of the TM-Bar Ranch…

CLOSE

ANNOUNCER: What will happen next? For fast action, for mystery and thrills, be sure to listen tomorrow when *Tom Mix and the Ralston Straight Shooters* return to the air. Tom Mix has been presented by Ralston; Ralston in the famous red and white checkerboard box for cowboy energy. Parents, you can help Uncle Sam in the war by buying defense bonds. You can buy them at your bank, post office or ask your newspaper carrier or retailer for them. Don't forget to tune into *Tom Mix* tomorrow night at 5:45. Good night from *Tom Mix and the Ralston Straight Shooters*. This is Mutual.

THEME MUSIC: Up full then fade out.

414. Top Secret

Ilona Massey as Karen Gaza, a World War II undercover agent for Central Intelligence. Sponsored by NBC. NBC, 1950. Roy Shields composed the theme, "Top Secret."

OPEN

ANNOUNCER (Fred Collins): This story is *Top Secret.*

THEME MUSIC: Up full then under...

ANNOUNCER: *Top Secret,* exciting stories of intrigue and espionage, brought to you transcribed by NBC and starring Ilona Massey as the Baroness Karen Gaza, a woman who fought without protection, without recognition, without fear for the forces of freedom. Tonight, as Assignment 10, "The Case of the Tattooed Pigeon."

KAREN: Assignment 10 began and ended with tragedy. I had been assigned by Central Intelligence to trace leaks of important top secret information from the Department of Internal Security in London... [The story follows her efforts as her investigation leads her to German Intelligence in Berlin.]

CLOSE

THEME MUSIC: Up full then under...

ANNOUNCER: You have just heard Ilona Massey as the Baroness Karen Gaza in another transcribed story of intrigue and espionage brought to you by NBC. Here is Miss Massey to tell you about next week's show.

ILONA: Next week, a story of a church that shouted evil, a trip to Brussels and a secret story called "The Church Without a Cross."

ANNOUNCER: *Top Secret* is written, produced and directed by Harry W. Junkin. The music was composed and conducted by Dr. Roy Shields. This is Fred Collins speaking. *Take It or Leave It* provides gay entertainment for you next on NBC.

THEME MUSIC: Up full then out.

SOUND: NBC chimes. N-B-C.

415. Town Hall Tonight

Music and comedy set against the background of a town hall with comedian Fred Allen as the host. Sponsored by Ipana and Sal Hepatica. NBC, 1934–1939.

OPEN

THEME MUSIC: Up full then under...

ANNOUNCER (Harry Von Zell): An hour of smiles on *Town Hall Tonight,* folks. Sixty minutes of fun and music brought to you by Ipana Toothpaste and Sal Hepatica. Ipana for the smile of beauty, Sal Hepatica for the smile of health. Fun with our star comedian Fred Allen and his Mighty Allen Art Players, Peter Van Steeden and the Ipana Troubadours, the Town Hall quartet and a flock of new and eager amateurs, new voices, new music and new fun—it's *Town Hall Tonight.*

SOUND: People cheering.

ANNOUNCER: Listen to that crowd. They're cheering in the streets as Fred Allen leads his weekly parade to the old town hall. Here we are in front of the old town hall folks and there's Fred getting into his bullet-proof vest and addressing the crowd. Let's listen.

FRED (speech would vary by episode): If I had the wings of an angel, through these town hall doors I would fly folks.

SOUND: Fred greeting people as he enters the town hall.

ANNOUNCER: We're ready and willing, captain.

FRED: Okay Harry, tell Peter I'm opening with "Rise and Shine."

ANNOUNCER: Okay, let her go Pete.

SOUND: Peter Van Steeden's orchestra playing the song "Rise and Shine."

ANNOUNCER: Presenting Fred Allen in person.

SOUND: Applause.

FRED: Thank you, thank you and good evening ladies and gentlemen... [Fred would then begin the show.]

CLOSE

THEME MUSIC: Up full then under...

ANNOUNCER: We hope, ladies and gentlemen, that tonight's program has brought you all another hour of smiles and that you'll remember to be with us again next Wednesday. In the meantime, we hope you'll remember the products that make this Fred Allen show possible: Ipana Toothpaste for the smile of beauty and Sal Hepatica for the smile of health.

FRED: Good night ladies and gentlemen, and don't forget next Wednesday night for another hour of smiles in the old town hall. This is Fred Allen saying good night.

ANNOUNCER: This is the Red Network of the National Broadcasting Company.

THEME MUSIC: Up full then out.
SOUND: NBC chimes. N-B-C.

Note: In the summer of 1936, comedians Stoopnagel and Budd (F. Chase Taylor and Wilbur "Budd" Hulick) hosted the series when Fred Allen went on vacation. Here are the opening and closing segments from the episode of September 23, 1936.

OPEN

THEME MUSIC: Up full then under...
ANNOUNCER (Harry Von Zell): An hour of smiles in *Town Hall Tonight*, folks. Sixty minutes of fun and music brought to you by Ipana Toothpaste and Sal Hepatica. Ipana for the smile of beauty, Sal Hepatica for the smile of health. Fun with Colonel Stoopnagel and Budd, music with Peter Van Steeden and another amateur contest. New voices, new music, new fun, it's *Town Hall Tonight*.
THEME MUSIC: Up full then out.

CLOSE

THEME MUSIC: Up full then under...
ANNOUNCER: It's time to close the town hall doors for tonight, ladies and gentlemen, until next Wednesday when we invite you to join us for another happy hour of smiles from the old town hall. Good night. This is the Red Network of the National Broadcasting Company.
THEME MUSIC: Up full then out.
SOUND: NBC chimes. N-B-C.

416. Treasury Agent

Dramas that depict the work of the U.S. Treasury Department as seen through the cases of Joe Lincoln (Raymond Edward Johnson). Various sponsors. ABC, 1947–1948. Ralph Norman composed the theme, "Treasury Agent."

OPEN

ANNOUNCER: The American Broadcasting Company presents *Treasury Agent*.
THEME MUSIC: Up full then under...
VOICE: The United States Treasury, largest group of law enforcement agencies in the world.

VOICE: The United States Secret Service. We protect the president of the United States at all times, and protect the money of the United States from counterfeiters.
VOICE: United States Revenue Intelligence. Jurisdiction over tax fraud evasion.
VOICE: United States Bureau of Narcotics.
VOICE: Bureau of Customs, Alcohol Tax Unit
VOICE: United States Coast Guard—crimes committed on the high seas.
THEME MUSIC: Up full then under...
ANNOUNCER: *Treasury Agent*, based on the general modus operandi of United States Treasury agents operating here and all over the world. *Treasury Agent*, starring Raymond Edward Johnson as Joe Lincoln, chief United States Treasury agent.
THEME MUSIC: Up full then out.

CLOSE

THEME MUSIC: Up full then under...
ANNOUNCER: *Treasury Agent* with Raymond Edward Johnson starred as Agent Joe Lincoln is produced by Phillips H. Lord with original music composed and conducted by Ralph Norman. *Treasury Agent* is based on the official files of the United States Treasury Department. All names and places used in this dramatization are fictitious ; any similarity to real names or places is coincidental. Be with us again next week for another *Treasury Agent* story. This is ABC, the American Broadcasting Company.
THEME MUSIC: Up full then fade out.

417. The Trouble with the Truitts

Comic incidents in the life of Elmer Truitt, owner of the Bit of Cheery Greeting Card Company in the town of Hope Springs. Various sponsors. NBC, 1950–1951. John Dehner starred as Elmer Truitt with Constance Crowder as his wife, Gert; Barbara DuPar and Jane Webb as their daughter Gladys; Dawn Bender as daughter Maggie; and Eddie Firestone and Gil Stratton, Jr. as their son Clarence. William Lava composed "The Truitts Theme."

OPEN

ANNOUNCER (Eddie King): During the next half hour, we'd like you to meet the Truitts, a delightful American family who are all set to win their way into the hearts of the radio public. The Truitts are real people drawn from the broad canvas of contemporary life. They'll probably remind you of your neighbor down the street, or maybe you'll see reflected in them your own family and some of the fun and trouble you've had together. Radio audiences will be quick to identify themselves with the Truitts and add them to their list of favorite radio families. What's trouble for the Truitts can be good news for you. The National Broadcasting Company brings you *The Trouble with the Truitts*.

THEME MUSIC: Up full then under...

ANNOUNCER: Well, let's see what's troubling the Truitts this time...

CLOSE

THEME MUSIC: Up full then under...

ANNOUNCER: *The Trouble with the Truitts* was written by Frank and Doris Hursley and produced and directed by Bill Karn with original music composed and conducted by William Lava. The cast included John Dehner as Elmer, Constance Crowder as Gert, Dawn Bender as Maggie and Gill Stratton, Jr. as Clarence. Your announcer has been Eddie King. The National Broadcasting Company invites you to join us again next week for another laugh at *The Trouble with the Truitts*. This is NBC, the National Broadcasting Company.

THEME MUSIC: Up full then out.

SOUND: NBC chimes. N-B-C.

418. Truth or Consequences

Game show in which players must perform a stunt if they fail to answer a question correctly. Sponsored by Drene Shampoo, DUZ Detergent, Ivory Soap Flakes, Pet Milk, Philip Morris Cigarettes. CBS (1940; 1950–1951), NBC (1940–1950; 1952–1956). Ralph Edwards served as the host. Basis for the television series.

OPEN

CHORUS: D-U-Z, D-U-Z.

GIRL VOCALIST:
> Put DUZ in your washing machine,
> Take your clothes out bright and clean.
> When you DUZ your wash,
> You'll sing DUZ does everything.

ANNOUNCER (Harlow Wilcox): Hello there, we've been waiting for you, it's time to play *Truth or Consequences*. Yes, *Truth or Consequences*, the show that does everything on the air, is brought to you by DUZ, the soap that does everything in your wash. And here he is, the star of our show Ralph "Truth or Consequences" Edwards.

CLOSE

GIRL VOCALIST: Put DUZ in your washing machine

CHORUS: Work clothes come out so clean.

GIRL: No soap quite like DUZ before

CHORUS: DUZ is different, DUZ does more

GIRL: When you DUZ your wash you'll say

CHORUS:
> D-U-Z does everything.
> D-U-Z, D-U-Z.

RALPH: That was delightful, DUZ-lightful Kids, yes sir. And folks now listen. The truth is that today's crisis for used kitchen fats are [*sic*] higher, much higher than last summer. Everybody save every drop of used fat. It's worth your while. This is Ralph Edwards speaking on behalf of our sponsor, the makers of DUZ. Good night everybody.

ANNOUNCER: Why has Hollywood star Merle Oberon switched to new, improved Drene Shampoo? Because compared to dulling soap shampoos, the wonderful new Drene reveals up to 33 percent more sheen. Follow Merle's secret for shining hair—

GIRL VOCALIST:
> It's new Drene
> For Hollywood sheen,
> Improved Drene
> For Hollywood sheen.
> Your hair can have
> That Hollywood sheen
> The very first time
> You use new Drene.
> Get wonderful new
> Drene Shampoo, new Drene.

ANNOUNCER: This is Harlow Wilcox speaking for Procter and Gamble, makers of DUZ. Ralph Edwards' *Truth or Consequences* came to you from Hollywood. This is NBC, the National Broadcasting Company.
THEME MUSIC: Up full then out.
SOUND: NBC chimes. N-B-C.

419. The Twenty-First Precinct

Crime drama centered around the activities of the Twenty-First Police Precinct in New York City. Sustaining. CBS, 1953–1956. Everett Sloane starred as Captain Frank Kennelly with Ken Lynch as Lt. Matt King.

OPEN

SOUND: Switchboard telephone ringing.
VOICE: Twenty-First Precinct, Sergeant Collins.
CAPTAIN: You are in the Muster Room of the Twenty-First Precinct, the nerve center. A call is coming through. You will follow, by transcription, the action taken pursuant to that call from this minute until the final report is written in the 124 Room of the Twenty-First Precinct.
ANNOUNCER (Art Hanna): *The Twenty-First Precinct*. It's just lines on the map of the city of New York. Most of the 173,000 people wedged into the nine-tenths of a square mile between Fifth Avenue and the East River wouldn't know if you asked them if they lived and worked in the Twenty-First. Whether they know it or not, the security of their homes, their persons and their property is the job of the men of the Twenty-First Precinct.
CAPTAIN: The Twenty-First—160 patrolmen, 11 sergeants and four lieutenants of whom I am the boss. My name is Kennelly, Frank Kennelly, I'm captain in command of the Twenty-First.

CLOSE

CAPTAIN: And so it goes, around the clock, through the week, every day, every year. A police precinct in the city of New York is a flesh-and-blood merry-go-round. Anyone can catch the brass ring—or the brass ring can catch anyone.
ANNOUNCER: *The Twenty-First Precinct*, a transcribed, factual account of the way police work in the world's largest city, is presented with the official cooperation of the Patrolman's Benevolent Association, an organization of more than 20,000 members of the police department, city of New York. Everett Sloane stars as Captain Kennelly, Ken Lynch is Lieutenant King. Written and directed by Stanley Niss. Art Hanna speaking. This is CBS, the Columbia Broadcasting System.

420. Two Thousand Plus

Chilling science-fiction stories set in the future. Various sponsors. Mutual, 1950–1952. Milton Kaye composed the theme, "Two Thousand Plus."

OPEN

SOUND: Voice giving a one-line summary of the evening's story.
VOICE: I have received word of a strange invention. What it can do will amaze science and strike terror to the world.
THEME MUSIC: Up full then under…
ANNOUNCER (Ken Marvin): *Two Thousand Plus*, science fiction adventures from the years beyond. Two thousand A.D. Tonight, *Two Thousand Plus* presents "The Insect." [Strange story about a scientist who creates a machine called the "growth ray" to enable him to enlarge insects so he may better study them.]

CLOSE

THEME MUSIC: Up full then under…
ANNOUNCER: Next week a strange drama of a silver rocket and an unseen visitor from space. Be sure to listen to *Two Thousand Plus*, radio's different series. In today's cast, Joan Shay portrayed Betty, Larry Robinson was Joe, Ralph Bell was George and Bill Griffis was the Dean. Music composed and played by Milton Kaye. This is Ken Marvin speaking. This program came to you from New York. This is the Mutual Broadcasting System.
THEME MUSIC: Up full then fade out.

421. The Unexpected

Stories of how fate influences people's lives. Sustaining. Syn., 1948.

OPEN

THEME MUSIC: Up full then under…

ANNOUNCER (Hal Sawyer): Lurene Tuttle in *The Unexpected.*

LURENE: It was like a bad dream, a monsterous, terrifying dream. I was caught in a fantastic nightmare. I knew that I had to escape or go mad. I had met "the unexpected."

ANNOUNCER: The unexpected, a secret future, a hidden destiny waiting for you? Where? When? Who knows. Tomorrow, today or an hour from now. Perhaps in just a few moments you too will meet—

VOICE: The unexpected.

ANNOUNCER: And now radio's most famous actress, Lurene Tuttle, in "Nightmare," a drama of *The Unexpected.*

THEME MUSIC: Up full then out.

CLOSE

THEME MUSIC: Up full then under…

ANNOUNCER: You think the story is over, don't you? But wait, wait for—

VOICE: The unexpected.

ANNOUNCER: "Nightmare," a drama of *The Unexpected*, starred Lurene Tuttle and featured Daws Butler and Stanley Waxman. This is Hal Sawyer inviting you to listen again soon when another of your favorite motion picture stars meets—

VOICE: The unexpected.

ANNOUNCER: *The Unexpected* is a Hamilton-Whitney Production transcribed in Hollywood.

THEME MUSIC: Up full then out.

422. Valiant Lady

Daily serial about Joan Scott, an actress who relinquished her career to marry noted plastic surgeon Truman Scott. Sponsored by Bisquick, Gold Medal Flour and General Mills. CBS (1938; 1942–1946), NBC (1938–1942),

ABC (1951–1952). Joan Blaine, Joan Banks and Florence Freeman played Joan Scott with Charles Carroll, Bartlett Robinson and Martin Blaine as Truman Scott. General Mills, sponsors of this episode from June 6, 1944, relinquished its commercial time in response to the D-Day invasion.

OPEN

THEME MUSIC ("Estrellita"): Up full then under…

ANNOUNCER (Dwight Weist): *Valiant Lady.*

THEME MUSIC: Up full then under…

ANNOUNCER: Joan Scott, the Valiant Lady; brought to you by Cheerios, a product of General Mills, creators of new foods and new ideas for a better world.

THEME MUSIC: Up full then out.

ANNOUNCER: Today, we are a nation united as perhaps we have never been united before. In the mind of everyone of us, there are the same anxious thoughts. How is the fighting going and how can I help. Compared with the sacrifices the men of our invasion forces are making now, it doesn't seem very much for us to do. To give money and get the outcome of a battle may be decided by the amount and kind of equipment with which our men are supplied. We can help today by buying war bonds—war bonds to provide money for equipment that will continue to give our men the overwhelming superiority we need and want them to have on the invasion front. We can help this very minute. By not just the bonds that we can well afford, but those that we may have to pinch and scrape to buy. And we can keep on buying war bonds with every penny we can spare, backing up our invasion armies until the victory is won.

THEME MUSIC: Up full then under…

ANNOUNCER: And now *Valiant Lady*, the story of a brave woman and her brilliant but unstable husband. The story of her struggle to keep his feet planted firmly up the pathway to success.

CLOSE

THEME MUSIC: Up full then under…

ANNOUNCER: Don't miss tomorrow's story of *Valiant Lady* presented by Cheerios. This is

Dwight Weist saying goodbye until then and inviting you to listen to *Light of the World* which follows immediately.

THEME MUSIC: Up full then out.

NEWSCASTER (interrupting the theme): We bring you this late dispatch from the CBS News headquarters in New York. President Roosevelt will go to the air at ten o'clock tonight, Eastern War Time, with the hope that the nation will join him in a prayer he has written for the occasion. Columbia will bring you the President's broadcast at ten o'clock this evening, Eastern War Time. Before that, at three P.M. Eastern War Time, we hope to bring you a broadcast by King George VI of Great Britain. This dispatch has come to you from CBS World News. We resume our scheduled programs.

423. The Vaughn DeLeath Show

Early variety series hosted by singer Vaughn DeLeath, believed to be the first woman to have sung on radio. Sustaining. CBS (1931–1932; 1935–1936), NBC (1934–1935; 1936–1937), Blue (1938–1939). The song "Red Sails in the Sunset" was used as the theme.

OPEN

THEME MUSIC: Up full then under…

VAUGHN (singing):
> Red sails in the sunset,
> Way out on the sea,
> Please carry my loved one
> Home safely to me.

THEME MUSIC: Under…

ANNOUNCER: Ladies and gentlemen, Vaughn DeLeath, radio's first singing sensation with next year's styles in songs as up to the minute as tomorrow's newspaper.

CLOSE

THEME MUSIC: Up full then under…

ANNOUNCER: You have been listening to Miss Vaughn DeLeath, radio's first singing sensation. This is the Columbia Broadcasting System.

THEME MUSIC: Up full then fade out.

424. Vic and Sade

Humorous dialogue about incidents in the lives of the Gook family: Vic (Art Van Harvey), a bookkeeper at Plant 14 of the Consolidated Kitchenware Company; his wife, Sade (Bernadine Flynn); and their adopted son, Rush (Billy Idelson, Johnny Coons, Sid Koss). Sponsored by Crisco Shortening, Fitch Shampoo and Lava Hand Soap (also sustaining at times). NBC (1931–1934), CBS (1941–1943; 1945), Mutual (1941–1946). The song "Chansom Bohemienne" by J.D. Boldi was used as the theme.

OPEN

THEME MUSIC: Up full then under…

ANNOUNCER (Ed Roberts): And now get ready to smile again with radio's home folks, *Vic and Sade*, written by Paul Rhymer. Yes, here again folks, your good friends *Vic and Sade*, brought to you by the makers of Crisco.

THEME MUSIC: Up full then out.

SOUND: Street noises.

CRISCO SPOKESWOMAN (Betty Ruth Smith): Hello Nancy, what's your rush?

NANCY: Oh, hello Mrs. Smith. I just passed my Girl Scout cooking test.

MRS. SMITH: That's grand.

NANCY: I baked a cake and Mrs. Green, she's our scout leader, said it tasted wonderful.

MRS. SMITH: What kind did you make.

NANCY: Orange layer. There was orange in the cake and I put orange in the frosting too. Mmmmm, it was so good.

MRS. SMITH: Stop Nancy, you're making me hungry.

NANCY: Wish I had some for you. It was so light. Mother said that new kind of shortening would make my cake especially light.

MRS. SMITH: What new kind of shortening, Nancy?

NANCY: The new Sure Mix Crisco. Mother heard about it on the radio. They said it was a different kind of shortening and that no other shortening at the store was made like this new Crisco. That's why it gives lighter cakes.

MRS. SMITH: But Nancy, how can a shortening make a difference in the lightness of cakes?

NANCY: It's the way it works. You see, this new

Crisco is an active blender. When you take a tablespoon of Crisco and a tablespoon of water and mix them together, Crisco takes the water right up. That's active blending. And Crisco does the same thing with eggs and flour when you're mixing a cake. Why I got the smoothest cake batter you ever saw with Crisco when I made my orange cake. And Mother says that's why it turned out so light.

ANNOUNCER: If you want lighter cakes, it's simply up to you. Crisco is waiting to give them to you. Make one of your favorite cakes. Use the same ingredients, use the same recipe. Change nothing but your shortening. This time use new Sure Mix Crisco. You have our promise, no other shortening we know of will give you cakes as light. Crisco gives you lighter cakes than any other shortening.

THEME MUSIC: Up full then under...

ANNOUNCER: And now let's see what's happening at the little house halfway up the next block... [The episode would then begin.]

<h3 align="center">CLOSE</h3>

THEME MUSIC: Up full then under...

ANNOUNCER: That concludes another brief interlude at the small house halfway up the next block. And so we leave *Vic and Sade* until the next time. Don't forget to listen.

THEME MUSIC: Up full then out.

ANNOUNCER: Tell me how many of you ladies listening in actually use Lava Soap? Well, all of you who use Lava can't help but like it. But what I'm really getting around to is we'd like to hear from you. We'd like to hear why you like Lava and any new uses you found for it. Send your letters to Lava Soap, care of Procter and Gamble, Cincinnati, Ohio. And ladies, always remember this. When it comes to getting extra dirty, housework-soiled hands really clean, quickly, easily, safely, no other soap you ever used equals Lava. That's the truth. Lava soap actually gets extra dirty hands shades whiter in only twenty seconds. Lava Soap, L-A-V-A, only a few pennies at dealers everywhere. Get some today and remember, let us know how you like it.

THEME MUSIC: Up full then under...

ANNOUNCER: This is Ed Roberts speaking.

THEME MUSIC: Up full then fade out.

425. The Voyage of the Scarlet Queen

Adventure series about Phil Carney, captain of the *Scarlet Queen*, and his first mate, Red Gallagher. Sustaining. Mutual, 1947–1948. Elliott Lewis played Phil Carney with Ed Max as Red Gallagher. Richard Aurandt composed the theme, "Voyage of the Scarlet Queen." See also *The Log of the Black Parrot*.

<h3 align="center">OPEN</h3>

SOUND: Wind blowing.

THEME MUSIC: Up full then under...

VOICE: Stand by to make sail.

THEME MUSIC: Up full then under...

PHIL: Log entry, the ketch *Scarlet Queen*, Philip Carney, Master. Position: 10 degrees, 20 minutes north; 107 degrees, 45 minutes east. Sky fair, wind fresh.

ANNOUNCER (Charles Arlington): *The Voyage of the Scarlet Queen*, written by Gil Dowd and Bob Talman and starring Elliott Lewis. The *Scarlet Queen*, proudest ship to plow the seas, bound for adventure. Every week, a complete entry in the log, and every week, a leap further in *The Voyage of the Scarlet Queen*.

THEME MUSIC: Up full then out.

<h3 align="center">CLOSE</h3>

SOUND: Wind hitting sails.

THEME MUSIC: Up full then under...

PHIL: Log entry, the ketch *Scarlet Queen*, five thirty P.M. Wind, brisk; sky fair. Ship secured for the night. Signed, Philip Carney, Master.

THEME MUSIC: Up full then under...

ANNOUNCER: Mutual invites you to sail into further adventures on *The Voyage of the Scarlet Queen* next week at this same time.

THEME MUSIC: Up full then under...

ANNOUNCER: *The Voyage of the Scarlet Queen* stars Elliott Lewis as Phil Carney with Ed Max as Gallagher. Music scored and conducted by Richard Aurandt. *The Scarlet Queen*, produced by James Burton, is written by Gil Dowd and Bob Talman.

THEME MUSIC: Up full then out.

ANNOUNCER: This program came to you from Hollywood. Stay tuned now for another Mutual favorite, *Quiet Please*, which follows in just a moment. Charles Arlington speaking. This is the Mutual Broadcasting System.

426. The Walter Winchell Journal

News items, gossip and commentary by Walter Winchell, an ex-vaudevillian turned newspaper columnist. Sponsored by American Razor, Gruen, Hudnut Products, Kaiser-Frazier Cars. ABC (1949–1955), Mutual (1955–1957).

OPEN

SOUND: Car horns.
ANNOUNCER (Hugh James): That means Kaiser-Frazier.
SOUND: Telegraph keys.
ANNOUNCER: That means Walter Winchell. *The Walter Winchell Journal* is brought to you by the men who sell and service Kaiser Automobiles and the Frazier. You, yes you, could win one of the 145 prizes in the great new Kaiser-Frazier contest. Every prize winner will receive $1,000 toward the purchase price of a new 1949 Kaiser or Frazier. Here is all you have to do. Go to your nearest Kaiser-Frazier dealer and ask for your entry blank. On it you will find one simple statement to complete in 25 words or less. Then mail your entry as directed. That's all there is to do and good luck. But now Kaiser-Frazier, builders of cars that make automotive history, presents the reporter of news that makes history. So who, what, when, where and why from the man America listens to most, Walter Winchell.
SOUND: Telegraph keys.
WINCHELL: Good evening Mr. and Mrs. North and South America and all the ships at sea, let's go to press…

CLOSE

THEME MUSIC: Up full then under…
ANNOUNCER: Kaiser-Frazier, builders of cars that make history, has presented this evening's broadcast of *The Walter Winchell Journal*. Be sure to visit your nearest Kaiser-Frazier dealer for your chance to win $1,000 toward the pur-

chase of a brand new 1949 Kaiser or Frazier. Until next Sunday, then, this is Hugh James wishing you a good evening from Kaiser-Frazier. This is ABC, the American Broadcasting Company.
THEME MUSIC: Up full then fade out.

427. We Who Dream

Stories based on dreams as told by the sexy-voiced Dream Girl (Claire Niesen). Sponsored by the Englender Company. CBS, 1944.

OPEN

THEME MUSIC: Up full then under…
ANNOUNCER: This is the Englender program. Englender, for more than 50 years, the name that stands for the most luxurious rests and sleeps.
THEME MUSIC: Up full then under…
DREAM GIRL: Sleep. The curtain of the day comes down but the play goes on. Behind the veil of sleep, the actors speak and posture and emit the day gone by. They whisper things to come in dreams.
THEME MUSIC: Up full then under…
ANNOUNCER: The Englender Company, manufacturers of America's most luxurious mattresses, presents *We Who Dream*, a program of plays that deal with the strange recesses of the unconscious mind. For the mind at sleep is not cut off from life. It dreams and lives another life linked with all our waking hours. This is a program about people who dream. For these dreams, however real or fantastic, are somehow, somewhere based on life, as all dreams must be.
THEME MUSIC: Up full then out.

CLOSE

THEME MUSIC: Up full then under…
ANNOUNCER: You have been listening to the Englender program, *We Who Dream*. Be with us again next Friday when the Englender Company, manufacturers of America's most luxurious mattresses, will again present *We Who Dream* featuring Claire Niesen. This is the Columbia Broadcasting System.
THEME MUSIC: Up full then fade out.

428. Wendy Warren and the News

Serial drama that related events in the life of Wendy Warren, a radio newscaster. Various sponsors (Maxwell House Coffee was a frequent sponsor). CBS, 1947–1958. Florence Freeman played Wendy Warren.

OPEN

SOUND: Telegraph signals.

ANNOUNCER (Hugh James): Maxwell House, the coffee that's good to the last drop, brings you *Wendy Warren and the News*.

WENDY: Hello, folks, this is Wendy Warren with news reports from the women's world, but first here's Douglas Edwards with the latest headlines... [An actual newscast by Douglas Edwards is given, followed by Wendy's news report for women.]

SOUND: Telegraph signals.

ANNOUNCER: You know, even the most easy-going person won't tolerate a cup of poor coffee and there is really no need to, not when you can enjoy all the flavor-packed goodness of Maxwell House Coffee for just a fraction of a penny more per cup than the lowest priced coffee sold. Rich, vigorous flavor, mellow, smooth goodness in every cup, that's Maxwell House. And you can credit the masterful blending skill of Maxwell House experts for their good to the last drop flavor. Next time, ask your grocer for Maxwell House, the coffee that's always good to the last drop.

SOUND: Telegraph signals (at which time the news show ends and Wendy's private life is depicted).

CLOSE

THEME MUSIC: Up full then under...

ANNOUNCER: Be sure to listen at this same time tomorrow for—

SOUND: Telegraph signals.

ANNOUNCER: *Wendy Warren and the News*, brought to you by Maxwell House, the coffee that's bought and enjoyed by more people than any other brand. Maxwell House, the coffee that's always good to the last drop.

THEME MUSIC: Up full then out.

SOUND (man singing):
    Coconuts, Baker's Coconut,
    Coconuts for sale,
    Delicious Baker's Coconut.

ANNOUNCER: It's the Coconut Man with that wonderful Baker's Coconut to make good candies even better. Add tender, delicious Baker's Coconut to your fudge and you'll have a treat that family and guests will love; grand in cupcakes and cookies too. So make good treats better with Baker's Coconut.

THEME MUSIC: Up full then under...

ANNOUNCER: Be sure to listen again tomorrow for *Wendy Warren and the News*. This is CBS, the Columbia Broadcasting System.

THEME MUSIC: Up full then fade out.

429. When a Girl Marries

Daily serial about marrieds Joan and Harry Davis. Sponsored by Baker's Coconut, Calumet Baking Soda, Carnation Evaporated Milk, General Foods, and Prudential Life Insurance. CBS (1939–1941), NBC (1941–1951), ABC (1951–1957). Noel Mills and Mary Jane Higby played Joan; John Raby, Robert Haag, Whitfield Connor and Lyle Sudrow played Harry. The theme, "Serenade," was composed by Richard Drigo.

OPEN

THEME MUSIC: Up full then under...

ANNOUNCER (Charles Stark): *When a Girl Marries*, a tender, human story of young married life dedicated to everyone who has ever been in love.

THEME MUSIC: Up full then out.

ANNOUNCER: *When a Girl Marries*, brought to you by that double-acting baking powder Calumet. Calumet for double protection, double perfection. Look for the big red can with the Calumet Indian chief. Calumet is famous for its double leavening action; the finest cooks have chosen it for more than 50 years. Yes, dependable, double-acting Calumet Baking Powder is the key to baking success for any woman who gets it in the big, bright red can with the picture of the Calumet Indian chief. For Calumet gives your baking double perfection: raises biscuits and batter twice: first in the mixing bowl when you add liquid to dry ingredients; and second, in the oven when your baking hits the heat. Remember, lady, the key to baking success is Calumet. Calumet for the very best baking yet.

THEME MUSIC: Up full then under...

ANNOUNCER: And now, *When a Girl Marries*, the story of Joan and Harry Davis.

CLOSE

THEME MUSIC: Up full then under...

ANNOUNCER: Until tomorrow at this same time, we leave the story of *When a Girl Marries* with Mary Jane Higby and written by Elaine Carrington. Your narrator was Charles Stark.

THEME MUSIC: Up full then under...

ANNOUNCER: This program was brought to you by that double-acting baking powder, Calumet. Calumet for double protection, double perfection. Look for the big red can with the Calumet Indian chief.

THEME MUSIC: Up full then out.

SONG:

> Coconuts, Baker's Coconut,
> Coconuts for sale,
> Delicious Baker's Coconut.

ANNOUNCER: It's the Coconut Man reminding you that Baker's Coconut makes swell desserts. So tonight, how about a delectable coconut pie—smooth, creamy coconut custard, topped with snowy white Baker's Coconut. Remember, it's better if it's made with Baker's Coconut.

THEME MUSIC: Up full then under...

ANNOUNCER: This is NBC, the National Broadcasting Company.

SOUND: NBC chimes. N-B-C.

430. Which Is Which?

Game show in which contestants must determine whether a famous celebrity voice is the real thing or an imposter. Sponsored by Old Gold Cigarettes. CBS, 1944–1945. Ken Murray served as the host.

OPEN

ANNOUNCER (Bob Williams): Don't let little an-

noyances get you down. Why be irritated? Light an Old Gold; its tobaccos are specially conditioned to help guard against cigarette dryness to give you more smoking pleasure.

THEME MUSIC: Up full then under...

ANNOUNCER: From Hollywood, California, the makers of Old Gold Cigarettes present *Which Is Which?* with our host Ken Murray, Richard Himber and his orchestra and are they real or a reasonable facsimile thereof—Carmen Miranda, Akim Tamiroff, Henry Busey and Fred Allen.

THEME MUSIC: Up full then under...

ANNOUNCER: And here's the star of our show, Ken Murray.

SOUND: Applause.

KEN: Thank you very much, ladies and gentlemen and good evening... [Ken begins the show. The stars mentioned in the theme were the guests for this particular show.]

CLOSE

ANNOUNCER: When little annoyances get you down, why be irritated? Light an Old Gold; enjoy the extra flavor of this fine cigarette plus its special protection from cigarette dryness. You see, Old Gold's fine blend of many superb tobaccos is conditioned with apple honey to help retain the natural moisture, to help guard against cigarette dryness. So keep it in mind, Old Gold, the better, cleaner smoke. But keep this in mind too, if you can't find a pack right off, please remember even though we're producing all the cigarettes we can without sacrificing any of Old Gold's high quality, the men and women of our armed forces get first consideration. But we're doing our utmost to assure fair distribution of all remaining Old Golds. So, if you had to be content today with substitute brands, remember tomorrow if you ask, your dealer may possibly have Old Golds.

THEME MUSIC: Up full then under...

KEN: This is Ken Murray saying good night for Old Gold.

ANNOUNCER: And don't forget, don't let little annoyances get you down, why be irritated? Light an Old Gold, its tobaccos are conditioned to guard against cigarette dryness to give you more smoking pleasure. Bob Williams saying good night for Old Gold.

This is CBS, the Columbia Broadcasting System.

THEME MUSIC: Up full then fade out.

431. The Whisper Men

Radio commentator Max Chandler's battle against the Whisper Men, Communist party members who infiltrate organizations to recruit members. Various sponsors. Mutual, 1945–1946. Karl Swenson and Joseph Curtin played Max Chandler.

OPEN

THEME MUSIC: Up full then under…

ANNOUNCER: The Mutual Broadcasting System presents the adventures of Max Chandler featuring Karl Swenson in the role of the famous broadcaster-reporter whose assignments bring him in constant conflict with—

VOICE (echo effect): *The Whisper Men.*

THEME MUSIC: Up full then out.

CLOSE

THEME MUSIC: Up full then under…

ANNOUNCER: Next week at this time, the Mutual Broadcasting System will bring you another in this series, *The Whisper Men*, based on the stories appearing in *Liberty* magazine. Tonight's program was produced by Dan Seymour and directed by Tony Leader. Karl Swenson was heard as Max Chandler. Music was by Chet Kingsbury. This is the Mutual Broadcasting System.

THEME MUSIC: Up full then fade out.

432. The Whisperer

Crime drama about Philip Gault, a lawyer with damaged vocal cords who works undercover as the Whisperer to destroy organized crime. Sustaining. NBC, 1951. Carleton Young played Philip Gault with Betty Moran as Ellen Norris, the nurse who knows his dual identity. Johnny Duffy composed the theme, "The Whisperer."

OPEN

VOICE (in rattling whisper): *The Whisperer, The Whisperer.*

ANNOUNCER (Donald Rickles): Presenting *The Whisperer* starring Carleton Young. The Whisperer, a brilliant man who, losing his voice in an accident which crushed his vocal cords, worked his way deep within the crime syndicate to help destroy it from within. To the underworld, his familiar rattling hiss is the voice of authority to be obeyed without question. Then a miracle of surgery performed by Dr. Benjamin Lee restored his natural voice, enabling him to resume his real identity. Now, as Philip Gault, brilliant young attorney, he skirts the thin edges of death living his dual role—for as the Whisperer, he sets in motion the forces of the syndicate in Central City, then as Philip Gault, uses his knowledge to fight the organized network of crime which seeks to control the fate of millions in cities and towns across the nation.

THEME MUSIC: Up full then under…

ANNOUNCER: The only person besides Dr. Lee who knows the true identity of the Whisperer is the doctor's nurse, Ellen Norris.

THEME MUSIC: Up full then out.

CLOSE

VOICE: *The Whisperer.*

ANNOUNCER: *The Whisperer* is based upon stories and characters created by Stetson Humphrey. Any similarity to persons living or dead is purely coincidental. Carleton Young is heard as the Whisperer with Betty Moran as Ellen. Original music by Johnny Duffy. *The Whisperer* was written, produced and directed by Bill Karn. This is Donald Rickles inviting you to listen next week to another exciting adventure with—

VOICE: *The Whisperer.*

THEME MUSIC: Up full then out.

ANNOUNCER: This is NBC, the National Broadcasting Company.

SOUND: NBC chimes. N-B-C.

433. The Whistler

Mystery stories about the plight of people who are caught in a web of their own misdeeds. Stories are related by the Whistler, a mysterious man identified by the mournful whistling of the theme music, who knows many things "for I walk by night." Sponsored by Signal Oil (West Coast), Household Finance (East Coast). CBS West Coast, 1942–1955; CBS East and West Coast, 1946–1948. Joseph Kearns, Bill Forman, Marvin Miller and Everett Clarke played the Whistler. The theme, "The Whistler," was composed by Wilbur Hatch. Dorothy Roberts and Owen James performed the eerie 13-note whistle theme.

OPEN (early)

ANNOUNCER (Marvin Miller): And now stay tuned for the mystery program that is unique among all mystery programs because even when you know who's guilty, you always receive a startling surprise at the final curtain in the Signal Oil program *The Whistler*. Signal, the famous go-farther gasoline, invites you to sit back and enjoy another strange story by the Whistler.

THEME MUSIC: Up full then under...

WHISTLER: I am the Whistler and I know many strange things for I walk by night. I know many strange tales hidden in the hearts of men and women who have slipped into the shadows. Yes, I know the nameless terrors of which they dare not speak.

ANNOUNCER: Yes friends, it's time for the Signal Oil program *The Whistler*... [The episode is then introduced followed by the Whistler's narration of the story.]

CLOSE (early)

THEME MUSIC: Up full then under...

ANNOUNCER: Let that whistle be your signal for the Signal Oil program *The Whistler*. Each Wednesday night at this same time and brought to you by the Signal Oil Company, makers of Signal gasoline and motor oil and fine quality automotive accessories. *The Whistler* was produced by George W. Allen. This is Marvin Miller speaking for CBS, the Columbia Broadcasting System.

THEME MUSIC: Up full then out.

OPEN (later)

ANNOUNCER (Marvin Miller): And now stay tuned for the program that has rated tops in popularity for a longer period of time than any other West Coast program in radio history, the Signal Oil program *The Whistler*.

THEME SONG: Up full then under...

ANNOUNCER: Signal, the famous go-farther gasoline invites you to sit back and enjoy another strange story by the Whistler.

THEME SONG WHISTLE: Up full then under...

WHISTLER: I am the Whistler and I know many strange things for I walk by night. I know many strange tales hidden in the hearts of men and women who have slipped into the shadows. Yes, I know the nameless terrors of which they dare not speak.

THEME MUSIC: Up full then under...

ANNOUNCER: And now for the Signal Oil Company, the Whistler's strange story, "Curiosity Killed the Cat." [The Whistler would then begin the story: here about a man and a woman who plot to kill a miserly old sea captain for his mysterious treasure chest.]

CLOSE (later)

ANNOUNCER: As you know, Signal dealers are independent dealers. That means each Signal dealer has invested his own money in his own business. So naturally, being a small businessman, he knows what's made America great. He is a strong believer in America, the kind of citizen you can be proud to do business with. Each Signal dealer realizes that his income and success depend upon pleasing you so well you'll want to deal with him regularly. That's why your Signal dealer tries to give you such thorough, such conscientious service. If all this adds up to the kind of serviceman you'd like to have looking after your car, then here's a suggestion. Stop at the Signal dealer nearest you and exchange some little friendly words, such as how you enjoy this radio program, or the chuckle you get out of the cartoons on Signal billboards, or even the weather. You'll be getting better acquainted with a good fellow American who's in business there to serve you.

THEME MUSIC: Up full then under...

ANNOUNCER: Featured in tonight's cast were Bill Forman as the Whistler, Lamont Johnson, Peggy Webber and Charles Seel. *The Whistler* was produced by George W. Allen with story by Jack Kelsey. Music by Wilbur Hatch. It was transmitted overseas by the Armed Forces Radio Service. *The Whistler* is entirely fictional and all characters portrayed on *The Whistler* are also fictional. Any similarity of names or resemblances to persons living or dead is purely coincidental. Remember to tune in at this same time next Sunday when the Signal Oil Company will bring you another strange story by the Whistler entitled "Christmas Gift," in which a nice girl pays a high price for a simple mistake and then receives an unexpected Christmas gift. Marvin Miller speaking for the Signal Oil Company. Stay tuned now for *Our Miss Brooks*, which follows immediately over most of these stations. This is the CBS Radio Network.

THEME MUSIC: Up full then out.

Note: Lever Brothers sponsored the West Coast series in 1954 (to 1955) when Signal Oil dropped sponsorship. Gale Gordon played the Whistler in the audition episode. The national version is a bit confusing to sort out. Although broadcast to all parts of the country, the East and West Coast versions had different casts for the same story. Bill Forman was the Whistler in West Coast episodes for Signal Oil; Everett Clarke was the Whistler in East Coast episodes for Household Finance. As stated in the closings that were used, George W. Allen was the director—but only for the West Coast. William N. Robson directed the East Coast shows. Marvin Miller announced the West Coast shows while Donald Rickles or Bob Venable did the announcing on the East Coast shows.

434. Whitehall 1212

Crime stories based on items found in London's Black Museum. Sustaining. NBC, 1951–1952. James Davidson, the host, was played by Harvey Hayes. See also *The Black Museum*.

OPEN

VOICE: This is Scotland Yard.

THEME MUSIC: Up full then under...

ANNOUNCER: For the first time in history, Scotland Yard opens its secret files to bring you the true authentic stories of some of its most baffling cases.

VOICE: These are the true stories, the unvarnished facts, just as they occurred, reenacted

for you by an all British cast. Only the names of the participants have, for obvious reasons, been changed. The stories are presented with the full cooperation of Scotland Yard.

ANNOUNCER: Research on *Whitehall 1212* has been prepared by Perry Hoskins, chief crime reporter for the London *Daily Express*. The stories for radio are written and directed by Wyllis Cooper.

THEME MUSIC: Up full then under...

ANNOUNCER: New Scotland Yard, the London headquarters of the Metropolitan Police, is situated near the Embankment on Whitehall; part by Ten Downing Street and almost in the shadow of Big Ben. Here also is the headquarters of the CID, the Criminal Investigation Department, the body of men whose exploits for more than a hundred years have made the name Scotland Yard synonymous with brilliant detection of crime and unrelenting pursuit of the criminal. On the lower ground floor of New Scotland Yard is the famous Black Museum whose present custodian is Chief Superintendent James Davidson, a Scotland Yard veteran.

DAVIDSON: Good afternoon. This Black Museum of ours is rather unique. Everything in it was at one time connected with the successful solution of a crime. We possess an imposing collection of lethal weapons here, each carefully documented to indicate its origin... [Davidson would then pick up an item and relate a case based on it.]

CLOSE

THEME MUSIC: Up full then under...

ANNOUNCER: You have just heard an authentic story from the files of Scotland Yard on *Whitehall 1212*. Research is prepared by Percy Hoskins, chief crime reporter for the London *Daily Express*. The stories for radio are written and directed by Wyllis Cooper. Harvey Hayes is heard as James Davidson.

THEME MUSIC: Up full then out.

ANNOUNCER: Three chimes mean good times on NBC. Today, *The Silent Men* stars Douglas Fairbanks in a story called "The Enemy," another authentic case based on government files. Then *The Big Show* features Bob and Ray, Jack Carson, Vera Lynn and your glamorous hostess Tallulah Bankhead, with

Meredith Willson directing the orchestra and chorus. Tomorrow night and every weekday evening, Robert Montgomery brings you something different in news analysis as he presents *A Citizen Views the News*. *The Silent Men, The Big Show, A Citizen Views the News*. Yes, you can hear all three on NBC.

435. Wild Bill Hickok

Western adventure about Marshal James Butler "Wild Bill" Hickok and his sidekick, Deputy Jingles P. Jones. Various sponsors. Mutual, 1951–1956. Guy Madison played Wild Bill Hickok with Andy Devine as Jingles. Bill's horse was named Buckshot; Jingles had a horse named Joker. Based on the television series.

OPEN

THEME MUSIC ("Will Bill Hickok"): Up full then under…
ANNOUNCER (Charles Lyon): *Wild Bill Hickok*, adventures in the Old West, starring Guy Madison as Wild Bill Hickok and Andy Devine as Jingles.
CHORUS:
> Wild Bill Hickok,
> Wild Bill Hickok.
> Ride on, ride on,
> Wild Bill.

ANNOUNCER: And now the adventures of *Wild Bill Hickok* and Jingles in another exciting story of the Old West.
THEME MUSIC: Up full then out.

CLOSE

BILL (after completing an assignment): Let's go Buckshot.
JINGLES: Hey Wild Bill, wait for meeeee!
CHORUS:
> Wild Bill Hickok,
> Wild Bill Hickok.
> Ride on, ride on
> Wild Bill.
> When Bill guided those settlers west
> He made those wagons roll.
> Over hills and plains he led
> The Wagons to their goal.

> Ride on, ride on Wild Bill,
> Wild Bill Hickok, ride on.

ANNOUNCER: You have just heard another adventure in the exciting life of frontier marshal Wild Bill Hickok with Andy Devine as Jingles. Be sure to see *Wild Bill Hickok* on television. Check newspaper for time and channel in your area. This is Charles Lyon speaking. This is Mutual.
THEME MUSIC: Up full then fade out.

436. The Witch's Tale

Chilling stories related by Old Nancy, an elderly witch, and her wise black cat, Satan. Sustaining. Local N.Y. (1931–1934), Mutual (1934–1938). Adelaide Fitz-Allen, Miriam Wolfe and Martha Wentworth played Old Nancy. "Orgy of Spirits" by Alexander Ilyinski was used as the theme.

OPEN (early)

SOUND: Howling winds, bells chiming.
ANNOUNCER: *The Witch's Tale*. The fascination of the eerie, weird, blood-chilling tales told by Old Nancy, the witch of Salem, and Satan, her wise black cat. They're waiting, waiting for you.
NANCY: A hundred and twenty-two year old I be today, yes sir, a hundred and twenty-two year old. Satan, tell the folks to douse all lights so we can get down to business.
SOUND: Satan meows.
NANCY: Nice and dark and cheery now, just the way we like it when we tell you our bedtime stories… [Nancy would then begin the show with a story.]

CLOSE (early)

SOUND: Howling winds.
THEME MUSIC: Up full then under…
ANNOUNCER: *The Witch's Tale* with Old Nancy and her wise black cat, Satan, will be with you again next Thursday.
THEME MUSIC: Up full then out.

OPEN (later)

THEME MUSIC: Up full then under…

ANNOUNCER: We bring you *The Witch's Tale*, written and produced by Alonzo Deen Cole. And now let us join Old Nancy, witch of Salem, and Satan, her wise black cat.

THEME MUSIC: Up full then under. [Old Nancy would then begin the show with her story.]

CLOSE (later)

THEME MUSIC: Up full then under...

ANNOUNCER: *The Witch's Tale*, written, produced and directed by Alonzo Deen Cole, will return next Monday at this same time.

THEME MUSIC: Up full then out.

437. The Wizard of Oz

Adventure serial based on the book by L. Frank Baum about Kansas girl Dorothy Gale (Nancy Kelly) and her experiences in the Land of Oz. Sustaining. CBS, 1933–1934.

OPEN

THEME MUSIC: Up full then under...

ANNOUNCER: *The Wizard of Oz*. The great gates of Oz swing open. Come one, come all, down the yellow road to the Emerald City with the weird and scary creatures of Oz.

THEME MUSIC: Up full then under... (as the story begins).

CLOSE

THEME MUSIC: Up full then under...

ANNOUNCER: And so Dorothy has started off on her long, adventurous journey to see the Wizard of Oz in Emerald City. Strange and wonderful are the sights in Oz and some of its magic is terrible indeed. But Dorothy is protected. She has the Good Witch's kiss and the silver shoes and a basket which will always be filled. *The Wizard of Oz*, written and directed by John L. Coon, will come to you again tomorrow at this same time. And now, there goes Dorothy and her new friends, marching away to the music of Charles Paul and his Munchkin Music Men. And so good night. This is the Columbia Broadcasting System.

THEME MUSIC: Up full then fade out.

438. The World Adventurers' Club

Stories of adventure related by members of the World Adventurers' Club. Sustaining. Syn., 1932.

OPEN

THEME MUSIC: Up full then under...

ANNOUNCER: *The World Adventurers' Club* is on the air. Once again we welcome you to our luxurious lounge where members of this famous club meet periodically to relate tales of valor and mystery in places remote and strange. Grab your chairs and prepare to hear another unusual story of *The World Adventurers' Club*.

THEME MUSIC: Up full then out.

CLOSE

THEME MUSIC: Up full then under...

ANNOUNCER: And so concludes another strange tale of *The World Adventurers' Club*. Don't fail to listen in on the next meeting of this famous group when you will hear an equally strange story of a strange land.

THEME MUSIC: Up full then out.

439. X Minus One

Science-fiction dramas adapted from the pages of *Galaxy* magazine. Various sponsors. NBC, 1955–1958.

OPEN

THEME MUSIC: Up full then under...

VOICE: Count down for blast-off. X minus five ... four ... three ... two ... X minus one! Fire!

SOUND: Rocket ship blasting off.

ANNOUNCER (Fred Collins): From the far horizons of the unknown come transcribed tales of new dimensions in time and space. These are stories of the future, adventures in which you'll live in a million could-be years on a thousand may-be worlds. The National Broadcasting Company in cooperation with *Galaxy* science-fiction magazine presents—

ECHO EFFECT: X-x-x-x-x-x Minus-minus-minus-minus One-one-one-one.
THEME MUSIC: Up full then out. [The episode would then begin.]

CLOSE

THEME MUSIC: Up full then under...
ANNOUNCER: Tonight by transcription, the National Broadcasting Company in cooperation with *Galaxy* science-fiction magazine, has presented *X Minus One*. Your announcer, Fred Collins. *X Minus One* is an NBC Network Radio production.
THEME MUSIC: Up full then out.
SOUND: NBC chimes. N-B-C.

440. You Bet Your Life

Comical game in which contestants, interviewed by comedian Groucho Marx, attempt to answer questions for money. Sponsored by Elgin and DeSoto-Plymouth. ABC (1947–1949), CBS (1949–1950), NBC (1950–1956). Basis for the television series. The song "Hooray for Captain Spaulding" was used as the theme.

OPEN

THEME MUSIC: Up full then under...
ANNOUNCER (George Fenneman): Ladies and gentlemen, the secret word for tonight is head, h-e-a-d.
GROUCHO: Really?
ANNOUNCER: You bet your life! Elgin American, creators of America's most beautiful compacts, smartest cigarette cases, and finest dresser sets, presents Groucho Marx in the Elgin American show *You Bet Your Life*, the comedy-quiz series produced and transcribed in Hollywood. And here's that sterling Elgin American, the one, the only—
AUDIENCE: Groucho!
GROUCHO: Welcome to Elgin American compacts, Mr. Marx. Oh, that's me, Groucho Marx.
SOUND: Audience applause.
GROUCHO: Thank you, thank you. Tonight we have $1,000 for one of our couples... [Groucho would then interview the first couple.]

CLOSE

THEME MUSIC: Up full then under...
ANNOUNCER: The Elgin American show *You Bet Your Life* is a John Guedel production, transcribed from Hollywood, directed by Bob Dwan and Bernie Smith. Music by Jerry Fielding. Remember, next week's big question pays $1,500. Be sure to tune in next Wednesday night at this time for *You Bet Your Life* starring Groucho Marx, presented by the makers of America's most beautiful compacts, smartest cigarette cases and finest dresser sets. This is ABC, the American Broadcasting Company.
THEME MUSIC: Up full then out.

441. Young Dr. Malone

Daily serial about Dr. Jerry Malone and his wife, Anne, residents of the town of Three Oaks. Sponsored by Bran Flakes, General Foods and Procter and Gamble. Blue (1939–1940), CBS (1940–1942; 1943–1960), NBC (1942–1943). Alan Bunce, Carl Frank, Charles Irving and Sandy Becker played Jerry Malone with Elizabeth Reller and Barbara Weeks as Anne Malone. "Prelude in D" by W. Intersteen was used as the theme.

OPEN

SPONSOR'S THEME ("Crisco"): Up full then under...
MALE SINGER: C-R-I-S-C-O.
ANNOUNCER (Ron Rawson): It's Crisco's *Young Dr. Malone*.
SERIES THEME MUSIC: Up full then under...
ANNOUNCER: You are about to hear a page in the life of Anne Malone and her husband Jerry. Written by Julian Faunt. We'll return to the Malones in just a moment.
SPOKESMAN (Tom Ball): Have you been baking any pies lately, ladies? Try making a pie with Crisco and Crisco's pastry method. You'll get tender, flaky pie crusts every time the Crisco way. Even a beginner can turn out tender, flaky pie crusts with Crisco and the pastry method printed on the Crisco label. Crisco is pure and all vegetable, digestible itself. For tender, flaky pies, try Crisco, it's digestible.

THEME MUSIC: Up full then under...

ANNOUNCER: And now to our story of *Young Dr. Malone.*

CLOSE

THEME MUSIC: Up full then under...

ANNOUNCER: Listen again tomorrow to *Young Dr. Malone* and all the other Three Oaks people who are brought to you by pure all vegetable Crisco. Now this is Ron Rawson reminding you—

SONG:

> They're cookin' with Crisco
> From New York to Frisco.
> Cakes are so light,
> Fried foods digestible.
> With Crisco they're right
> So keep on cookin'
> With Cris-co.

SPONSOR'S THEME: Up full then out.

ANNOUNCER: This is CBS, the Columbia Broadcasting System.

442. Young Widder Brown

Daily serial about Ellen Brown, a widow and owner of a tea shop in Simpsonville. Various sponsors. NBC, 1938–1956. Florence Freeman and Wendy Drew played Ellen Brown. The songs "In the Gloaming" and "Wonderful One" were used as the theme.

OPEN

THEME MUSIC: Up full then under...

ANNOUNCER (George Ansboro): Time now for *Young Widder Brown.*

THEME MUSIC: Up full then under...

ANNOUNCER: The makers of Bayer Aspirin bring you *Young Widder Brown,* the story of the age-old conflict between a mother's duty and a woman's heart.

THEME MUSIC: Up full then out.

CLOSE

THEME MUSIC: Up full then under...

ANNOUNCER: Be with us again tomorrow when Bayer Aspirin will again present *Young Widder Brown.* Florence Freeman is heard as Ellen. *Young Widder Brown* is produced by

Frank and Anne Hummert with organ music by John Winters. George Ansboro speaking.

THEME MUSIC: Up full then out.

ANNOUNCER: This is NBC, the National Broadcasting Company.

SOUND: NBC chimes. N-B-C.

443. Your Hit Parade

Variety series that counted down the top songs of the week as determined by record and sheet music sales, songs played on the radio and songs played in juke boxes. Sponsored by Lucky Strike Cigarettes. NBC (1935–1936; 1947–1953), CBS (1936–1947). Frank Sinatra was a regular host from 1943 to 1945 and 1947 to 1949. Guests hosted at other times. Axel Stordah and his orchestra appeared when Frank was the host. Other orchestras were those conducted by Al Goodman, Johnny Green, Lennie Hayton, Richard Himber, Carl Hoff, Leo Reisman, Freddie Rich, Raymond Scott, Harry Sosnik and Orrin Tucker. Announcers were Andre Baruch, Martin Block, Kenny Delmar, Basil Ruysdael and Del Sharbutt.

OPEN

ANNOUNCER (Del Sharbutt): *Your Hit Parade* starring Frank Sinatra. Presented by Lucky Strike. For your own real deep smoking enjoyment remember—

VOICE: L.S.M.F.T.

ANNOUNCER: Lucky Strike means fine tobacco. And in a cigarette, it's the tobacco that counts.

VOICE: So smoke that smoke of fine tobacco, Lucky Strike, so round, so firm, so fully packed. So free and easy on the draw.

THEME MUSIC ("Lucky Day"): Up full then under...

ANNOUNCER: Lucky Strike presents *Your Hit Parade* with Axel Stordahl, the Lucky Strike Orchestra, Beryl Vaughn, Ken Lane and the Hit Paraders and starring Frank Sinatra.

SOUND: Audience applause and girls screaming... (after which Frank begins the show with a song).

CLOSE

ANNOUNCER: Men who know tobacco best, it's Lucky Strike two-to-one.

SOUND: Telegraph keys.

VOICE: L.S.M.F.T. L.S.M.F.T.

ANNOUNCER: You said it, Lucky Strikes means fine tobacco, so round, so firm, so fully packed, so free and easy on the draw. Lucky Strike has presented *Your Hit Parade* starring Frank Sinatra, with Beryl Vaughn, Ken Lane, Axel Stordahl and the Lucky Strike Orchestra. Be with us again next week when Lucky Strike presents *Your Hit Parade*. This is CBS, the Columbia Broadcasting System.

THEME MUSIC: Up full then out.

444. Yours Truly, Johnny Dollar

Crime Drama about Johnny Dollar, a high-priced insurance investigator. Mostly sustaining (Wrigley's Chewing Gum, 1953–54, and Philip Morris cigarettes, 1961, were sponsors). CBS, 1949–1962. Johnny Dollar was played by: Dick Powell (audition, December 4, 1948), Charles Russell (1949–1950), Edmond O'Brien (1950–1952), John Lund (1952–1954), Gerald Mohr (1954 audition), Bob Bailey (1955–1960), Bob Readick (1960–1961) and Mandel Kramer (1961–1962).

OPEN (Dick Powell)

THEME MUSIC: Up full then under...

ANNOUNCER: The Columbia Broadcasting System presents a thrilling new series starring Dick Powell.

THEME MUSIC: Up full then under...

VOICE: I'm an insurance investigator. My name is Johnny Dollar.

VOICE: What?

JOHNNY: You heard me, Johnny Dollar and I can pad an expense account with the best of them. Yup, I'm a freelance insurance investigator and I live in Hartford, Connecticut; at least that's where I pay rent. My work sees to it that I live anywhere except at home. At insurance investigations I'm an expert; at making out my expense account, I'm an absolute genius.

THEME MUSIC: Up full then under...

JOHNNY: Expense account submitted by investigator Johnny Dollar to home office, East Coast Underwriters, Terminal Building, Hartford, Connecticut. The following is an accounting of my expenditures in the investigation of Milford Brooks III for your company... (the story would then begin).

CLOSE (Dick Powell)

ANNOUNCER: And so with the final signature on his expense account, Dick Powell as Johnny Dollar has just closed the book on his first adventure in this new CBS series. Be sure to tune in again next week when the expense account covers special investigation Singapore— another unusual adventure starring Dick Powell in—

JOHNNY: *Yours Truly, Johnny Dollar.*

THEME MUSIC: Up full then under...

ANNOUNCER: This is CBS, the Columbia Broadcasting System.

OPEN (Charles Russell)

THEME MUSIC: Up full then under...

ANNOUNCER: This is another in the adventures of America's fabulous freelance insurance investigator, Johnny Dollar, starring Charles Russell. At insurance investigation, Johnny Dollar is only an expert; at making out his expense account, he's an absolute genius.

THEME MUSIC: Up full then under...

JOHNNY: Expense account submitted by special investigator Johnny Dollar to West Coast Underwriters, San Francisco branch. The following is an accounting of expenditures during my investigation of "The Little Man Who Wasn't There" or "The Unpaid Premium Payoff" (the story would then begin).

CLOSE (Charles Russell)

JOHNNY: Expense account total $942.08. Signed, Yours Truly, Johnny Dollar.

THEME MUSIC: Up full then under...

ANNOUNCER: *Yours Truly, Johnny Dollar* stars Charles Russell. Be sure to be with us again at this same time next week when another unusual expense account is handed in by—

JOHNNY: *Yours Truly, Johnny Dollar.*

THEME MUSIC: Up full then under...

ANNOUNCER: Stay tuned for *Vaughn Monroe and His Caravan* which follows immediately on most of these CBS stations. This is CBS, the Columbia Broadcasting System.

OPEN (Edmond O'Brien)

ANNOUNCER: And now from Hollywood, it's time for Edmond O'Brien as—
SOUND: Phone rings; receiver being pick up.
VOICE: Johnny Dollar.
THEME MUSIC: Up full then under...
ANNOUNCER: Edmond O'Brien in another adventure of the man with the action-packed expense account, America's fabulous freelance insurance investigator—
JOHNNY: *Yours Truly, Johnny Dollar.*
THEME MUSIC: Up full then under...
JOHNNY: Expense account submitted by special investigator Johnny Dollar to home office, Cosmopolitan All Risk Insurance Company. The following is an account of expenditures during my investigation of "The Hartford Alliance Matter" (the story would then begin).

CLOSE (Edmond O'Brien)

JOHNNY: Expense account total $180. Yours Truly, Johnny Dollar.
THEME MUSIC: Up full then under...
ANNOUNCER: *Yours Truly, Johnny Dollar* stars Edmond O'Brien in the title role. Edmond O'Brien can currently be seen in the Columbia Pictures production of *711 Ocean Drive.*
THEME MUSIC: Up full then under...
ANNOUNCER: There'll be a new adventure with *Philip Marlowe,* Raymond Chandler's famous private eye on most of these same CBS stations this Friday night. This is CBS, the Columbia Broadcasting System.

OPEN (John Lund)

ANNOUNCER: Wrigley's Spearmint Chewing Gum, the refreshing, delicious treat that gives you chewing enjoyment, presents for your listening enjoyment, John Lund as—
SOUND: Phone rings; receiver being picked up.
VOICE: Johnny Dollar.
THEME MUSIC: Up full then under...
ANNOUNCER: The makers of Wrigley's Spearmint Chewing Gum bring you John Lund in a transcribed adventure of the man with the action-packed expense account,

America's fabulous freelance insurance investigator—
JOHNNY: *Yours Truly, Johnny Dollar.*
THEME MUSIC: Up full then out.
ANNOUNCER: Wrigley's Spearmint Chewing Gum refreshes you, gives you real chewing enjoyment. Yes, for chewing enjoyment plus refreshment, it's Wrigley's Spearmint Chewing Gum. Healthful, refreshing, delicious.
THEME MUSIC: Up full then under...
JOHNNY: Expense account submitted by special investigator Johnny Dollar to Home Office, Hemispheric Life Insurance Company, Hartford, Connecticut. The following is an accounting of my expenditures during my investigation of "The Enoch Arden Matter" (the story would then begin).

CLOSE (John Lund)

JOHNNY: Total expenditures, $1,879.80. Yours Truly, Johnny Dollar.
THEME MUSIC: Up full then under...
ANNOUNCER: *Yours Truly, Johnny Dollar,* brought to you by Wrigley's Spearmint Chewing Gum, stars John Lund in the title role. *Yours Truly, Johnny Dollar* was transcribed in Hollywood. The makers of Wrigley's Spearmint Chewing Gum hope you enjoyed tonight's story of *Johnny Dollar* and that you're enjoying delicious Wrigley's Spearmint Gum everyday. This is Charles Lyon inviting you to join us again next week at this same time when from Hollywood, John Lund returns as—
JOHNNY: *Yours Truly, Johnny Dollar.*
THEME MUSIC: Up full then fade out.

OPEN (Bob Bailey)

ANNOUNCER: From Hollywood, it's time now for—
SOUND: Phone rings; receiver being picked up.
VOICE: Johnny Dollar.
THEME MUSIC: Up full then under...
ANNOUNCER: Tonight and every weekday night, Bob Bailey in the transcribed adventures of the man with the action-packed expense account, America's favorite freelance insurance investigator—
JOHNNY: *Yours Truly, Johnny Dollar.*
THEME MUSIC: Up full then under...

JOHNNY: Expense account submitted by special investigator Johnny Dollar to the Inner Allied Insurance Company, Hartford, Connecticut. Following is an account of expenditures of my investigation of "The Curse of Kamashet Matter" (the story would then begin).

CLOSE (Bob Bailey)

JOHNNY: Expense account total $985. Yours Truly, Johnny Dollar.

THEME MUSIC: Up full then under…

ANNOUNCER: *Yours Truly, Johnny Dollar* starring Bob Bailey is transcribed in Hollywood. Be sure to join us on Monday night, same time, same station for another exciting story of *Yours Truly, Johnny Dollar.* Roy Rowan speaking.

THEME MUSIC: Up full then fade out.

OPEN (Bob Readick)

THEME MUSIC: Up full then under…

ANNOUNCER: CBS Radio brings you Bob Readick in the exciting adventures of the man with the action-packed expense account, America's fabulous freelance insurance investigator—

JOHNNY: *Yours Truly, Johnny Dollar.*

THEME MUSIC: Up full then under…

JOHNNY: Expense account submitted by special investigator Johnny Dollar to the Continental Insurance Company, Boston office. Following is an account of expenses incurred during my investigation of "The Paperback Mystery Matter" (the story would then begin).

CLOSE (Bob Readick)

CHORUS:
Welcome aboard, welcome aboard,
The cleaner the tobacco,
The better it tastes,
Have a Commodore and see.

ANNOUNCER: Try new king size Philip Morris Commodores, made on a new machine, the Mach 8, that takes full, rich tobacco and gently vacuum cleans it—and the cleaner the tobacco, the better it tastes; noticeably better.

CHORUS: Have a Commodore, welcome aboard.

JOHNNY (after summing up the case): Expense account total, seventy bucks. Yours Truly, Johnny Dollar.

THEME MUSIC: Up full then under…

ANNOUNCER: *Yours Truly, Johnny Dollar* stars Bob Readick. Be sure to join us next week, same time and station for another exciting story of *Yours Truly, Johnny Dollar.* This is Art Harris speaking.

THEME MUSIC: Up full then fade out.

OPEN (Mandel Kramer)

ANNOUNCER: The CBS Radio Network brings you Mandel Kramer in the exciting adventures of the man with the action-packed expense account. America's fabulous freelance insurance investigator—

JOHNNY: *Yours Truly, Johnny Dollar.*

THEME MUSIC: Up full then under…

JOHNNY: Expense account submitted by special investigator Johnny Dollar to the Trinity Mutual Insurance Company, Hartford, Connecticut. Following is an account of the expenses incurred during my investigation of "The Phony Phone Matter" (the story would then begin).

CLOSE (Mandel Kramer)

THEME MUSIC: Up full then under…

ANNOUNCER: The CBS Radio Network has presented Mandel Kramer as the star of *Yours Truly, Johnny Dollar.* Be sure to join us next Sunday evening when we will bring you another adventure of the man with the unusual expense account on *Yours Truly, Johnny Dollar.* This is CBS, the Columbia Broadcasting System.

THEME MUSIC: Up full then fade out.

Appendix A: Sponsors and Programs

See the program mentioned for further information

Adler Elevator Shoes—*Henry Morgan Show*
Alka Seltzer—*Lum and Abner; Quiz Kids*
All Sweet Margarine—*Meet the Meeks*
American Hocking Glass—*Flashgun Casey*
American Home Products—*Our Miss Brooks*
American Razor—*Walter Winchell Journal*
Anacin—*The Big Show; Dean Martin and Jerry Lewis Show; Front Page Farrell; Just Plain Bill; Our Gal Sunday*
Anahist—*Counterspy*
Arrid Deodorant—*Meet Millie*
Auto Lite—*Everything for the Boys; Suspense*
Bab-O Cleanser—*David Harum*
Baker's Coconut—*Wendy Warren and the News; When a Girl Marries*
Bayer Aspirin—*Big Town; Lorenzo Jones; Mark Sabre; Mr. Chameleon; Second Husband*
Beechnut Foods—*Chandu, the Magician*
Benefax Multi Vitamins—*Romance of Helen Trent*
Bisquick Biscuit Mix—*Valiant Lady*
Black Flag Insect Killer—*Just Plain Bill*
Blatz Beer—*Duffy's Tavern*
Blue Bonnett Margarine—*Fred Allen Show; One Man's Family*
Blue Coal—*The Shadow*

Bond Bread—*The Lone Ranger*
Borden Milk—*Happy Island*
Bran Flakes—*Young Dr. Malone*
Brylcream Hair Tonic—*FBI in Peace and War*
Bristol Myers—*Duffy's Tavern; Henry Morgan Show*
Bromo Quinine—*Sherlock Holmes*
Bromo Seltzer—*Inner Sanctum Mysteries; The Saint*
Buster Brown Shoes—*Buster Brown Show; Smilin' Ed and His Buster Brown Gang*
Calumet Baking Soda—*When a Girl Marries*
Camay Soap—*This Is Hollywood*
Camel Cigarettes—*Abbott & Costello Show; Blondie; Jimmy Durante Show; My Friend Irma; Mystery in the Air; Richard Diamond*
Campbell Soup Company—*Campbell Playhouse; Grand Central Station; Meet Corliss Archer; The Saint*
Canada Dry Ginger Ale—*Canada Dry Program; Information Please*
Carnation Evaporated Milk—*When a Girl Marries*
Carter's Liver Pills—*Call the Police; Inner Sanctum Mysteries*

Casmere Cold Creme—*Kay Fairchild, Stepmother*

Chase and Sanborn Coffee—*Chase and Sanborn Hour; One Man's Family*

Cheerios Cereal—*The Lone Ranger*

Chesterfield Cigarettes—*Big Show; Bob Hope Show; Dean Martin and Jerry Lewis Show; Dragnet; Gunsmoke*

Chevrolet—*Gangbusters*

Chicklets Gum—*Bobby Benson and the B-Bar-B Riders*

Chrysler-DeSoto Cars—*It Pays to Be Ignorant*

Clipper Craft Clothes—*Crime Cases of Warden Lawes; Sherlock Holmes*

Clorets Breath Mints—*Defense Attorney*

Coca-Cola—*Coke Club; Spike Jones Show*

Cocomalt—*Buck Rogers in the 25th Century*

Colgate—*Bachelor's Children; Can You Top This?; Colgate Sports Newsreel; The Goldbergs; Mel Blanc Show; Mr. and Mrs. North; Romance*

Colgate Dental Creme—*Judy Canova Show; Steve Allen Show*

Colgate-Palmolive Company—*A Day in the Life of Dennis Day; Inner Sanctum Mysteries; Our Miss Brooks*

Colgate Tooth Powder—*Judy Canova Show; Kay Fairchild, Stepmother*

Continental Can Company—*Continental Celebrity Club*

Cream of Wheat—*Buck Rogers in the 25th Century; Grand Central Station; Let's Pretend*

Cresta Blanca Wine—*This Is My Best*

Crisco Shortening—*Right to Happiness; Vic and Sade; Young Dr. Malone*

Cue Magazine—*Gangbusters*

Cystex (medicine)—*The Nebbs*

Dentine Gum—*Bobby Benson and the B-Bar-B Riders; Dean Martin and Jerry Lewis Show*

DeSoto-Plymouth Dealers—*You Bet Your Life*

Dial Soap—*Dial Dave Garroway*

Dodge Autos—*Roy Rogers Show*

Dreft Detergent—*Brighter Day; Life of Riley*

Drene Shampoo—*Truth or Consequences*

Dr. Lyon's Tooth Powder—*Mark Sabre; Pursuit; Second Husband*

DuPont—*Cavalcade of America*

DUZ Detergent—*Road of Life; Truth or Consequences*

Easy Cut Electric Lawn Mowers—*Rogue's Gallery*

Elgin Products—*You Bet Your Life*

Englander Company (Mattresses)—*We Who Dream*

Eno Effervescent Salts—*Eno Crime Clues*

Eversharp Products—*Let Yourself Go*

Ex Lax—*Secrets of Scotland Yard*

Fatima Cigarettes—*Dragnet; Tales of Fatima*

Fitch Shampoo—*Fitch Bandwagon; Rogue's Gallery; Vic and Sade*

Florida Treat—*Harry Richman Show*

Ford Motor Company—*Adventures of Philip Marlowe; A Date with Judy; Lum and Abner; Pursuit; The Saint*

Formula 9 Shampoo—*Modern Adventures of Casanova*

Frigidaire Appliances—*Lum and Abner*

Gaffers and Sadler Appliances—*Thirty Minutes in Hollywood*

Gaines Dog Food—*Baby Snooks Show*

Gallen Kamp Shoes—*Pat Novak for Hire*

Gem Razor Blades—*The Falcon*

General Electric—*Adventures of Ozzie and Harriet*

General Foods—*Baby Snooks Show; Buck Rogers in the 25th Century; Father Knows Best; The Goldbergs; Joyce Jordan, M.D.; My Favorite Husband; When a Girl Marries; Young Dr. Malone*

General Mills—*Curtain Time; Light of the World; Silver Eagle; Valiant Lady*

General Motors—*Man Called X*

George Washington Coffee—*Sherlock Holmes*

Gold Medal Four—*Valiant Lady*

Goodyear—*Defense Attorney*

Griffin Shoe Polish—*Time to Shine*

Groves Nose Drops—*Flash Gordon*

Gulf Oil—*Counterspy*

Half & Half Pipe Tobacco—*Leave It to Joan*

Hallmark Greeting Cards—*Charlotte Greenwood Show*

Halo Shampoo—*Judy Canova Show; Mr. and Mrs. North*

Hazel Bishop Cosmetics—*Lorenzo Jones*

Hearst Newspapers—*Flash Gordon; Jungle Jim*

Heinz Foods—*Adventures of Ozzie and Harriet; Information Please; A Life in Your Hands; The Thin Man*

Hinds Honey and Almond Creme—*Hinds Honey and Almond Creme Program*

Hostess Snack Cakes—*Bachelor's Children*

Household Finance—*Sherlock Holmes; The Whistler*

Ipana Toothpaste—*Abbott and Costello Show; Duffy's Tavern; Fred Allen Show; Town Hall Tonight*

International Silver—*Adventures of Ozzie and Harriet*

Ironized Yeast Tablets—*Big Town; A Helping Hand; Henry Morgan Show*

Jell-O Gelatin & Pudding—*Aldrich Family; Jell-O Program; My Favorite Husband*

Jergens Hand Lotion—*Nero Wolfe; Romance; Time for Love*

Johnson Wax—*Call the Police; Fibber McGee and Molly*

Kaiser-Frazier Cars—*Walter Winchell Journal*

Kellogg's Cereals—*Adventures of Superman; Buck Rogers in the 25th Century; Mark Trail; Singing Lady; Tom Corbett, Space Cadet*

Kirkman's Soap Flakes—*Can You Top This?*

Kix Cereal—*Curtain Time; Defense Attorney*

Knox Company—*Deadline Mystery*

Kraft Foods—*Archie Andrews; Bobby Benson and the B-Bar-B Riders; The Falcon; Great Gildersleeve*

Kroger's Baked Goods—*Mary Foster, The Editor's Daughter*

L&M Cigarettes—*Fort Laramie; Frontier Gentleman; Gunsmoke; Have Gun—Will Travel*

LaRosa Macaroni—*LaRosa Theater of Stars*

Lava Hand Soap—*FBI in Peace and War; Vic and Sade*

Lever Brothers—*Adventures of Philip Marlowe*

Lifebuoy Soap—*Big Town; Call the Police; Henry Morgan Show; Lifebuoy Show*

Linit Beauty Bath—*Linit Bathclub Revue*

Lipton Tea—*Arthur Godfrey's Talent Scouts; Inner Sanctum Mysteries*

Listerine Mouth Wash—*Billie Burke Show; Grand Central Station*

Lucky Strike Cigarettes—*Information Please; Jack Benny Program; Your Hit Parade*

Lustre Creme Shampoo—*Blondie; A Day in the Life of Dennis Day; Our Miss Brooks*

Lux Soap Flakes—*Broadway Is My Beat*

Majestic Radios—*Majestic Master of Mystery*

Mars Candies—*Can You Top This?; Curtain Time; Inner Sanctum Mysteries; People Are Funny*

Maxwell House Coffee—*Adventures of Topper; Maxwell House Coffee Time; Maxwell House Show Boat; Wendy Warren and the News*

Miles Laboratories—*Roy Rogers Show*

Milkbone Dog Biscuits—*Adventures of Rin Tin Tin*

Molle Shaving Creme—*Mark Sabre; Molle Mystery Theater; Pursuit*

Nabisco Cereal—*Adventures of Rin Tin Tin; Straight Arrow*

Nescafe Instant Coffee—*FBI in Peace and War*

Nestlé's Chocolate—*Space Patrol*

Norwich Pharmaceutical—*The Fat Man*

Noxzema Skin Creme—*Mayor of the Town*

Old Dutch Cleanser—*Bachelor's Children*

Old English Floor Wax—*Our Gal Sunday*

Old Gold Cigarettes—*Melody and Madness; Songs by Sinatra; Which Is Which?*

Ovaltine Drink Mix—*Captain Midnight; Little Orphan Annie*

Oxydol Detergent—*Everyman's Theater; The Goldbergs; Ma Perkins*

Pabst Blue Ribbon Beer—*Eddie Cantor Pabst Blue Ribbon Show; Life of Riley; Night Beat; The Thin Man*

Pacific Coast Borax Company—*Death Valley Days*

Pal Mall Cigarettes—*Henry Morgan Show*

Palmolive—*Blondie; Gangbusters; Judy Canova Show; Our Miss Brooks; Steve Allen Show*

Pearson Pharmaceutical—*Inner Sanctum Mysteries*

Pepsi-Cola—*Counterspy*

Pepsodent—*Adventures of Philip Marlowe; Amos 'n' Andy Show; The Goldbergs; Man Called X; Meet Corliss Archer; Mr. District Attorney; My Friend Irma*

Pepto Bismol—*The Fat Man*

Pet Milk—*Pet Milk Show*

Petri Wines—*Case Book of Gregory Hood; Sherlock Holmes*

Pharmacraft—*Counterspy*

Philco Electronics—*Philco Radio Time*

Philip Morris Cigarettes—*Flashgun Casey; Hogan's Daughter; I Love Lucy; It Pays to Be Ignorant; Johnny Desmond Follies; Milton Berle Show; Philip Morris Playhouse*

Phillips Milk of Magnesia—*Amanda of Honeymoon Hill; Lorenzo Jones; Mark Sabre; Stella Dallas*

Pillsbury—*Grand Central Station; Today's Children*

Popsicle—*Buck Rogers in the 25th Century*

Post Cereals—*Adventures of Topper; Baby Snooks Show; Father Knows Best; Gangbusters; Gunsmoke; Roy Rogers Show; The Thin Man*

Prell Shampoo—*Life of Riley*

Procter and Gamble—*Abie's Irish Rose; Big Sister; Joyce Jordan, M.D.; Lorenzo Jones; Right to Happiness; Road of Life; This Is Hollywood; Young Dr. Malone*

Prudential Life Insurance—*When a Girl Marries*

Quaker Oats—*Lum and Abner; Roy Rogers Show; Sergeant Preston of the Yukon; That Brewster Boy; Those Websters*

Raleigh Cigarettes—*A Life in Your Hands; People Are Funny; Raleigh Room*

Ralston Cereals—*Space Patrol; Tom Mix Ralston Straight Shooters*

RCA Victor—*Big Show; Magic Key of RCA; Manhattan Merry-Go-Round; Private Files of Rex Saunders*

Reader's Digest—*Secrets of Scotland Yard*

Red Heart Dog Food—*Lassie*

Revere Cameras—*A Date with Judy*

Rexall Drugs—*Amos 'n' Andy Show; Jimmy Durante-Garry Moore Show; Jimmy Durante Show; Phil Harris-Alice Faye Show; Richard Diamond, Private Detective*

Rinso Detergent—*Amos 'n' Andy Show; Big Sister; Big Town; Call the Police; Grand Central Station; Mayor of the Town*

Rio Grande Oil—*Calling All Cars*

Rise Shaving Creme—*Meet Millie*

Roi-Tan Cigars—*Leave It to Joan*

Roma Wines—*Suspense*

Ronson Lighters—*Johnny Desmond Follies*

Royal Gelatins and Puddings—*One Man's Family; The Open Door; Royal Gelatin Hour*

Sal Hepatica Mouth Wash—*Abbott and Costello Show; A Date with Judy; Fred Allen Show; Town Hall Tonight*

Sanka Coffee—*Duffy's Tavern*

Schick Razor Blades—*Duffy's Tavern*

Schlitz Beer—*Halls of Ivy*

Schutter Candy—*Counterspy*

7-Up—*Fresh Up Show*

Shell Gasoline—*Henry Morgan Show*

Signal Oil Company—*The Whistler*

Silvercup Bread—*The Lone Ranger*

Sloane's Liniment—*Gangbusters*

Spry Shortening—*Aunt Jenny's Thrilling Real Life Stories*

Standard Oil Company—*Flywheel, Shyster and Flywheel*

Super Suds—*Blondie; Judy Canova Show*

Swan Soap—*Joan Davis Show*

Sweetheart Soap—*Backstage Wife; Strange Romance of Evelyn Winters*

Swift and Company—*Archie Andrews; Meet the Meeks*

Teel Dentifrice—*Life of Riley*

Tender Leaf Tea—*Fred Allen Show; One Man's Family*

Tetley Tea—*Stella Dallas*

Texaco—*The Fire Chief; Jumbo Fire Chief; Texaco Star Theater; Texaco Town*

Toni Home Permanents—*Flashgun Casey; Grand Central Station; Meet Corliss Archer; One Man's Family; Our Miss Brooks; People Are Funny*

Treasury Department—*Guest Star*

Tums Anacid—*Me and Janie; Mr. and Mrs. Blandings*

TWA (Trans World Airlines)—*Mr. and Mrs. Blandings*

U.S. Steel—*Theater Guild on the Air*

Vaseline Petroleum Jelly—*Dr. Christian*

Vitalis Hair Tonic—*Mr. District Attorney*

Vitamin Consumer Service—*Secrets of Scotland Yard*

Wesson Oil—*One Man's Family*

Wheatena—*Popeye the Sailor*

Wheaties Cereal—*Armstrong of the S.B.I.; Jack Armstrong, the All-American Boy; Night Beat; Sara's Private Caper*

White King Soap—*Chandu, the Magician*

Wild Root Creme Oil—*Adventures of Sam Spade; Dark Venture*

Wonder Bread—*Bachelor's Children; Renfrew of the Mounted*

Woodbury Facial Soap—*Mr. and Mrs. North*

Wrigley's Spearmint Gum—*Broadway Is My Beat; Life with Luigi; Mr. Chameleon; Pursuit; Rogers of the Gazette; Romance, Yours Truly, Johnny Dollar*

Appendix B: Product Slogans and Jingles

Auto Lite Car Products

ANNOUNCER: Remember, you're always right with Auto Lite.

Barbasol Shaving Creme

MALE VOCALIST: Barbasol.
CHORUS: Barbasol.
MALE VOCALIST:
The brushless shaving creme,
Leaves your face so smooth and clean.

Buster Brown Shoes

SOUND: Dog barking.
BUSTER BROWN: That's my dog Tige, he lives in a shoe. I'm Buster Brown, look for me in there too.

Chase and Sanborn Coffee

ANNOUNCER: The superb blend of the world's choicest coffees, which is so reasonably priced.

Chesterfield Cigarettes

ANNOUNCER: Chesterfield packs more pleasure because it's more perfectly packed.
CHESTERFIELD SONG:
Smoke dreams
From smoke rings
While a Chesterfield burns.

Colgate Tooth Powder

SONG:
Don't take a chance
With your romance
Use Colgate Tooth Powder.

Cresta Blanca Wine

ANNOUNCER: Whenever you dine, dine with wine and make it the best wine. C-R-E-S-T-A ... B-L-A-N-C-A ... Cresta ... Blanca, Cresta Blanca.

Crisco Shortening

ANNOUNCER:
Keep on cooking with Crisco.

It's all vegetable.
It's digestible.

Dial Soap

ANNOUNCER: Dial, the soap that stops odor before it starts.

Dreft Detergent

ANNOUNCER: Don't get left, use Dreft.

DuPont

1940S SLOGAN: Makers of better living through chemistry.
1950S SLOGAN: The DuPont Company, makers of better things for better living through chemistry.

DUZ Detergent

SONG:
> Put DUZ in your washing machine
> Take clothes out bright and clean.
> When you DUZ your wash
> You'll sing
> DUZ does everything.

Eversharp Pens

SLOGAN: The pen that's guaranteed not for years, not for life, but guaranteed forever.
SONG:
> Buy Eversharp, buy Eversharp
> For writing pleasure.
> Buy Eversharp, buy Eversharp,
> They'll be forever.

Fitch Shampoo

SONG:
> Don't despair;
> Use your head,
> Save your hair,
> Use Fitch Shampoo.

Gallen Kamp Shoes

SONG:
> Cinderella lost a shoe

And so she got a mate.
With lovely shoes
A girl can't lose
In Gallen Kamps she'll rate.

Gem Razor Blades

ANNOUNCER: Avoid five o'clock shadow.
VOICE: Use Gem Blades, use Gem Blades, use Gem Blades.

General Mills

ANNOUNCER: General Mills, creators of new foods and new ideas for a better world.

Gillette Razor Blades

Announcer: Look sharp, feel sharp, use Gillette Razor Blades.

Hallmark Cards

EARLY SLOGAN: A Hallmark card will best express your perfect tastes, your thoughtfulness.
LATER SLOGAN: Hallmark, when you care enough to send the very bet.

Halo Shampoo

SONG:
> Halo, everybody, Halo.
> Halo is the shampoo
> That glorifies your hair.
> Halo everybody, Halo,
> So Halo Shampoo, Halo.

International Silver

ANNOUNCER: The silver with the beauty that lasts forever.

Ivory Soap

ANNOUNCER: Ivory Soap, ninety-nine and forty-four one hundredths percent pure. It floats.

Jell-O

SLOGAN: Jell-O Puddings, real old-fashioned puddings made a new-fashioned way.

SONG:

>Oh the big red letters
>Stand for the Jell-O family.
>That's Jell-O, yum, yum, yum,
>Jell-O Puddings, yum, yum, yum.
>Jell-O Tapioca Puddings,
>Yes sir-reeeee.

Kaiser-Frazier Cars

ANNOUNCER: Kaiser-Frazier, builders of cars that make history.

Kroger's Baked Goods

SONG:

>Kroger's, Kroger's, Kroger's
>Everything from bread to cake
>It's better if it's
>Kroger baked.
>Kroger's, Kroger's, Kroger's.

L&M Cigarettes

ANNOUNCER: L&M is best, stand out from all the rest.

Lucky Strike Cigarettes

SLOGAN: L.S.M.F.T., Lucky Strike means fine tobacco.

SONG:

>Light up a Lucky,
>It's light-up time.
>Be happy, go Lucky,
>It's light-up time.

Lustre Creme Shampoo

SONG:

>Dream girl, dream girl
>Beautiful Lustre Creme girl,
>You owe your crowning glory to
>A Lustre Creme shampoo.

Maxwell House Coffee

ANNOUNCER: America's favorite brand of coffee, always good to the last drop.

Nestlé's Chocolate

ANNOUNCER: N-E-S-T-L-É-'S, Nestlé's makes the very best—

VOICE: Chocolate.

Pabst Blue Ribbon Beer

SLOGAN: Pabst Blue Ribbon Beer, finest beer served anywhere.

SONG:

>Thirty-three fine brews
>Blended into one great beer.

Pall Mall Cigarettes

ANNOUNCER: Outstanding! And they are mild.

Pepsi-Cola

ORIGINAL SONG:

>Pepsi-Cola hits the spot
>Twelve full ounces,
>That's a lot.
>Twice as much
>For a nickel too,
>Pepsi-Cola is the drink for you.

REVISED SONG:

>Pepsi-Cola hits the spot
>Two full glasses
>That's a lot.
>Why take less
>When Pepsi's best.

Petri Wine

ORIGINAL SLOGAN: The Petri family, the family that took time to bring you good wine.

REVISED SLOGAN: You can't go wrong with Petri wine because Petri took time to bring you good wine.

Philip Morris Cigarettes

JOHNNY THE BELLBOY:

>Call for Philip Mor-rees,
>Call for Philip Mor-rees.

Post 40% Bran Flakes

ANNOUNCER: They're so good and so good for you.

Post Toasties Cereal

SONG:

> We toast 'em crisp,
> We toast 'em light.
> You can tell by the taste
> We toast 'em.
> Post Toasties.

Prell Shampoo

GIRL VOCALIST:

> I'm Tallulah
> The tube of Prell.
> I'll make your hair
> Look swell.
> It'll shine, it'll glow.
> For radiant hair,
> Get a hold of me,
> Tallulah, the tube of Prell.

Raleigh Cigarettes

ANNOUNCER: The pack with the coupon on back.

RCA

ANNOUNCER: World leader in radio, first in recorded music, first in television.

Rinso Detergent

GIRL VOCALIST:

> Rinso white,
> Rinso bright,
> Happy little washday song.

Roi-Tan Cigars

ANNOUNCER: Man to man, smoke a Roi-Tan, the cigar that breathes.

Roma Wines

ANNOUNCER: Roma Wines, made in California for enjoyment throughout the world.

Ronson Lighter Fluid

ANNOUNCER:

> Ronson all, Ronson all,

> Lights any flint lighter
> Best of all.

Schlitz Beer

ANNOUNCER: The beer that made Milwaukee famous.

7-Up

ANNOUNCER: Fresh up with 7-Up. You like it, it likes you.

Spry Shortening

ANNOUNCER: Rely on Spry.

Super Suds

SONG:

> Super Suds, Super Suds,
> Lots more suds
> With Super Suds.

Tide Detergent

CHORUS:

> Tide's in, dirt's out.
> Tide's in, dirt's out.

ANNOUNCER: Tide gets clothes cleaner than any other soap. T-I-D-E, Tide!

Tums Antacid

ANNOUNCER: Tums for the tummy.

Wheaties Cereal

ANNOUNCER: Wheaties, breakfast of champions.

Wild Root Creme Oil

ANNOUNCER: The choice of men who put good grooming first.

Wonder Bread

ANNOUNCER: The bread that's doubly fresh. Fresh when you buy it, fresh when you eat it.

Appendix C: World War II Announcements

See the program mentioned for further information

The Adventures of Father Brown (Merchant Marine recruiting)
The Adventures of Ozzie and Harriet (tin can salvage)
Amanda of Honeymoon Hill (WAVE recruitment)
Bachelor's Children (gasoline rationing)
Everything for the Boys (automatic pilots; the Red Cross)

Fibber McGee and Molly (support for President Truman)
The Judy Canova Show (used fats)
Light of the World (war bonds drive)
The Man Behind the Gun (Army Medical Corps)
Mystery Playhouse (service message)
Texaco Star Theater (scrap metal)
This Is My Best (Victory gardens)
Valiant Lady (war bonds)

Index

References are to entry numbers